Exploring Civic Innovation for Social and Economic Transformation

This edited collection examines the globally rising phenomenon of civic innovation. Combining nuanced theory with rich empirical examples, this book defines the dynamic and complex process of civic innovation as the multiple economic, political and social processes where people, organizations, movements and ideas are shaping struggles for global justice on the interface of capitalism.

Exploring Civic Innovation for Social and Economic Transformation reflects the increasingly holistic approach to development in terms of both teaching and research, and illustrates how civic innovation happens everywhere; at the global and institutional level as well as in communities and for individuals. Through conceptual debate and narrative accounts, this book explores the new practices emerging from varying economies, transformative empowerment strategies in global value chains, local politics of social movements and the struggles for rights in regards to race, gender and sexuality.

Bringing together scholars from a range of disciplines, this book will be of interest to post-graduate students of development studies, with an interest in social research.

Kees Biekart is Associate Professor of Political Sociology at the International Institute of Social Studies of Erasmus University in Rotterdam, The Netherlands.

Wendy Harcourt is Associate Professor in Critical Development and Feminist Studies at the International Institute of Social Studies of Erasmus University in Rotterdam, The Netherlands.

Peter Knorringa is Professor of Private Sector and Development at the International Institute of Social Studies of Erasmus University in Rotterdam, The Netherlands.

Routledge Studies in Development Economics

For a complete list of titles in this series, please visit https://www.routledge.com/series/SE0266

114 Developmental Macroeconomics
New developmentalism as a growth strategy
Luiz Carlos Bresser-Pereira, José Luis Oreiro and Nelson Marconi

115 Industrial Innovation, Networks and Economic Development
Informal information sharing in low-technology clusters in India
Anant Kamath

116 Employment and Inclusive Development
Rizwanul Islam and Iyanatul Islam

117 Growth and Institutions in African Development
Edited by Augustin K. Fosu

118 Public Finance and Economic Growth in Developing Countries
Lessons from Ethiopia's reforms
Stephen B. Peterson

119 Peripheral Visions of Economic Development
New frontiers in development economics and the history of economic thought
Edited by Mario Garcia-Molina and Hans-Michael Trautwein

120 The Political Economy of Natural Resources and Development
From Neoliberalism to resource nationalism
Edited by Paul A. Haslam and Pablo Heidrich

121 Institutional Innovation and Change in Value Chain Development
Negotiating tradition, power and fragility in Afghanistan
Holly A. Ritchie

122 China's War against the Many Faces of Poverty
Towards a New Long March
Jing Yang and Pundarik Mukhopadhaya

123 Exploring Civic Innovation for Social and Economic Transformation
Edited by Kees Biekart, Wendy Harcourt and Peter Knorringa

Exploring Civic Innovation for Social and Economic Transformation

Edited by
Kees Biekart, Wendy Harcourt
and Peter Knorringa

LONDON AND NEW YORK

First published 2016
by Routledge

2 Park Square, Milton Park, Abingdon, Oxfordshire OX14 4RN
52 Vanderbilt Avenue, New York, NY 10017

Routledge is an imprint of the Taylor & Francis Group, an informa business

First issued in paperback 2019

British Library Cataloguing in Publication Data
A catalogue record for this book is available from the British Library

Library of Congress Cataloging in Publication Data
Names: Biekart, Kees, editor. | Harcourt, Wendy, 1959- editor. |
Knorringa, Peter, 1964- editor.
Title: Exploring civic innovation for social and economic transformation /
edited by Kees Biekart, Wendy Harcourt and Peter Knorringa.
Description: Abingdon, Oxon ; New York, NY : Routledge, 2016.
Identifiers: LCCN 2015046766| ISBN 9781138936331 (hardback) |
ISBN 9781315676913 (ebook)
Subjects: LCSH: Social action. | Political participation. | Social movements. |
Civil society.
Classification: LCC HM831 .E97 2016 | DDC 306.2--dc23
LC record available at http://lccn.loc.gov/2015046766

ISBN: 978-1-138-93633-1 (hbk)
ISBN: 978-0-367-87404-9 (pbk)

Typeset in Times New Roman
by Taylor & Francis Books

Contents

List of illustrations   vii
List of contributors   viii

1 Introduction: giving meaning to civic innovation   1
  KEES BIEKART, WENDY HARCOURT AND PETER KNORRINGA

2 The institutional foundations of civic innovation   20
  GEORGINA M. GÓMEZ AND HOLLY A. RITCHIE

3 Change actors and civic innovators: who triggers change?
  Systematising the role of interlocutors in civic innovation
  processes   41
  ALAN FOWLER

4 Can consultants be civic innovators? Exploring their roles as
  auditors and allies   67
  SYLVIA I. BERGH AND KEES BIEKART

5 Between state, market and civil society: what constitutes the
  social in social entrepreneurship?   87
  A.H.J. (BERT) HELMSING

6 Civic innovation in value chains: towards workers as agents in
  non-governmental labour regulation   109
  KARIN ASTRID SIEGMANN, JEROEN MERK AND PETER KNORRINGA

7 Civic innovation by family farmers in the face of global value
  chain inclusion: between material conditions and imagined
  futures   132
  LEE PEGLER AND WANESSA MARQUES SILVA

8 Exploring embodiment and intersectionality in transnational
  feminist activist research   148
  WENDY HARCOURT, ROSALBA ICAZA AND VIRGINIA VARGAS

9 Towards new perspectives on labour precarity and decent work for sex workers'   168
SILKE HEUMANN, KARIN ASTRID SIEGMANN AND EMPOWER FOUNDATION

10 Resistance and hope: Youth responses to the economic crisis in Southern Europe   192
PAULINA (SAT) TREJO-MENDEZ, PAULA SÁNCHEZ DE LA BLANCA,
LAURA SANTAMARÍA BUITRAGO, EMMA CLAIRE SARDONI, GUILIA SIMULA
WITH WENDY HARCOURT

11 Civic activism and social accountability: a quantitative approach   215
ANDERSON MACEDO DE JESUS AND IRENE VAN STAVEREN

12 Minding the gap between activism and academia – or bridging it? Reflections on how to do civic innovation research   233
KEES BIEKART AND KARIN ASTRID SIEGMANN

13 Conclusion: moving agendas forward   251
WENDY HARCOURT, KEES BIEKART AND PETER KNORRINGA

Index   267

Illustrations

Figures

2.1	Linking beliefs, values, habits and rules	24
2.2	The institutionalist action-information loop	26
2.3	Institutional innovation and change	30
3.1	Interlocution schematic	53
11.1a–d	Scatter plots between relevant variables	226
11.2	Model with service delivery determinants	229
12.1	Researchers discussing how to do civic innovation research at CIRI retreat, Hilversum, The Netherlands, August 2014	244

Tables

I.1	Messages from the CIRI Building	7
I.2	Central CIRI concepts and how these might be related	9
3.1	Summary of interlocution cases	54
11.1	Variables	225
11.2	Results	230

Contributors

Sylvia I. Bergh is an Assistant Professor (Senior Lecturer) in Development Management and Governance at the International Institute of Social Studies (ISS). She holds a D.Phil. in Development Studies from the University of Oxford. Her main expertise is on issues of rural development and local governance in Morocco, including as staff at the World Bank's Morocco country office. Her work experience also includes a year in the President's office at the World Bank and various consultancy assignments, including for UNIFEM (now UN Women) and the Dutch Ministry of Foreign Affairs. She is currently conducting research on local social accountability initiatives in the Middle East and North Africa region.

Kees Biekart is Associate Professor of Political Sociology at the International Institute of Social Studies (ISS) of Erasmus University in Rotterdam, The Netherlands. He has worked for many years in Latin America, including as a research co-ordinator and consultant with the 'scholar-activist' Transnational Institute (TNI). His MA studies at the University of Amsterdam focused on democratization, NGOs, and political change in Chile, and his Ph.D. was on the role of international NGOs in the political process in Nicaragua, El Salvador, Guatemala, and Honduras. His research focus is on civic-driven change, social movements, and the political role of change agents. He also works with his ISS students on developing participatory action research techniques.

Alan Fowler is a pracademic. As well as researching civic innovation and citizen driven change, he has been advising and writing about nongovernmental organizations and civic society more widely. His numerous books and articles are post-graduate texts in this field. Currently an emeritus professor, he has held elected positions on the boards of the International Society for Third Sector Research (ISTR) and Civicus, the World Alliance for Citizen Participation. He is a co-founder of the International NGO Training and Research Centre (INTRAC). Ongoing studies take a citizen's eye view of socio-political processes in polycentric governance and the effectiveness of multi-stakeholder initiatives. In addition to qualifications in engineering and education, he holds a D.Phil. in development studies.

Georgina M. Gómez is Senior Lecturer in Institutions and Local Development at the International Institute of Social Studies of Erasmus University Rotterdam, The Netherlands. She obtained a PhD with distinction with a thesis on Community and Complementary Currency Systems in Argentina. She has published and supervises doctoral candidates on the local economic development in Latin America, social and solidarity economy, institutional and evolutionary economics, and social monetary innovations.

Wendy Harcourt is Associate Professor in Critical Development and Feminist Studies at the International Institute of Social Studies (ISS), Erasmus University in The Hague, The Netherlands. Dr Wendy Harcourt joined the ISS in November 2011 after 20 years at the Society for International Development, Rome as Editor of the journal *Development* and Director of Programmes. At the ISS she is a member of the civic innovation research initiative management team and co-coordinates the Sexuality Research Initiative. She has edited ten books and her monograph: *Body Politics in Development: Critical Debates in Gender and Development* published by Zed Books in 2009, received the 2010 Feminist Women Studies Association Book Prize. She is series editor of Palgrave's Gender, Development and Social Change book series and is actively involved in several journal boards and feminist movement organizations and gender and development networks.

A.H.J. (Bert) Helmsing is Professor of local and Regional Development at the International Institute of Social Studies of Erasmus University Rotterdam. His Ph.D. in economics is from Tilburg University. He has worked for nearly 40 years in development studies education, capacity building and policy advice on local and regional development in Latin America and Sub Saharan Africa. He has published 30 articles in peer reviewed journals, contributed 21 chapter to edited books and published/edited ten books. He specialized in the areas of decentralization to local governments and markets, meso level economic analysis of firms, chains and clusters and the roles of NGOs and (social) entrepreneurship in economic development. His current research focuses on the study of local institutional change processes.

Silke Heumann is a Sociologist and Assistant Professor in Women's and Gender Studies at the International Institute of Social Studies of Erasmus University Rotterdam, The Netherlands. Her research interests include gender, sexual politics and (their relation to) social justice; social movements; and discourse analysis.

Rosalba Icaza is a Mexican feminist academic-activist who conducts research and teaches on social movements, epistemic justice and indigenous people resistance and autonomy. Her pedagogical practice has been focused on making the classroom as space to share ideas-as-incarnated-experiences about the academy as a colonizing institution and/or emancipatory possibility. Her latest publication in English is 'The Peoples Permanent Tribunals and indigenous people's struggles in Mexico: between the coloniality of international law and epistemic justice?' *Palgrave Communications Journal* available at: http://www.palgrave-journals.com/articles/palcomms201520. She is Senior Lecturer in Governance and International Political Economy at the Institute of Social Studies, Erasmus University of Rotterdam.

Peter Knorringa is Professor of Private Sector & Development at the International Institute of Social Studies of Erasmus University in Rotterdam, The Netherlands. His main interest concerns the diverse roles and impacts of business on development. He investigates to what extent socially responsible and environmentally sustainable forms of development are possible under capitalism.

Anderson Macedo de Jesus is a Ph.D. researcher at the Institute of Social Studies of Erasmus University Rotterdam. He is an international development professional with experience in academia, federal and local government agencies in Brazil, and multilateral organizations such as UNICEF, UNDP, and UNESCO. He was one of the Brazilian coordinators of the National Human Development Report in 2010 and author of many articles in peer reviewed journals such as *Revista Psicologia Reflexão e Crítica, Revista de Administração Pública, Brazilian Political Science Review*. In 2013, he was awarded the Science without Border (CAPES) Scholarship, the Santander Cambridge Scholarship (Cambridge Trust) and the Claremont Evaluation Center & EvalPartners Scholarship.

Wanessa Marques Silva holds a master degree in Globalization and Development from the University of Antwerp. Her Masters dissertation was part of the Governance of Labour and Logistics for Sustainability (GOLLS) research project, a joint initiative between the Institute of Social Studies of the Erasmus University Rotterdam, in The Hague, the Institute of Development Policy and Management (IOB) in Antwerp, and several universities and organizations in Brazil. GOLLS project studies commodity chains' dynamics that link Brazil and the main ports of Europa, aiming to assist the promotion of labour rights, human security and social improvements to populations involved in global value chains.

Jeroen Merk is Research Associate at the International Institute of Social Studies. His research explores the conditions under which social movements, trade unions and networks of NGOs are (re-)framing and contesting common sense understandings of global governance institutions, agendas and priorities.

Lee Pegler spent his early career working as an economist with the Australian Labour Movement. Recent times have seen him researching labour implications of 'new' management strategies of TNCs in Brazil. This interest has expanded to a focus on the implications of value chain insertion on labour, both for formal and informal workers. Trained as an economist and sociologist (Ph.D. from LSE), he currently works as lecturer (Work, Organization and Labour Rights) at the International Institute of Social Studies.

Project work includes consultancies on Decent Work in Global Food Chains (ILO) and on cluster/social inclusion promotion in Brazil (World Bank). He also coordinates a project (GOLLS) concerning sustainable value chains – one which links ports and logistics (in the Netherlands) with production and livelihoods in Brazil. This project has significant implications for Government, civil society and companies concerning CSR/sustainability. Such experience has led to Pegler's involvement in exercises to develop responsible chain diagnostics.

Holly A. Ritchie is a research fellow at the International Institute of Social Studies of Erasmus University Rotterdam, with an interest in gender, institutions and economic development in fragile environments. Her Ph.D. (ISS Cum Laude, Best Ph.D. Thesis Erasmus University 2013) focused on women's enterprise in Afghanistan and institutional change. An active member of the IS Academy on Human Security in Fragile States (2009–2014), Wageningen University, she works as a development consultant with experience in Afghanistan, Brazil and East Africa.

Paula Sánchez de la Blanca, Spain, is an MA student (2014/5) at the ISS/EUR, the Netherlands.

Laura Santamaría Buitrago, Colombia, has an MA from ISS/EUR (2013/4) and is currently working in peace building projects with young men and women in Bogotá and other regions of Colombia.

Emma Claire Sardoni, Italy is in her penultimate year at Tasso Classical High School in Rome, Italy.

Karin Astrid Siegmann works as ISS Senior Lecturer in Labour and Gender Economics. Her research is concerned with the intersection of global economic processes with local labour markets, stratified by varying degrees of security of work, gender, and other social identities.

Guilia Simula, Italy, is an MA student (2014/5) at the ISS/EUR, the Netherlands.

Irene van Staveren is professor of pluralist development economics at the Institute of Social Studies of Erasmus University Rotterdam. She is also member of the think tank Sustainable Finance Lab. She is the director of the online database Indices of Social Development (www.IndSocDev.org), which measures the strength of civil society and the extent of equality and inclusion in societies across the world. Her books include, with Jan Peil, the *Handbook of Economics and Ethics* (Edward Elgar, 2009) and, with Peter Knorringa, the edited volume *Beyond Social Capital* (Routledge, 2008). In 2014, she received the Thomas Divine Lifetime Achievement Award from the Association of Social Economics. Recently, she published a pluralist economy cis textbook titled *Economics after the Crisis* (Routledge, 2015).

Paulina (Sat) Trejo-Mendez, Mexico, is a Ph.D. student at the ISS/EUR, The Netherlands.

Virginia (Gina) Vargas is a sociologist and feminist activist in Peru and Latin America, and is founding board member of the Centro 'Flora Tristan' in Lima. She has published several books and many articles, has been a visiting professor at various universities in Europe, USA and Latin America. She is also part of numerous networks and various feminist initiatives in Latin America and worldwide. For the Fourth World Conference on Women, held in Beijing, China, in 1995, she was named coordinator of the Latin America and the Caribbean NGO Forum. Now she is actively involved in the World Social Forum since its inception, representing the Articulación Feminista Marcosur.

1 Introduction

Giving meaning to civic innovation

Kees Biekart, Wendy Harcourt and Peter Knorringa

Introduction

What is the link between mainstreaming the Fair Trade movement, mobilizing solidarity around gender-based violence at Tahrir Square in Egypt in 2011, and experimenting with new forms of decision-making at one of the Occupy camps in the Global South? We think all three examples are interdisciplinary, multi-level and interconnected social change processes that can be defined as civic innovations. Recognizing civic innovation when one sees it is one thing, but developing a clear definition and demarcation is quite something else.

This introductory chapter describes and reflects upon the search for the meaning of civic innovation. It is written by three academic colleagues coming from different fields of interest, disciplines and backgrounds. The process of writing has been an experiment in how to generate knowledge by taking into account our diverse histories and stories, the methodology we use, reflecting on the questions we ask and the language we employ. We have tried to keep it an open, respectful collaboration, producing knowledge that is not locked into particular methodologies as we cross the boundaries of our different disciplines.

In the process we have tried, as much as possible, to call attention to the differences, similarities and also tensions among the different ways we approach civic innovation. Indeed, we see those tensions or what we have called 'frictions' as productive ways to open up possibilities for new forms of analysis and research.

For example, viewing civic innovation from an economics perspective, mainstreaming of the Fair Trade movement is a useful case study as it can illustrate the importance of analytical tools that will help us to interpret the changing characteristics of civic innovations over time. From an intersectional embodiment perspective we would zoom in on which type of gendered bodies are engaged in the process. What difference does class, race, ethnicity, age and gender make in terms of the people engaged in growing, buying and selling? What tastes and desires are being defined by which cultures and histories? Who does the buying in the supermarkets, who does the marketing for which consumers? What are the gendered, racialized and sexualized imaginaries created around Fair Trade? From a politics perspective it would be important to analyse the ways in which farmers managed to organize in such a way to influence power relations favourably with their international partners.

An example from the intersectional embodiment perspective is solidarity around gender-based violence in Tahrir Square. What Tahrir Square 2011 reveals for understanding civic innovation is the mobilizations that link local actions with global arenas across cultures around the issue of gender based violence. When the calls for democracy in Tahrir Square protests failed to include women's rights to protest in safety and security there was a global outcry. The global connections forged by women's rights movements to end gender based violence were immediately called on to provide solidarity with the women on the streets who were attacked and raped, not only by police but also by fellow protestors. Women's rights were defended via social media and exposed the discrimination against women protestors. Tahrir Square is one example of body politics that is linked via feminist histories and actions to other civic innovations defending women's rights to security and integrity through on the ground politics and via Internet. These struggles demand an end to embodied and structural gender based violence that are embedded in patriarchal economic, social and political power.

Questions to be raised here are about whether global interventions are interfering in local cultures and customs. How does solidarity support in the long term generate social change? We hope that research in this area of civic innovation consolidates and supports the actions of women's rights movements working to end gender based violence aware of the fragilities and difficulties of looking into issues of body politics.

Our third example is another important imaginary as we give meaning to civic innovation. Occupy Wall Street (OWS) moved spectacularly into the public realm in September 2011, and became one of the widest global responses to the recent financial crisis, rapidly expanding to all the major squares of the world, and then suddenly ending a few months later. What it demonstrated was its rapid expansion as a form of protest combining social media and the square, creating a hybrid from of action between the offline and online world in thousands of physical locations. On these squares a new form of decision-making was practised, countering the top-down methods of the financial system that had negatively affected 99 % of the world population. From a politics perspective the movement demonstrated a sense of empowerment of those mostly affected by the greed of the few. From an economics perspective Occupy Wall Street was an uncomfortable signal to the financial sector that had lost much of its legitimate role of a professional class preaching 'confidence' and 'calm' in order to maximize profits. Here the frictions were around: how was the financial sector going to regain its prestige, if ever? Was its legitimacy not more damaged than it was after the downfall of the 1929 crisis?

From an intersectional embodiment perspective questions to the Occupy movement would be, for example: What are the bodily experiences played out in Occupy camps? What were the different gendered relations? Were there racial tensions? And what about generational issues? Were there conscious efforts to have women and men as leaders and facilitators? Were there tensions around leadership (in terms of gender, race, age)? In designing the actions were there specifically 'feminine' and 'masculine' roles that were challenged of the 1% and played out in the different actions? Were there discussions around traditionally 'feminine' issues around care and cleaning? How were sexual violations and bodily integrity taken into account among the camp dwellers? How were people of different ages, genders, race, ethnicities and sexual orientation treated by police and by the media?

This introductory chapter uses the above examples to engage further with key concepts that underpin civic innovation. We look first at how we move beyond the crisis narrative in order to set the scene of how a civic innovation research agenda allows us to creatively use the inevitable frictions arising from trying to develop alternatives at the edges of global capitalism. We then introduce the state of play on the concepts that constitute civic innovation, followed by an experiment with the usefulness of these concepts when we elaborate our three examples: Tahrir Square, Fair Trade, and the Occupy Movement. We follow this with a discussion of the methodology of doing civic innovation research, and conclude by setting out possible research agendas for civic innovation to be explored by the Civic Innovation Research Initiative (CIRI).

Moving beyond the crisis narrative

Civic innovation is about focusing on what is positive, creative and imaginative in the face of a world that seems beset by crisis narratives, whether financial, economic, ecological, social or cultural. As development researchers we see the mainstream development community responding with difficulty to this crisis narrative – awkwardly speaking of the failure of the Millennium Development Goals (MDGs) while setting up a new set of Sustainable Development Goals (and a new acronym – the SDGs – currently being decided mostly by expert groups and officials in the United Nations bureaucracy). Underlining these discussions are deep concerns about the viability of the development project in the new conditions of today. In exploring the term civic innovation we suggest this helps us to give a useful alternative to overwhelming crisis narratives. We are not looking for a new theory and practice that will lead to a 'grand transformation' of neoliberal capitalism but rather at how to build a mosaic of responses by looking at what is happening 'on the ground' where people are living the contradictions of development. We argue that we need to question pre-determined ideas of what measures to take and go beyond universal policy solutions, in order to look with openness at the actions on the ground. This also means going beyond the strictures of development aid and its logics. Civic innovation acknowledges the contradictions and failures but also looks at what is possible in how people live their everyday lives in twenty-first-century neoliberal capitalism.

As our three opening examples show, we are interested in exploring the shifts and possibilities in politics, local economics and in gender and sexuality emancipatory movements (Fraser 2013) that move us away from dominant capitalist narratives that predominate in development discourse. We are interested in how innovative practices of community and solidarity economies, sometimes in alliances with transformative empowerment strategies in global value chains, local politics of social movements and rights movements around the body, gender and sexuality are allowing new imaginaries of well-being and possibility to flourish. These alternative discourses connect in interesting ways: the private and public, the domestic and national, local and the global, the emotional with the technical. They try hard and sometimes selectively succeed to create inroads into the mainstream development discourse. Most importantly, they contain the potential for social change that needs to be understood and acted upon, instead of just talking about crisis.

In that spirit, our chapter aims to contribute to progressive and creative thinking that offers the possibility to understand better (and imagine more confidently) alternatives to oppressive doom and gloom scenarios. While still acknowledging the fears, doubt and uncertainties, we aim to build connections and openings for social change. In this search, we need to confront the many frictions that are coming to the fore in depressing and ugly ways. We do not dispute the depth of inequalities, the dysfunction in our societies, nor the destructive pressure on our environments and the level of social despair about the future. Our sense of hope is that there are many people, in various institutions, cultures and societies who are eager to address these issues. The diversity of how to approach multiple levels of dysfunction is at the same time part of the messiness as well as part of the possibility for change. If we move away from a search for one overarching approach or solution, such as the SDGs, and instead look at how to bridge and forge connections among the different approaches, we can learn from a wealth of innovative ideas and practices. In looking at the productive interfaces we can step away from tired ideologies that drag us down with their inability to explain what is happening today. Working with the frictions we can understand how development can engage with what is going on today as people work through the systemic contradictions, the pain, the everyday difficulties in their lives. CIRI works with inter-disciplinarity in order to go beyond the confines of single disciplines challenging Western universalism and social science that relies too much on the principles of logical positivism. CIRI looks at the real-life intersections between these and other paradigms as sources of friction that energize civic innovation in domains of action with institutional effects[1].

Our examples show how studies of civic innovation seek to weave together non-hegemonic narratives about how people on the ground are overcoming profound obstacles in their direct challenge to social, political, economic and cultural inequalities. Through exploring these narratives we analyse the obstacles and break through possibilities for social change.

Our use of the term civic innovation acknowledges that social change happens everywhere in society, at the global level as well as in communities, in governments, in markets, in families, as well as for individuals. We see civic innovation as a generic term that is crosscutting but also inspiring.

The 'civic' element was developed from the civic-driven change work at the ISS (see Fowler and Biekart 2008). Civic-driven implied a key role for citizens as well as civic agency, something we considered to be present throughout society. This '24/7 citizen' in peace time broke fast as a family member (or tax payer) in the morning, went to work in the household, or as an employee, or entrepreneur in the streets, or to the farms, or to study or legislate and there grew food to sell, cared for the family and community, sold produce as a trader or bought as a consumer, contributed to governance activities and in the evening and holidays participated in family and community activity. This same citizen has the potential of being a change agent in all these realms, thereby emphasizing that 'civic agency' is not by definition linked to civil society, markets, or governments. It has at least the potential to be crosscutting as well as bridging and connecting.

The 'innovation' concept has an intuitive meaning – as a term used in social and technology sciences to refer to new approaches, tools, as well as policies that are creative and are 'Making Things Better' (the slogan of Dutch firm Philips in the 1990s). We are taking innovation in a positive sense, aware that innovation can be negative in both quality and meaning. So, we are using the term innovation to refer to creative forms of cultural political and economic resistance and pathways to social change. We do not mean however 'social innovation'. Recent years have seen the use of 'social innovation' as a flag for social entrepreneurs to explore new ways of contributing to more responsible businesses. Social innovation does not directly take on board the political and rarely gives priority to gender/sexuality and embodiment. As Fowler (2013) warns, high expectations of the concept social innovation are not justified:

> The tricky bit is that the current state of social innovation is so plural as to permit multiple uses and users of the term that may be diametrically opposed to one another. In addition, current definitions, formulations and interpretations of the concept are politically under dimensioned, if not naïve.

Learning from engagements at the CIRI Forum, October 2013

In order to explore the 'real life intersections' of civic innovation and their frictions at the interface of capitalism, we brought together researchers in three 'strands' of research in October 2013 at the CIRI Forum in The Hague on 'Theories and Practice in Civic Innovation: Building bridges among politics, markets and gender/sexuality'. The first strand of research explores how civic innovation can play a role in making markets more socially responsible and environmentally sustainable with a focus on commercial and civil society actors. The research looks at complementary currency systems, social entrepreneurship, the role of institutions, the rights of workers at the bottom of value chains; and at possibilities to re-politicize business–society relationships. The second strand focuses on how to embody the political economy by discussing the political and economic use of gendered bodies from an intersectional perspective in order to understand the lived bodily experiences in the struggle for democratic power. The research looks at how organizations and individuals mobilize in different places as well as across national borders, to change understandings and practices of embodiment/sexuality/gender in an intersectional framing. The third strand explores civic driven change investigating the nature of micro-macro socio-political connections in upscaling of civic agency and the recent wave of global activisms, from Egypt to Brazil, and from Occupy to Gezi Park, looking at the role of social media, and the new types of inter-mediary and politically activist groups who are operating outside traditional political boundaries.

In each of these strands we aim to explore civic innovation from our different situated positions as researchers working and engaged in research that we see as contributing to social change. We therefore use a situated standpoint, conscious of our role in our interventions as researchers and reflecting on the process of research in which we are engaging as part of the civic innovation. In this we follow feminist ontology – consciously scrutinizing and asking questions about our personal and political research interests, as well as seeking to disclose our own subjectivities that include gender blind, racist, sexist and heteronormative assumptions about work and relations, including in our own development practice and research.

This type of research means recognizing the frictions, contractions and contesting energies and what Catherine Walsh (2016: 36) calls the 'construction of the otherwise today' – thinking with alternatives in order to forge ways to 'live together a different world and a new agenda'. An important methodo-logical approach to civic innovation is therefore co-production of knowledge with an awareness of difference (inside and outside academe, across age, race and gender) even to the extent of blurring the boundaries of what is acceptable academic research.

The 2013 CIRI Forum was a process of self-reflective ontological research, adopting somewhat unusual participatory techniques in an academic envir-onment that claims objectivity in knowledge production processes. In order to ensure creative frictions would emerge at the Forum we used non-traditional academic ways to keep a lively discussion going on 'civic innovation'. At the start of the Forum we deliberately chose to avoid using opening keynote addresses and started instead our discussions with a self-facilitating 'open microphone' brainstorm discussion on 'civic innovation'.

It was notable that in the brainstorm several participants contested the term 'civic'. Someone argued that 'the civic' in Latin America often represented the efforts by external actors (such as the European Union) to individualize citi-zenship and hence to undermine social movements. Someone else suggested the concept of conflict was excluded in the term 'civic': so who decided what was civic or not, and how could conflicts and power struggles within the 'civic' be made more explicit? The debate also pointed to a difference between 'social movement action' and 'civic innovation action'. Some participants, for example, categorized the recent urban mobilizations in Brazil as 'civic action', as many participants seemed to make claims towards the state about changes in policies. It was felt this was not the same as game changing mobilizations that have been seen in other Brazilian social movements.

The CIRI Forum process tried to move people out of their comfort zone by encouraging people to share what was exciting, confusing and even annoying about the term 'civic innovation'. For example, asking questions about gender and sexuality and embodiment in relation to issues such as Fair Trade, solidarity economies and supply chain processes was for some participants not intuitive.

The interactive methodologies in the CIRI Forum included participatory conversations, a World Café and an interactive dinner with local 'civic innovators' in a squatted high school. In these intense discussions, key concepts informing the CIRI future agenda emerged from a politics, markets and gender/sexuality perspective constructing a CIRI 'building' of cardboard boxes made up of hand written tweets, questions, issues and statements for a research agenda on civic innovation. At the end of the forum participants were asked to prioritize these messages (a selection is presented in Table I.1).

Listening to the debates at the CIRI Forum, we realized that it will be important to research the different forms of civic innovation in action, conflict and movement building in order to deepen the debate and clarify our meaning of 'civic innovation' in different places, economies, historical times and social turning points. As one participant commented, the CIRI Forum encouraged participants to think differently about knowledge institutions and recognize different experimental knowledges in social movements and at the same time challenge the embodied subjectivities we have as academics, which are increasingly marketized.

Table I.1 Messages from the CIRI Building

Positive and/or encouraging remarks:	Negative and/or critical remarks:
Innovation: changing the game or changing rules of the existing game?	Where is capitalism in this story?
Process matters (on methodology)	Mainstreaming good, bad or ugly?
Why not civic 'transformation' rather than 'innovation'?	Civic innovation: old wine in new bottles?
Can the state promote civic innovation and participation?	Where is the *art* in our process?
Good idea of problematizing the civic and citizenship: individual vs collective	Let's talk more about the *practice* of civic innovation
Keep on breaking through fixed mindsets!	Innovation for business as usual or timely transformation?
Actors are embodied and that has consequences for power	Doesn't most innovation and social change come from 'uncivil' ideas and practices?

Source: CIRI Forum participant remarks – October 2013

Identifying key concepts underpinning civic innovation

From our discussions at the CIRI Forum, and building on the civic-driven change approach, we recognized the need to step out of the traditional silos of civil society/market/state if we are to understand how people are challenging the assumptions of dominant patriarchal capitalism as they respond to injustices and form alternatives to dominant political, economic, social and cultural practices. We realized we were approaching the concept of civic innovation from various epistemologies. We had different perceptions, associations, as well as emotions, when hearing concepts like 'state', 'body' or 'markets'. We knew we had to be clearer about these frames of thinking as well as to find a language to understand (and communicate with) those coming from other traditions and paradigms, despite the fact that we all worked in interdisciplinary fields. After the CIRI Forum we opened up a frank discussion about the meaning of key concepts, also when beginning to put together this paper and to prepare the book.

We felt the process of discussion on how we understood civic innovation was generating a 'puzzle' of interrelated concepts, which could be presented as a 'mosaic', in which we could build a language that cut across our different entry points. We started with the metaphor of a 'jig-saw puzzle' but dropped that as we felt that even if the puzzle was solved, we would always encounter new puzzles. We therefore adopted the image of a 'mosaic' in order to explain how we are variously responding to concepts like embodiment, which for researchers working on gender and sexuality is key and central to understanding civic innovation processes, whereas to those working on markets is on the margins of the analysis. Or again for those working on political movements, public sphere is not seen as a useful concept whereas for those working on markets it is a key term. 'Mainstreaming' was also understood in very different ways, whereas the concept 'institutions' cuts across all areas of our research.

We started to put forward possible key concepts and tried to see to what extent they allowed space for our various epistemological perspectives. What we present below is an intermediate result after a number of iterations, in one of our CIRI team meetings following the Forum. We deliberately limited the maximum number of concepts in the mosaic to a dozen in order to force each other to actually make argued choices as well. The following dozen concepts presented in Table I.2 constitute the beginning of a mosaic of civic innovation which we feel offers scope for a fruitful interdisciplinary content discussion. This process continues to be fluid and open, and we deliberately leave one space free in order to encourage readers to consider participating in the creation of the mosaic.

Below we briefly locate these concepts in their relationships. The idea is that each contribution to this volume engages with a combination of these concepts in more detail, both conceptually and empirically. The present set of concepts is therefore not cast in stone. We hope and expect that some of the contributions will lead us to think afresh about the constituting elements of civic innovation. The volume as a whole then allows us – as a collective – to arrive at a sharper and more shared conceptualization of civic innovation.

Table I.2 Central CIRI concepts and how these might be related

Interlocutors	Embodiment	Scale
Institutions	Intersectionality	Knowledge
Activism	Agency	Establishment
Values	?	Power

Power and *values* are two fundamental building block concepts underlying civic innovation. We aim to analyse change processes, and investigate how individuals and groups of people engage in *activisms* – to exercise *agency* towards changing what they perceive as the *establishment*. In such change processes we need to be acutely aware of various types of vertical and horizontal power, and we need to be systematically self-critical about values – who determines which means and ends of activisms are justified and would contribute to the common good (and who decides what is the common good)? So, activists do not by definition aim for the 'good', nor does the establishment automatically represent the 'bad'.

At a less abstract level of analysis, civic innovation processes are co-shaped by the institutional setting within which they take place, by available types of *knowledge*, and by actors' experience of *embodiment*, identity and levels of *intersectionality*. This is a two way process in that civic innovation may also generate, for example, new or reconfigured *institutions*, and that civic innovation can be targeted at fighting interlocking forms of oppression and shaping new ways forward.

At the more operational level of analysis we look at the actors involved, with a focus on the *interlocutors* who inspire and knit together the needed network of actors to synergize the change process. Finally, as will be illustrated in the Fair Trade example, to bring civic innovations to *scale* poses yet another major challenge. Upscaling or mainstreaming a civic innovation implies it starts to become part of the establishment. That raises the question to what extent such upscaling is also likely to partly destroy some of its original values from the initial activism phase, and to what extent the values of the establishment might adjust.

In the following three sections we use our three illustrative cases to experiment with how sub-sets of these key concepts can be used to give meaning to civic innovation.

Three examples of civic innovation

Solidarity over gender based violence in Tahrir Square

Returning to the example of solidarity around gender based violence (GBV) in Tahrir Square. Our interest is in understanding further the way civic innovation operated in the activism of transnational networks of solidarity that were brought into play over the violations in the Square when women protestors were seen to threaten male power and privilege. The event is one illustration of activism by women's rights groups to bring about change to gender based violence within the framework of human rights. With reference to the fundamental CIRI concepts the event is about body politics or how embodiment is politicized through civic action in defence of bodily integrity and against patriarchal power. In this case, power operates on two levels. It is hierarchical oppressive and patriarchal as men – police (the state) and other men demonstrators – abused the women. And it is also horizontal as women's rights activists used their agency and power to call on others (within the state and outside) to defend their rights to demonstrate safely in the square. The acts of solidarity in Tahrir Square were not just a one off, flat event but rather an outcome of historical transnational activism of women's human rights groups that have built strong networks of solidarity to counter gender based violence. It was this history and connection that the women in Tahrir Square could call on instantly through digital connected networks. It was an example of how civic innovation has used global international communication technology and movement building over the last decades around women's human rights to support these local incidences of violations. Through these locally linked, global processes of civic innovation, activists in defence of women's rights and bodily integrity have brought the issue of gender based violence to the global and national public sphere for legislation, punitive action and prevention. Civic innovation around GBV includes campaigns to end sexual violence of all kinds (domestic violence, rape, intimate partner violence, rape as a weapon of war, female genital cutting, femicide and sexual harassment in the work-place). The global response to gender based violence in Tahrir Square is an important example of civic innovation that built on years of negotiation among women's rights groups around the world to make visible GBV (Antrobus 2004: Moghadam 2005). This form of civic innovation largely led by women's rights movements has created possibilities for social change, and in the process has changed establishment attitudes to gender relations and vio-lations making what was once private visible.[2] Transnational feminist solidarities linked local protests via personal connections and via social media created the possibilities for the immediate responses of feminist networks to the sexual violence in Tahrir Square. The events in Tahrir Square in this sense, radiated outward from the Square itself, to be part of the global protest movements that are challenging national and transnational cultures of sexism and domination.

The work of ending gender violence as the example in Tahrir Square suggests is not straightforward. Activism around the issue is not always easy. It is painful and difficult to speak about and to act to end it takes courage and knowledge of legal and other systems. It can also be dangerous political work when GBV campaigns deal with major economic forces such as the black economy of sex trafficking and pornographic industry and cyberstalking.

Even though there is public recognition of GBV and there is considerable knowledge about its forms, and legal and punitive systems set up to try to combat it, deep sexism continues to lead to violations.

Let us go a little deeper in our analysis of solidarity in Tahrir Square. The global outrage via press and social media that women were targeted for sexual violence and harassment in Tahrir Square also suggests some frictions. To read Tahrir Square through the prism of transnational feminist solidarity is a tricky task given the emotions that continue to ride high both in Egypt and globally around what are appropriate forms of political solidarity in such explosive situations (Mohanty 2004; Biekart and Fowler 2013). What does such global attention do for local political movements? Is such global attention useful for local women living the violations? Does the global interfere with the local? What is the role of 'cyber' protest and solidarity?

It is a sensitive and difficult task for those outside to support women in location and to avoid falling into the trap of objectifying and instrumentalizing women's bodies in a discourse of otherness where 'vulnerable women' need to be 'rescued' in the name of rights. It is important to avoid inappropriate 'maternalism', a sort of mirror reversal of the patriarchal claims of rapists and violators claiming the right to control and punish female bodies in the name of culture or religion. Here an intersectional awareness is important – it is not only gender but also age, race, politics and religion that is played out on women's bodies. The feminine bodies of young Egyptian women are 'disciplined and regulated through discourses of patriarchy, Islamism and secular modern masculinity' (Hafez 2014: 172). In Tahrir Square these bodies became also sites of dissent and revolution. The tension around Islamist, liberal secularism and claims of western freedom centred on disciplining the bodies of these young Egyptian women in ways that could not be fully understood in the global press and global social media. The fallen woman prone beneath the boots of soldiers in the Square became a media icon, but as the revolution in the Square continued, more and more women were harassed, assaulted and tested for virginity in callous and humiliating processes. The bodies of female protestors were seen as transgressive, unregulated and unruly being controlled by men in what women activists in the Square described as 'sexual terrorism' (Hafez 2014: 184).

Tahrir Square provides an interesting example of how embodiment plays out in political civic innovation. Judith Butler (2011) in her article on Tahrir Square, discusses how bodies on the streets are connected in important ways to those who are virtually engaged in the protests. In order for the people on the streets to be effective they require those watching and monitoring what is going on. They need the bodies holding the cameras, typing on the screens, making the tweets, sending messages on networks and signing the e-petitions, creating a global public that reacts. Some of those using the cameras or sending messages via Internet are risking, like those on the streets, being violated and punished if that typing, filming and sending of messages is traced. But the point here is not who is on the frontline or not. Tahrir Square and other social movement protests such as Occupy are about connecting local and global action; the sense of public space expands and contracts between the local, national and global. How the global process is shaping local events is something that needs to be understood not as the global dominating and misunderstanding the local but rather that the global is in the local. When women in Tahrir square reported sexual violence by tweeting, sending email messages, and You Tube films, they connected not only to local, national feminist groups but also to global networks, often personally knowing to whom they were reaching out. Those reporting from Tahrir Square on the sexual violence (including those who were harassed and attacked) ensured that in this public space violence against women was visible, challenged and fought against. The feminist networks connected via social media gave support, knowing the violence experienced on their own and others' bodies. Transnational feminism was not outside of what was happening, but part of the events, supporting the possibility for women to negotiate, to listen, to protest and to bring knowledge of other ways of fighting violations in other Squares.

Tahrir Square illustrates how civic innovation happens in bodily ways, connecting the local with the global, the political with the sexual – combining resisting patriarchal oppression, sharing emotional concern and values and building knowledge of strategies for change.

Has scaling up the Fair Trade movement killed it?

Fair Trade is among the most commonly recognized examples of civic innovation. Its very success raises some uncomfortable issues in terms of its ongoing commitment to its original values and aims. Has this civic initiative, originally developed by activists in rich and poor countries, been taken over by mainstream commercial companies, i.e. the economic establishment? And if so, or at least partly so, has that altered the values in the economic exchange relationships between producer cooperatives in the Global South and retailers and consumers in the Global North? What types of change are being brought about now by Fair Trade – for whose benefit? How do we see gender being played out? We now turn to explore further the frictions of the civic innovation process by looking more at Fair Trade.

The example of Fair Trade helps us to look at how civic innovation can often be different from what it might seem to promise initially. Fair Trade illustrates how civic innovations are difficult to institutionalize and upscale. They often initially depend on one or a few charismatic change agents – interlocutors – who create a momentum for change, but it is usually less clear how that change is to be consolidated and institutionalized. And if such a change process does become 'mainstreamed', it risks losing its original values and can become part of the establishment.

Fair Trade started as a movement committed to offering small producers in developing countries an alternative to capitalist exchange relations. Fair Trade products were initially distributed through non-commercial outlets.

From the 1960s onwards, Fair Trade movements in Europe and the US tried to develop mutually respectful and fair exchange relations with producer cooperatives, with coffee from Central America as the most well-known example. The initiators of this alternative might be seen as archetypical civic innovators. In the following decades people in and outside the Fair Trade movement started to debate the pros and cons of upscaling: how to reach and convince more consumers of Fair Trade so that more small producers could benefit (Barrientos, Conroy and Jones 2007). This led to the establishment of two schools of thought within Fair Trade: the so-called 'fundis' and the 'realos'. Fundis emphasized the importance of strictly adhering to 'doing things differently' and not becoming 'infected' with capitalist logic of up-scaling and accumulation. Realos emphasized the importance of reaching a broader audience and used Fair Trade to demonstrate to mainstream brands that 'it' can be done differently while also up-scaling. In the Netherlands the realos eventually became dominant and also ventured into positioning Fair trade products in mainstream supermarkets.

The demonstration effect of Fair Trade products in supermarkets was successful in that most branded competitors and supermarket chains themselves felt compelled to either adopt the Fair Trade label or developed their own ethical labels. These company-based ethical labels are often fiercely criticized by Fair Trade staff for being 'light-versions' of the real Fair Trade label. Representatives of these company-based labels retort that their labels might not yet have reached zero-tolerance, but that their improvement-oriented approach allows for small producers to grow into the system. Moreover, they argue that it is more important to provide modest and sustainable benefits to millions of small producers versus the Fair Trade model that provides relatively larger benefits to a much smaller and stable group of producers and cooperatives that have been in the system for decades.

How do we see Fair Trade as civic innovation? Has the Fair Trade movement lost its 'soul' when it started to sell products in supermarkets? After all, in the mainstream nobody is talking anymore about providing an alternative to capitalist development, but people focus on 'ticking the boxes' of eradicating child labour, and equal treatment of men and women. While these are crucial development indicators, the process of certification has become instrumentalized.

Or has the mainstreaming and up-scaling been particularly successful because it has forced mainstream businesses to adopt at least something that (claims to) resemble Fair Trade? Proponents argue that Fair Trade has successfully transformed markets for products like coffee, tea, chocolate and bananas. Ethical concerns are now not a concern for a few idealists, but have become an inescapable element in any premium brand strategy. One might therefore argue that a 'watered down' version of Fair Trade principles has become the new norm in the establishment, especially among A-brands that are vulnerable to public criticism from those who cling to the original alternative values. One might thus argue that the realos and fundis play complementary roles. Fundis continue to work on developing credible alternatives and keep up the pressure towards mainstream business, and realos work with firms in the establishment to integrate additional ethical concerns in their business strategies.

The Fair Trade movement has traditionally been male centred, focusing for example on providing male farmer heads of households with various types of training while most of the actual farming was done by women. Moreover, Fair Trade has struggled with power differences within cooperatives, where board members do not always share information and benefits with the actual producers. So, while the idea of Fair Trade is powerful and long-lasting, its practices have inevitably been more unruly. This by no means disqualifies Fair Trade. On the contrary, it helps us to see how actual implementation at local level, and especially attempts at up-scaling to make its ideals part of common practice in the establishment, raise challenges to practitioners and also to researchers on how to interpret, define and demarcate civic innovation.

In the example from Tahrir we saw how local civic innovations are supported and linked to global struggles and how internal violations of power can be obscured or made invisible in the light of the larger social goals. The Fair Trade example shows how it is important to scrutinize what is successful and what is not and how we can interpret measures of something as subjective as success. We now turn to the Occupy movement that looks at issues of decision-making and generational difference in civic organizing.

The temporality of Occupy Wall Street

Occupy Wall Street (OWS) is a third important imaginary as we give meaning to civic innovation. As mentioned earlier, Occupy Wall Street was one of the most visible global responses to the recent financial crisis. It became apparent in September 2011 when the New York OWS occupation was soon followed by a dozen similar protests throughout the United States and hundreds of other occupations worldwide. What was the source of all this civic energy, and was it only a temporary eruption of civic action from the so-called '99 %'? Or is the Occupy movement still present, though latent? What has been its relationship with other protests in the recent wave of post-2010 activisms (Biekart and Fowler 2013)? And how do we analyse the global Occupy campaigns from a perspective of 'markets' and 'sexuality'?

In order to answer these questions, a brief recollection of the global spread of Occupy is helpful. The idea to stage a 'Day of Global Occupation' to protest against the institutions and people responsible for the financial crisis emerged somewhere in the first half of 2011. Inspired by the protests on Tahrir Square (and other Arab Spring rebellions) but also triggered by the widespread bottom-up activisms in Portugal, Spain, and Greece where the so-called 'indignados' rallied creatively and with assembly-led movements against the impact of the crisis, the first Occupy protest in lower Manhattan was planned. The idea was to organize a big demonstration and then to occupy Zucotti Park (close to Wall Street in New York) for a few months; it was actually never the intention of the Occupy activists to stay in the park forever (as was suggested later by their critics).

After the first marches and the occupation of Zucotti Park, things went quickly as the images were swiftly circulated in the social media. Within a week Occupy camps were set up in a dozen other US cities and this number rapidly increased to six hundred US cities within a few weeks. Even though the activists were largely young and middle-class students and professionals, the Occupy movement was quite diverse as it also included middle-aged union members, unemployed 50-plus workers, Afro-American activists as well as Iraq and Afghanistan war veterans. What brought them together was a joint rejection of the 1 % of the population who had been responsible of the financial crackdown. The slogan 'we are the 99 %' was powerful, went viral and also triggered Occupy protests globally: on the Global Day of Action occupy protests were staged in over 1,500 cities all over the world.

Even though the protestors were violently evicted from Zucotti Park a month later, the movement had shown a vast impact; in the first place by demonstrating different ways of organizing and leading a multitude of people. Occupy introduced and experimented with new forms of horizontal decision-making and deliberation in order to show what real democracy was about (Castells 2012). Inspired by the protests in Egypt and Spain in particular, the Occupy activists explicitly wanted to explore new forms of collaborative and transparent forms of decision-making that had been so absent in the run-up to the financial crisis. A horizontal system of deliberation through councils, working groups, and a general assembly, was intended to prevent that any individual would be able to manipulate decision-making. Castells (2012: 184) observes: 'the Occupy movement is challenging the current practice of political institutions in the US, while reaching back to the founding principles of community-based democracy as one of the sources of the American Revolution'.

The constraint of the Occupy movement was that it had no clear or concrete demand that could be negotiated. Sure, the assemblies voted for a range of proposals (on mortgages, student loans, environmental projects, etc.) but these did not evolve into single demands towards the international financial establishment. Young people dominated the debates in the movement, but their demands were not always heard. There was also a group of feminist peace activists within the movement that started a campaign Occupy Patriarchy 'to provide a supportive, global space for feminist analysis, response and organizing and networking within the world-wide Occupy movement'[3], which attracted quite some support in the social media. Many Occupy participants even considered it essential not to make any specific demands, as they felt the mere existence of Occupy was powerful enough, but also to avoid a situation where demands were made on behalf of 'others'. This certainly was a strength of the movement, but it would also lead to its disintegration by the end of 2011. As one observer noted: 'After the last Occupier went home and the parks were hosed down, OWS seemed to suffer a prolonged hangover.'[4]

We should therefore also pose a few more critical questions in relation to the OWS aftermath. The first constant critique has been that its viral nature made OWS a movement of young people, excluding anyone who was not a 'digital native'. The response to this argument is that OWS implemented a new type of activism in which the boundaries between online and offline have been blurred: the separation is no longer relevant. In addition, many non-digital natives have found the social media to be a crucial forum for discussion and action, so at least this has triggered a changing attitude. Another major criticism was that OWS did not achieve anything substantial other than publicity and sympathy. The reaction of OWS activists has been that new types of 'Robin Hood' tax legislation have been initiated and implemented in a dozen (mostly European) countries since the OWS campaign. In the United States similar legislation has not yet been realized, out of fear for companies leaving the country.

The question thus remains: what was the 'civic innovation' of the Occupy movement? Here the most important achievement is probably that it managed to institutionalize itself within the social media. Rather than being vulnerable to physical counter-reactions (as we have seen in the Kiev protests) Occupy went back to where it was conceived. In that sense we can consider this temporality of the 'square & park presence' as a real civic innovation which will very likely have its impact on global activisms (as we witness for example in Gezi Park in Istanbul).

Which methodologies to use?

Our three examples trigger three burning questions in relation to civic innovation and will form a key part of the basis for a more coherent CIRI research programme.

The example on gender-based violence in Tahrir Square demonstrates that there are complex stories and issues within collectivities striving for social transformation and that internal power relationships often are obscured in order to prioritize 'larger' social goals. This is exactly what we want to question in the framework of civic innovation research. In particular this generates the question about how to account for the complexity of intersectionality and embodiment in social movement dynamics and actions, i.e. how to understand the lived bodily experiences in the struggle for democratic power. As the example of Tahrir Square shows, our understanding of civic innovation is responding to how social science is struggling to develop new methods that can 'perform' and capture the fluidity of changing understandings of identities, bodies, emotions, networks, power relations and knowledge in today's 'messy' world. This is particularly important when looking at how gender and sexual relations are changing in places that defy easy capturing in social science framing. Current methodologies, for example, find it hard to describe the complexities of intersectional embodiment in relation to changing economies, geographies, cultures, networks of communications, experiences of pleasures, of visible and invisible interactions.

CIRI is looking at using methodologies of co-partnership and ways to build a co-generation of new understandings and knowledges around embodiment and intersectional analysis of civic innovation through reflexive learning processes. Understanding civic innovation requires a horizontal sharing of knowledge where all expertise and knowledges are valued and understood as coming from a particular positionality. Reflexive learning means valuing and respecting differences (of approach, age, experience, gender, race, education) without denying the role that power and acts of governing play in shaping those differences (Harcourt 2013; Harcourt and Icaza 2014).

The Fair Trade example shows that things often do not turn out to be what they initially seem to be: so assessing new developments also requires close scrutiny of these results (for which we need new concepts and new assessment criteria). So the question here is: In which cases have processes of institutionalization and up-scaling of civic innovations been more successful, and what generalizable lessons can be drawn from those experiences? As our Fair Trade example has shown, to answer this research question we need to analyse both the specific activisms that aim to generate change, as well as assess the extent to which practices in the establishment have been altered or adjusted as a consequence. Moreover, we need to reflect on how values evolve, both over time and when implanted in other institutional settings.

The Occupy example shows that civic innovation can be often rather vague, diffuse and invisible, and that it seems to be linked to institutionalization of success. Even though this is generally not easy to assess (see the previous point). For Occupy, the question was and is whether these experiments worldwide with new forms of horizontal deliberation and decision-making will have an impact on a new generation of decision-makers who grew up as digital natives. In other words: how can we make sure civic innovation processes are not generating outcomes that exclude some of the actors for which the change process was meant?

Conclusion: civic innovation as a mosaic

We see civic innovation as part of future critical narratives for social change built from bottom up perspectives. By adopting an ontological approach – learning from doing – we see the study of civic innovation as an instructive way to look at how people adapt and try to move forward. Through seeking to understand civic innovation we chip away at the big narratives of global patriarchal capitalism and its failures and go to the underlying pulse of change in the multiple forms of alternatives at the edges of mainstream global capitalism.

In order to operationalize a civic innovation mosaic we have introduced a preliminary set of constituting concepts, and the idea is that each contribution to the book engages with and explores the usefulness of a combination of some of these concepts, both conceptually and empirically.

This introductory chapter brings together some key questions on how to shape a civic innovation agenda and sets out why those concepts in the mosaic are key. We have asked first, how can we avoid that civic innovation processes generate exclusionary and disempowering outcomes for those it was intended to benefit? Second, how can we account for the complexity of intersectionality and embodiment in social movement dynamics? And third, which types of civic innovations are more likely to endure and can be brought to scale without losing their identity?

The chapters that follow show how this first experiment in civic innovation has allowed us to develop new methods that can capture the fluidity of changing understandings of identities, bodies, emotions, networks, power relations and knowledge in today's 'messy' world. The 11 chapters that make up the book give meaning to civic innovation through different conceptual approaches and studies from locations around the world. In the conclusion we highlight the main findings and point to what we see as the conceptual innovations of this foundational work on civic innovation research as well as our reflections on the process and methodology of doing civic innovation research. We invite those who are curious to turn to those concluding remarks, but first we would encourage you to take a journey through these very different descriptions and analysis of civic innovation presented in the following chapters.

Notes

1 See the short statement about CIRI on the ISS website: http://www.iss.nl/fileadmin/ ASSETS/iss/Research_and_projects/CIRI/Documents/CIRI_Public_Briefing_Note_ Final.pdf (accessed 18 January 2016).
2 Some global GBV campaigns are '16 Days of Violence Against Women,' the 'Billion Rising Campaign', 'Women Living Under Muslim Law', and 'Women's Rights Defenders' (Harcourt 2013).
3 See http://www.feministpeacenetwork.org/; as well as http://www.occupypatriarchy. org/ (accessed December 2015).
4 http://againstausterity.org/blog/world-pure-imagination-how-occupy-turned-anarchy# sthash.v6pB887f.dpuf (accessed December 2015).

References

Antrobus, P. (2004) *The Global Women's Movement, Origins, Issues and Strategies.* London: Zed Books.
Barrientos, S., Conroy, M. E. and Jones, E. (2007) 'Northern social movements and Fair Trade'. In L. Raynolds, D. Murray and J. Wilkinson (eds) *Fair Trade: The Challenges of Transforming Globalization.* London: Routledge, 51–62.
Biekart, K. and Fowler, A. (2013) 'Transforming activisms 2010+: Exploring ways and waves'. *Development and Change* 44(3): 527–546.
Black, A. and Burstein, R. (2013) *The 2050 City: What Civic Innovation Looks like Today – and Tomorrow.* Report for the New America Foundation.
Butler, J. (2011) 'Bodies in alliance'. Lecture given at Bryn Mawr College,14 November 2011. Text of an essay 'Bodies in alliance and the politics of the street' may be found at http://www.eipcp.net/transversal/1011/butler/en (accessed 2 April 2014).
Castells, M. (2012) *Networks of Outrage and Hope: Social Movements in the Internet Age.* Cambridge: Polity Press.

Fowler, A. (2013) 'Social innovation: new game, new dawn, or false promise?' (*mimeo*, August).

Fowler, A. and Biekart, K. (2008) *Civic-Driven Change: Citizen's Imagination in Action*. The Hague: Institute of Social Studies.

Fraser, N. (2013) *Fortunes of Feminism: From State-managed Capitalism to Neoliberal Crisis*. Brooklyn, New York: Verso Books.

Hafez, S. (2014) 'The revolution shall not pass through women's bodies: Egypt, uprising and gender politics'. *The Journal of North African Studies* 19(2): 172–185.

Harcourt, W. (2013) 'Transnational feminist engagement with 2010+ activisms'. *Development and Change* 44(3): 621–637.

Harcourt, W. and Icaza, R. (2014) 'Going beyond the comfort zone: conference report of the Interculture Dialogues on Sexuality, Reproductive Health and Rights in Development'. *Gender, Technology and Development* 18(1): 131–145.

Moghadam, V. M. (2005) *Globalizing Women: Transnational Feminist Networks*. Baltimore: John Hopkins University Press.

Mohanty, C. T. (2004) *Feminism Without Borders: Decolonizing Theory, Practicing Solidarity*. Durham: Duke University Press.

Walsh, C. (2016) 'On gender and its otherwise'. In W. Harcourt (ed.), *Palgrave Handbook on Gender and Development: Critical Engagements in Feminist Theory and Practice*. London: Palgrave, 34–47.

2 The institutional foundations of civic innovation

Georgina M. Gómez and Holly A. Ritchie

The institutional content of civic innovation

The Introduction to this book presented the concept of civic innovation illustrating that social change happens everywhere in society, at the global level as well as in communities, governments, markets, and families. This chapter will unpack the concept of civic innovation from an institutional perspective towards the development of a theory of actor-driven social change. Civic innovation depends on the '24/7 citizen' described in the introduction as the central actor, a representative agent that engages in public and civic actions towards social transformation. This chapter centres on the 24/7 citizens that are constituted by the institutions prevalent in a particular space and time, and which install a tendency or inclination to act in a certain way. The 24/7 citizen does not exist independently from the social context: it is an agent who breakfasts as a family member according to the patterns of food consumption in the area, gets dressed according to the social customs of gender and local custom, engages in work – paid or unpaid – in line with the work ethic of his or her corresponding class and status, and participates in the evening in a traditional ceremony according to the conventions in the community. He or she may also attend a trade union meeting or a demonstration where attendants would scream and distribute pamphlets or walk in absolute silence, in line with the applicable rules of action for that specific setting. The actions of our protagonists have followed uncountable social rules throughout the day. Even the size of the pillow upon which their heads rests and drifts into sleep follows the prescriptions of what is accustomed and expected for someone in that specific social position, gender, time, space, and so on.

No actions of our agents are independent of the institutions that create an inclination to do things in a particular way. Our agents may be more aware of some rules than others. Some rules seem wrong to some agents, but the nor- mative content, or the values underpinning those rules and related social expectations, may be too strong to ignore or to disobey or the agent may not be troubled enough by them. Hence most of the time agents willingly or unwillingly accommodate to the prescribed rules and conform. A few rules, however, are perceived to be so constraining, outdated or wrong, that some agents seek to change them at a social level and this is where civic innovation begins. When our socially configured 24/7 agents decide to engage in political action to precipitate social change, we will refer to these actions as 'civic innovation'. Its first basic element is a clash of institutions and the values that these represent. The second basic element includes the mechanisms that are used to change the institutions that entail collective action in the public space, as opposed to a private act. Neglecting one traffic light does not mean that our citizen wants to abolish traffic lights as an institution that coordinates traffic priorities. The origin of civic innovation is thus the initial identification of a conflict in values and a contestation of the normative contents of institutions: citizens (in plural) recognise that an institution clashes with the values and interests of their group or network. The process of civic innovation is then one fed by collective action. This is not because agents know what they want and act instrumentally to achieve pre-determined goals. Rather, in order to make progress towards civic innovation, cooperation is instrumental to clarify actor goals as well as their attainability. That means that they collectively problematise an issue and frame alternatives to the status quo. The conflict results from the fact that some institutions contradict emerging values; and that in response, related agents may promote their own institutions instead, or simply resist the institutions of others. The key elements in our definition are: institutions, a socially structured agent, political motivations, and collective action. In this chapter we will explore each one of these elements in detail.

The concept of civic innovation is approached from an institutional point of view and a preference for the perspective of the Old Institutionalism (including Thorstein Veblen, John Commons, and Clarence Ayres), and the more recent works of Geoffrey Hodgson, Masahiro Aoki, and others. It will present civic innovation as one particular type of institutional change, incorporating both political conflicts between institutions and emerging values, and collective action/agency to resist and change those institutions. 'What's in an institution?' will conceptualise institutions and the ways in which they regulate behaviour and constitute agents. 'Towards a theory of institutional change' proposes a tentative model of how institutions change, in general, and 'Civic innovation as endogenous institutional change' explores how agents engage in contentious actions to push for institutional change and disseminate it within their social setting, or 'tessera' of the social mosaic referred to in the Introduction. The chapter concludes with a conceptualisation of 'civic innovation' and the identification of the characteristics that distinguish it from other forms of institutional innovation. The discussion addresses specifically the concepts of institutions, values, agency, power and scale described in Table I.1 of the Introduction to this book.

What's in an institution?

Institutions shape human behaviour and provide structure in society. Whilst central to human societies, there is still little consensus on a common definition of institutions or how to do institutional analysis (Hollingsworth 2002).

Nobel Prize for Economics winner Douglass North famously defined institutions as the 'rules of the game' (North 1990: 4), including the incentives and disincentives to behave in certain ways. Other authors describe institutions as 'structured processes of interaction among individuals, relatively enduring and recognised as such' (Lawson 2003: 182). With an emphasis on coordination, Ostrom (2005: 3) views institutions as 'prescriptions' that are used to organise 'all forms of repetitive and structured interactions' within families, communities, organisations and markets, across social, cultural, political and economic realms. Institutions present possible paths of action for economic agents to decide about employment, production, exchange and the options between abiding by rules and shirking. With some variation in the focus of the definition, institutions are invariably characterised as social structures (Wells 1970) that are regularities that give stability and meaning to human action (Crespi 1994). Hodgson (2006: 2) argues that institutions are 'the kind of structures that matter most in the social realm, and comprise "the stuff of social life"'. He distinguishes institutions, which are 'socially embedded systems of rules' from other social structures, which are simply *any* regularity in social relations. So, while all institutions are social structures, the opposite is not true. Institutions are specific types of social structures that are distinctly embedded in societal values and indicate a socially acceptable action.

Institutions as systems of rules

Hodgson's definition of institutions as 'systems of rules' gives a first hint to understand what makes them a special type of regularity in social life. As rules, institutions have the format 'in circumstances X, do Y' (Hodgson 2006: 3). Rules refer to 'an injunction or disposition' that guides human behaviour. The durability of rules comes through the capacity of institutions to 'create stable expectations of the behaviour of others' and permit 'ordered thought, expectation and action' (Hodgson 2004: 425). While human nature makes various actions possible in circumstances X, society indicates one specific action Y as the accepted one within a particular social setting, time and place, and this creates an inclination to behave in a certain way. In this way, rules are 'considered, acknowledged, or followed without much thought' (Hodgson 2006: 3). Max Weber similarly pointed out that 'some rules are followed without any subjective formulation in thought of the rule' (Weber 1978: 105). For example, language structures communication, and individual property rights permit for-profit behaviour in economics.

Rules, however, are not merely guides for action within specific sets of values and conditions, they are also potentially codifiable and have normative content related to core social values and expectations. On the normative content, agents may ignore the dispositions to act as the rules indicate, but their choice does not mean that the inclination does not exist, and at a social level any transgression will be seen as a deviation – or breach of the rules – which could be sanctioned. 'Potentially codifiable' means that the action is socially acceptable, and under specific conditions may be articulated through discourse to both inform other agents and support the transmission amongst them. Knowledge of rules can also be tacit. Whilst sociologists have theorised that people follow rules to avoid sanctions, rules also generate positive effects such as facilitating interaction with strangers, permitting trust and social cooperation (Seabright 2010). Such rules of action – or 'social norms', their close equivalent in sociology – enable agreements in 'situations in which there is an inherent conflict between individual and collective interests' (Biccheri 2010: 298). In relation to civic innovation, being codifiable is a precondition to the organisation of collective action. The normative content of rules addresses the meaning of what is expected by others.

Since knowledge of the rules may be tacit, it can be difficult to determine whether behaviour is a result of complying with rules or a natural instinct. It may be useful to distinguish instinct, habit and actual behaviour. Instinct is a genetically inherited inclination, while habit is a socially acquired inclination, and behaviour is the physical conduct of actors. Instinct explains just a small part of the variety of human actions and interactions, while habits are ubiquitous and make institutions work without need for deliberation. This distinction denies the 'natural' character of any prevailing social order as a biological determination and underlines the role of habits as dispositions to engage in previously adopted or acquired behaviour, triggered by 'specific stimuli or contexts' (Hodgson 2003: 556). Habits create immanent or unreasoned dispositions to act in a certain way, like propensities or inclinations, and sustain the rules as codifiable and normative components of institutions. In the meantime, behaviour is the factual action, including a possible non-response, i.e. in not taking any action. In this way, insights from Dewey (1922: 40) are taken up by Hodgson to explain that institutions both reflect and shape habits (Hodgson 2004: 656). Within economic sociology, Powell and DiMaggio (1991: 26) revisit Bourdieu's cognitive concept of *habitus,* related to people's common histories and backgrounds, as leading to shared thoughts, dispositions and strategies of action, and which was critically influenced by Veblen's conceptualisation of habit (O'Hara 2007; Wäckerle 2014). As expressed by O'Hara, institutions, habits and instincts come together in a 'realist analysis of the structure, contradictions and unstable reproduction of economic systems, paying particular attention to the link between agency and institutions, habits and instincts in an environment of uncertainty, ignorance and bounded rationality' (O'Hara 2007: 35).

Unpacking institutional components

Taking a closer look at institutional building blocks, the social embeddedness of institutions marks a relation to ethics, morality and related social values, which express themselves in the rules that make up an institution. For instance, the cultural beliefs and values around gender and caring add moral implications to the rules that drive family life and these can be enforced based on moral arguments (van Staveren 2007). Values define 'good personhood' within a specific cultural setting and, by definition, the institutions under which family life is recreated. Beliefs, history and cultural experience constitute the general frame into which institutions exist. The complex interplay between rules of action and underlying values, belief systems, and their cultural heritage shape how agents interact with, and develop institutions. In a similar vein, Weber's (1930) classic *Protestant Ethic* earlier postulated a religious foundation (related to work values) to capitalist behaviour. But such a cultural determinant approach to economic practices subsequently came under attack in the 1960s and 1980s from a number of scholars in the neo-Marxist and post-modernist traditions, as noted by Fukuyama (2003: 4). In recent decades, culturalist explanations of economic behaviour have been revisited in different contexts. Platteau, for example, drew attention to African societies and the origins of highly egalitarian norms with restraints on individual wealth, which he argues has led to 'cultural' obstacles to accumulation and subsequent economic growth (Platteau 2000). Fukuyama (2003) elaborated on a wide range of areas of human behaviour that are in fact non-rational in origin (i.e. non-optimising behaviour) such as actions based on religious belief, as well as inherited social habits and other deeply embedded cultural values. Emphasising the influence of historical experience on subsequent institutional development, Greif (2006) pointed to the 'community responsibility system' as an existing institution that functioned in Europe from medieval to modern times, which fostered gradual institutional development through 'self-governed communes'. Douglas (1986: 91) draws attention to human cognition and its dependence on institutions, with institutions built by 'squeezing each other's ideas into a common shape' to gain legitimacy by 'sheer numbers'. Douglas describes the stabilisation of institutions and the gaining of legitimacy through 'distinctive grounding in nature and reason'. This may explain why actors may behave in certain ways and reproduce social structures, influencing institutional development.

Figure 2.1 endeavours to capture the relationship between beliefs, values, habits and rules (or social norms) as the basic ingredients of institutions. At

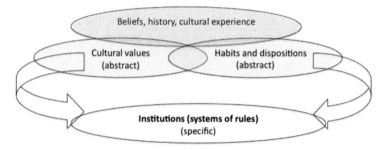

Figure 2.1 Linking beliefs, values, habits and rules
Source: Derived from Ritchie 2013

the fundamental level, societal beliefs are entrenched in history and cultural experience. These subsequently drive abstract or conceptual evolving cultural values, and social habits and dispositions. Ultimately, these then shape practical and concrete institutions, or specific systems of social rules. Recognising the influence of culture and beliefs in later work, North (2003: 4) has drawn attention to the cultural heritage of individuals, i.e. the deeply embedded institutions and aggregated beliefs 'carried forward' over generations (path dependent patterns), in addition to new positive and negative experiences. Clearly, it is critical to appreciate the background of a society and cultural heritage (and the dynamic shifts as societies evolve) to understand the emergence of dynamic institutions with 'complex chains of causality', and particularly the 'interplay' between the formal rules and the informal norms (North 2003).

Towards a theory of institutional change

Institutions establish systems of rules, according to which individuals interact, frame their agency and dispose agents to certain actions. Advancing theoretical arguments on structure and agency, and going beyond this dichotomy, Hodgson (2004) has elaborated a cognitive conception of agency, describing agency as the capacity of agents to 'reflect and deliberate upon the context, options, purpose and possible outcomes of action'. With an emphasis on habit, Hodgson described the relationship between agency and structure as distinct but 'connected in a circle of mutual interaction and interdependence' (Hodgson 2004: 446). Hodgson hence proposes an evolutionary dimension in a 'non-conflationary and casually interactive' approach that tries to capture how individual intentions or preferences change, suggesting that individuals become agents in the social context that constitutes them and not as isolated entities. As we anticipated, the 24/7 agent in the Introduction is in itself a social product.

Institutions and agents

In earlier work, Hodgson (1998) depicted the interaction between agents and institutions as a stable loop that reproduces itself as long as the equilibrium lasts. Hodgson follows several works of Veblen (1919) in analysing the interactions between individuals and institutions as a relationship of causality in both directions, although agents and institutions exist at different ontological levels. Institutions inform individuals on what actions Y are acceptable in circumstances X and individuals are inclined to act in that way. The repetition of the action, in turn, reinforces the institutions that continue being enacted and their embeddedness in that particular social setting of values, intentions and preferences. The double loop addresses the fact that institutions guide and shape agents, but at the same time the actions of the agents affect institutions by reproducing them. We will first study this stable situation, before adding complexity in the next section exploring what happens when individuals resist the institutions and attempt to change them.

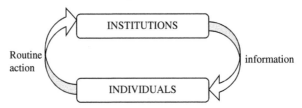

Figure 2.2 The institutionalist action-information loop
Source: Hodgson 1998: 176

The loop in Figure 2.2 discloses an understanding of institutions as a point of equilibrium, in the sense that the rules of action in an institution have become stable, are being repeated without much thought and have stopped mutating. The inclination to abide by the rules is internalised by individuals and at the same time it has meaning at the social level, so that others expect these to be followed, too. This reciprocal expectation constitutes an incentive for agents to reproduce the relevant institutions, as Greif and Kingston (2011) express it, because 'interactions create the structure that motivates obedience. The behaviour of others motivates behaviour'. Shared expectations on each other's actions become 'self-enforcing', Greif and Kingston (2011) continue, in the sense that agents will generally follow the equilibrium rule of action as long as the others follow it as well.

> From each decision-maker's perspective, the others' expected behavior constitutes the structure motivating her to conform to the behavior expected of her. But by conforming, she contributes to motivating others to conform too. Thus, the structure is self-perpetuating, and although it is beyond the control of each decision maker, it is endogenous to all of them taken together.
>
> (Greif and Kingston 2011: 27)

Examining agency, institutional diversity and change

In developing the model, we consider that a first element that could be further theorised in this reasoning is the outcome of rule-following. As long as rule-following leads to the expected outcomes, no further reflection need ensue – institutions are points of equilibria in terms of the coincidence between expectations and actual outcomes – but this may not be the case. Aoki (2007: 3) refers to 'the *consequence function*' that specifies 'particular (physical) consequences of concern to some or all the agents [contingent on the state of nature]'. In the logical form of the rule mentioned above, 'in circumstances X do Y', there is a certain expected outcome Z that should result from the individual's rule-following action. The logical form of an institution as equilibrium could be expressed as 'in circumstances X do Y and expect Z'. In this way, if Z occurs after doing Y in circumstances X, agents will be inclined to continue repeating the action. The failure of Z to happen, however, may trigger a reflection on what went wrong or what needs to be reviewed in the equilibrium loop.

A second point that is not specifically included in the institution-action loop in Figure 2.2 is diversity. Equilibria at the macro level (the overall 'cognitive framework' guiding individuals to behave and relate to institutions) may differ from the meso or micro level in which agents – individually or collectively – enjoy relative autonomy and live in contexts imbued with meanings. Along that line of thinking, Aoki (2007) and Greif and Kingston (2011) hint that institutions are only *partial* equilibria, in the sense that they represent equilibria with relevance to a specific time, space, and social group in terms of ethnicity, class, gender and other dimensions of differentiation. Chang (2002) argues that competing cultures and traditions exist within one society, so institutions are points of equilibria only within the limits of each one of these. In relation to the Introduction to this volume, our reasoning speaks to the metaphor of societies as a mosaic, and argues that different individuals are affected by the institutions in their particular sphere, or *tessera* or tile. Partial equilibria co-exist because different agents acquire the institutions from others who had been following these before them and among whom the various agents have been shaped.

The human actions in each *tessera* are regulated by a set of institutions applicable to a group or network. Mark Granovetter and Richard Swedberg (1992: 4) emphasised the importance of networks to explain the configuration of agents and agency, and defined networks as a regular set of contacts or similar social connections among groups or individuals. A network transmits situated institutions and the values and habits on which these institutions rely, within a cultural and historical experience as depicted in Figure 2.1. For example, some networks are biased towards self-interest and sustain a number of institutions consistent with those values, while other networks are driven by common interest and generate institutions that guide agents to a common goal. These learning processes, however, are ultimately individual, so by definition agents' behaviour is not necessarily uniform, equal or 'given' (Hodgson 1998) even within a single network. Agents may choose to ignore rules, resist them or challenge them, so individual action is never fully predictable. To complicate it further, agents move across *tesserae* because they are part of different networks at the same time (workplace, family, trade union, and so on).

Apart from this horizontal institutional diversity, there is also a hierarchical arrangement of institutions. Several scholars have elaborated on the layers of institutions. For example, Ostrom (1990: 52) used the innovative concept of 'nested' rules to describe the linkages between rules, and their capacity for change. In later work, Ostrom (2005: 58) presented a hierarchical arrangement with five layers of rules, depending on the type of action that they guide. The 'operational rules' guide day-to-day interactions, 'collective-choice rules' establish procedures for choosing operational rules, 'constitutional rules' govern the selection of collective-choice rules, the 'meta constitutional rules' regulate over choices of constitutional rules and the biophysical world is

situated at the top level. When agents perceive that the rules over their interactions at one level are unsatisfactory, they are driven to 'shift levels' in search
of information and guidance to change those rules. Ritchie (2013) added
insights to Ostrom (1990) by elaborating on the nature of the interdependence
of 'nested' rules in enterprise in relation to the spheres of applicability, scope
of variation, and enforcement with overall control firmly resting with powerful actors (entrepreneurs and local authorities). Layering institutions is critical
to understand that some of them change relatively quickly, while others are
extremely durable and institutional change at that level is 'overwhelmingly
incremental' (North 1990: 89). At the same time, it explains why institutions are
path-dependent: 'the consequence of small events and chance circumstances
can determine solutions that, once they prevail, lead one to a particular path'
(North 1990: 94).

A third point that could be further theorised in the reasoning depicted in
Figure 2.2 is the implication that institutions are fixed and individuals continue
enacting them *in eternum*. In other words, agents in Figure 2.2 are trapped in
a loop of repeating actions. That is obviously not the case, although more
slow-moving evolutionary processes may be ongoing, and the question of how
institutions change has been the object of a rich research agenda. At the same
time, Figure 2.2 does provide a principle to theorise institutional change from
an evolutionary perspective, because it links agency back to institutions. If
individuals do not enact the rules, they may seek different ways of thinking,
understanding and behaving in a situation X. Institutional change is based on
agency and is defined as the creation of new inclinations to guide the actions
of a number of individuals. These new institutions would be formalised as
rules to behave in a certain way Y' in circumstances X. Per our definition of
institutions, the new rules will eventually acquire normative content, too, will
be codifiable, reflect certain values and gain resilience to stay unchanged for a
certain period of time. We emphasised that institutions are layered horizon-
tally and vertically, which implies that an action is reproduced repeatedly but
need not be permanent. Institutions are demi-regularities, a term coined by
Lawson (1997) which describes elements that are only stable within a certain
scope of time, space and positionality.

Evolutionary insights and collective agency

Moreover, our approach is evolutionary in the sense that new institutions
emanate from existing institutions of a higher layer that define what is possible
and what is not for agents to think, understand and experiment. Greif and
Kingston (2011: 39) note that past institutional elements are 'the raw material
on which new institutions are based', while Sugden (1989) argues that agents
engaged in institutional change coordinate their strategies to achieve it but
'generally adopt rules which are analogous to rules with which they are already
familiar'. In other words, familiarity relates to habits as inclinations and preferences that limit the scale and scope of the change process. Consequently,

new institutions resemble older, familiar institutions because they contain elements inherited from or inspired by past institutions. Several scholars (Campbell 2004; Gomez 2008) elaborated that actors create new institutions through a process of 'bricolage', a term first used by Lévi-Strauss (1966: 16) to explain how agents recombine elements in their institutional repertoire 'with devious means' and deal with obstacles with 'some extraneous movement' before they return to the usual path. Campbell (1997) also suggests that institutional change evolves through a process of delimited selection, as permitted by the existing arrangements, in addition to prevailing power relations. Friedland and Alford (1991: 251) describe existing institutions as affecting both institutional change processes and their outcomes.

Along this evolutionary reasoning, institutional change starts when agents do not follow the rule and resort to acts of experimentation conditioned by the prevailing institutions, on the one hand, and by networks of agents as sources of information and inspiration, on the other. In the Introduction to this volume, the civic innovation type of institutional change was described with terms such as 'institutional setting' and the 'activisms' in which people engage to exercise agency. We are arguing, in turn, that networks shape intentions and interests, which affect the reasoning to search for new solutions. So while habits provide the cognitive means by which information is sought and interpreted, the networks of belonging – including the activisms – define what experimentation is possible and later support its repetition until it becomes a new rule of action. While agents are elements of a lower ontological level than institutions, they can affect those at a higher level in a process that Hodgson (2002) terms reconstitutive upward causation. The inverse process is termed reconstitutive downward causation, when institutions inform and contribute to the formation of individual habits by defining 'what has meaning and what actions are possible' in experimentation (Powell 1991: 9). Greif (1989) and Greif, Milgrom and Weingast (1994) have argued that organisations inherited from the past and cultural beliefs shape the choices among alternative institutions, among other reasons, because the interaction with specific networks determines whose identity is known to whom, and where information flows, while cultural beliefs coordinate expectations.

This conceptualisation of institutional innovation is depicted in Figure 2.3. The information–action loop of Figure 2.2 is now reconfigured into two loops. In the first loop (top), agents do rule-following and a routine situation X leads to a routine action Y. It is an action already experienced as acceptable and leading to an expected outcome Z. Routine action is repeated mechanically in the *reproduction loop*. But the model is now reconfigured to include a second loop in which agents face new or unknown situations X or understand that Z is unacceptable. Insufficient or unacceptable information do not define an appropriate course of action. Other higher-level institutions and networks hold a role as enablers and persuaders of action and inform what experimentation is possible and adequate for the social setting. An *evolutionary loop* (bottom) thus appears in which reflexive action takes over

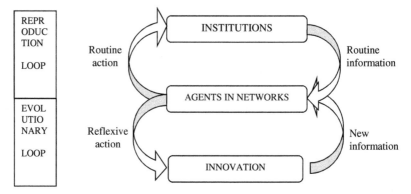

Figure 2.3 Institutional innovation and change

routine rule-following and the 'skilful actors' begin their innovation and learning. Experimental actions are embedded in networks that influence both the interpretation of the situation and the final decision-making. In the long run, if the response Y' is tested and perceived as suitable to achieve acceptable results Z' every time that circumstances X are present, then the action is repeated for that situation and eventually becomes the accepted course of action, which may be imitated by others in the network and may cement as institutions in the long run. Institutions hence do not grow out of infallible design and in fact they can be the outcome of mistake, speculation, coincidence, and erratic behaviour, but once in place as acceptable actions, they acquire stability and resilience.

Economic action in the face of new information is basically an experimental process guided by pragmatism, previous experience, values, and sometimes the pursuit of a specific goal (Beckert 2003), because agents are not perfectly rational but driven by bounded experimentation and learning. Their actions are guided by 'rational learning' meaning that while they are engaged in a rational process, by the very act of learning not all information is possessed, so intuition, emotions and ideals play a role. In the same vein, given that learning is an individual process, agents are diverse in themselves and diversely positioned in social networks, so the economic agent is not 'a given'. Learning is conceived as more than just acquiring information; it is the development of new habits, means and modes of cognition, calculation and assessment. Learning and experimenting are transformative and reconstructive processes, involving the creation of new habits, preferences, propensities and conceptual frameworks. The methods and criteria of optimisation are themselves learnt. Jens Beckert (2003) provides a theory of action in economic contexts of complexity and novelty. Uncertainty not only makes it impossible to identify a 'best' solution but to link accurately the causal relationship between means (strategies) and outcomes. Every situation has several readings judged as adequate by the actors. In turn, decisions depend on joint interpretations of the situation within networks of belonging. This is where inter-subjectivity and networks play a role, since orientations, perceptions of values and beliefs are formed with the expectations brought on them by the social surrounding where they are embedded (Granovetter and Swedberg 1992; Uzzi 1996). In the process of (institutional) innovation by experimentation, possible future states are considered along with the strategies to reach them. Experimentation represents a creative achievement on the part of the actors that demands imagination and judgement, taking a reflexive distance from rule-following. Outcomes are evaluated and tested until an acceptable solution is reached. The term 'acceptable solution' notes that it need not be 'optimal' but one that resolves a situation and/or represents an equilibrium, or re-stabilisation in combination with the conditions of power. We expand on this point below.

When actors succeed in framing a new mode of action and repeat it in similar situations, then 'something new enters the world' (Joas 1996: 128). Aoki (2007: 11) defines the process of configuring new institutions as an 'equilibrium displacement and its reconstruction', which represents the transition from one stage of equilibrium to a stage of experimentation, followed by another state of equilibrium represented by a new institution. Aoki considers that once an institution acquires a linguistic or symbolic representation recognised and reproduced by other agents, it may be regarded to have existence as an objective reality, which implies that it has evolved into a viable institution. Greif and Kingston (2011: 25) state that a social situation is 'institutionalized' when it 'motivates each individual to follow a regularity of behavior in that social situation and to act in a manner contributing to the perpetuation of that structure'. For an institution to be perpetuated, they continue, 'its constituent elements must be (1) confirmed (not refuted or eroded) by observed outcomes (2) reinforced by those outcomes (in the sense that its ability to be self-enforcing does not decline over time) and (3) inter-temporally regenerated by being transmitted to newcomers.' Institutions, therefore, can be conceived as points of equilibrium and stabilisation when they have climbed a step on the ladder, in the words of Brousseau and Raynaud (2011), and reach a new alignment between the pre-existent institutions, and prevalent values, expectations and outcomes in a particular social setting, they start to be reproduced without much reflection. Hollingsworth (2002: 6) draws attention to Legro (1997) in highlighting the differing strengths of institutions as indicated by their 'simplicity' (in how well they are interpreted and ease of application), their 'durability' (in terms of how long they were in existence and their legitimacy), and their 'concordance' (in terms of the breadth of application). These elements are characteristic of a state of equilibrium and stabilisation – with slow evolutionary processes ongoing – and may last for a very long time and seem indefinite.

Civic innovation as endogenous institutional change

The approach presented in Figure 2.3 refers to any type of institutional change at an abstract level and follows recent empirical insights on institutional change that integrate an evolutionary approach with network considerations. There are several instances of institutional change, depending on whether its trigger is novelty (a new situation), or whether it is exogenously or endogenously driven. This section will look into these three cases and subsequently delve into the conceptualisation of civic innovation as the endogenous type of institutional change.

The first instance of institutional change is when situations are new or incongruent with the information that individuals may associate with existing institutions because the situation is completely unknown. The circumstances are new or different (X is unknown), so there is no clear inclination on what path of action Y to follow. A response needs to be formulated. The second instance of institutional change is the exogenously driven one, in which following a rule Y does not lead to the expected outcome Z, because there have been recent changes in the environment that have reduced the applicability of the institution. In order to still obtain Z in circumstances X or X', a different path of action (Y') needs to be sought. The third instance is the endogenously driven institutional change one, in which the social values underpinning an institution have changed in such a way that they are inconsistent with the path of action Y or the outcome Z. In other words, following the rule has become unacceptable and in the situation X, agents seek a different path of action Y' to obtain an acceptable Z'. Greif and Kingston (2011) refer to this situation as an 'institutional disequilibrium' which results when an institution ceases to represent an accepted alignment between beliefs, cultural values and experiences, on the one hand, with courses of actions, expectations and outcomes, on the other.

Networks and interests

The endogenous institutional change stems from the introduction of new values and ideas, and a political conflict that compels agents and their networks to take actions in search of new institutions. For example, slavery was widely accepted 200 years ago, but it then became unacceptable to some (i.e. due to a change in beliefs and values). Eventually it was subsequently banned by law (a change in formal institutions). Agents resist the prevailing institutions and experiment with different courses of action collectively, sometimes with organised collective action or through simple non-compliance. In the long run the consistent deviation from a rule may void it of its normative content and allow others to experiment with different courses of action. This can occur either due to exogenous shocks or due to endogenous modifications in the habits that occur gradually over time as a result of the erosion of the institutions, and may ultimately make them obsolete (Greif and Laitin 2004). Organised resistance may be part of the configuration of a new rule as well. The Introduction to this volume made reference to the 'activisms' in which people engage 'to exercise agency towards changing what they perceive as the establishment'. These activisms occur within networks that condition and support experimentation towards the construction of new institutions.

The Introduction also made reference to the co-shaping of civic innovation by the 'institutional setting within which it takes place, by available types of knowledge, and by the actor's experience of embodiment, identity and levels of intersectionality'. Civic innovation corresponds to the third type of institutional change presented in this chapter. It originates in a clash of values, is highly politicised and is related to a number of elements. The first ingredient of civic innovation is the interest to act in the political arena. It is not enough to disagree or feel uncomfortable with an institution; civic innovation requires motivation to take action against a rule. Several scholars have studied this issue and Beckert (1999), for example, explores integrating 'interest-driven behaviour in institutional change' to institutional organisation theory. Beckert critically advances an understanding of the role of 'strategic agency' as the 'systematic attempt to reach conceived ends through the planned and purposeful application of means' (Beckert 1999: 783). The author suggests that institutional rules and agency act as 'antagonistic mechanisms that contradict each other', and destabilise each other but remain interconnected. Other authors refer to 'intentionality' of action as guiding conscious deliberation and self-reflexive reasoning (Lawson 1997). Joas (1996: 158) defines intentionality as 'self-reflective control which we exercise over our current behaviour'.

Power struggles and change agents

A key characteristic of civic innovation is a dialogue of power asymmetries, in which existent rules embed power and there are degrees of resistance in an attempt to configure new rules. Civic innovation is the type of institutional change that unequivocally involves power struggles between different groups as they wrestle to gain control over the 'rules of the game', and build 'asymmetries' in their favour (Marglhin 1991). From an Institutional Political Economy perspective, several scholars (e.g. Bardhan 1989; Bowles and Gintis 1993, and Perrow 1986) have elaborated on the role of power in shaping institutions. As advanced in the Introduction of this volume, the study of civic innovation needs to be 'acutely aware of various types of' power. Drawing from Emerson (1972), Molm (1990: 429) distinguished two levels of power including structural power, as the 'potential power created by the relations of dependence among actors in exchange networks', and the strategic use of power by actors, influencing outcomes of exchange. Towards overcoming the dichotomy of power driven by agents or structure, Gaventa (2003) draws attention to Foucault (1998), with power perceived as beyond either individuals and institutions, and rather 'dispersed and subject-less' and 'ubiquitous': 'Power is everywhere: not because it embraces everything, but because it comes from everywhere' (Foucault 1998: 63). In this view, power may be a major source of social discipline and conformity, so the control over the rules of the game is as critical as the space to exercise agency. Our 24/7 citizens, therefore, do not just want to be able to decide when to abide by the rules and when to deviate. The 24/7 citizens want to create new rules of the game they play with others and perhaps shift to an entirely different game if the new institutions eventually reach an equilibrium, or restabilisation, with a different balance of power.

Among the 24/7 citizens that aspire to achieve different rules, some actors may perform critical roles as leaders or change agents. In the field of organisational studies, there has been a rich discussion on 'institutional entrepreneurs', a term coined by DiMaggio in 1988 to define the actors that are involved in transforming existing institutions or creating new institutions. Using a resource-mobilisation argument, the leading agents may draw on resources to influence others and to support prevailing institutions (the status-quo) or to formulate new institutions. Towards a more elaborate definition, Battilana, Leca and Boxenbaum (2009: 72) describes 'institutional entrepreneurs' as individuals or organisations that 'initiate, and actively participate in the implementation of changes that diverge from existing institutions, independent of whether the initial intent was to change the institutional environment and whether the changes were successfully implemented'. Such changes may be within organisations, or within their existing environment. Gomez (2008) highlights the characteristics of such entrepreneurs as 'skilful and resourceful' and notes their capacity to engage in 'collective action'. Yet 'change agents' may have diverse capacities and influences (Ford, Ford and D'Amelio 2008). In emerging enterprises, Ritchie (2013) elaborates a typology that includes socially motivated trailblazers permitting liberal institutional processes, and self-oriented gatekeepers endeavouring to retain control and limit institutional access and development.

With disagreements between the rational choice proponents (Axelrod 1984) and sociological institutionalists that dwell on actors' interpretation shaped by structure, Fligstein advances a number of theoretical propositions that aim to better incorporate people's interests and power in institutional change processes (Fligstein 2001). Firstly, skilled social actors are critical to gain the cooperation of others in an emerging field and to change agents – we have referred to them as institutional entrepreneurs. Secondly, skilled actors can establish new cultural frames by establishing 'compromise identities' which appeal to many groups. Thirdly, skilled actors that are part of existing powerful groups may draw on existing rules and resources to 'reproduce their power'. Fourthly, skilled actors in challenger groups may create niches and avoid dominant groups. Fifthly, where there is more stability and less external threats, actor social skills may matter less. Sixthly, skilled actors in dominant groups may tend to stand by the status quo, even in a crisis. And finally, new frames may emerge from 'invader' or 'challenger' groups, and thus they may either establish a political coalition, or create new frames that 'reorganise interests and identities'. Yet whilst these propositions expand our thinking on the various possible strategies of 'skilled groups', they do not incorporate more diverse actor motivations (and capabilities) that may lie beyond power-oriented incentives. Bringing about a change may require important collective action from a large number of individuals, as well as cooperation from others and strategies to overcome the opposition of those who stand to lose from the change. Such contingent alliances of collective action and cooperation may be generated by persuasion, through the use of new or existing organisations, or, according to Greif and Kingston (2011: 36), 'less commonly, through the rise of a charismatic leader'. Meanwhile going beyond 'institutional entrepreneurs' as critical actors, Battilana, Leca and Boxenbaum (2009) draw attention to Eisenstadt (1980) who argued that these agents may be just one 'variable' among a 'constellation' of others in the change process and may not be a critical ingredient in organising resistance.

Besides the political interests, the conflicts around the configuration of new institutions, and the skilful actors that may give voice to the process, the fourth element of civic innovation is the network that nests and nourishes the resistance, the 'activisms'. In moving away from individualism and towards exploring collective agency, Granovetter and Swedberg (1992) posit that 'stable' economic institutions emerge as growing 'clusters of activity' around existing personal networks. They theorise that the level of network fragmentation and cohesion, or 'coupling and decoupling' is a significant indicator of potential outcomes, and that actors whose networks straddle the largest number of institutional spheres will have the most advantage. Fligstein (1996) theorised that new paths of action could be opened up and institutionalised by 'skilful actors' by repeated learning within networks. Meanwhile Hollingsworth and Boyer (1997: 451) have described collective action as required to overcome the 'hysteresis of inefficient institutions'. Hage and Alter (1997: 120) further expand upon the motivation for inter-organisational evolution in the formation of linkages and alliances (within and between sectors) in more 'complex forms of coordination'. And they suggest that this may be driven by economic incentives (North 1990), the importance of innovation, and the 'reduction of adaptive costs'. Grabowski (1999) looked at the impact of networks on market integration and theorised that the process of 'integration' is believed to occur through 'bridging holes in social networks' and is carried out predominantly by entrepreneurial middlemen.

The process of civic innovation, as a special case of institutional change, is entrenched in actors' control over the configuration of institutions and depends on framing interests, engaging with power in the political arena, and conforming groups of interests with or without actors that will give a voice to the process. Civic innovation is by definition bottom-up and it is located among the citizens that resist rules, the values and the power embedded in them. That means that it stems from the needs, demands, and conscious interests of the citizens and their activisms. However, institutional change may also be initiated by external civic innovators that successfully insert themselves among those that pursue actions of resistance and manage to operationalise and stabilise a range of local actors around these other values, such as NGOs (Ritchie 2013). In that case, local agents may be further reinforced in their own agency, or be able to garner collective agency. Or if unsupported, in less amenable conditions, they can equally be thwarted by others' agency. In empirically grounded research of women's businesses in Afghanistan, Ritchie (2013) has advanced the critical role that NGOs can specifically play as institutional innovators and guides; the need for legitimacy in reshaping and ongoing institutional development, led by the entrepreneurs; and the importance of gaining the support of local authorities (as local power holders). Ultimately the research underscores the value of attaining cognitive synergies between these major players in a receptive and stable context to permit institutional change and development. Yet the social and political motivations of dominant local actors may influence their ongoing evolution, and the scope of equitable outcomes.

Towards understanding institutional sustainability, Brousseau and Raynaud (2011) highlight the influence of 'time and space' on institutional flexibility and strength, with earlier stage institutions more adaptable but (still) threatened by alternative rules. They discuss institutional options that may be available from different localities. They describe the launching of a competitive process, as institutions created locally by self-interested actors participate in a 'race for generalization'. They suggest that local lower level institutional arrangements tend to seek to become part of 'higher order institutions' in the overall institutional framework, 'climbing the ladder' of institutions. Yet as indicated by empirical research (Ritchie 2013), actor interests may be more nuanced than this, and actors may be further influenced by environmental effects or even other actors. Chang (2011) further describes broader processes of development as influencing the nature of institutions themselves, and actor motivations towards change. He describes economic development in particular as triggering agents to demand new and better quality institutions, and permitting the 'affordability' of these new institutions.

Conclusions

Institutions are important social phenomena because they can constrain or enable social change. They can be the target of civic change or the vessel for civic change. We first proposed a definition of institutions as socially embedded systems of rules (Figure 2.1), with two constitutive elements: (1) rules or norms prescribing socially acceptable behaviours, and (2) underlying values, habits and dispositions shaped by beliefs and ethical representations, sometimes triggering hidden, tacit, and implicit reactions when challenged. In some institutions, there is a critical moral content and in others there is not. Likewise, in some institutions the power dimension is critical and in others it is not. In all cases, institutions structure social life and create dispositions among agents to behave in certain ways, although agents may deviate from these rules.

We analysed the process of institutional change in a double loop (Figures 2.2 and 2.3). The institution–action loop in Figure 2.2 discloses an understanding of institutions as points of equilibria, in the sense that the rules of action are stable and are being repeated without much thought. However, we identified that this representation needs to be further theorised in a number of areas, namely the role of outcomes upon human representations of the rules, the diversity of institutions, and the complexities of institutional change. We differentiated horizontal and vertical diversity of institutions to capture the variety of institutions that apply to different individuals and their networks of belonging, on the one hand, and the hierarchical layering of institutions with varying degrees of durability. We followed the metaphor of the mosaic presented in the Introduction to this volume, specifying that different institutions apply to agents in several spheres or *tesserae*. By layering institutions hierarchically, we were able to introduce a principle of institutional change, in which new institutions are only partially new, in the sense that they emanate from the prevailing institutions of a higher hierarchical order. This allowed us to delve into the complexities of institutional change, which we depicted in Figure 2.3. Moreover, layering gives an indication of the scale of collective action needed to challenge institutions of different hierarchical levels.

We emphasised the role of experimentation, learning and networks in the process of institutional transformation and differentiated among three types of institutional change, namely novelty, exogenously driven and endogenously driven. The first one refers to situations which are completely new and for which a repeated action is formulated as the most acceptable one. The second one refers to changes in the circumstances that lead to a certain action and which have changed the outcome of the rule-following to one which is different to the one expected. A new rule of action therefore needs to be configured. The third instance of institutional change is the endogenously driven, in which the values that sustain the rules of action have changed, and the actions or their outcomes have become unacceptable. This is the instance of civic innovation which has a high dose of political motivation and collective action (organised or not). Civic innovation takes place in networks of belonging or activisms. It represents a confrontation of power asymmetries embedded in the rules and related to the control over making rules. Its first basic element is a clash between institutions and the values these represent. The second basic element includes the actions that are used to change the institutions that entail collective action in the public space, as opposed to a private act, and collective learning. While some agents promote their own institutions, others may simply resist the institutions of others. The process is ongoing – equilibria are always unstable agreements between groups that uphold institutions and groups that challenge them – so social structures are never to be seen as unchangeable. At the same time, (evolving) institutions are points of relative stability within specific groups in times and places, so institutions are 'out there' with ontological weight, which means that they have real impact on agents' actions and can be studied.

References

Aoki, M. (2007) 'Endogenizing Institutions and Institutional Changes', *Journal of Institutional Economics*, Vol. 3, No. 1, pp. 1–31.

Axelrod, R. (1984) *The Evolution of Cooperation*. New York: Basic Books.

Bardhan, P. (1989) 'The New Institutional Economics and Development Theory: A Brief Critical Assessment', *World Development*, Vol. 17, No. 9, pp. 1389–1395.

Battilana, J., Leca, B. and Boxenbaum, E. (2009) 'How Actors Change Institutions: Towards a Theory of Institutional Entrepreneurship', *The Academy of Management Annals: A Journal of the Academy of Management*, Vol. 3, No. 1, pp. 65–107.

Beckert, J. (1999) 'Agency, Entrepreneurs, and Institutional Change: The Role of Strategic Choice and Institutionalized Practices in Organizations', *Organization Studies*, Vol. 20, No. 5, pp. 777–799.

Beckert, J. (2003) Economic Sociology and Embeddedness: How Shall we Conceptualise Economic Action?, *Journal of Economic Issues*, Vol. 37, No. 3, September, pp. 769–785.

Biccheri, C. (2010) 'Norms, Preferences and Conditional Behavior', *Politics, Philosophy and Economics*, Vol. 9, No. 3, pp. 297–313.

Bowles, S. and Gintis, H. (1993) 'The Revenge of Homo Economicus: Contested Exchange and the Revival of Political Economy', *The Journal of Economic Perspectives*, Vol. 7, No. 1, pp. 83–102.

Brousseau, E. and Raynaud, E. (2011) 'Climbing the Hierarchical Ladders of Rules: A Life-cycle Theory of Institutional Evolution', *Journal of Economic Behavior and Organization*, Vol. 79, No. 1–2, pp. 65–79.

Campbell, J.L. (1997) 'Mechanisms of Evolutionary Change in Economics Governance: Interaction, Interpretation and Bricolage'. In Magnusson, L. and Ottosson, J. (eds) *Evolutionary Economics and Path Dependence*. Cheltenham: Edward Elgar.

Campbell, J.L. (2004) *Institutional Change and Globalization*. Princeton: Princeton University Press.

Chang, H.-J. (2002) 'Breaking the Mould – An Institutionalist Political Economy Alternative to the Neo-Liberal Theory of the Market and the State', *Cambridge Journal of Economics*, Vol. 26, No. 5, pp. 539–559.

Chang, H.-J. (2011) 'Institutions and Economic Development: Theory, Policy and History', *Journal of Institutional Economics*, Vol. 7, No. 4, pp. 473–498.

Crespi, F. (1994) 'Hermeneutics and the Theory of Social Action'. In Sztompka, P. (ed.) *Agency and Structure: Reorienting Social Theory*. Abingdon and New York: Routledge, pp. 125–142.

Dewey, J. (1922) *Human Nature and Conduct: An Introduction to Social Psychology*, 1st edn. New York: Holt.

Douglas, M. (1986) *How Institutions Think*. Syracuse, NY: Syracuse University Press.

Eisenstadt, S.N. (1980) 'Cultural Orientations, Institutional Entrepreneurs, and Social Change: Comparative Analyses of Traditional Civilizations', *American Journal of Sociology*, Vol. 85, No. 3, pp. 840–869.

Emerson, R.M. (1972) 'Exchange Theory, Part I: A Psychological Basis for Social Exchange' and 'Exchange Theory, Part II: Exchange Relations and Networks'. In Berger, J., Zelditch, M. and Anderson, B. (eds) *Sociological Theories in Progress 2*, Boston: Houghton- Mifflin.

Fligstein, N. (1996) 'Markets as Politics: A Political-Cultural Approach to Market Institutions', *American Sociological Review*, Vol. 61, pp. 656–673.

Fligstein, N. (2001) *The Architecture of Markets*. Princeton: Princeton University Press.

Ford, J.D., Ford, L.W. and D'Amelio, A. (2008) 'Resistance to Change: The Rest of the Story', *The Academy of Management Review*, Vol. 33, No. 2, pp. 362–377.

Foucault, M. (1998) *The History of Sexuality: The Will to Knowledge*. London: Penguin.

Friedland, R. and Alford, R.R. (1991) 'Bringing Society Back in: Symbols, Practice, and Institutional Contradictions'. In Powell, W. and DiMaggio, P. (eds) *The New Institutionalism in Organizational Analysis*. Chicago, IL: University of Chicago Press.

Fukuyama, F. (2003) 'Still Disenchanted? The Modernity of Postindustrial Capitalism'. *Center for the Study of Economy and Society Working Paper Series Paper* 3.

Gaventa, J. (2003) *Power after Lukes: A Review of the Literature.* Brighton: Institute of Development Studies.

Gomez, G. (2008) *Making Markets: The Institutional Rise and Decline of the Argentine Red de Trueque.* The Netherlands: Shaker Publishing BV (PhD Thesis).

Grabowski, R. (1999) 'Market Evolution and Economic Development: The Evolution of Impersonal Markets', *American Journal of Economics and Sociology*, Vol. 58, No. 4, pp. 699–712.

Granovetter, M. and Swedberg, R. (eds) (1992) *The Sociology of Economic Life.* Boulder: Westview Press.

Greif, A. (1989) 'Reputation and Coalitions in Medieval Trade: Evidence on the Maghribi Traders', *The Journal of Economic History*, Vol. 49, No. 4, pp. 857–882.

Greif, A. (2006) 'History Lessons–The Birth of Impersonal Exchange: The Community Responsibility System and Impartial Justice,' *The Journal of Economic Perspectives*, Vol. 20, No. 2, pp. 221–236.

Greif, A. and Kingston, C. (2011) 'Institutions: Rules or Equilibria?' In Schofield, N. and Caballero, G. (eds) *Political Economy of Institutions, Democracy and Voting.* Berlin Heidelberg: Springer, pp. 13–43.

Greif, A. and Laitin, D.D. (2004) 'A Theory of Endogenous Institutional Change', *American Political Science Review*, Vol. 98, pp. 633–652.

Greif, A., Milgrom, P. and Weingast, B. (1994) 'Coordination, Commitment and Enforcement: The Case of the Merchant Guild', *Journal of Political Economy*, Vol. 102, No. 4, pp. 745–776.

Hage, J. and Alter, C. (1997) 'A Typology of Interorganizational Relationships and Networks'. In Hollingsworth, J.R. and Boyer, R. (eds) *Contemporary Capitalism: The Embeddedness of Institutions.* Cambridge and New York: Cambridge University Press.

Hodgson, G. (1998) 'The Approach of Institutional Economics', *Journal of Economic Literature*, Vol. 36 (March 1998), pp 166–192.

Hodgson, G. (2002) 'Reconstitutive Downward Causation: Social Structure and the Development of Institutional Agency'. In Fullbrook, E. (ed.), *Intersubjectivity in Economics: Agents and Structures.* London: Routledge.

Hodgson, G. (2003) 'John R. Commons and the Foundations of Institutional Economics', *Journal of Economic Issues*, Vol. XXXVII, No. 3, September, pp. 547–576.

Hodgson, G. (2004) *The Evolution of Institutional Economics: Agency, Structure and Darwinism in American Institutionalism.* London: Routledge.

Hodgson, G. (2006) 'What are Institutions?', *Journal of Economic Issues*, Vol. 40, No. 1 (March), pp. 1–25.

Hollingsworth, J.R. (2002) 'Some Reflections on How Institutions Influence Styles of Innovation'. Paper for *Swedish Collegium for Advanced Study of the Social Sciences*, 26 September. Available online at http://history.wisc.edu/hollingsworth/documents/Some_Reflections_on_How_Institutions_Influence_Styles_of_Innovation.htm (accessed December 2015).

Hollingsworth, J.R. and Boyer, R. (1997) (eds) *Contemporary Capitalism.* Cambridge: Cambridge University Press.

Joas, H. (1996) *G. H. Mead: A Contemporary Re-examination of his Thought.* Cambridge: The MIT Press.

Lawson, T. (1997) 'Realism, Explanation and Science'. In Lawson, T. (ed.) *Economics and Reality.* London: Routledge.

Lawson, T. (2003) 'Institutionalism: On the Need to Firm up Notions of Social Structure and the Human Subject', *Journal of Economic Issues*, Vol. XXXVII, No. 1, March 2003, pp. 175–207.

Legro, J. (1997) 'Which Norms Matter? Revisiting the "Failure" of Internationalism', *International Organization*, Vol. 51, pp. 31–63.

Lévi-Strauss, C. (1966) *The Savage Mind*. Chicago: University of Chicago Press.

Marghlin, S. (1991) 'Understanding Capitalism: Control versus Efficiency'. In Gustafsson, B. (ed.) *Power and Economic Institutions*. Aldershot (England): Edward Elgar.

Molm, L. (1990) 'Structure, Action, and Outcomes: The Dynamics of Power in Social Exchange', *American Sociological Review*, Vol. 55, No. 3, pp. 427–447.

North, D. (2003) 'The Role of Institutions in Economic Development', *ECE Discussion Papers Series* 2003(2).

North, D. (1990) *Institutions, Institutional Change and Economic Performance*. Cambridge: Cambridge University Press.

O'Hara, P.A. (2007) 'Principles of Institutional-Evolutionary Political Economy: Converging Themes from the Schools of Heterodoxy', *Journal of Economic Issues*, Vol. 41, No. 1, pp. 1–42.

Ostrom, E. (1990) *Governing the Commons: The Evolution of Institutions for Collective Action*. Cambridge: Cambridge University Press.

Ostrom, E. (2005) *Understanding Institutional Diversity*. Princeton and Oxford: Princeton University Press.

Perrow, C. (1986) *Complex Organizations: A Critical Essay*. New York: Random House.

Platteau, J.P. (2000) *Institutions, Social Norms, and Economic Development*. Amsterdam, The Netherlands: Harwood Academic Publishers.

Powell, W. and DiMaggio, P. (1991) *The New Institutionalism in Organizational Analysis*. University of Chicago Press: Chicago.

Ritchie, H.A. (2013) *Negotiating Tradition, Power and Fragility in Afghanistan: Institutional Innovation and Change in Value Chain Development*. PhD thesis, Rotterdam: ISS Erasmus University.

Seabright, P. (2010) *The Company of Strangers: A Natural History of Economic Life*. Princeton: Princeton University Press.

Sugden, R. (1989) 'Spontaneous Order', *Journal of Economic Perspectives*, Vol. 3, No. 4, pp. 85–97.

Uzzi, B. (1996) 'The Sources and Consequences of Embeddedness for the Economic Performance of Organizations: The Network Effect', *American Sociological Review*, Vol. 61 (August 1996), pp. 674–698.

Van Staveren, I. and Odebode, O. (2007) 'Gender Norms as Asymmetric Institutions: A Case Study of Yoruba Women in Nigeria', *Journal of Economic Issues*, Vol. 41, No. 4, pp. 903–925.

Veblen, T. (1919) *The Place of Science in Modern Civilization and Other Essays*. New York: Huebsch.

Wäckerle, M. (2014) *The Foundations of Evolutionary Institutional Economics: Generic Institutionalism*. Abingdon: Routledge.

Weber, M. (1930) *The Protestant Ethic and the Spirit of Capitalism*. Translated by T. Parson. New York and London: Taylor & Francis e-library, 2005.

Weber, M. (1978) *Max Weber: Selections in Translation*. Edited and introduced by W.G. Runciman. Cambridge: Cambridge University Press.

Wells, A. (1970) *Social Institutions*. London: Heinemann.

3 Change actors and civic innovators: who triggers change?

Systematising the role of interlocutors in civic innovation processes

Alan Fowler

Introduction

For good or ill, societies are never static. Imagination, hope and despair, injustice, learning, contagions, conflicts, embodied experiences, the economic imperatives of gaining a livelihood, population change, technological advances and climate dynamics all feed pressures that motivate people to change the way things are. Over long historical time, people's reactions to these and myriad other domestic and external forces interact to produce institutionalised patterns of norms, behaviours, economic and power relations – commonly treated as societal structures – that are never stable, nor fully predictable or controllable (Beinhocker 2006). This uncertain movement of society by society generates leaders and followers, winners and losers, as well as systemic dysfunctions (e.g. Group of Lisbon 1995) with different consequences for individuals, age and social groups, classes and genders. And, because a society's institutions cannot operate in isolation, the lack of predictability in why, when and how they change leads to 'frictions' – understood as disruptions to established social norms, structures, their configurations and interactions – which challenge the prevailing order.

Frictions often translate into human ingenuity and energy to redirect processes of structuration towards a preferred future condition. Such inspirations involve a normative position which needs collective action to make change happen. While recognising that human agency can be uncivil, even for civic ends (Biekart and Fowler 2013), the changes of interest in this chapter are civic innovations that seek to bring a society closer to fairness and social justice for all, allied to a sustainable natural ecology required to do so across generations. The contribution of this chapter is to question if and how this direction of multi-institutional effort is brought about and to fruition through the concept and functions of an *interlocutor*, an actant gaining significance in addressing intractable social dilemmas.[1]

In doing so, the treatment here expands on an analysis of attributes seen in organisation forms across the world which are evolving to better fulfil interlocution roles in formal multi-stakeholder processes (Fowler 2014). The approach is one of exploring systematisation of the phenomenon which, for example, includes interlocution processes and effects of civic activism operating at any number of scales.

A working proposition is that, where an interlocution role is appropriate, the task is bound to feature significant relational competencies. Why? Because by their very nature, institutions, organisations, fields, sectors, domains, industries, communities – call them want you will – are made up of embodied interacting agents operating according to competing and cooperative logics. While an individual entrepreneur, activist or civic innovator may have a winning socio-economic idea to 'change the world', or a meaningful part of it, she or he alone will not bring about significant societal effects; the building and expanding of relationships will be critical. For example, a recent study argues that barriers to scaling innovation products and services for those near or at the bottom of the economic pyramid are such that an 'industry facilitator' is needed to help make this transition happen (Koh, Hegde and Karamchandani 2014). A contrasting micro-relational example is a phone-in programme of a local radio station in Uganda acting as an interlocutor between disgruntled voters and their local member of parliament challenging the issuing of fishing licences to foreign companies (Tembo 2013: 7). In actor-network theory and the terminology of Latour (2005) the radio technology involved constitutes an actant – it is a party to the interaction between citizens and their political representative. A similar story can be applied to cellular and internet technologies.

Such micro-level grassroots agency is not necessarily limited to local space but can orchestrate wider relational effects seen, for example, in the transnationalism of Slum Dwellers International (Batliwala 2004: 64). Networked relationships playing interlocutory roles are seen in transnational social movements such as the coalition group Mobilization for Social Justice that orchestrated participation of diverse actors and interests in protests targeting multilateral institutions (Escobar 2004; Murphy 2004: 40) and 'Spinning the Green Web' of transnational environmentalism (Torrance and Torrance 2006: 101).

Each instance of interlocution contains power and influence – none are neutral in the processes with which they engage. Experience shows that in struggles for social and ecological justice, those playing this type of role can exhibit a power of translation designed to 'erase' knowledges, meanings and world views that do not correspond to a dominating modernising world order (Vázquez 2011). This shadow side needs to be borne in mind.

The power analysis required in systematising an interlocutor role follows the categorisation of spaces for citizen engagement delineated by Cornwall (2002) and Gaventa (2006). They articulate a graduated division between interlocutors who are: (a) invited to do so in spaces and with rules pre-established by others; (b) claim space to instigate social change; and (c) occupy closed spaces denied to outsiders. Instigation, invitation and closure can seek to retain the *status quo ante* against destabilising forces (though there may be innovation involved in doing so). Operating across this space/power spectrum does not mean that an interlocutor is a civic innovator *per se*. Interlocution can in itself be innovative in new ways of configuring relationships, applying technologies and so on. But more often than not interlocution is the facility needed by civic innovators to reach out, gain support and generate social traction. Whatever the case, we begin with a summary of a basic set of interlocutor attributes involved in bringing about inter-organisational collaboration. This leads to a critical discussion of the limitations of organisationally formalised arrangements for establishing a robust systemic framework. After locating the concept of interlocution in wider social, economic and political processes, a systematising framework is established and its application is illustrated with seven cases from this volume and other sources.

An interloculator's multi-stakeholder role – AGEing and attributes

Bringing about socio-political changes as a conscious act or 'project' is often described in linear cause–effect logical positivist terms as having a beginning, a process and an intended 'knowable' end, but which, from a complexity perspective, may initiate emergent outcomes that create a new beginning in a never ending action spiral of its own initiation. In multi-stakeholder settings interlocution can be seen in both lights. On the one hand, starting collective action means bringing about an ostensibly 'linear' process that Assembles interested parties, Guides and aligns collaboration across their institutional and/or organisational interfaces and helps to Embed in society the wanted changes. On the other hand, institutional inter-connectedness means that embedding generates a new dynamic that can invite innovation anew. Navigating these dynamics depends on an interlocutor having the necessary role-playing capabilities. Comparisons of different organisational approaches to bring about AGEing in practice suggest a number of common attributes that inter-locutors deploy and are described below. It is clear that these formalised settings offer only one window into the functions involved.

Interlocutor attributes

Previous research on social accountability (Tembo 2013) identified an inter-locutor as a critical role player that was 'defined' by purpose and context. With this concept in mind, subsequent research by this author involved comparative study of interlocutor-type behaviour of newly emerging organisations in many walks of life. They were analysed in terms of the attributes brought to bear in making multi-stakeholder initiatives effective. Paraphrasing Fowler (2014: 22–24), seven attributes were identified that were not present to equal degrees.

Servant leadership in making conflict productive

By and large, collaborative arrangements and processes seen, for example, in the Global Alliance for Improved Nutrition (GAIN), the Global Alliance

Against Female Genital Mutilation (GAAFMG) and the Global Water Partnership (GWP) rely on voluntary participation. Leaders of collaborative arrangements and processes have little in the way of formal authority and must rely on gaining influence in other ways. This typically means attaining participants' respect when establishing and applying the rules which shape the psycho-social behaviour of groups, creating a safe space for expressing differences, negotiating shared aims and holding each other to agreed contributions. The term 'servant leadership' is often applied to this type of behaviour (e.g., Barbuto and Wheeler 2006; Spears 2010). In addition to expressing a compelling vision, leadership provided by an interlocutor must anticipate inter-stakeholder conflict as a starting point for collaboration, a condition which must be transcended over time. Put another way, leading is both sensitive towards and competent in managing disputes. Disagreements are turned into productive forces for change and innovation. Recognising that conflicting interests will be in play, as a pre-emptive move, the Scaling up Nutrition (SUN) Initiative commissioned an organisation to draft a conflict management protocol that, when all internal processes failed, anticipates the use of external mediators (GSO 2013).

Both trustworthy and a trust builder

Stakeholders in collaborative arrangements and processes inevitably harbour implicit or explicit pre-dispositions towards other members. An essential task is to establish trustworthiness in the interlocutor and trust between members. The former condition can arise from the recognition of technical competence, from reputation and from a collective mandate. Whatever the foundation of trustworthiness, an interlocutor's task calls for demonstrating and maintaining integrity while working on establishing bonding social capital between members that translates into binding commitments of the organisations to which participants belong. Often this feature of an interlocution process involves careful attention to sequencing and scale of collective 'win wins' with practical experiences of deeds matching words. Such a process can gradually erode prejudicial stereotypes which mistrust the motives of others. This being said, interlocution also calls for a healthy scepticism. Participants may be appointed against their will or better judgment, or are designated to act as 'guardians' preventing encroachment over their institution's interests.[2]

System sensitivity and scaling

A framing task for an interlocutor is to see the 'big picture' in which an innovation – often at a micro-starting point – has to find a systemic home. Typically, this attribute calls for a multi-disciplinary pre-disposition and openness.[3] This work includes determining sites and forms of resistance to change as 'normal' (Harich 2010) and, more importantly, correctly assessing viable entry points for gaining institutional effects along the lines identified by

Donna Meadows (1999). Put another way, system analysis – how the whole works and why – needs to be part and parcel of an interlocution process that has institutional change as its test of an innovation's effectiveness.

Awareness of polycentric governance, distributed authority and power

Reading a social system in order to change it means clarity about intention: to change the rules of the game the system relies on or to change the game itself (Tembo 2013: 7–8). For example, making markets more just by bringing moral considerations into corporate 'shared value' chains is akin to the former (Porter et al. 2012). Moving a system to the shared ownership principles of a social solidarity economy, described later, is more the latter (Kawano 2013). Each case calls for awareness of the sites of power and governing likely to be involved. And each case is likely to need the vision and competencies of institutional entrepreneurs and entrepreneurship. This is a concept of how people's agency can shape institutions, while simultaneously being constrained by them, cognitively, normatively and through regulation and sanction (e.g., DiMaggio 1998; Scott 2008).

Neutrality, time-bound presence and the long haul

A question for debate and explored in more detail in the following section is the extent to which an interlocutor needs to be a 'neutral' party in interactions between stakeholders, or have presence in the sense of being implicated in and belonging to the outcomes of collaboration. The notion of *presence* means letting go of a position of external observer of, say, a collaborative group, in order to re-engage in a more insightful way. It invokes the idea of being *implicated*; letting go of pre-conceived and secure realities to re-locate oneself within processes which re-institutionalise the never ending interplay between structure and agency in ways that 'unroot' rather than ameliorate causes of social dilemmas (Senge et al. 2007: 219). In reality, the choice is likely to be as much pragmatic as one of principle. Probable determinants are the scale and duration of the processes required, the complexities to be encountered in terms of the intended outcome and the time frames involved. A perspective of collaborative arrangements and processes seen in many global initiatives is the creation of a purpose built 'secretariat' to hold and guide the processes required until the end. In contrast, multi-stakeholder processes that seek to bring about local rearrangements of power, such as social accountability, appear to need neutral facilitation.[4] In order to make headway a case study of business innovation spoke of the need to have both a committed insider allied to a trusted outsider, in this case an academic (Bessant, Kaplinsky and Morris 2003). The general point is that the type of interlocutor needs to be 'fit for purpose' with neutrality or presence being a key variable. Another common sense variable is an ability to listen to and communicate in the 'languages' of different parties – understanding the acculturated meaning of the vocabularies they use to the knowledges they employ and the information they trust and rely on.

Polyglot: the attribute of many tongues

Participant diversity of the type associated with social dilemmas brings diverse frames of reference with multiple jargons and vocabularies where the same words cannot be relied on to mean the same thing to everyone. A competent interlocutor needs attributes of a polyglot, speaking and 'reading' actant communications which can have multiple meanings. Advances in technologies that satisfy multi-lingual requirements should help, but understanding the geo-institutional and organisational life worlds of participants will remain a human competency. Case examples suggest the significance of adequate and timely 'translational' communication that keeps everyone in the loop without belittling those less educated or les empowered or uncomfortable in vocalising, which is a typical problem faced by women in strongly patriarchal societies. Experience of a Collaborative Intermediary Organisation connecting communities with Cape Town City planners and national policy makers speaks to this attribute (Fowler 2014: 17). Without care, technologies can create exclusion and amplify the voice of some parties over others. The task is to open information flows and reduce the hierarchy of access feeding the transparency needed for trust.

Sovereignty and financing: he who pays the piper

A further attribute is the nature of governance that the interlocutor is subject to. It needs to ensure an interlocutor's behavioural 'sovereignty' on the one hand but with accountability on the other. By this is meant a clear allocation of decision rights that do not compromise independence of thought and action towards a partisan or prescriptive interpretation. As with many other attributes, the scope for 'sovereignty' is co-determined by conditions attached to an interlocutor's financing. Cases involving self-financed foundations playing this role differ from their grantees doing the same and differ yet again from a cost-sharing agreement between the parties involved. The political-economy of interlocutor financing is likely to be a pivotal feature of effectiveness, of trust and of conflict management.

Discussion

The 'limitless' objectives of collaboration and of collaborators make it highly unlikely that an effective 'generic' interlocutor or interlocution process can be defined a priori. As Tembo has written 'the kind of collective-action problem determines what can be called a 'game changing' characteristic, and hence *we cannot categorise any organisation as an interlocutor away from the action and context*' (Tembo 2013: 8, emphasis added).

First, this quote implies that at issue for interlocution roles and processes is the extent to which they are directed at changing the 'game' played by society to something significantly different – a deeply systemic change, for example one that ends patriarchy – or seeks to alter the rules of the existing game by, for example, making the existing capitalist economic system and its processes more inclusive and fair. In both cases, who in society determines what the 'game' is anyway and how is a collective decision reached? A civic driven change (CDC) perspective on the answer is to treat society as a political project populated by embodied agents in continual interaction both creating and mediated by institutionalised norms and rules that are themselves subject to contestation and change. The extent to which a political system allows for 'democratic' aggregation of preferences and imagined futures driving agency will depend on how power is distributed which defines 'the game' and how this prevailing condition can be challenged (Biekart and Fowler 2012).

From a perspective of systemisation, these directionalities of agency imply a 'bifurcation' (Laszlo 2012) between applying a radical imagination (Haiven and Khasnabish 2014) and timely transformation (TT) of society, or pursuing an (incremental) agenda to reform business as usual (BaU). This distinction offers polarities to, for example, understand the range of objectives that interlocution can serve, driven by the imagined futures inspiring individual and collective agency (Fowler and Biekart 2008). An open question remains, however. This is whether or not conditions exist where the incremental rule-changing latter can lead to the game changing former – that is to a systemically disruptive tipping point or phase shift to a new relative stability (Cilliers 1998).

Second, also at issue is the extent to which interlocution can be detrimental to the interests of those acting to change or sustain the world they live in. A theoretical explanation of this problem has already been alluded to. In the terms of de Sousa Santos (2014), a selective knowledge-constraining application of interlocution is a form of epistemic violence which 'erases' the meaning and embodiment of the world views of (some of) the actors involved. A constraining interpretative process by an interlocutor brings subordination to the epistemic territory declaimed and imposed by modernity as the norm of the world order. In this reading, interlocutors function as guardians of modernity's epistemic borders to prevent encroachment by contending discourses. Interlocution operates against people's struggles to live other meanings of social justice and ecological affinity (Icaza and Vázquez 2013). This reading of an anti-interlocutor stance is exhibited by the Zapatistas' insistence to self-determine the nature of the Chiapas uprising in terms of a locally located ontological expression of knowledges that had to be comprehended in their own right, not as 'reactions against' modernity familiar to judgements made about mass activisms seen in Tahrir Square and Occupy Wall Street (Icaza and Vázquez 2013: 686). Other examples of rejecting or removing interlocutors are reported in the struggles that grassroots movements, such as Slum Dwellers International (SDI) and Women in Informal Employment: Globalizing and Organizing (WIEGO), have mounted against NGOs that sought to speak on their behalf

(Batliwala 2004). These perspectives invite caution in determining if and when interlocutor systemisation is relevant, but also invite questioning of why this is not the case – what is going on that makes this so?

Third, an interlocutor is as much of a role as it is of a discrete entity or individual. A recent comparative study of interlocutors is starting to illuminate the diversity of ways in which the role is enacted and who the players are. For example, a multi-stakeholder initiative in Kyrgyzstan called for interlocution to be spread across stakeholder categories – one 'host' could not be found or co-constructed. The study also showed that the relative significance of attributes may change over time, becoming more intense as Embedding draws closer (Biekart and Fowler 2015). As the study only looked at a limited number of countries and cases, future research on these dimensions will be needed. For the moment we can best rely on examples and common sense to speculate about the relationship between attributes and the existing range of players that fulfil an interlocutor role in whole or in part. This is the substance of the following section.

The players in play – horses for courses

The notion of interlocution – etymologically, a process of engaging with parties in a conversation – is far from new. Nor new are those, the interlocutors, who fulfil such a role. While this chapter takes the modern organised world as its frame of reference, it is useful to locate the function in a wider time and space. Doing so provides a vantage point from which to see and understand the ontology of contemporary ways of undertaking this relational function.

Interlocution over time and space

At its core, interlocution is about purposeful involvement in relational processes between actants that can occur at any number of combinations and scales. For reasons alluded to above, there is little point in thinking that a generic definition of an interlocutor will be useful in terms of prescribing the specificities of what is required. More practical would be to describe an interlocutor as a role player with attributes, rather than as an entity. Before taking this route, it is important to have a wide appreciation of this function in daily life across the globe in politics, economics and complex modern-day relational processes.

Since time immemorial, third parties and go-betweens have been a common frame of relational reference. Faiths invoke and ask deities to intercede in worldly conditions and relational affairs, attributing earthly changes to their responses. Socio-culturally, interceding in relationships can have political (side) effects. For example, negotiation of dowries in Africa is typically an indirect process between families who deploy a go between from each side. The processes involved establish extended family ties and norms of reciprocity as a mainstay of the economy of affection which co-determines governance on the continent (Hyden 1989). Today, for many poor people and struggling middle classes, the pathway to (public) resources and (private) employment is often mediated by middle-men and women, as well as community based and non-governmental organisations, who navigate and open up access to (rent seeking) gate keepers and decision makers. Studies of the underclass in India's cities offer many examples where intermediary actors can themselves perpetuate and become part of the patronage system to which poor people are subjected (e.g., De Wit and Berner 2009). In West Africa using intermediaries to negotiate petty corruption is a normal feature of daily life (Olivier de Sardan and Blundo 2006). Closer to home, the Dutch speak of a *kruiwagen* (a wheel barrow) alluding to an interlocutor who transports, so to speak, the supplicant through obstacles of access. In societies, interlocutor types and roles are part and parcel of micro-politics. The modern era may have transformed elemental mediating roles into professions for hire, but their socio-political and cultural origins co-form webs of inter-personal experience: the wefting and weaving of socio-political fabric.

As with politics, economic life is essentially relational, be it in collaboration or in competition. Sometimes referred to as 'boundary spanners', inter-organisational theory recognises the importance of internal functions that are designed, skilled and mandated to reach out to the external environment and bring it inside (Alexander 1995: 118). This relational task is relatively straight-forward when the organisations concerned share similar logics, incentives and performance measures, like market share and competitive profit-making. Contracting is a typical way that these relationships are formalised. But collaborative arrangements can extend to strategic alliances, economic clusters (Knorringa and Nadvi 2014) and voluntary association in trade groups to influence public policy deployed, for example, by the pharmaceutical and other industries.[5] Public Private Partnerships (PPPs) co-created with the help of consultants acting, say, as brokers, are a contracting model that involves at least two types of stakeholders – business and governments – but can include more. Multi-stakeholder initiatives (MSIs) and partnerships (MSPs) are formed to promote the sustainable use of natural resources and typically contain a rich diversity of partners who may not see eye to eye but whose common interest can converge in forms of private governance seen, for example, in (transnational) co-regulation between business and non-profit organisations (Pattberg 2005).[6] Subsequent moves from private to public governance involving interlocutors can also be seen when the voluntary adoption of minimum standards for workers in international supply chains becomes enshrined in national labour law (Knorringa 2014).

Collaborating becomes more complicated for interlocution when the multiple factors already affecting relatively straightforward partnerships increase in a factorially compounded way. Three categories of collaborating entity – government, business, civil society – involves six relational combinations, add the academy and four types brings twenty four relational combinations, five types bring one hundred and twenty and so on. Theoretically and practically, the task of interlocution grows in difficulty, but also increases in value, as the number of collaborating agents and the degree of their interdependence to achieve results increases (Chrislip and Larson 1994). Evidence from many collaborations arising from the World Summit on Sustainable Development suggests that getting interlocution right is both a necessary and ongoing challenge.

> The overall picture that emerges is rather sobering. Multi-stakeholder partnerships have, by and large, not lived up to their promise. There are certainly some that perform excellently and have had impressive impacts on their issue areas but these should be considered as anomalies.
>
> (Pattberg and Widerberg 2014: 16).

Multi-stakeholder arrangements typically bring together diverse types of institutional players around a common agenda. They can be dialogues based on periodic exchanges or collaborations with mutual dependencies and responsibilities (Biekart and Fowler 2016: 54–60). In many (global) instances, an MSI creates a sort of 'host' secretariat providing a focal point and platform for partners' interaction overseen by forms of 'representative' governance.[7] Depending on the specific set up, selected attributes of an interlocutor can be hired or are provided by an 'internal' entity mandated for the purpose. Specialist working and task groups made up of participants is not uncommon. For example, the Global Partnership for Oceans relies on dedicated teams to create Public Private Partnerships (PPPs). But, even in the latter situation, relation-building services can be helpful, if not a prerequisite, for actors to effectively couple and apply their varied perspectives and competencies.

Today's organisational scene is well populated with individuals and entities whose invited services are relied on by stakeholders to assist collective efforts towards realising shared agendas. While specific skill sets and competencies often overlap and blend with each other, distinct 'marketing' niches are occupied by Facilitators, Intermediaries, Mediators, (Partnership) Brokers, Convenors, Change Agents, Orchestrators and Activators (Fowler 2014: 9). They may be stand-alone 'branded' operations, such as the Boston Consulting Group; may function as consultants located within accounting and audit firms; or, like the Partnering Initiative, have transformed from a for-profit to a non-profit entity joining others who started out in that way.[8] However, the professional services-for-hire mainstream obscures interlocutors who are not invitees but who as professionals or 'amateurs' are claimants and instigators deploying their civic agency with institutional change in mind. Unmasking this tendency is, therefore, one purpose of this chapter.

By and large, the examples and the interlocutor attributes described so far are being applied to change the rules of existing institutional games, not changing the game itself. Hence, they do not fully reflect interlocutors and processes that have this latter agenda. With these different motivations in mind, the following section explores an interlocution model that can aid in a systemic understanding of where interlocutors or 'hosts' are located and what they want to assist in achieving.

Interlocution – towards a systematic understanding

This chapter's approach to the concept of interlocution has its origins in research on social accountability. The concept was then applied to new types of organising to bring about formalised multi-stakeholder processes. A next step is to explore and expand the concept of an interlocutor in the direction of civic agency and civic innovation for social change at any scale. It does so by, in previous sections, recognising the ingrained, complex nature of 'inter-mediations' which are deeply woven into an ever changing web of social relations and behaviours as well as in the institutions to which they give rise. In addition, interlocution is problematised in terms of the power relations inherent to all human interactions, which play out in the dynamic exchanges that feed social structuration.

In multi-stakeholder initiatives, to be effective an interlocutor selects and deploys a range of attributes that match and over time adapt as progress alters the conditions of reaching a shared objective. The driver of many forms of collaboration for civic innovation is to address and redress problems of the day – poverty, inequality, gender-based violence and so on – and prevent from occurring those, like political instability, global warming and climate change, which are anticipated for tomorrow. However, as will be argued later, it cannot be assumed that all interlocution efforts share this perspective of the future and actively seek to present a different narrative. Whatever the case: 'A society's ability to confront the conflicts potential inherent in modern life depends on the capacity of its citizens to cooperate for mutual benefit' (Chrislip 2002: 22). In doing so, Ostrom (2005) identifies issues of gaining collective action under conditions where individuals – including organisations – choose to exert their agency in interdependent situations, which are increasing as globalisations bring greater inter-reliance to the world's relational dynamics. The problem is that, unless negotiated and connected in some way, such choices produce sub-optimal outcomes for the whole. Her central argument is that the root of social dilemmas stem from: 'a conflict between individual rationality and optimal outcomes for a group … Even if some individuals cooperate, the others are predicted to "free-ride" on the contributions of the cooperators (Ostrom 2005: 3–5; Ostrom 2009). Consequently, and bearing power differences in mind, a fundamental task of an interlocutor is to bring parties to a point of adequately forgoing their own optimal outcome to one of a sufficiently satisfactory outcome for the group.

Applying this insight to the intractable nature of many of today's societal problems has spurred active debate about solutions that overly rely on technical fixes. Such a tendency, referred to by Morozov (2013) as 'solutionism', is reflected, for example, in the apolitical character of laboratories dedicated to social innovation (Kieboom 2014) which is distinguished from civic innovation by the latter's attention to the centrality of citizen-driven politics in action. The pre-disposition of social innovators is associated with contestation about whether or not the rules, systems and power relations currently constituting the world order can be modified enough to provide 'solutions', or is something more radical required: a transformation in human thinking, expectations, and behaviour, particularly towards the ecosystem. Crudely framed, as alluded to previously, is a collaborative quest, one of changing the rules of the local to global game or changing the game itself – a World Shift[9] towards a supposedly poorly defined alternative.[10]

> We demand a paradigm transformation from the current neoliberal economic model of development, which prioritizes profit over people, and exacerbates inequalities, war and conflict, militarism, patriarchy, environmental degradation and climate change. Instead, we call for economic models and development approaches that are firmly rooted in principles of human rights and environmental sustainability, that address inequalities between people and states, and that rebalance power relations for justice so that the result is sustained peace, equality, the autonomy of peoples, and the preservation of the planet.[11]

The function of interlocutors can be charted within this paradigmatic framing as well as in relation to the power associated with their involvement depicted by Cornwall (2002) and Gaventa (2006) as three spaces for citizen engagement: invited, instigated and closed.

Consequently, a systematic approach to interlocutors would pose four questions:

What conversation/type of change in society do they aspire to/align with?
Where do they figure in the distribution of power space in society?
What trajectories of change do they pursue over time?
When is interlocution not appropriate?

Figure 3.1 illustrates these three elements of systematisation. After an explanation, working from left to right, seven examples are used to demonstrate application. Table 3.1 summarises the seven cases.

Following Gaventa (2006) the lower spectrum spans the power associated with an interlocutor's (initial) positioning – the space they rely on to act, which may be a blend described below. The upper spectrum is an offset overlap of the type of change being aspired to: none at all, rule change or game change as previously explained. The connecting lines allude to seven examples of interlocution processes over time selected to illustrate a diversity of positioning and trajectories. Such processes are seldom linear involving changes in direction as lessons are learned, resistances are felt, and adaptation takes place. Each case located in the figure is briefly explained. More detailed enquiry will be required to fully test against attribute mixes and their evolution as a case proceeds.

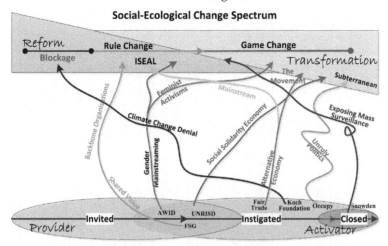

Figure 3.1 Interlocution schematic

Association for Women's Rights in Development

Now more than twenty years old, the Association for Women's Rights in Development (AWID) is an interesting case of interlocutor movement across roles and spaces advancing a conversation within society about gender equity and women's rights. Today, AWID is developing as a transnational feminist movement whose history has led to a complex dualism in holding the tensions between old modes of professional organising associated with donor-funded, rule-changing NGO-ism towards new modes of game-changing activism and claim making against patriarchal institutional inspirations and behaviours. The process emerges as a creative response to what was a potential 'split' between institutional reformist and radical feminist trajectories within the evolution of a transnational women's movement originating from the gender mainstreaming. Such energising tensions were anticipated by Peggy Antrobus and Gita Sen.

> Not everyone in the women's movement is comfortable about feminism. There is tension between feminists and other women within women's movements who are more ambivalent about challenging prevailing gender relations and certainly about some of the feminist language and analysis of these relations. ... The issue of asymmetry of power between women within the movement must be acknowledged and addressed honestly and with integrity.
>
> (Antrobus and Sen 2006: 153–154)

This complex, dualistic rule + game changing outcome is part-attributed to AWID Forums operating as meshworks providing a holding space for diversity of women's political formations and engagement (Harcourt 2013; De Landa n.d.).

Table 3.1 Summary of interlocution cases

Interlocutor	Interlocutor	The 'Conversation'	Power space	Change spectrum	Interlocution/Trajectory
AWID	NGO –Feminist Movement	Advancing women and gender issues in socio-political processes and debates	Originally invited into international public policy space	Initially rule change by mainstreaming gender in public policy	Through forums shifting to game change in structural patriarchy
Fair Trade	NGO – social enterprise	Intermediating values-driven connections between 'rich' consumers with poor farmers in developing countries	Originally instigated by NGOs North–South	Game to change to a fairer economic system for primary producers	From activism, main-streaming splits inter-locutors into rule changing standards makers and alternative economy advocates
FSG	US NPO/ Consultancy	Values-based stimulation of innovation in organi-sations acting as inter-locutors to refine capitalism in pro-social directions.	Blend of invited non-profit and self-instigat-ing philanthropies	Rule change towards corporations adopting shared value principles in supply chains abetted by a new type of interlocutor: 'backbone' actants	Protagonist towards shared value and catalytic philanthropy being tempered by 'backlash' from tradi-tional grant makers.
Koch Brother Foundation	US Foundation	Conservative influence on public debate as well as on politicians and policy makers	Instigated from a pri-vately owned corporate foundation	Blocking rule change on climate issues	From overt to more covert financing of 'denialist' public disinformation about climate change.

Interlocutor	Interlocutor	The 'Conversation'	Power space	Change spectrum	Interlocution/Trajectory
OWS	Social Movement	Vehicle for disillusioned citizens to engage with political and economic elites	Self-instigated activation on mass across multiple geographies	Transformatory overhaul of the prevailing political and economic system: another world is possible	Mass public, non-violent protest and unruliness to more subterranean net-enabled provocations and formation of alternative political parties
UNRISD	UNRISD	Connecting 'activitist' researchers to innovate ideas in the UN System	Blend of instigating within an invited space of the UN	Towards a game change in the economic order	Research driven conferences moving into a Task Force across the UN system
Snowden	Individual	Advance public debate about personal privacy and technology	Closed power of state security	Towards a game change in how security services are overseen.	Media exposure of state malpractice in mass surveillance with protective self-exile.

Note: AWID (Association for Women's Rights in Development); FSG (Foundation Strategy Group); NPO (non-profit organisation); OWS (Occupy Wall Street); UNRISD (United Nations Research Institute for Social Development)

'AWIDS's evolution away from the mainstream development Washington-consensus positioning reflects a profound discontent of NGO reality and the failure of advocacy and NGO project work to make any real change to world poverty and inequalities' (Harcourt 2013: 635).

The mix of AWID's interlocutor attributes has shifted. Initially AWID was a relatively safe, elite feminist leadership deploying professional NGO techniques 'on behalf of women' towards political and economic power holders. Today, AWID is characterised by its catalytic stimulation of distributed networks of locally conceived more risky activism with sensitivity to conflict awareness and its 'management'. AWID's transnationalism and its space-generating convening role has established a networked foundation of trust that self-driven feminist agency could rely on. Hence a role shift from technical guidance on instrumentalist gender-based delivery and implementation of UN related projects and programmes to creating enabling conditions for local action by, especially young, women that is globally connected and operates across multiple languages and scales.

Foundation Strategy Group

Foundation Strategy Group (FSG) is a US-based non-profit organisation co-founded in 2000 in Boston, MA by Harvard Professors Michael Porter and Mark Kramer, originally as a way to give strategy and practical substance to their notion of creating shared value (CSV) to redress social problems by bringing moral principles to economic processes (Porter and Kramer 2006).

> As FSG expanded, we began to offer a wider range of services to a more diverse clientele, including corporations, nonprofits, and governments around the world, so we shortened our name to FSG and opened an office in Geneva, Switzerland. In 2006, we became a nonprofit organization to better reflect our mission. And in 2009, we launched a strategic learning and evaluation division to help build the field through new approaches to evaluation that could better support strategy.[12]

Extending beyond the ambit of corporate social responsibility (CSR), FSG's originating value proposition in societal change – an instigated conversation directed towards business – is that each location in a value chain needs to generate social benefits and well as economic gains. 'In a nutshell, CSV proposes to transform social problems relevant to the corporation into business opportunities, thereby contributing to the solving of critical societal challenges whilst simultaneously driving greater profitability' (Crane et al. 2014: 1). In tackling societies' intractable problems, FSG is avowedly 'solutionist' applying a broad mix of expertise towards changing the rules driving exploitive economic relations, hence 'fixing' the problem of mistrust in capitalism.

In the space of some ten years, FSG has evolved in the direction of an innovator in and beneficiary of US philanthropy. This advance has enabled the organisation to be both an invitee by corporations that are interested in rule change towards social goals and an instigator of what are argued to be game changing advances through catalytic philanthropy and social investing. Doing so places significant emphasis on the attribute of a polyglot that can speak languages of business, nonprofits, government, academia and communities with increasing attention to scale transnationally.

More recently, from shared value, with support from philanthropic foundations, FSG has been experimenting with 'backbone organisations', specifically designed to play interlocutor roles. Backbones do so by providing a skeletal infrastructure that social innovators can rely on to bring about collective/ multi-stakeholder impact. In terms of attributes, greatest emphasis is placed on leadership which needs to be: visionary; results-oriented; a collaborative relationship builder; focused while adaptive; charismatic influential communicator; politically savvy; and humble – a servant leader (Turner et al 2012: 7). It is in the area of collective impact – focused collective effort of combined stakeholders – that FSG is seeking to instigate a movement of like-minded people and organisations.

The FSG approach relies on an implicit assumption that as more corporations embrace and apply the concept, the scaling of sharing-oriented rule change will lead progressively to system change. This process is deeply questioned.

> CSV also suffers from a number of serious shortcomings that will erode any real possibility for the more fundamental change aimed at by the authors. That is, it is unoriginal, it ignores the tensions between social and economic goals, it is naïve about the challenges of business compliance, and it is based on a shallow conception of the role of the corporation in society.
> (Crane et al 2014: 130)

With these weaknesses in mind, wide-spread attention to and adoption of CSV is liable to crowd out other narratives, marginalising those with an alternative, game changing approach to 'fixing' capitalisms dysfunctions.

Finally, FSG now complements CSV with three other approaches – collective impact, catalytic philanthropy and strategic evaluation. These additions might signal recognition of weaknesses in the original conceptualisation of CSV as business-only solution to the need for types of collaboration that in turn stimulate the emergence of dedicated interlocutors, like Backbones.

United Nations Research Institute for Social Development

Founded in 1963, the United Nations Research Institute for Social Development (UNRISD) is an autonomous think tank type complement to the United Nations University (UNU).

> UNRISD was established in 1963 as an autonomous space within the UN system for the conduct of policy-relevant, cutting-edge research on

social development that is pertinent to the work of the United Nations Secretariat; regional commissions and specialized agencies; and national institutions.[13]

It is highly regarded for its critical research inputs across the UN system – sometimes seen as institutionally critical and provocative. While invited to provide intellectual and knowledge backing, in determining a research agenda the Institute can instigate processes directed at rule or game change, the former usually being more comfortable for UN agencies. Deploying interlocutor attributes of name recognition, trust and track record in identifying cutting edge research opened up a potentially game changing initiative. This was an investigation of a social solidarity economy (SSE).

> The Social Solidarity Economy is an alternative to capitalism and other authoritarian, state dominated economic systems. In SSE ordinary people play an active role in shaping all of the dimensions of human life: economic, social, cultural, political, and environmental. SSE exists in all sectors of the economy — production, finance, distribution, exchange, consumption and governance.[14]

A series of Forums has now led to the establishment of an Intercontinental Network for the Promotion of Social Solidarity Economy (INPSSE) dedicated to building SSE as an alternative model of development.

> RIPESS is an intercontinental network that connects social and solidarity economy networks throughout the world. As a network of networks, it brings together continental networks that, in turn, bring together national and sectoral networks. RIPESS believes in the importance of global solidarity in order to build and strengthen an economy that puts people and planet front and center.[15]

The proposed network is a practical example of how an initial interlocutor – UNRISD – transfers this function to another type of 'hosting' entity, with attributes better able to move forward on outreach and scaling.[16]

Fair Trade

As a normative condition for the operation of value chains between primary producers and consumers, Fair Trade is explained as a Norm Cycle Model of emergence, cascading and internalisation or industry mainstreaming of civic values in market relations (Finnemore and Sikkink 1998: 898, cited in Knorringa 2014: 370). Some fifty years ago, Fair Trade's instigators as leaders of an interlocution process were nongovernmental development organisations actively promoting 'solidarity' with agricultural and handicraft producers. The original proposition was to replace the capitalist economic structure operating between poor primary producers and richer consumers in favour of the former. The practical civic innovation was to morally persuade consumers to pay a premium price for ethical goods on the one hand, with local cooperatives providing assurance of equitable distribution of the higher monetary value of produce on the other. The notion of empowerment of producers through self-governing mechanisms shows a polycentric power analysis of the value chains involved. This analysis appears to have neglected gender intersectionality between those who do the agricultural work – women – and those who usually govern cooperatives – male land owners – for their own ends. Over time the school of thought which advocated for and actively pursued scaling-up of the model won the day, creating a bifurcation between mainstreamers and movementalists (Biekart, Harcourt and Knorringa, in this volume). However, the 'success' of mainstreamers has, it is argued, brought very marginal benefits to producers (Sylia 2014). Gains disproportionally accrue to the wealthy economies where consumers spend.[17]

By cascading 'fairness' into the consumer mainstream, supermarket promotion and marketing of many 'ethical' commodities has systemic effects by feeding an inflation of ethical certification, branding and labelling. Today, the ISEAL Alliance brings together some twenty self-initiated certification organisations.[18] Their positioning is one of interlocutors between corporations and consumers. They rely on a political-economy of providing 'trust services', legitimising the sellers of products independently validated as 'fair' or 'sustainable', free of child labour and so on. Such a service is bolstered by those who remain agitators for and instigators of alternatives to this 'new normal' of consumer preferences and expectations. This example of interlocution choices suggests that mainstreaming and scaling can generate unwanted emergent effects that turn civic innovation back on itself.

Koch Foundation

Philanthropic foundations in America have a lot of scope in terms of the causes they subscribe to and the influence they try to exert on public perceptions and government policies. The National Committee for Responsive Philanthropy tracks what foundation ideologies support. Philanthropic finance to think tanks is a common vehicle to promote a funder's ideological position and policy agenda. An illustration of this self-financed power to instigate and inject think tanks as interlocutors in public debates in order to block change is provided by the Koch Foundation.

> Billionaire oilman David Koch used to joke that Koch Industries was 'the biggest company you've never heard of.' Now the shroud of secrecy has thankfully been lifted, revealing the $67 million that he and his brother Charles have quietly funnelled to climate-denial front groups that are working to delay policies and regulations aimed at stopping global warming.[19]

As the quotation shows, the Koch Brothers are dedicated to preventing policy or socio-political changes that are predicated on the notion of global warming and climate change more broadly. The advantage of Foundation funding is that it can be consistently applied over long periods that outlive changes in the political party in power. A conservative Foundation's ability to shift or block narratives and shape public discourse has proven itself in the past when their concerted effort effectively removed the notion and vocabulary of 'solidarity' from America's political language (Covington 1997). Here, the interlocutor's 'epistemic' role is to counter and erase the messaging of ideological opponents.

Occupy Wall Street

The Occupy Wall Street (OWS) movement was citizen self-instigated and game changing in its ambition. Unlike AWID, in its activism OWS could not rely on previously constructed international networks to transmit its 'we are the 99 percent' conversation about economic injustice. OWS origins speak to the emergence of a communication-rich transnational self-consciousness and collective 'global' identity, allied to an energising imaginary of a more just and humane world order that inspires the 'will to become an actor' (Pleyers 2010: 16). Flowing from the financial crisis of 2008 was a sharpened perception among the West's middle classes of the precariousness of their livelihoods, the insecurity of their savings, the duplicity of financial institutions, especially banks, and failures of a 'light touch' financial regulatory system. This discomfort was abetted by disaffection with representative politics and widespread mistrust of (corrupted) politicians. The formation of OWS and its *indignados* counterparts in Europe started to act as instigating interlocutors between threatened socio-economic groups and the political and economic elites responsible for the economic disillusionment and broken promises of capitalist democracy. It was civic agency at scale, fully aware of the multiple locations at which public and private governance had aided and abetted the 1% to arise: illustrated in the capture of America's public policy by the economic elites and corporate lobbyists, where US voters have negligible traction (Gilens and Page 2014).

The polyglot attribute of interlocution was readily provided by the bi-lingualism of multi-country activists, with English as *lingua franca*. But OWS also brought to the fore the communication power of shared symbolisms, Guy Fawkes masks being one of the best known. This case illustrates interlocution through the 'politics of the mask', creating a 'vocabulary' of political universalism and global agency.[20]

Another OWS interlocution attribute – temporariness or presence – invites a question: when a movement stops moving in its overt public forms does it relinquish this descriptor or accolade? Is its *presence* too temporary to have a lasting impact or do we need to look below the media-attractive surface to the subterranean politics that bubbles up in new types of 'internetted' political parties – The Pirates in Germany, The Five Star Movement in Italy?[21] Do these expressions signal a step change in collective awareness that cannot be eradicated as if it did not happen because it has not, overtly, succeeded? From an interlocution perspective, does an ostensible 'failure' to bring about substantial institutional change feed a social latency of resentment described by Hirschman (Biekart and Fowler 2014)? That is a reservoir of popular antipathy is created which can be triggered at any moment without apparent intentional cause – self-immolation and the Arab Spring being a recent example.

Finally, OWS sovereignty of action relied on volunteering, but cash was needed too. The OWS happening and imaginary attracted spontaneous financing from passers-by as well as the attention of critics to see if it had big backers, like George Soros. The attribute of civic resourcing poses its own problems of transparency and capture by moneyed elites. But, it is a critical aspect of interlocution that should not be an afterthought.[22]

Edward Snowden

A 'whistle-blower' illustration of interlocution is provided by Edward Snowden, instigated from out of the closed space of national security. His exposure of mass surveillance by the security services gave added impetus to public conversations about not just states spying on their citizens but also about personal privacy in the era of social media and big data. A hope was to transform the system of oversight of security services as well as tightening justifications for collection of private communications. His actions have given rise to legal challenges about the constitutionality of mass surveillance. In keeping with other whistle-blowers, Snowden has faced the wrath of the institution that employed him. The kinks and turns in his trajectory – branded as both traitor and hero – led eventually, via Hong Kong, to asylum in Russia. His case illustrates that interlocution can be a (personally) risky undertaking.

Final reflections

This chapter systematises the concepts of an interlocutor and interlocution by expanding from formalised settings of multi-stakeholder processes to include less formalised engagement in public affairs and debates as additional sites of civic innovation. The diversity of examples from contributions to this volume and from other sources, suggest that the systemic categories proposed – power location, rule or game changing intention, and tracking trajectory of effort anticipated and realised over time – allied to an examination of attributes can help to better understand an interlocution function. This preliminary conclusion needs to be tested in at least two ways. One is to critically examine the seven attributes for robustness and completeness, particularly with respect to inter-relational competencies. Another is detailed studies to interrogate if and how attribute weightings alter as AGEing proceeds, from which effectiveness can be improved.

The examples illustrate the far from straightforward nature of how diverse power origins of civic innovation can be translated into a 'hosting' function that holds, gives momentum to, and guides interlocution processes. This includes negotiation and separation of trajectories towards and away from rule changing or game changing options as political strategies and tactics of civic agency. It also alludes to and invites caution in assuming that any civic agency would benefit from interlocution if its intentions or unanticipated effects are to subordinate knowledges of particular groups by, for example, speaking on their behalf. In other words, interlocution may not always be a suitable way to address collective action problems. Be that as it may, gaining collective traction in civic innovation will, *ceteris paribus*, typically call for some way of bringing parties together and an agent to do so – the two are intimately related.

At the time of writing, the United Nations has endorsed Sustainable Development Goals (SDGs) whose attainment will rely on multi-stakeholders processes.[23] An implication is one of a growing need for more and better quality interlocutors. This chapter offers pointers to what this requirement might entail in practice and the work needed to better understand when and when not to rely on them to change the rules of the game or the game itself.

Notes

1 The term 'actant' follows Latour's (2005) inclusion of technologies as an actor in their own right.
2 I am grateful to Joe McMahon for pointing out this feature of participant behaviour.
3 See, for example, http://sigknowledgehub.com.
4 http://blogs.worldbank.org/governance/category/tags/multi-stakeholder-initiatives.
5 http://www.huffingtonpost.com/2009/07/21/phrma-pfizer-lead-in-heal_n_241702.html.
6 http://www.idhsustainabletrade.com.
7 An internet search shows that out of twenty-three examples of global MSIs, nine are 'hosted' by a non-profit organisation, thirteen by an official body and one by a social enterprise.
8 http://thepartneringinitiative.org/.
9 http://worldshift2012.org/profiles/blogs/worldshift-2012-making-history (downloaded 31 July 2014).
10 Roberto Unger's interview on the 20th November 2013 BBC programme *Hardtalk*, sets out criticism of the TINA– There Is No Alternative – angle on this debate in some detail. http://www.bbc.co.uk/podcasts/series/ht/all (accessed 22 January, 2014).
11 http://www.socialwatch.org/sites/default/files/feminist-post-2015-declaration.pdf (accessed 1 September 2014).
12 www.fsg.org/our-story.
13 www.unrisd.org.
14 http://www.ripess.org/wp-content/uploads/2015/05/RIPESS_Global-Vision_EN.pdf (accessed 12 January 2016).
15 http://www.ripess.org/about-us/?lang=en (accessed 30 September 2015).
16 http://www.ripess.org/about-us/?lang=en (accessed 7 October 2014).
17 This author calculates that only three cents of every dollar more paid by America's consumers actually reaches producers – most stays within the chain and its certifiers (*Economist*, 5 July 2014: 76).

18 http://www.isealalliance.org/ (Accessed 1 August 2014).
19 http://www.greenpeace.org/usa/en/campaigns/global-warming-and-energy/pollute rwatch/koch-industries/ (accessed 21 September 2014).
20 http://www.critical-theory.com/politics-mask/ (Accessed, 4 August 2014).
21 http://blogs.lse.ac.uk/europpblog/2012/10/20/subterranean-politics-europe/ (accessed 4 August 2014).
22 http://observer.com/2011/10/more-money-more-problems-how-occupy-wall-stree t-is-really-funded/ (accessed 4 August 2014).
23 SGDs 17.16 and 17.17 http://www.un.org/sustainabledevelopment/sustainable-deve lopment-goals/ (accessed 4 August 2014).

References

Alexander, E. 1995, *How Organizations Act Together: International Coordination in Theory and Practice*, Gordon and Breach Publishers, New York.
Antrobus, P. and Sen, G. 2006, The Personal Is Global: The Project and Politics of the Transnational Women's Movement, in Batliwala, S. and Brown, D. (eds), *Transnational Civil Society: An Introduction*, pp. 142–158, Kumarian Press, Bloomfield, CT.
Barbuto, J. and Wheeler, D. 2006, Scale Development and the Construct Clarification of Servant Leadership, *Group and Organization Management*, Vol. 31, No. 3, pp. 300–326.
Batliwala, S. 2004, Grassroots Movements as Transnational Actors, in Taylor, R. (ed.) *Creating a Better World: Interpreting Global Civil Society*, pp. 64–82, Kumarian Press, Bloomfield, CT.
Beinhocker, E. 2006, *The Origin of Wealth: Evolution, Complexity and the Radical Remaking of Economics*, Random House, New York.
Bessant, J., Kaplinsky, R. and Morris, M. 2003, Developing Capability through Learning Networks, *Journal of Technology Management and Sustainable Development*, Vol. 2, No. 1, pp. 19–38.
Biekart, K. and Fowler, A. 2012, A Civic Agency Perspective on Change, *Development*, Vol. 55, No. 22, pp. 181–189.
Biekart, K. and Fowler, A. 2013, Transforming Activisms 2010+: Exploring Ways and Waves, *Development and Change, Forum Debate*, Vol. 44, No. 3, pp. 527–546.
Biekart, K. and Fowler, A. 2014, Civic Energy as a Trigger for Collective Citizens' Action, paper presented at conference 'Citizenship and Cooperation – Trend or Hype?', Royal Netherlands Academy of Arts and Sciences (KNAW), Amsterdam, 28 February.
Biekart, K. and Fowler, A. 2016, Country Ownership – Building From Within, Volume I, Task Team CSO Multi-Stakeholder Studies, International Institute of Social Studies, The Hague.
Chrislip, D. 2002, *The Collaborative Leadership Fieldbook*, Jossey Bass, San Francisco.
Chrislip, D. and Larson, C. 1994, *Filling a Hole: Collaborative Leadership – How Citizens and Civic Leaders Can Make A Difference*, Jossey Bass, San Francisco.
Cornwall, A. 2002, Making Spaces, Changing Places: Situating Participation in Development, *Working Paper* 170, Institute of Development Studies, University of Sussex.
Cilliers, P. 1998, *Complexity and Post Modernism*, Routledge, London.
Crane, A., Palazzo, G., Spence, L. and Matten, D. 2014, Contesting the Value of the Shared Value Concept, *California Management Review*, Vol. 56, No. 2, pp. 130–153.

Covington, S. 1997, *Moving a Public Agenda: The Strategic Philanthropy of Conservative Foundations*, National Committee for Responsive Philanthropy, Washington, DC.

De Landa, M., nd, Meshworks, Hierachies and Interfaces, http://www.t0.or.at/delanda/meshwork.htm (accessed 4 August 2014).

de Sousa Santos, B. 2014, *Epistemologies of the South: Justice Against Epistemicide*, Paradigm Publishers, Boulder.

De Wit, J. and Berner, E. 2009, Progressive Patronage? NGOs, Community-Based Organizations, and the Limits to Slum Dwellers' Empowerment, *Development and Change*, Vol. 40, No. 5, pp. 927–974.

DiMaggio, P. 1998, Interest and Agency in Institutional Theory, in Zucker, L. (ed.), *Institutional Patterns and Organizations*, pp. 3–22, Balinger, Cambridge.

Escobar, A. 2004, Beyond the Third World: Imperial Globality, Global Coloniality and Anti-Globalization Social Movements, reprint from *Third World Quarterly*, Vol. 25, No. 1, pp. 207–230. http://www3.nd.edu/~druccio/Escobar.pdf (accessed 7 January 2016).

Finnemore, M. and Sikkink, K. 1998International Norm Dynamics and Political Change, *International Organization*, Vol. 52, No. 4, pp. 887–917.

Fowler, A. 2013, *Social Innovation: New Game, New Dawn or False Promise?*, Hivos, The Hague. http://www.hivos.net/Hivos-Knowledge-Programme/Themes/Social-Innovation/Publications/Social-Innovation-New-Game-New-Dawn-or-False-Promise (accessed 7 January 2016).

Fowler, A. 2014, Innovation in Institutional Collaboration: The Role of Interlocutors, Working Paper, 584, International Institute of Social Studies, Erasmus University, Rotterdam. http://hdl.handle.net/1765/51129 (accessed 7 January 2016).

Fowler, A. and Biekart, K. (eds) 2008, *Civic Driven Change: Citizen's Imagination in Action*, Institute of Social Studies, The Hague. www.iss.nl/cdc (accessed 7 January 2016).

Gaventa, J. 2006, Finding the Spaces for Change: A Power Analysis, *IDS Bulletin*, Vol. 37, No. 6, pp. 23–36.

Gilens, M. and Page, B. 2014, Testing Theories of American Politics: Elites, Interest Groups and Average Citizens, *Perspectives on Politics*, Vol. 12, No. 3, pp. 564–581.

Group of Lisbon1995, *Limits to Competition*, MIT Press, Cambridge, MA.

GSO2013, Engaging the SUN Movement: Preventing and Managing Conflicts of Interest, Working Paper, 6, Global Social Laboratory, Geneva.

Haiven, M. and Khasnabish, A. 2014, *The Radical Imagination: Social Movements in the Age of Austerity*, Zeb Books, London.

Harcourt, W. 2013, Transnational Feminist Engagement with 2010+ Activisms, *Development and Change*, Vol. 44, No. 3, pp. 621–638.

Harich, J. 2010, Change Resistance as the Crux of the Environmental Sustainability Problem, *Systems Dynamics Review*, Vol. 26, No. 1, pp. 35–72.

Hyden, G. 1989, Reciprocity and Governance in Africa, in Wunsch, J.S. and Dele, O. (eds), *The Failure of the African State*, Westview Press, Boulder, pp. 245–269.

Icaza, R. and Vázquez, R. 2013, Social Struggles and Epistemic Struggles, in Biekart, K. and Fowler, A. (eds), *Transforming Activisms, Forum Edition, Development and Change*, pp. 35–72, Institute of Social Studies, The Hague.

Kawano, E. 2013, Social Solidarity Economy: Towards Convergence across Continental Divides. http://www.unrisd.org/unrisd/website/newsview.nsf/%28httpNews%29/F1E9214CF8EA21A8C1257B1E003B4F65?OpenDocument (accessed 7 January 2016).

Kieboom, M. 2014, *Lab Matters: Challenging the Practice of Social Innovation Laboratories*, Kennisland, Amsterdam. http://www.kennisland.nl/filter/publicaties/lab-matter s-challenging-the-practice-of-social-innovation-laborat (accessed 7 January 2016).

Knorringa, P. 2014, Private Governance and Social Legitimacy in Production, in Payne, A. and Phillips, N. (eds), *Handbook of the International Political Economy of Governance*, pp. 361–378, Edward Elgar, Cheltenham.

Knorringa, P. and Nadvi, K. 2014, Rising Power Clusters and the Challenges of Local and Global Standards, *Journal of Business Ethics*, Published online 19 September. http://link.springer.com/article/10.1007%2Fs10551-014-2374-6#/page-1 (accessed 7 January 2016).

Koh, H., Hegde, N. and Karamchandani, A. 2014, *Beyond the Pioneer: Getting Inclusive Industries to Scale*, Monitor Deloitte. http://www2.deloitte.com/content/ dam/Deloitte/global/Documents/Financial-Services/dttl-monitor-Beyond-the-Pio neer-2014-04.pdf (accessed 7 January 2016).

Laszlo, E. 2012, Global Bifurcation: The 2012 Decision Window, in Hubbard, B., *Birth 2012 and Beyond; Humanity's Great Shift to the Age of Conscious Evolution*, pp. 147–154, Shift Books.

Latour, B. 2005, *Reassembling the Social: An Introduction to Actor–Network Theory*, Oxford: University Press, Oxford.

Meadows, D. 1999, *Leverage Points: Places to Intervene in Systems*, Sustainability Institute, Hartland, VT.

Morozov, E. 2013, *To Save Everything, Click Here: The Folly of Technological Solutionism*, Allen Lane, London.

Murphy, G. 2004, The Seattle WTO Protests; Building a Global Movement, in Taylor, R. (ed.) *Creating a Better World: Interpreting Global Civil Society*, pp. 43–63, Kumarian Press, Bloomfield, CT.

Olivier de Sardan, J.-P., with Blundo, G. 2006, *Everyday Corruption and the State: Citizens and Public Officials in Africa*, Zed Books, London.

Ostrom, E. 2005, The Complexity of Collective Action Theory, Workshop on Political Theory and Policy Analysis, Centre for the Study of Institutions, Population and Climate Change, Indiana University, Bloomington.

Ostrom, E. 2009, Beyond Markets and States: Polycentric Governance of Complex Economic Systems, Nobel Prize Lecture, Workshop in Political Theory and Policy Analysis, Indiana University, Bloomington, IN, and Center for the Study of Institutional Diversity, Arizona State University, Tempe, AZ, 8 December. http://www. nobelprize.org/nobel_prizes/economics/laureates/2009/ostrom_lecture.pdf (accessed 7 January 2016).

Pattberg, P. 2005, The Institutionalization of Private Governance: How Business and Nonprofit Organizations Agree Transnational Rules, *Governance: An International Journal of Policy, Public Administration and Institutions*, Vol. 18, No. 4, pp. 589–610.

Pattberg, P. and Widerberg, O. 2014, Transnational Multi-stakeholder Partnerships for Sustainable Development: Conditions for Success, IVM Institute for Environmental Studies, Amsterdam. http://link.springer.com/article/10.1007%2Fs13280-015-0684-2#/pa ge-1 (accessed 7 January 2016).

Pleyers, G. 2010, *Alter-Globalization: Becoming Actors in the Global Age*, Polity Press, London.

Porter, M. and Kramer, M. 2006, Strategy and Society: The Link Between Competitive Advantage and Corporate Social Responsibility, *Harvard Business Review*, pp. 78–93, December.

Porter, M., Hills, G., Pfitzer, M., Patscheke, S. and Hawkins, E. 2012, *Measuring Shared Value; How to Unlock Value by Linking Social and Business Results*, Foundation Strategy Group, Washington, DC.

Scott, W. 2008, *Institutions and Organizations: Ideas and Interests*, Sage, London.

Senge, P., Scharmer, C., Jaworski, J. and Flowers, B. 2007, *Presence: An Exploration of Profound Change in People, Organizations and Society*, Doubleday, New York.

Spears, L. 2010, Character and Servant Leadership: Ten Characteristics of Effective, Caring Leaders, *The Journal of Virtues and Leadership*, Vol. 1, No. 1, pp. 25–30.

Sylia, N. 2014, *The Fair Trade Scandal: Marketing Poverty to Benefit the Rich*, Pluto Press, London.

Tembo, F. 2013, *Rethinking Social Accountability in Africa: Lessons from the Mwananchi Programme*, Overseas Development Institute, London.

Torrance, W. and Torrance, A. 2006, Spinning the Green Web: Transnational Environmentalism, in Batliwala, S. and Brown, L. (eds), *Transnational Civil Society: An Introduction*, pp. 101–123, Kumarian Press, Bloomfield, CT.

Turner, S., Merchant, K., Kania, J. and Martin, E. 2012, *Understanding the Value of Backbone Organizations in Collective Impact*, Foundation Strategy Group, Boston, MA.

Vázquez, R. 2011, Translation as Erasure: Thoughts on Modernity's Epistemic Violence, *Journal of Historical Sociology*, Vol. 24. No. 1, pp. 27–44.

4 Can consultants be civic innovators?

Exploring their roles as auditors and allies

Sylvia I. Bergh and Kees Biekart

Introduction

This chapter looks at the changing role of 'development professionals' in an international aid system that is challenged by external observers, but increasingly also from within the aid system itself. In particular, we focus on development consultants who are often hired for a temporary period of time to provide advice and feedback. They work within the virtual reality of the international aid system which has been coined *Aidland* by Apthorpe (2011), Mosse (2011a), and others. Aidland is a 'macro construct' which has 'its own mental topographies, languages of discourse, lore and custom, and approaches to organizational knowledge and learning' according to Apthorpe (2011: 199). He adds: 'it even has its own handed-down secular-inspirational ten commandments: the "thou shalt" UN Millennium Development Goals.'

As 'development researchers' at the International Institute of Social Studies, the Netherlands (ISS), we are also part of this virtual reality and we are familiar with the international professional communities of Aidland into which we move in and out for shorter or longer periods. For example, Sylvia Bergh has worked for two years as a World Bank staff member in both Washington DC and Morocco, and regularly takes on short-term consultancy assignments. Kees Biekart worked for four years as an independent development adviser for a range of European aid agencies, largely implementing evaluations on development effectiveness in the early 2000s. In the professional Aidland communities, a wide range of players are active: donor aid officials, technical advisors, NGO workers, academic researchers, and consultants from diverse academic, professional, and geographic backgrounds. What they have in common is that they are mediators and brokers of this virtual Aidland, 'translating' as Mosse (2005: 23) calls it, 'global policy into the different languages of state, donor, NGO and other agencies involved, and diverse practices back into global policy'. Mosse (2011a) and Eyben (2012) and others have analysed this translation process from global to local and back again in order to spell out the disjuncture (between rationalising global policies and complex local practices) and what they point to as the contradictions of the international aid system. Easterly (2014: 6) argues that this has generated a 'technocracy', which he essentially describes as a form of authoritarian development run by autocrats and advised by technical experts.

In this chapter our interest is in 'civic innovation' and how progressive social change is triggered and realised *despite* the particularities and limitations of Aidland. In doing so, we are building on the civic-driven change (CDC) framework which elaborates why aided processes of social change seldom lead to structural changes in power balances (Fowler and Biekart 2013). We are also interested in how drivers of civic change operate in multiple sectors of society: apart from mediating between donors and recipients, aid consultants also cross boundaries between state, civil society and markets. Even though often originating in Aidland, they are generally not confined to those boundaries, especially when they pursue a commonly shared view (for example with social movements) of a different 'imagined future'.

We agree with Hindman and Fechter (2011: 4–5) that 'the individual life situations and motivations of aid workers matter in how their work is accomplished [...] as they are enmeshed in networks that include other aid workers, local interlocutors, and their own families.' This chapter therefore aims to contribute to the growing literature on aid workers as 'mediating actors' whose transformative work is analysed in order to help explain the gaps between project design and implementation, and ultimately outcomes. Following Harrison (2013: 273), we build on the concept of 'brokerage' (Bierschenk 1988; Long and Long 1992; Mosse and Lewis 2006; Rossi 2006) which interrogates the ways in which a wide spectrum of actors involved in aid and development relate to and understand one another. We see 'Aidland' not as a bubble but as a range of places and situations in which relations of power are played out. Drawing on Actor Network Theory (Latour 2005), work on brokerage enables an understanding of how power and politics are played out in practice (see Harrison 2013: 273). This literature has its foundations in Norman Long's 'interface' approach, and aims to counteract the predominant view (inadvertently helped by the concept of governmentality and the focus on the discursive work of aid), that the individual agency of aid workers, including consultants, does not matter when it comes to evaluating project and programme success or failure, but rather, that these experts are mere 'tools' and therefore replaceable and interchangeable (Hindman 2011: 172; Hindman and Fechter 2011: 6).

The chapter explores these ideas in a series of sections: the next section clarifies the focus and research methodology followed by a brief literature review on the rise of consultants in international aid and the various constraints under which they are working. This is followed by a presentation of the empirical findings on the circumstances under which consultants can or could be acting as change agents. In the final reflections, we share some implications of these findings for civic innovation processes and research.

Focus and methodology

Our focus is on the group of mediators and brokers that are often not visible in development studies, but are often quite influential: development consultants working for Northern aid agencies (and often based in the Global

North). We aim to define a typology of these consultants, building on earlier work on development workers. Stirrat (2008) distinguishes mainly between two stereotypes of the development worker: *mercenaries* and *missionaries*. However, Stirrat (2008: 407) is quick to acknowledge that 'while there are individuals who can be recognized as approximating to [each stereotype], in general people veer between them, at different points in their careers and even at different points on the same day!'. As for the first category, it refers mainly to 'development professionals', those who work permanently or as consultants on a fixed-term basis for the major international development banks and donor agencies.

> This stereotype represents these development professionals as simply being interested in the material benefits they gain from working in the aid industry. They have no commitment to eradicating poverty or whatever, but simply to their own self-interest. As their title suggests, they are motivated solely by this self-interest and not by any higher morality.
>
> (Stirrat 2008: 407)

We would include here – perhaps unjustly so, as they may indeed have a personal moral commitment – the consultants employed by big audit and consulting firms such as PriceWaterhouseCoopers (PWC) or Deloitte.

Pratt (2013) notices about these 'auditing consultants':

> To save transaction costs, DFID, like many other official donors, now package more individual tasks or jobs into very large contracts. So whereas previously a DFID administrator would hire several smaller organisations or individuals to perform very specific tasks, these are now assembled into grand, multi-million pound programmes. Inevitably this means that very few companies (and even fewer NGOs) are of the size to finance the proposal writing and cover cash flow, given that payment is made in arrears for many contracts. This means that DFID and other donors are now in the hands of very large consultancy companies who charge higher rates per day, but can afford to cover the expenses required in advance. This has inflated many of the rates paid, and led to the dominance of the sector by very large companies, including financial multinationals with no previous experience except in auditing. These companies are driven by profits and are more concerned about meeting the last letter of their Terms of Reference (ToR) rather than achieving lasting social change.

Stirrat's second stereotype is the missionary, exemplified by the NGO worker, who is committed and enthusiastic, eschewing the world of executive lounges, expensive hotels and air-conditioned vehicles in favour of a direct meeting and identification with the 'real people'. As Stirrat (2008: 412) puts it, 'in this sector of the development world, people are motivated not by money but by a personal moral commitment.' This commitment is based on values such as participation, empowerment, gender sensitivity and the importance of indigenous knowledge with the aim of liberating people from poverty, marginalisation and social injustice. They see themselves as activists, as individuals who are committed to changing society (Stirrat 2008: 414).

However, there are a number of similarities between the mercenary and the missionary: first, there is no evidence to suggest that NGO personnel develop closer contact with 'the people' than development professionals. Second, the same is true for the claim that NGO personnel have a better grasp of local conditions. Both groups are dependent on counterparts or local employees to generate the information on which they base their actions. Third, 'it is becoming increasingly difficult to distinguish between an NGO and a commercial consultancy company, and this is having a major impact on the sort of personnel employed by NGOs' (Stirrat 2008: 413). Linked to this is the trend of missionaries frequently becoming mercenaries.

In the course of the research for this chapter we came up with a similar typology – but we felt that specifically for today's development consultants it would be more appropriate to re-label Stirrat's stereotypes as the *auditors* (corresponding to Stirrat's mercenaries) and the *allies* (Stirrat's missionaries). Both categories of consultants can be considered as 'interlocutors' in civic innovation processes according to Fowler (in this volume). The more specific roles of these interlocutors in fostering civic-driven change need further examination. The auditors are generally employed by one of the large consultancy companies (PWC, Deloitte, KMPG, McKinsey, etc.), as described above. They are often recent economics, management or accountancy graduates and lack any development-related expertise except for knowledge of budgets and financing models. In addition, they charge substantially higher fees to their clients than the *allies* as the invoices carry the logo of their consultancy companies, which until recently had undisputed reputations. In future research, we will have to analyse the emergence of this category in more detail, as it is rapidly growing in importance, but from a civic innovation perspective we are far more interested in the second category: influential and well paid Northern born/based consultants acting as *allies* for social change. The *allies* are the consultants often involved in collective learning processes, policy advisory missions, as well as capacity building activities. They are often hired by Northern and Southern NGOs, bilateral donors and Southern governments. They tend to be critical inhabitants of Aidland, but still very much depend on it for their income.

All of the consultants in any of these two categories – auditors or allies, can have the potential to be 'interlocutors', with varying degrees of willingness and power to bring about AGE processes: **A**ssemble interested parties, **G**uide and align collaboration across their institutional and/or organisational interfaces and help to **E**mbed in society the wanted changes (Fowler, this volume, p. 43). These changes can be either systemic ('changing the game') or merely changes in the rules of the existing game. To achieve such processes, Fowler stresses that the type of interlocutor needs to be 'fit for purpose', with neutrality or presence being a key variable, along with an ability to listen to and communicate in the 'languages' of different parties' (Fowler this volume, pp. 45–6). When it comes to consultants, Fowler states that 'consultants are typically invited and paid to provide services [...]. Permanent engagement is seldom consistent with their role, while their work is likely to improve the functioning of collaboration within the existing game rather than change the game itself.'

The aim of this chapter is to find out whether there may nevertheless be development consultants who do aim to change the game, and not (only) the rules of the game. Since we also have been active as 'allies' in this consultancy world, our intention in writing this chapter was to collect experiences from other allies who have been active in Aidland for many years. We wanted to find out whether there are any specific conditions which facilitate or hinder their work in bringing about AGE processes.

Our research approach has been to collect opinions and narratives from four consultants whom we consider to be highly experienced and to be acting as *allies*. We had in-depth interviews with them, *in situ* as well as via Skype, which often transformed into long and inspiring (group) conversations.[1] When examining civic innovation, it is important to explore views from consultants who see themselves also as change agents in Aidland. Nevertheless, they also were self-critical enough to position themselves at times outside Aidland, for example when working directly with social movements or activist groups which were not part of the international aid system. The four interviewees were selected within our own networks as well as by 'snowballing': asking suggestions from the participating consultants. In order to begin the conversations, we used a set of (provocative) statements about the role of consultants in bringing about political and societal change. Given that the international consultants' world can be quite small, and to enable our interviewees to respond freely, we changed the names of the four interviewees into fictitious ones in this chapter.

Consultants and their constraints in the current aid paradigm

Hindman and Fechter (2011: 3–5) argue that, 'development work is being transformed by processes such as deskilling, outsourcing, and neoliberal approaches to staffing' which amount to 'depoliticize "best practices" of employment and efficiency'. Indeed, much of development work 'has been reduced to a set of technical problems to be resolved by experts.' There has been a shift 'in the demographic profile of aid workers from development professionals deployed abroad with their families, to single technical specialists on short-term contracts' (Hindman 2011: 186). The processes of professionalisation and of commodifying development expertise reduces development projects to a series of unconnected micro processes and thereby alienates the expert from the projects themselves (Hindman 2011: 171), let alone from the socio-political contexts in which they are implemented. Another effect of this trend is that different types of experts can now access different salaries and daily rates, leading to 'a decline in a shared sentiment about the value of the work they were doing'; the short-term consultant and long-term career aid worker are no longer 'in it together' to help the local people but rather preoccupied with their own bonuses and per diems (Hindman 2011: 176). As Edward put it when we spoke to him, 'I rolled into what I do not really regard as a profession but as an atomized worker in an atomizing labour circumstance.'

Related to this observation is the type of knowledge that is valued in the current aid paradigm. As Sillitoe (2010: 16–17, 24–25) points out, the domi-nant capitalist-informed view of development, as largely a technological and market issue, relates to a particular epistemology that sees the world in uni-versalistic terms that ignores local (indigenous) knowledges and alternative views of development. Agencies assume that they have knowledge relevant to advancing development, and that approaches such as 'integrated rural develop-ment' or 'sustainable livelihoods' can be applied globally. When the under-standing of the 'beneficiaries' conflicts with these dominant views, the latter are side-lined, or worse. In fact, agencies often behave as if they do not trust local people's knowledges or the soundness of decisions they reach, and can manipulate their participation in order to ensure the dominance of the agency views. Local populations then reciprocate with distrust, particularly when promised developments rarely seem to materialise for the poor. Sillitoe therefore argues that there is a need for aid workers to foster trust in the knowledge that informs their development interventions. This demands awareness of epistemic cultural context and anticipation of misunderstanding and contradictions as people privilege 'everyman's' understanding when evaluating options above 'expert' views.

It is an open question as to what extent aid consultants can play a role in fostering this trust, and by extension contribute to the emergence of alternative, and potentially more transformative, views of development, given the time and other constraints they are working under. Indeed, consultants derive a large part of their status and potential influence from learning and using the 'right' type of knowledge and language – what Cathy Shutt (2006: 79) calls 'Aidlish'. What is more, Shutt (2006: 85) argues, based on her own personal experience as an aid worker, 'it is easy for those who enter the international aid system [Aidland] with honest intentions of "empowering" people in developing countries to unwittingly reproduce the inequitable social relations of power that they seek to challenge.' This is mainly due to the desire to acquire 'symbolic capital' and higher salaries that the knowledge of donor rules and procedures confer. Such rules and procedures are part and parcel of 'Aidlish'; they include the models widely used by aid consultants, such as the logical framework matrix and the management for results frameworks, with an emphasis on quantitative impact indicators and neglecting issues of power and context. As Mosse (2011b: 12–13) puts it, 'what is striking is the capacity of professionals [...] to sustain neoliberal institutionalist models as structure of representation, an accepted interpretation of what is going on and what can be accomplished.' These professionals serve as bearers of 'context-free ideas with universal applicability' (ibid.: 16). Or in other words, 'in deferring to the instrumentality of expert models, professionals are required to deny context, contingency, compromise, even their own agency, and to suppress the relational' (ibid.: 21; see also Kothari 2005).

The way these requirements are specified and imposed on consultants is often through restrictive Terms of Reference (ToR) governing their assignments. As Stirrat (2000: 36) mentions, they 'typically spell out a series of empirically defined issues and call for action-orientated responses. There are also various "checklists" which list the sorts of questions and the sorts of information which should be addressed in particular situations.' He goes on to cite the example of World Bank guidelines that spell out not only the structure of the report that the consultant is expected to deliver, but even the chapter and section headings. In fact, for Stirrat (2000: 37), the ToR and report formats represent part of a 'culture of consultancy' which

> is premised on what are seen as modernist principles of objectivity and rationality. The assumption on which development consultancy work is based is that consultants can somehow penetrate to the 'truth', the essence of what is going on in the world they are seeking to change, and that they can do this with the analytical tools which their 'modernity' puts at their disposal. Furthermore, what they aim to do is to change the world so that it more closely approximates the world which is imagined in terms of their modernism.

However, some potentially countervailing trends are observable in Aidland. Since the beginning of the 2000s, analytical tools such as Political Economy Analysis (PEA), Social Development Assessments (emphasising concepts such as social capital and empowerment), or 'Drivers of Change' (in the case of Department for International Development (DfID)) have emerged which emphasise the importance of context, distribution of power, and informal governance institutions in partner countries, as tools that may positively impact on the effectiveness of development interventions. They could thus also potentially serve as a basis for transformative views and strategies of development, but they seem to have been either abandoned or emptied of their political dimensions, and therefore remain marginal in the aid business. Fisher and Marquette (2014: 10) note that donors have increasingly externalised PEA in recent years, abandoning earlier ambitions to cultivate a generation of in-house development officials who are able to instinctively 'think politically'. Instead, external (both Western and Southern) consultants have steadily become the de facto suppliers of political analysis and training for donors. Fisher and Marquette (2014: 10) further state that 'having started as a transformative vision for the way donors think about the way they do their job, PEA has instead become a multimillion dollar industry focused around a product – PEA^{TM}. [...] Its transformative vision for internal change may be being lost as a result.'

Edward, one of the consultants interviewed for this study, recalls his own experience with the Dutch version of this tool, called SGACA (Strategic Governance and Corruption Analysis):

> I was almost asked to do one of these when I was in Pretoria for the Dutch Embassy. But then at the last minute the embassy decided not to do it, as they preferred to hire a local auditor (from PWC or so) to lead us through a technical exercise on corruption of South African elites. This gave me the feeling that these new models and mechanisms are actually extremely sensitive. Late last year I read in a blog of the former ECDPM Director that the European Commission has decided to drop the use of all of these mechanisms because they are too tricky and too dangerous.[2] They raised issues about what foreign embassies or aid consultants are doing asking political questions and probing relationships between companies and elites. So the future of these frameworks may be limited.[3]

Indeed, the European Commission is no longer investing in PEA, mainly because it has recognised that

> understanding the political and economic reality in which we operate belongs among the core tasks of desk officers and staff in delegation and the EEAS [European External Action Service]. Therefore the method should make more use of the staff of DEVCO and EEAS and avoid the use of external consultants. Secondly, there is an inherent political risk of pulling together detailed information on the political context into a single report.
>
> (EU official writing on the Capacity4dev website, cited in Fisher and Marquette 2014: 16[4])

PEA has effectively been 'depoliticised' and incorporated into the 'aid effectiveness' agenda, as donors are using it merely to assess fiscal and reputational risk and to identify 'easy wins', thereby excluding recipient voices from the development enterprise as well as minimising PEA's transformational potential. As Andrew Natsios, a former USAID Administrator, has noted, 'those development programs that are most precisely and easily measured are the least transformational' (Natsios 2010: 3 cited in Fisher and Marquette 2014: 17). A final reason why PEA and other such tools have been marginalised is that

> the 'political economy approach' to assistance generally entails building networks and facilitating discussions across a range of local actors who then, themselves, push forward reform agendas. This requires a lot of time and effort – but it spends much less money than building schools and hospitals.
>
> (McCulloch 2014)

This point refers to Sogge's (2002: 89) fundamental insight about the aid industry, namely that the 'prosperity of aid institutions and the careers of people who run them depend on making funds flow'.

In the case of other donor agencies such as the World Bank, it has signed Articles of Agreement that forbid it from 'interfering in the political affairs of any member' and thus inherently political social development ideas such as social capital and empowerment are framed in economistic terms so as to depoliticise them. This allows for the expert design of technical interventions for social reorganisation through neoliberal models of self-help, self-organisation and 'responsibilisation' (Mosse 2011c: 90–91 and footnote 18, citing Li 2007, 2011, and Rose 1999).

A further, more practical, constraint on consultants' political agency is their 'hypermobility' (Verma 2011: 59), as they move from country to country, negotiating with development agencies on a contract-to-contract, project-to-project basis. During their careers, they may also change their sectoral focus 'to fit various postings, organizational strategies, and donor demands' (Verma 2011: 60). This, and the fact that development practitioners generally tend to socialise mostly with other such international practitioners as 'escape mechanisms' in order to normalise their hypermobile lifestyles (also called 'fishbowls' or 'islands'), means that it may be difficult if not impossible for consultants to build up relations with relevant local social actors in the first place (Verma 2011: 73). In other words, consultants who want to be change agents must first overcome various disconnects with the people they are supposed to 'develop', i.e. 'gaps and lack of meaningful interface, interaction, communication, understanding, connection, and congruent meaning between domains of people, individuals, or [...] epistemic cultures' (Verma 2011: 74). This links to the point made earlier about the importance of 'Aidlish'; i.e. the fact that expatriate development consultants not only acquire but also continuously adapt technical knowledge associated with 'modern', scientific ideas (forms of cultural capital) in order to maintain their status and legitimise their interventions. 'In this way, the separation between "expert" and "local" knowledge and an intellectual distance between donor and recipient is maintained' (Kothari 2005: 428).

We have tried to outline the contours of the current aid paradigm in which aid workers, including consultants, are operating. Essentially, this boils down to the persistent quality of development as an 'anti-politics machine' that works by 'insistently reposing political questions of land, resources, jobs, or wages as technical "problems" responsive to the technical [and we could add, globally applicable] "development intervention"' (Li 2011: 58 citing Ferguson 1994: 270). As a result, while most staff in development agencies – and by extension, consultants – are concerned *about* the political context they operate in, they usually feel they should not themselves be concerned *with* politics in a development context (Hout and Schakel 2014: 621 citing Unsworth 2009). This is of course rather problematic and formed the basis of our enquiries.

Perspectives from Northern-based consultants as allies of social change

Given this rather pessimistic assessment of the scope for transformative action on the part of development workers, can we identify consultants who would be (consciously or unconsciously) acting as potential change agents? And if so, how do they position themselves in this context? What are their strategies to fight the 'anti-politics machine'? Or as Kothari (2005: 444) puts it, 'how can critical voices be effective within a neoliberal development agenda?' This is the question we put forward to our interviewees. The first two responded with the following experiences.

Edward worked for a wide range of donor NGOs and bilateral agencies in Southern Africa:

> (...) before I even had any inkling of this world of consultants, there was an emergency in Southern Mozambique in January 1984, a storm for which the Dutch, Danish and Swedish together with the Mozambican col- leagues mounted a big help operation, over 2–3 months, for a particular zone, with a lot of money. There was suddenly the need for a report for these donors: how did it work, what happened, what were the strong and weak points? Somehow, via via, it came to me; because I was available, I had three weeks to go and talk to people, I knew the terrain, I spoke Portuguese, and meet some of the people. That was an unexpected opportunity that I did not seek but that came to me.

This is similar to Peter's experience who worked as a consultant to pay for his passion to write books and who later became an influential actor in an inter- national process designed to resolve one of Africa's most thorny conflicts. When asked whether he was able to influence processes of social change as an 'ally consultant', Peter replied:

> As a consultant, you're hired to do a specific job, not to bring a particular bias [...]. Somebody wants an evaluation of Volkswagen, you evaluate the Volkswagen, according to whatever terms of reference you are given. [...] So I'm not sure that the actual consulting work is where the kind of activism might most manifest itself. [...] Maybe it's a bit like teaching, if you think of teachers. I mean you are supposed to teach the curriculum, but you can do a lot of other things besides that, as a teacher, you can work with students after school, outside the classroom, you can write... From my perspective, I think it's been the writing that has been the most [influential].

To the same question, Edward replied:

> Let's take my love-hate relationship with Angola. I began consulting work in Angola in the 1980s, and I was there about 6–7 times, out of an argument that I made to myself: this is one country where there might

actually be a chance for some counter-hegemonic force to develop. Pure delusion in those years, but still with a grain of plausibility. And so in the course of time, I kept at it and realized that this country is not going to be the new star of a progressive Africa. But then a new argument emerged, which is one voiced by many, which was, 'well, if you stay with it, and accept assignments like little NGO things etc., perhaps you can add to greater knowledge of the Angolans'; and part of my attraction there was, you came up against a handful of extremely impressive Angolan intellectuals who were leaders of, call them social movements – they had jobs in NGOs – but they were leaders of a kind of oppositional force. And for one thing or another, you are interested in them, your loyalties are with them, you are interested in the country. And you build up a set of arguments that kept me interested in that country. Now I find myself being asked to write articles about 'what went wrong with Angola and the solidarity of Angola?'

Edward emphasised a point here, which comes back in our conversations: why do you do this type of consultancies as someone who has an agenda of progressive social change, but also sees the limitations? Edward: 'There is something to consider here, in terms of motivation, the kind of stories that consultants tell themselves to justify their arguments about being relevant in a political sense, relevant in social change, but which probably risk being exaggerated.' Caroline strongly reacted to this as she disagrees with the underlying assumptions. Caroline:

> It assumes that this is what a consultant – even a social change consultant – wishes to do. It assumes that this is our agenda. I can't say that I have ever taken on a consultancy job thinking 'Can I contribute to social change here?'. It never crossed my mind! I find it interesting in Edward's recounting of his history, that for you, it was very important to think 'Is there space in this country for social change?'. I have never thought of countries as my unit to consider a job. (...) It depends whether the consultant is somehow committed or linked to the movement where he or she works.

In contrast to Caroline who worked with the (global) women's movement for many years, the links between Edward's consultancy work and activism were less strong, both in his professional life and in his mind:

> Solidarity activism was largely a separate world, with the exception of personal contacts: I was sometimes asked in the context of anti-apartheid work or my association with the solidarity movement as someone they could trust to give them the kind of report they wanted to see. So that's the overlap; but an initiative that I want to be a consultant to provide progressive insights into problems of social change, never crossed my mind.'

This points to the fact that a consultant can have several roles (shifting back and forth between auditor and ally roles as interlocutors; see also the point made by Stirrat above), and acting in spheres of influence that may not necessarily connect. In fact, our interviewees did a lot of unpaid/pro bono work for NGOs or movements that they cared about and which could not afford to pay them as consultants.

Another interviewee whom we call Max started working as a consultant in a partnership-based consultancy firm he founded in Eastern Africa in the early 1980s, mainly out of frustration at the lack of expertise on 'professional' NGO management. He consulted for a range of African NGOs on management, organisation, and funding issues, with a concern for 'learning from ourselves, as opposed to being taught by others'. He then was involved in setting up training courses aimed at developing a proper style of organisational management:

> (...) if you look at the process of what participatory development and community empowerment is about, it's simply not a commodity. And therefore your points of reference of what you are trying to do and how you measure change and how you measure performance is simply much more complicated than it is for for-profits.

A further dimension of consultants as potential change agents lies in the way they conduct their work, even when it is governed by increasingly stringent and non-negotiable ToRs. Caroline emphasised that she is more a facilitator of group processes:

> I believe in people doing self-evaluations, so I always try to maximize involving people to do their own evaluations, or experiment with different methods and lots of group work. Also because my loyalty is more towards the organization than to the one that is paying... I remember an example of an association working on family planning in the Balkans where I had to do a straight-forward evaluation, but even before I started I tried to be in touch with people inside that organization to decide what they wanted and what they needed. Otherwise you are like the inspector who is flown in, does the job, and flies out. For me that is useless. I try to involve the various groups in such a way that it is useful for them, because I believe in the people and in group dynamics to create something new or to get something out of the way that is a problem. Sometimes it works better than other times.'

This leads to the question about the consultant's influence or impact. Are his or her reports read at all by those who could effect change? This assumes that the reports are meant to bring about change in the first place. Stirrat (2000: 41) notes:

> while at one level the rationale for development consultancies is that they should have a practical impact, at the same time there is an acceptance

that they do not and that they are not expected to. While explicitly short term consultants are hired to deal with specific empirically defined problems, implicitly the situation is rather different. Frequently it appears that they are hired to tell their clients what they want to hear, and even more frequently their advice or their findings are ignored.

Apthorpe (2011: 207) gives an example where a consultancy mission that he was heading had the full support of the minister concerned as well as other key staff in the government and outside (United Nations Development Programme), so that the draft recommendations were discussed at a large representative and public meeting and turned into a Cabinet paper afterwards. Soon after that, the new policy was determined and introduced. As Apthorpe puts it, this experience stood in contrast to the usual 'highly intrusive surgical shock event perpetrated by aliens from another planet perhaps with their own agenda.'

Peter recounted the routine of such 'shock events' in his experience working with a major bilateral aid agency:

> You would go out to do an evaluation of a project [...]. What I would often find is that there were design problems; the thing wasn't working very well because it hadn't been designed very well in the first place, or because the donor was inflexible in terms of changing directions when it became obvious that had to take place. So if you were at all critical of the donor, you started to get into trouble. The donor really did not want to hear that they had made any mistakes at all. So what kind of evaluation can you do, if either you can't be honest or they don't want honesty.[...] I think a lot of consultants do whatever the employer wants, and don't raise any questions.

Peter then compared this narrow focus of the 'auditor' type of consultant to working as a dentist:

> I think a lot of consultants see themselves as dentists. I mean you go in, you got your teeth cleaned, you got your tooth drilled, and you go home; that's one after the other. It's not about changing dental health, it's not about changing the dental community or the association of dentists or anything else; it's really 'just do the teeth'.

However, as was already suggested by Max, there are cases where it's not just 'about the teeth', but where there is the possibility for consultants to influence donor organisations to change the ways in which they 'deliver' aid. Caroline: 'If you think about contributing to social change, you also have multiple influences. You tend to think about influence on the local NGO setting etc., but far more important as a consultant is having influence on a (donor) organisation like ICCO.' Edward agreed with this, saying, 'That is one of the stories I keep telling myself as "my modest contribution". If I get a few people in this organisation to listen it will nudge things.' Caroline added to that by saying 'If I think of my influence in Hivos, I think about my links with social movements where Hivos staff also walks around, and where I speak to them in an informal way as well. In that sense I have influence in Hivos', or through conducting workshops presenting the consultant reports:

> That's why I love doing workshops. For example with ICCO, they told me I had raised important questions which were not directly related to the evaluation, but still valuable for ICCO. They then asked me to go to a brainstorm meeting to discuss these questions, and so I did. That is when you actually have an influence.

Max serves as a good example of someone who thought to influence the aid sector at the global level, by joining several international boards of global networks. He continued to work as a consultant in order to be able to take on these unpaid positions, as he felt that he could have more strategic influence through them than through his consultancy work. He also emphasised the importance of being in it for the long haul.

> I don't do one-offs much anymore: that is part of the old repertoire. [...]. So unless there is something of a long game, but that is only really possible because of the networks of people whom I have known for years who are still in these big international NGOs at reasonably senior levels. [...] Influence over time is of course essential; on thinking processes [and] language use.

Max refered to his strategy work for a major international NGO by saying, 'I am outsider enough to provide critical feedback, but there is also a degree of trust.' This is very similar to Peter's view: 'I think the kind of consultancy where you can make more difference is where they are hiring you to do a look at the future, the strategic planning.' In addition, developing a long-term relationship is important, as Peter explained:

> A lot of organisations hire consultants in a serial fashion; so you hire this one for that, and another one and another one, but I found that if you develop a long-term relationship with two or three organisations regularly, they like it better and you tend to have more influence. [...] I know what they can tolerate and what they can't. I'm more likely to tailor recommendations and reports to reality than to some dreamland.

The bottom line is that 'allied consultants' such as Edward and Caroline do not consider themselves to be change agents when doing consultancies. They stress that they might be contributing to change processes of organisations or movements in an implicit way, but that this is not central to their motivations.

In fact, they also depend very much on how these movements themselves develop. Caroline made this point:

> I went to a large international women's conference in 2012, and I had a very interesting conversation with a Pakistani woman. We both concluded that, for us, a lot of the fun of what we were doing, also as consultants, was getting less and less. We attributed that to the demise of the international women's movement. (...) If a movement is in decline, the funders become more important, so the movement no longer has its own agenda; it has to follow someone else's agenda. And then your job as a consultant is becoming less interesting.

Similarly, Max argued: 'in my consultancy life I do not really consider myself to be a "change agent", as I provide services for which I get paid. In my non-consultancy life I can be a "catalyst".' Alan Fowler, in his chapter in this volume, makes a similar point. He maintains that interlocution and civic innovation are not the same thing. So if someone is invited to somebody else's table, the chances are that that person is not going to be a civic innovator (in the sense of changing the game). He or she is more likely to be asked to change the rules of the game. But, Fowler argues, someone can be an inter-locutor and a civic innovator at the same time if that person is not trying to provide a service but chooses to use his or her experience to influence parti-cular processes, for example by writing a paper or a blog.[5] In that sense, civic innovation can also be a way to maintain the status quo; after all, civic innovation does not always mean pro-social change, or changing the game itself.

In our conversations with some of the consultants this triggered an intense debate about the role of Southern-based consultants: is it possible for a socially engaged consultant to work as a translator of Southern voices and to insert that into Northern debates? Do we have examples that this is effectively happening? Caroline answered in the affirmative:

> Sure: the international women's movement! The way things were discussed, and the agenda items (especially in the 1990s), you can see this as a very powerful force. Voices came from countries like the Philippines, where the movement was also strong because of migrant communities. Or India, which was big but also with the UK connection. Many movements with different voices, such as from Southern Africa, Eastern Africa, Brazil, came together at the international level. One of their key achievements was 'women's rights are human rights', which was agreed at the 1993 Vienna summit because we campaigned so hard for it.

Edward suggested another example:

> Consultants from Brazil came for a longer period to Angola, sometimes even up to six months, and often were very successful, also bringing their

activist experiences. The circumstances certainly were not optimal: Angolan NGOs can be quite conservative and opportunistic, just working within the aid system. The lesson is that the choice is right from a political and activist milieu like Brazil (but also for example Shack Dwellers International), there you have some very fruitful cross-fertilisation. That is, under certain circumstances consultants can be really delivering and contributing to progressive social change.

This led the conversation towards the question why we had largely selected Northern-based consultants for this study, all of which seem to be linked to 'Aidland'. Our response was that we were looking indeed at consultants largely trained in Northern (academic) institutions, including those Southern consultants we have had, for example, as students at the International Institute of Social Studies in The Hague. However, Caroline saw it differently:

> But it is not true that all consultants have been trained in the North, as I know a number which have really progressive agendas. For example some of my consultant friends based in Zimbabwe, none of them have ever been trained in a Northern or a Western university. I think of a good friend of mine who was educated in Zimbabwe and then did a degree in South Africa; she has very different ideas about consultancies and development aid. Also some of my Indian friends who come from the smaller women's groups and who have been for example very critical of the growing NGO-isation of social movements (which is a very Indian discussion).

Eventually this is what we all seem to agree on: contributing to social change has multiple aspects. In Caroline's words, 'As a consultant, you tend to think only about your influence on a local NGO setting, though far more important is having influence on a donor or social organisation itself.' Edward: 'I would agree, and that is one of the stories I keep telling myself as "my modest contribution" as an activist. If I can only get a few people in a (donor) organisation to listen, it will nudge things.'

Final reflections

This chapter has explored the role of development consultants in processes of civic innovation. Are they able to trigger change processes at all, or are they basically reconfirming existing power relations within Aidland? Our literature review suggested that we had to make a proper typology of development consultants, so we proposed the category of 'auditors', of whom there are an increasing number in Aidland and who largely monitor efficiency and evaluate effectiveness. And we proposed a more activist type of consultant which we called 'allies', as they were often also linked to particular agendas of social change, even though often working under multiple constraints, not least financial ones. We had long conversations with a few Northern-based 'allies', who seem to be doing their most influential work outside of their consultants' roles. However, they also admitted being in need of their experiences and incomes as such (including as 'auditors'), otherwise they would not be able to perform a role as change agents. What exactly have they achieved? Here we have to be modest, although in particular settings consultants indeed have been 'influential'. Peter:

> many consultants complain that maybe they have not achieved very much, but maybe this obscures that you actually have achieved something. Maybe we are all a bit too ambitious? Maybe we all want to build Saint Paul's Cathedral and we miss the fact that we actually train some stone masons who will do it themselves?

There are three important implications of these findings for civic innovation processes and for further research in particular on consultants as change agents. The first is that it underlines again why our civic innovation agenda is actually not really focusing on Aidland (nor on its potential futures). In all our discussions so far it is clear that we want to explore the boundaries that are appearing in the cracks of the international aid system, opening up new opportunities for new coalitions and innovative strategies that are not depending on external aid agendas and resources. A second, and related, implication is that the development consultants we have analysed in this chapter are constantly exploring the contradictions as well as the distrust generated by the aid system, whilst at the same time trying to offer a critical voice. Sometimes they are heard, but often it is not easy to offer an alternative view or strategy. We therefore have to be careful to give too much of a change agent role to these 'allies', even though we can come up with a number of examples, and a broader review will likely find new ones. However the third, and most important implication, is probably the need to shift our focus more to those consultants as 'allies' of (Southern) social change processes that have been rather autonomous from Aidland. This is either because they were trained at local academic institutions or research centres, or because they had stronger links with local social movements and activist groups. This also offers new challenges for those of us working in Northern-based institutes, like ISS and the Institute of Development Studies in Brighton, where we train Southern researchers to become the new drivers of local processes of civic innovation. A future research agenda on civic innovation therefore will have to be securely rooted into these interesting and important initiatives that are trying to trigger change beyond (and despite) the dynamics of the aid system, bringing together a whole new generation of globally connected 'allies'.

Notes

1 All consultants involved have different nationalities; interviews were held by Skype and in person between August to September 2014.

2 For the interview transcript with ECDPM's Head of Strategy, Jean Bossuyt, see http://ecdpm.org/talking-points/is-there-a-future-political-economy-analysis-europea n-commission/ (accessed 7 January 2016).

3 In the case of SGACA, Hout and Schakel (2014: 621, 625) explain the demise of the tool in the Dutch Ministry of Foreign Affairs within the time span of only one four-year policy cycle (2007–2009) mainly by the proponents' inability to convince embassy staff that their involvement would outweigh the costs of their participation. Some embassy as well as HQ staff also feared that the SGACA might have a fall-out on their day-to-day work or on their relations with government officials and other donor agencies working in the country.

4 The message was deleted very soon after it was posted, see http://ecdpm.org/ta lking-points/is-there-a-future-political-economy-analysis-european-commission/ (accessed 7 January 2016).

5 See for example http://devballs.yolasite.com/ which is anonymous but clearly written by someone or several people who used to work for DfID.

References

Apthorpe, R. (2011) 'With Alice in Aidland: A seriously satirical allegory?', in Mosse, D. (ed.) *Adventures in Aidland*, New York, Oxford: Berghahn Books, 199–219.

Bierschenk, T. (1988) 'Development projects as arenas of negotiation for strategic groups: A case study from Benin', *Sociologia Ruralis* 28(2/3): 148–160.

Easterly, W. (2014) *The Tyranny of Experts: Economists, Dictators, and the Forgotten Rights of the Poor*, New York: Basic Books.

Eyben, R. (2011) 'The sociality of international aid and policy convergence', in Mosse, D. (ed.) *Adventures in Aidland*, New York, Oxford: Berghahn Books, 139–160.

Eyben, R. (2012) 'Fellow travellers in development', *Third World Quarterly* 33(8) 1405–1421.

Fechter, A.M. and Hindman, H. (eds) (2011) *Inside the Everyday Lives of Development Workers: The Challenges and Futures of Aidland*, Sterling, VA: Kumarian Press.

Ferguson, J. (1994) *The Anti-Politics Machine: 'Development', Depoliticization, and Bureaucratic Power in Lesotho*, Minneapolis: University of Minnesota Press.

Fisher, J. and Marquette, H. (2014) 'Donors doing Political Economy Analysis[TM]: From process to product (and back again?)', Developmental Leadership Program Research Paper 28, available at: http://www.delog.org/cms/upload/pdf-pea/Donors_ Doing_Political_Economy_Analysis_-_From_Process_to_Product_and_Back_Aga in.pdf (accessed 7 January 2016).

Fowler, A. (2014) 'Innovation in institutional collaboration: The role of interlocutors', *CIRI Working Paper*, No. 3. The Hague: Institute of Social Studies.

Fowler, A. and Biekart, K. (2013) 'Relocating civil society in a politics of civic-driven change', *Development Policy Review* 31(4): 463–483.

Harrison, E. (2013) 'Beyond the looking glass? 'Aidland' reconsidered', *Critique of Anthropology* 33(3): 263–279.

Hindman, H. (2011) 'The hollowing out of Aidland: Subcontracting and the New Development Family in Nepal', in Fechter, A.M. and Hindman, H. (eds) *Inside the Everyday Lives of Development Workers: The Challenges and Futures of Aidland*, Sterling, VA: Kumarian Press, 169–192.

Hindman, H. and Fechter, A.M. (2011) 'Introduction' in Fechter, A.M. and Hindman, H. (eds) *Inside the Everyday Lives of Development Workers: The Challenges and Futures of Aidland*. Sterling, VA: Kumarian Press, 1–20.

Hout, W. and Schakel, L. (2014) 'SGACA: The rise and paradoxical demise of a political-economy instrument', *Development Policy Review* 32(5): 611–630.

Kothari, U. (2005) 'Authority and expertise: The professionalization of international development and the ordering of dissent', *Antipode* 37: 425–446.

Latour, B. (2005) *Reassembling the Social: An Introduction to Actor Network Theory*, Oxford: Oxford University Press.

Li, T. (2007) *The Will to Improve: Governmentality, Development, and the Practice of Politics*, Durham, NC: Duke University Press.

Li, T. (2011) 'Rendering society technical: Government through community and the ethnographic turn at the World Bank in Indonesia', in Mosse, D. (ed.) *Adventures in Aidland*, New York, Oxford: Berghahn Books, 57–80.

Long, N. and Long, A. (eds) (1992) *Battlefields of Knowledge: The Interlocking of Theory and Practice in Social Research and Development*, London: Routledge.

McCulloch, N. (2014) 'Can a Political Economy Approach explain aid donors' reluctance to think and work politically? Guest post from Neil McCulloch', From Poverty to Power blog, 27 March 2014, available at: http://oxfamblogs.org/fp2p/can-a-poli tical-economy-approach-explain-aid-donors-reluctance-to-think-and-work-politica lly-guest-post-from-neil-mcculloch (accessed on 2 June 2014).

Mosse, D. (2005) 'Global governance and the ethnography of international aid', in Mosse, D. and Lewis, D. (eds) *The Aid Effect: Giving and Governing in International Development*, London: Pluto Press.

Mosse, D. (ed.) (2011a) *Adventures in Aidland: The Anthropology of Professionals in International Development*, New York, Oxford: Berghahn Books.

Mosse, D. (2011b) 'Introduction: The anthropology of expertise and professionals in international development', in Mosse, D. (ed.) *Adventures in Aidland*, New York, Oxford: Berghahn Books, 1–32.

Mosse, D. (2011c) 'Social analysis as corporate product: Non-economists/anthropologists at work in the World Bank in Washington D.C.', in Mosse, D. (ed.) *Adventures in Aidland*, New York, Oxford: Berghahn Books, 81–102.

Mosse, D. and Lewis, D. (eds) (2006) *Development Brokers and Translators: The Ethnography of Aid and Agencies*, Bloomfield, CT: Kumarian Press.

Natsios, A. (2010) 'The clash of the counter-bureaucracy and development', Center for Global Development essay, Washington DC: Center for Global Development, available at: http://www.cgdev.org/files/1424271_file_Natsios_Counterbureaucracy. pdf (accessed on 17 January 2016).

Pratt, B. (2013) 'The use of consultants in development'. *INTRAC Blog* No. 34: http:// www.intrac.org/blog.php/34/the-use-of-consultants-in-development (accessed 7 January 2016).

Rose, N. (1999) *Powers of Freedom: Reframing Political Thought*, Cambridge: Cambridge University Press.

Rossi, B. (2006) 'Why donors and recipients should not be compartmentalized into separate "worlds of knowledge"', in Mosse, D. and Lewis, D. (eds) *Development Brokers and Translators: The Ethnography of Aid and Agencies*, Bloomfield, CT: Kumarian Press.

Shutt, C. (2006) 'Power in aid relationships: A personal view', *IDS Bulletin* 37(6): 79–87.

Sillitoe, P. (2010) 'Trust in development: some implications of knowing in indigenous knowledge', *Journal of the Royal Anthropological Institute (N.S.)* 16: 12–30.

Sogge, D. (2002) *Give & Take: What's the Matter with Foreign Aid?* London: Zed Books.

Stirrat, R.L. (2000) 'Cultures of consultancy', *Critique of Anthropology* 20(1): 31–46.
Stirrat, R.L. (2008) 'Mercenaries, missionaries and misfits: Representations of development personnel', *Critique of Anthropology* 28(4): 406–425.
Unsworth, S. (2009) 'What's politics got to do with it? Why donors find it so hard to come to terms with politics, and why this matters', *Journal of International Development* 21(6): 83–94.
Verma, R. (2011) 'Intercultural encounters, colonial continuities and contemporary disconnects in rural aid: An ethnography of development practitioners in Madagascar', in Fechter, A.M. and Hindman, H. (eds) *Inside the Everyday Lives of Development Workers: The Challenges and Futures of Aidland*, Sterling, VA: Kumarian Press, 59–82.

5 Between state, market and civil society

What constitutes the social in social entrepreneurship?

A.H.J. (Bert) Helmsing

Introduction

In the past decade, social entrepreneurship has become a new theme in international development debates. A considerable volume of literature deals with social entrepreneurship in relation to the social needs and problems and dealing with these in the social sector, but in the past five years attention has extended to include changes in and transformation of the capitalist market economy. Although historically its conceptualisation originated in localised experiences of constructing alternative economies, nowadays then, social entrepreneurship is appealing to a broad ideological spectrum. A recent bibliometric study on the subject covering the period 1991–2010 showed that the meteoric rise of journal publications began in 2004/5 (Granados et al. 2011). It is my impression that it is precisely this extension of the purview of social entrepreneurship from the social sector to transformative change in and of the market economy that is responsible for this rapid rise in the literature. In relation to international development, I particularly refer here to social entrepreneurial initiatives at the 'Base of the Pyramid'[1], or for short BoP.

This broad appeal across the ideological spectrum seems contradictory and calls for clarification of concepts and contexts in which these are applied. Currently, if anything, the academic field of social entrepreneurs, entrepreneurship and enterprise is characterised by an enormous diversity of perspectives and explanations, though certain perspectives and academic disciplines dominate. This will be reviewed below in the section 'Why has social entrepreneurship become an issue?'.

The growing popularity of the concepts has not gone unchallenged. For example Nichols (2011) and many others who are critical see social entrepreneurship as a privatisation of what is essentially collective and/or public in which previously civil society, participation and active citizenship played a central role and is now marginalised. Are then social entrepreneurs 'uncivic'? Or formulating the question more positively: How is the social constituted in social entrepreneurship?

The concern expressed by Nichols has in part been triggered by a dominant current in the social entrepreneurship literature, which glorifies the individual entrepreneur whilst de-emphasising the importance of social (and political) processes. This monological conceptualisation of the social entrepreneur and its critique is reviewed in the section 'Defining social entrepreneurship'.

To uncover the social in social entrepreneurship it is important to elaborate on the social entrepreneurial process in different contexts. Here we will contrast the social entrepreneurial process in the social sector with social entrepreneurial initiatives at the BoP. This will be done in the section on 'Social entrepreneurial processes'.

The chapter concludes that the 'social' not only refers to the mission of social entrepreneurs but also resides in processes by which these initiatives are conceived and made sustainable. Here there are important differences between the social sector and the BoP domain of emerging market economies.

This chapter then clearly connects to a sub-set of the central CIRI concepts from the Introduction chapter (see p. 8). Social entrepreneurs can be an example *par excellence* of interlocutors who exercise their agency to push for civic innovations, in the social and in the economic domain. This would, amongst others, depend on the extent to which their values are well intentioned but individual, or have gone through or rely on deliberative processes to reflect real societal needs. Social entrepreneurs are cross-sectional or hybrid phenomena. Finally, they are likely to challenge established structures and processes in the social and economic domain through various forms of activism and at the same time engage state, civil society and market in order to develop sustainable social enterprises.

Why has social entrepreneurship become an issue?

Different authors point to different factors that explain the relevance and emergence of social entrepreneurship. Some authors who look at the phenomenon from the perspective of civil society, stress negative factors, such as the crisis of the welfare state and increase in unmet social needs (e.g. by researchers of the European Network on Social Enterprise research EMES, such as Defourny and Nijsens (2008) and Borzaga and Defourny (2004)). Perrini and Vurro (2006) argue in relation to the social sector that the rise of social entrepreneurship is clearly associated with the economic slowdown, which triggered the crisis of the welfare state, and the rise in unemployment, which simultaneously resulted in rising unmet social needs. The crisis of the welfare state is not only a fiscal issue but related to a fundamental redesign of social policies through privatisation and decentralisation.

The reduction in state subsidies for international development cooperation available for non-profit organisations such as development oriented NGOs is another important factor. This has increased the competition between these NGOs and in turn has triggered a search for market-based sources of funding for their social activities (Dees 1998; Dees, Emerson and Economy 2002; Kieng and Quack 2013). In addition, the increasing demand for efficiency in the use of public monies resulted in increased competition between NGOs.

They respond by searching for new ways to address social needs. Furthermore, the critique about the lack of effectiveness of their development interventions has induced NGOs to search for market-based interventions as a way to increase sustainability and this in turn has led NGOs to explore social entrepreneurship. This coincides with the emergence of new ways of poverty alleviation (e.g. fair trade and inclusive business). A related factor concerns the 'dependency syndrome' and disempowerment effects associated with state and NGOs subsidised programmes. Last but not least the current pro-business 'zeitgeist' has made social entrepreneurship more fashionable. Social entrepreneurship is not necessarily the solution to the signalled trends. Kieng and Quack warn that social entrepreneurship may not be a really new concept but rather a financial issue. Indeed, financial pressures may lead to 'mission drift' as NGOs struggle to make ends meet and they adjust the portfolio of activities to suit their sources of finance.

Others, like Becchetti and Borzaga (2010), stress positive factors to explain the rise of social entrepreneurship, such as the global increase in advocacy movements and the growing awareness of the downsides of globalisation as well as the rise in voluntary activities to provide goods and services to disadvantaged groups that are neglected by state and market. They also see the increasing awareness of responsible consumers who are receptive to social entrepreneurial approaches to provide goods and services (e.g. the rise of fair and eco-labels) as well as the more responsible behaviour of for-profit enterprises. In more general terms other authors stress the complexity of current developmental problems, which need a different kind of actor and actor configurations to address these (Fowler 2014).

Many of the above authors see social entrepreneurship to be clearly associated with civil society and the social sector (Hulgard 2010; EMES), while others, more recently, see social entrepreneurship in relation to the market economy. Authors of the latter group tend to argue that corporate social responsibility (CSR) has not delivered on its promises and has effectively been marginalised by corporations, which often have reduced CSR to corporate philanthropy.

In relation to the economy, one can distinguish two rather distinct lines. Some authors see social entrepreneurship as striving to replace the capitalist market economy, often in association with the rise of the solidarity economy (e.g. Utting 2013; Perez de Mendiguren Castresana 2013). Others see social entrepreneurship aiming for transformation in and of capitalism itself (Porter and Kramer 2011). The latter authors see social entrepreneurship as a temporary or transitional phenomenon in making conventional for-profit enterprises refocus themselves on creating social value (see interview with Michael Porter in Driver 2012). Shared value creation (not to be confused with social value creation) has been put forward as the principal driver (Porter and Kramer 2011). This strand recognises that for-profit enterprises do generate social value (providing goods and services, incomes and employment for people) but that 'financialisation' has made that the pressure for short term financial returns has taken precedence over the drive to create social value. In international development this line of social entrepreneurial activity concentrates on the Base of the Pyramid in emerging market economies.

Bieckman (2013) is less optimistic that social entrepreneurship has a chance of becoming a driving force of change of capitalism. It has to compete with conventional for-profit enterprises, which engage in a competitive race to the bottom. Social enterprises that seek to pay fair wages and fair prices to suppliers will not become viable and be able to mainstream unless governments steps in with regulatory policies to level the playing field by changing the tax structure for conventional enterprises and by rewarding social enterprises. In contrast, Depedri (2010) argues that social enterprises have clear competitive advantages over commercial enterprises. This competitive advantage may stem from several factors. Close relations with clients and their search for locally specific solutions may help reduce waste of resources and make their operations more efficient. Social enterprises attract employees who are intrinsically motivated and who often accept lower pay. Moreover social enterprises very often have volunteers and this significantly reduces operating costs. A further competitive factor is the non-distribution of profits resulting in lower capital costs. Last but not least, a social enterprise generally has a better alignment between individual and organisational goals and this results in lower monitoring and management costs. In contrast Hudson (2009) argues that many social entrepreneurial initiatives at the margins of the market economy suffer from competitive tensions that reduce their viability.

From the above it can be concluded that there are different types of institutional configurations or types of social enterprises. First of all there are: i) social enterprises that operate *in* the market and that are the result of collective action (co-operatives, mutual societies). These produce what some call 'general interest' goods and services. These are institutionally quite distinct from ii) social enterprises *outside* the market; in other words: self help through collective action; Furthermore there is a growing institutional category of iii) social business ventures in the market; these produce private goods that have a merit character, i.e. they are excludable/rival but have intended external social effects. Last but not least there are iv) 'hybrids' as a combination of 'iii' with 'i' or 'ii'.

From the above it can also be concluded that explanations of social entrepreneurship are very diverse. While the concept may have originated in the social sector in terms of market-based solutions to social problems, it increasingly is also seen in relation to the transformation in and of that very same market economy. It has become a cross-sector concept that seeks to build bridges between conventional domains of state, market and civil society. To some authors this very hybridity and multiple meanings makes scientific advance difficult as the concept lacks rigour, but one can also take this in positive terms: it may permit more 'intersectionality' and recognise agency, which are central concepts that give meaning to civic innovation in Chapter One.

Defining social entrepreneurship

There is quite a diversity in the way in which social entrepreneur(ship) and enterprise are defined. For example, the volume edited by Mair, Robinson and Hockerts (2006) contains 15 contributions that have 12 different definitions.[2] Also other authors acknowledge the lack of agreement on a definition and cite a wide range of definitions to illustrate this (Becchetti and Borzaga 2010; Borzaga and Tortia 2010). As mentioned earlier, some see this as problematic (e.g. Dacin, Dacin and Tracey 2011) while others consider this a characteristic feature of an emerging field that still lacks consolidation (Mair and Noboa 2006; Mair, Robinson and Hockerts 2006; Granados et al. 2011).

Cheriakova (2013) gives an overview and links certain definitions to different 'schools of thought'. The first two, which originate in the USA, use basic formal definitions such as 'non-dividend enterprises pursuing a social objective' and definitions that focus on new forms of cooperation (between social entrepreneurs and private enterprise) and use innovative ways to create social value and address social problems. The third definition comes from the European Research Network on Social Enterprises (EMES). It has a focus on the social enterprise, more than on the social entrepreneur. It defines the social enterprise as being engaged in the production of goods and services with economic risk and minimal paid work aiming to benefit a local community and which has a participatory or democratic governance structure. Some authors in this school stress its civil society association (Hulgard 2010). Others in this school see social enterprises at the cross section of civil society, state and market (Nyssens 2006). A fourth definition comes from Dees. For this hallmark author in the US tradition the social entrepreneur is a change agent, i.e. not just tackling one problem but creating socio-economic structures that sustain social benefits (Dees 1998, 2001). In doing so, social entrepreneurs are driven by their relentless pursuit of new opportunities to further their mission to create social value, by their continuous drive to innovate; and by their boldness and their refusal to accept resource limitations (Elkington and Hartigan 2008). To this Peredo and Mclean (2006) add the capacity of the social entrepreneur to take and endure economic risks. As this literature expanded it has put more and more emphasis on the entrepreneur.

Mair, Robinson and Hockerts (2006) argue that in defining social entrepreneurship one needs to clarify not only the entrepreneurial but also the social element. They disagree with a dichotomous conceptualisation where the social is related to non-profit orientation or to altruism. The generation of profit can make a social enterprise more sustainable. Moreover, the entrepreneur can have personal or professional fulfilment as an important driver alongside his/her social mission. For Mair and colleagues the social element resides in the mission of the entrepreneur to create social value rather than economic value. Social entrepreneurship is 'a process involving the innovative use and combinations of resources to pursue opportunities to catalyse social change and/or address social needs' (Mair, Robinson and Hockerts 2006: 37).

Other authors (Peredo and McLean 2006) stress that social entrepreneurship should be understood in relative terms along a continuum between full social exchange and purely commercial exchange. Under such an approach even corporate social responsibility becomes a relevant category. But most authors utilise more restrictive definitions.

Dacin, Dacin and Tracey (2011) are critical of the concept of social entrepreneur and entrepreneurship. They see the concept appealing to people who have become 'sceptical about the ability of governments and businesses to meaningfully address pressing social problems such as poverty, social exclusion and the environment' (ibid.: 1203). Definitions of social entrepreneurship often cover the following four aspects: i) the personal characteristics of the entrepreneur; ii) their sphere of operation; iii) the processes and resources they use and, iv) their mission to create social value. They argue that the first three are context dependent and hence are not helpful in the search for a general definition. Only the fourth one can serve that purpose: creating social value to address social problems. Such social value creation does not negate the importance of economic value creation for reasons of sustainability. The focus on social mission achievements would imply turning attention to the outcomes and social impacts of social enterprise activity and a comparative analysis of similar social impacts by different types of organisations would make the academic research more robust. This may however be easier said than done as contexts could well vary and different organisations may target different segments or social domains.

Dacin, Dacin and Tracey (2011) observed that many empirical studies that feed the academic debate are predominantly singular case studies in which '*heroic individuals*' who are 'capable to change the world' are the main focus. Elkington and Hartigan (2008) who formulated ten characteristic features of social entrepreneurs would be a clear illustration in this regard. These features include amongst others, a professional and practical rather than ideological orientation, innovativeness, risk taking and tenacious determination to get things done, etc. Dacin and colleagues argue that this focus on the successful entrepreneur generates three biases: i) bias against learning from failures; ii) bias to limit the analysis to micro level factors; and iii) a bias in terms of (altruistic) motives and social mission of the social entrepreneur, ignoring that there may be a 'dark side' to social entrepreneurship.

Furthermore, they note that the social entrepreneurship conceptualised as 'heroic individual' fits well in the neo-liberal ideology: portraying the individual effort conveniently ignoring the structural political economic and other contextual factors. Indeed, social entrepreneurs can also manipulate social entrepreneurial values to capture power in politics. To this they add that concentration of social entrepreneurial activity in a few individuals and organisations may lead to abuse of their leading position in the public debate to successfully mobilise resources to further enhance their own position, power and influence. The powerful but subtle role of 'philanthro-capitalists', examined by Michael Edwards (2008), would be a notable example illustrating their concerns.

Dacin, Dacin and Tracey (2011) have suggested several promising lines of research, which include the link between social movements and social entrepreneurial activities (also put forward earlier by Hockerts 2006). In terms of our main question, this would ask to what extent social entrepreneurs interact with social movements for developing their social value proposition. This derives from the empirical finding that social activism is a recognised source of social entrepreneurial activities. Social movements can be a source of inspiration and ideas and can legitimise such social entrepreneurial activity. Lastly, social movement organisations have also considerable potential in terms of lobby and advocacy to support the required changes in institutional arrangements and of the institutional environment for social entrepreneurial activity to become more effective and/or sustainable.

A second important line of research put forward by Dacin, Dacin and Tracey (2011) concerns the role of networks in social entrepreneurship. Social entrepreneurs pursue their social mission by sharing their ideas and knowledge. That means that networks play a key role. This raises several important questions: How do social entrepreneurs form their networks and to what extent are these locally embedded? What is the scale-ability of social entrepreneurial activity and what role do networks play therein? Last but not least, networks constitute a source of power that social entrepreneurs can use (but also abuse to keep competitors out) (ibid.). Other lines of research advocated by Dacin and colleagues refer to culture and the role of rituals, issues of identity and celebrity and cognitive structures and processes. Networking and implied embedding of social entrepreneurial activity in relations with others is an important way in which 'the social' gets constructed. We will turn to this issue below.

A powerful threefold critique comes from Cho (2006). It is important to note that Cho adopts the more restrictive definition of the social entrepreneur as formulated by Dees (see above). This definition, Cho argues, is exclusively defined in terms of the entrepreneur but not in terms of the social. The entrepreneur defines the social value (s)he will pursue. This leads to the first point of criticism: 'The social entrepreneurs have their own divergent subjective visions for the rest of society and rationally mobilize resources in order to enact their agendas' (Cho 2006: 46/47). If the social is not generated from a collective process, it is not more nor less than a private vision of the social. 'This monological stance is simultaneously the social entrepreneur's greatest asset and its greatest challenge' (ibid.). The author points to the possible disjuncture between the entrepreneurial objectives and processes and the need to engage in participatory deliberation to negotiate between conflicting visions for social transformation. This disjuncture need not necessarily arise but Cho has correctly identified this as a blind spot in SE research: how do social entrepreneurs identify their social mission. Is this flowing from his/her own 'can do mentality' or is it derived from some form of social consensus? However, Cho poses a strict criterion that the social mission must be generated through a collective deliberative process. This position disregards that there is also 'on the shelf' socially constructed knowledge on which the social entre-preneur can base the social value proposition. There is for example ample social agreement that potable or purified water can be regarded a recognised social need (or even a human right as it forms part of an adequate standard of living). The vision that people have access to potable water need not be (re-)constructed. The question then remains how the social entrepreneurial process to enact this vision takes shape. This issue we will discuss below.

A second point of criticism of Cho follows from the first, namely that well-intentioned social entrepreneurs may displace social processes and strategies that may be more appropriately positioned to achieve discursively negotiable common objectives. Difficult and complex collective choice processes get dis-placed by the 'can do' entrepreneurial result oriented social value proposition, and bad social entrepreneurial investments decisions may in the end result in waste or lower social value than otherwise achievable. The implicit assump-tions of Cho are that there is no state of civil society failure to which the social entrepreneur responds, and that collective choice processes are indeed inclusive.

The third point raised by Cho is that the social entrepreneur begins with the wrong question. Faced with a social problem and the inability of social actors to solve this problem, the social entrepreneur will seek to mobilise resources and find innovative ways to address the problem; however the real question according to Cho is 'Why is the state unwilling or unable to tackle the problem?' This in his view is in the first place a political question rather than a problem derived from market failure: 'social entrepreneurship is a means to an end: it is not itself capable of defining social needs or assessing whether the burdens of meeting these are being shared equally. These are fundamentally political questions' (Cho 2006: 49). By applying private social entrepreneurial strategies to meet social needs, the social entrepreneur bypasses political processes in favour of subject centred and sometimes market oriented approaches to the definition and achievement of social objectives (ibid.). Is the social entrepreneur a substitute to state and market?

> The implicit treatment of social entrepreneurship as a substitute for rather than a complement to concerted public action raises troubling issues related to the distribution of burdens. Social entrepreneurs identify service gaps and efficiently mobilize resources to fill them. In doing so however they may privilege addressing symptoms over resolving more fundamental root causes, such as social inequality, political exclusion and cultural marginalization.
>
> (Cho 2006: 51)

The public sphere ceases to be the pilot of society's steering mechanism; instead civil society begins to take its direction from the mechanistic opera-tions and failures of markets and states. This reversal of agency lies at the heart of the theoretical problem of social entrepreneurship, according to Cho:

social entrepreneurship may divert attention away from the possibility that more basic structural reforms might be necessary to address social problems, particularly where governance is weak and exclusionary.

The author concludes that social entrepreneurs may produce immediate and impressive gains but this cannot replace sustained public engagement with social issues. It may even have unexpected perverse outcomes: 'while social entrepreneurship addresses local symptoms of deeper political and institutional malaise – poverty, exclusion, marginalization, environmental degradation – it may also avoid discursively mediated processes that could produce more inclusive and integrative systemic solutions' (Cho 2006: 53/54).

Cho suggests that social entrepreneurs should not underestimate the importance of participation in processes intended to broker and articulate social compromises; The public sector is to be seen more a partner than a competitor in social service delivery. In places where governance is weak, social entrepreneurs may have to support movements designed to improve and rehabilitate the capacity of the public sector to define and meet social needs. Lastly, social entrepreneurs should not isolate themselves from other key actors but actively search for opportunities to cooperate with and support their partners.

Social entrepreneurial processes

How do social entrepreneurs in the distinct domains go about their activities? Why do they engage in it in the first place? How do they define their social mission and how do they formulate the social value to be created by their innovations? Furthermore, how socialised is this process? To what extent are other groups and stakeholders involved and in what ways? In examining this process we look at two distinct domains, one is the social domain and the other is the 'Base of the Pyramid' segment of the market economy. The social domain is characterised by a wide range of actors, organisations and institutions, which are involved in problems of social deprivation and poverty. The BoP segment of the market economy refers to the bottom segment of the economy, which consists of poor consumers and large numbers of low productive and informal micro and small enterprises.

Social entrepreneurship in the social domain

From within the social sector, Hockerts (2006) argues that with regard to social value opportunities one can distinguish between three different sources: a) activism, where activists are the main actors whose economic value proposition is to provide moral legitimisation to the social enterprise; with communication and distribution through activists' networks; the social concerns championed by the activist group shape the social value proposition; b) self-help as another important source: the beneficiaries themselves are the social entrepreneurs. The economic value proposition is based on cheap labour and marketing;

cheap and patient capital and loyal and patient clients; their social value proposition is the social need or concerns of the main beneficiaries of the social enterprise; lastly, c) philanthropy as an important source: donors are the main actors; their economic value proposition is charitable grants and donations; business development advice and networking with other entrepreneurs; the social value proposition is based on the social issues defined by the donors. The first two represent social value propositions that are derived from a social or group based consensus. For the third source the critique formulated by Edwards (2008) on 'Philanthrocapitalism' is relevant. Large donors can unduly influence the debate, develop top down propositions of social value creation and in the process disempower particular social groups.

Robinson (2006) argues that social entrepreneurial opportunities in the social sector represent a different kind because the social sector, if perceived as a market, is not simply one characterised by conventional economic barriers of entry (such as capital requirements; cost advantages; switching costs; distribution access; and proprietary assets) but also by social and institutional barriers of entry. This makes the social entrepreneur very different from the conventional entrepreneur. Social barriers of entry prevent the social entrepreneur from using the social network of relationships that exist within a market to his/her advantage, e.g. in relation to business owners, professional associations, civic organisations, political and labour markets organisations. Often these relationships have evolved and stabilised over time and constitute localised networks and it requires considerable tacit knowledge to be able to enter and use these networks for new innovative social ventures. Institutional barriers of entry prevent the entrepreneur from knowing or accommodating the rules, norms and values that contribute to the culture, order and practices of the market. These form the institutional structure of the market. The core of social sector markets consists of interdependencies between the public (centralised and decentralised public agencies) and decentralised forms of private and civic activity.

The perceptions of social entrepreneurs about these barriers of entry and of the social opportunities are central to the entrepreneurial decision. Prior experiences of the entrepreneur are crucial: some entrepreneurs have had previous 'life experiences' that allow them better to see and assess social and institutional barriers of entry; while business experiences enable the entrepreneur to better assess the social venture as a sustainable business proposition. The lack of life experiences in an area (if the entrepreneur comes from elsewhere or from outside the sector) may make that the entrepreneur is unable to see the social and institutional barriers of entry and this may also obscure the social opportunities. Lack of knowledge may act as deterrent, while familiarity with these social and institutional barriers of entry may help identify the opportunities. Especially in the social sector these social and institutional barriers are very important as an entrepreneur seeks to cope with local expressions of specific social problems. Thus, the issue is not simply an innovative entrepreneurial strategy but also how social entrepreneurs are able to navigate these barriers in order to make their social venture work. Institutional barriers of entry originate in formal rules and organisations defined by government policies (e.g. decentralisation of social policy within the public domain and the liberalisation of social service delivery), while social barriers of entry refer to local cultural perceptions and divergences between the social groups and the social service providers. In order to be able to understand and navigate these barriers, the would-be social entrepreneur would have to interact with other actors in the community and other public, civic and private players in the particular social arena. This is what, according to Robinson (2006), makes social entrepreneurial process so special and distinct from the conventional understanding of the entrepreneurial process. Social entrepreneurs engage a range of stakeholders to identify and navigate the barriers of entry and in that process formulate their social value proposition. This therefore constitutes some form of socialisation of the value proposition or at least a consensual process of dialogue and coordination. An important question here is to what extent the social groups whose problems the social venture is to address are excluded or included in such a deliberative process.

It could be argued that Robinson's analysis is neither more nor less than the realisation that economic relationships are embedded in social relationships as formulated by Granovetter (1985). To some extent this is correct as also social entrepreneurs deploy their networks of social relationships to develop their social enterprise, to contact potential clients, providers of capital, suppliers and competitors. However, Robinson further elaborates on two issues. Firstly, that such social networks matter as these enable the social entrepreneur to learn about the social problems as experienced and perceived by disadvantaged groups. That is, how personal intrinsic motivation of the social entrepreneur combines with how social needs are experienced by the social group concerned and how these can be addressed, thus contributing to formulation of the social value proposition itself. Furthermore, these social networks matter to mobilise other resources critical to the realisation of the social venture, which the social entrepreneur on his/her own cannot muster. In the specific case of social policy, relationships with central and decentralised public agencies responsible for social policy and its corresponding rules and regulations and its financing are critical to navigate institutional barriers of entry. Thus relationships with government have to be forged in order to learn how public and social entrepreneurial activity can be complementary rather than conflicting. The emphasis is on mutual accommodation of public policy and social entrepreneurial goals. The social entrepreneur is not an isolated provider who can stay at 'arm's length' from other stakeholders and the target group. Furthermore, engaging in such a social process helps to acquire legitimacy rather than displacement.

Social entrepreneurship at the Base of the Pyramid

While Robinson specifically seeks to advance our understanding of how social entrepreneurs operate in the social sector, other more recent authors have focused on social entrepreneurship to achieve transformations in the market economy, particularly in relation to the 'Base of the Pyramid'.

Social entrepreneurial activity at the Base of the Pyramid faces, according to Desa and Koch (2014), three types of market failures. Firstly, market failure on the supply side applies in particularly to the lack of financial resources for social business ventures; furthermore, BoP producers, traders and distributors lack competency, resources and technologies to produce required quantity and quality of inputs and their lack of resilience forces them at times to divert inputs or products or to side sell (Kubansky, Cooper and Barbary 2011). Secondly, failure on the demand side has to do with the high volatility of BoP markets. BoP consumers have low, insecure and often irregular incomes and face unforeseen large cash outlays which crowd out other expenditures and they lack resilience to withstand this volatility. Affordability is a critical issue also for social entrepreneurial ventures. Markets are thin both in economic and spatial terms. The third type of market failure occurs in distribution of goods and services, which for reasons just mentioned faces severe 'last mile' distribution problems, i.e. when distribution costs become prohibitive in relation to volume and price. All these factors influence sustainability of social business ventures. How do social entrepreneurs contend with these challenges in their business models? The Monitor Group in its report on BoP business models in Sub-Saharan Africa (Kubansky, Cooper and Barbary 2011) stresses that products and services in their design must be BoP friendly. That is to say, they must be delivered on a pay per use basis, imply pared down services and no frills or frugal products; business models have to bring down complexity through para-skilling and use shared channels for distribution. A second set of business models create external economies of scale through aggregation and networking of large numbers of BoP producers *and* lower costs by drawing on their collective and relational assets. Here, one refers to aggregation platforms and value chains connecting small farmers, producers and deep distributor networks of micro enterprises and informal shops to reach BoP consumers. This second set of business strategies can only be realised if the social entrepreneurs are capable of engaging other stakeholders and community groups to promote group formation and provide capacity building and education in awareness building. Mobilising collective and relational assets of the poor producers, traders and distributors means that social entrepreneurs have to engage them and their organisations. The very success of the social ventures depends on it. In many instances the social entrepreneurs and their organisations undertake these tasks themselves but in many other instances they seek the support of NGOs and/or of local governments or other public agencies. This would further 'socialise' their social value proposition. The latter is even more so in the case of goods and services in the so-called 'push' category. That is, those products that require a high level of awareness building and education of potential customers (e.g. preventive health care). These products contrast with so-called 'pull' products of which BoP consumers readily see the benefits (like specialised uses of texting on cell phones and specialised apps on smart phones).

The above analysis corresponds with Alvord, Brown and Leffs (2004) who took an empirical route to understand the social entrepreneurial process and studied seven successful initiatives of social transformation (among these are BRAC, SEWA [Self Employed Women's Association, India], Grameen, and Plan Puebla) and then worked backwards to elicit common features in terms of social innovations and entrepreneurship. They see social entrepreneurs as change agents who aim to achieve social transformation. They conclude that social innovations are often clustered or multi-dimensional (economic, cultural and political) and can take various forms: 1) building local capacity; 2) dissemination of a package of innovations through reconfiguring products, resources and management practices to better match local specifics; and 3) building a movement giving voice to marginalised groups. In the process these social ventures mobilise tangible and intangible assets of poor groups and emphasise systematic learning and knowledge sharing by individuals and organisations. Networking is fundamental: social entrepreneurs showed their capacity to build bridges among very diverse stakeholders from different domains, often based on their own experiences in these diverse domains.

Di Domenico, Haugh and Tracey (2010) made an important contribution that is relevant here as well. They use a broader conception of social entrepreneurship and a 'blended value creation' approach. They define social entrepreneurship with five characteristics: i) own revenue generation through trading; ii) pursuing social and/or environmental goals; iii) blended value creation – that is to say to deliver goods and services which have additional goals such as increased social capital or social cohesion; iv) active role of stakeholder participation in formulating the social enterprise venture, its governance structures and procedures – i.e. locally embedded and downwardly accountable; v) active in a range of contexts but closely associated with communities with limited access to resources.

An important characteristic feature of such social enterprise is that it operates in severely constrained resource environments. This implies that social entrepreneurs engage in what the authors call 'social bricolage'. They have to 'make do' with existing resources and institutions and make something new out of them (e.g. an old unused building, discarded materials, food with expired freshness etc.). Creation of social value is often altering existing inadequate institutional arrangements. Resource scarcity demands resourcefulness and social entrepreneurs have to improvise. The refusal to accept limitations is needed in order to counteract or overcome political and institutional resistance; this may entail subverting limitations by showing the social value that is created (Newth and Woods 2014). Engaging stakeholders is often essential in order to overcome resource and institutional constraints. This may be done via social network activity or by adapting the governance structure of the enterprise so as to get access to resources or to get access to expertise and/or by persuading stakeholders to leverage resources for the social enterprise. Social value creation is central to social bricolage and stakeholders participate in its formulation, realisation and accountability. By implication social entrepreneurship is by far not a mono-logical process.

This applies even more so at the 'Base of the Pyramid' in poor economies. Maas (2013) studied the promotion of social entrepreneurship among Bangladeshi women over a period of several years The author adopted and extended Di Domenico's framework, and pointed out that the refusal to be limited by structural constraints (resources and institutions) stresses the agency of the social entrepreneur as against taking these structural constraints for granted. He noted that network-building gives rise to spontaneous collective action, as networks reach 'critical mass'. This becomes a new resource created in the process. Maas (2013) argues that sharing knowledge and learning in networks is a characteristic of social entrepreneurship and dis-tinguishes it from for-profit entrepreneurship, which thrives on creating and maintaining information asymmetries. For the 'social' in social entrepreneurship this would be a distinguishing feature.

Perrini and Vurro (2006) also emphasise that social entrepreneurship entails an inter-sectoral dynamic: 'social entrepreneurial initiatives ideally break up boundary lines among organizational clusters, configuring themselves as hybrid organizations' (ibid.: 61). Social entrepreneurs identify social opportunities through a combination of external and internal drivers: own life experiences in combination with perceived social needs define the social value proposition. They follow Hockerts' (2006) classification of sources of social opportunities and Alvord, Brown and Leffs' (2004) definition of types of social innovations (see above). The authors argue that social entrepreneurs have in common with conventional for-profit entrepreneurs their aptitude, risk taking tolerance and strong control desire, but are different in their desire for concrete social change rather than preference for status quo and for their aptitude for net-working and cooperation with other stakeholders. Except in exceptionally favourable circumstances, social entrepreneurs realise that they cannot expand their social value proposition on their own.

Scale and scaling

For upscaling and growth social entrepreneurs are dependent on networking and the ability of other partners to deliver complementary contributions. Moreover as social ventures are covering new ground and breaking boundaries, their outcomes are rather uncertain and this demands considerable flexibility on the part of the social entrepreneur. Other authors add that up-scaling requires alliances with other stakeholders, especially social movements.

Dees, Anderson and Wei-Skillern (2004) raised the issue of scaling already a decade ago. For social innovations to result in real transformations scaling was deemed to be essential. It can take place in various forms: through horizontal spreading over a larger area and through deepening the social innovation, extending it to more spheres or activities within the same area. Much depends, according to the authors, on what the social innovation consists of:

a concrete organisational model with an overarching structure, governance, resources and goals and ideas about how the programme is to work; or a programme with a specific set of concrete tools or a set of principles of a more general nature which can be tailored to local specific circumstances. Spreading impact can be realised in three ways, according to these authors: through dissemination of ideas by providing information and training modules, sometimes with technical assistance. Alternatively it can take place by affiliation, i.e. a more formal relationship with the originator as a kind of 'social franchise'. Lastly the organisation can form branches in new locations. The authors develop a set of criteria (the 5 'Rs') to assess the best strategy in particular circumstances.

The issue of scaling is even more important at the BoP, not only so as to achieve the desired social transformation by spreading impact but also because reaching scale can be critical in order to achieve economic sustainability. Desa and Koch (2014) examine scaling of social innovations at the Base of the Pyramid. Central to upscaling is not just increasing social impact but also strengthening sustainability by lowering cost. They distinguish 'breadth' and 'depth' scaling which more or less corresponds to the two types identified by Dees, Anderson and Wei-Skillern (2004). Breadth scaling is about quantitative expansion and organisational upscaling, generating economies of scale, raising efficiency and effectiveness leading to greater sustainability by lowering unit costs. Reaching scale often demands dealing with institutional barriers for which the collaboration of government and/or civil society organisations is important. Depth scaling finds it origin in organisational slack and underutilised assets, which can be deployed by diversifying activities resulting in economies of scope. The social mission can become more sustainable when combined with other compatible activities.

In both instances scaling implies mobilising additional resources, adapting organisational procedures and social entrepreneurial adjustment. But the manner in which this occurs varies. In breadth scaling resources can be attracted if the programme has been made immune to localised site specific problems; in depth scaling bricolage may pose limits to the kinds of additional resources that can be mobilised. Operating procedures in breadth scaling concern how the social innovation can be replicated elsewhere while in depth scaling the issue is how these can be flexible and adapted to a range of goods and services. Social entrepreneurial adjustment also varies: 'in breadth impact social innovation is defined in a narrow focused way and clear functional strategies are developed to address marketing, manufacturing, sales, finance and human resources' (Desa and Koch 2014: 166). In depth scaling the key criterion is learning to define

> the business in an inclusive way and outlining adaptive strategies based on local community engagement and transformation through social and economic empowerment. Challenges to the social mission are addressed

with an emphasis on factors that develop trust and address power
relationships within the value chain.

(ibid.: 166)

Other authors add that for up-scaling alliances with other stakeholders and
with social movements are critical. Social movements provide legitimacy to
the social value proposition of the venture and their strengths in lobby and
advocacy becomes vital to break institutional and cultural constraints.

Zahra et al. (2009) developed a typology of three different social entrepreneurial processes that is also connected to scale. They distinguish between
three different types of social entrepreneurs and social entrepreneurial processes. The first one, the 'social bricoleur' operates at a very localised scale,
addressing social needs that are not easily recognised, involving tacit knowledge not accessible to outsiders. Its social significance lies in creating social
harmony. Social bricoleurs are 'at the right time at the right place', using
whatever resources available that they can mobilise. That gives them the
autonomy and independence from resource stakeholders (e.g. local food
banks which spread in the face of declining social welfare). A second type is
social constructionists who exploit knowledge and see opportunities for systemic change not seen by others: 'they build, launch and operate ventures
which tackle those social needs that are inadequately addressed by existing
institutions, businesses, NGOs and government agencies' (ibid.: 525). They
face limited competition in the delivery of their programmes and often
'leverage the resources and capabilities of for-profit and not-for-profit organizations that generate mutually beneficial outcomes' (ibid.: 526). Negotiation
with these stakeholders is part and parcel of the social entrepreneurial process. Lastly, there is a third type, denominated, social engineers who address
complex social problems and thereby challenge fundamental institutions,
which implies that they face considerable political opposition from established
groups and interests. This means that social entrepreneurs of this kind have to
be more political and engage in advocacy and/or seek support from advocacy
movements and other stakeholders as they seek large fundamental social
transformations.

In terms of our classification of institutional types of social enterprises,
formulated above, the social bricoleur typically operates outside the market
through local (individual and collective) action for self-help both for social
and economic purposes. Social constructionists and social engineers are more
likely to be associated with social enterprises operating in the market, be this
through collective action (like a cooperative venture) or by means of individual business ventures that are replicated on a large scale. Fair trade and
micro-finance would be examples of the last mentioned types.

Following the typology of Zahra et al. (2009), Smith and Stevens (2010)
recently argued that the degree of embeddedness varies from high for local
bricoleurs to low for the social engineer for reasons that geography limits the
scope and intensity of developing human interaction and ties. Embedded ties,

as distinct from arm's length ties, require reciprocal social obligations and hence cost more time and effort to be realised. The social 'bricoleur' can bank on his/her embedded ties to gather local tacit knowledge on specific social needs and mobilise scarce resources to address these, while the social engineer operating on a larger (e.g. global) scale would develop a more formalised social value proposition to mobilise more distant but like minded groups and resources. The social bricoleur would by implication be able to go for depth scaling within the same locale and community, while the social constructionist and engineer would be more likely to expand his/her innovative venture on a larger geographical scale.

Concluding reflections

There are diverse explanations about the rise of social entrepreneurship, which often tend to use different definitions and meanings of social enterprises. Looking for a single definition in this institutionally diverse field would not very helpful and may in fact obstruct further scientific advances, but it is also not helpful to be content with the current confused state of affairs.

There are different types or institutional configurations of social enterprises. First of all there are: a) social enterprises that operate *in* the market and that are the result of collective action (cooperatives, mutual societies). These produce or provide what some call 'general interest' goods and services. These are institutionally quite distinct from b) social enterprises *outside* the market; in other words, self-help through collective action; Furthermore there is a growing category of c) social business ventures in the market: these produce private goods that have a merit character, i.e. they are excludable/rival but have intended external social effects. Last but not least there are d) 'hybrids' as a combination of 'c' with 'a' or 'b'.

Disagreements about explanations may in fact result from different implicitly held views of the type of social enterprise. Thus, while Borzaga and Defourney (2004), Borzaga and Tortia (2010) and others of the EMES network refer to social enterprises of the 'a' type; others (e.g. Di Domenico, Haugh and Tracey 2010) refer to enterprises of type 'b'. When Borzaga and Tortia (2010) discuss competitiveness of social enterprises they refer to type 'a' enterprises while Hudson (2009) and Desa and Koch (2014) refer to issues of competitiveness of social ventures (type 'c') in the market. Cho's critique of social entrepreneurs is based on a social business venture providing goods and services in the social sector displacing the public and civil society sectors. Clearly the critique would not the same were civic driven social enterprises of the type 'a' and 'b' to fill a social gap not attended by the State. Again others when examining a particular aspect sometimes include a mixture of different types of enterprises (e.g. Hockerts 2006; Alvord, Brown and Leffs 2004). A better systematic understanding is needed of these different institutional configurations and the setting in which social entrepreneurs seek to achieve their social goals.

There is healthy scepticism about social entrepreneurship in the academic world as well as in discussions among development practitioners. This scepticism in part stems from debates concerning reform in the social sector. Does the social entrepreneur privatise what ought to be a collective process and replace the latter with a subjective individual vision about how to address social needs? In the past ten years social entrepreneurship is increasingly applied to transformations in the capitalist market economy and especially at the base of the pyramid. Clearly the same critique would not apply here. Newth and Woods (2014) make a similar point. Social entrepreneurship is much more contested where it applies to social needs previously attended by the public or civil society sector than it is in the market or at the BoP. These authors add that such social entrepreneurs have to contend with many more stakeholders than conventional entrepreneurs would in the market. Conventional entrepreneurs need to convince the providers of capital and their targeted customers. Social entrepreneurs face more stakeholders (socio-cultural and community leaders, media, other social care actors), precisely because it concerns the social domain. Furthermore the social value proposition may be more diffuse and less circumscribed than a commercial proposition that focuses on a concrete product or service.

When examining social entrepreneurship at the BoP of the market economy, sustainable business models point to the need to leverage tangible and intangible assets of poor producers, traders and distributors in order to lower costs and produce and provide accessible, available and affordable products to poor consumers. By their very nature, therefore, social entrepreneurial processes are negotiated with (groups of) BoP producers and distributors in order for the social venture to become sustainable as well as with other stakeholders, especially as regards 'push' products, for which social ventures often requires complementary action by NGOs and/or public agencies for capacity building and awareness raising.

The scepticism about social entrepreneurship in the social sector gained more force as business management literature that portrayed the social entrepreneurs as 'heroic individuals' gained prominence. This literature tends to disregard the context and structures within which social entrepreneurship takes place. The concept of 'heroic individual' is essentially what Granovetter (1985) would characterise as an *undersocialised* view of social entrepreneurship. Cho is correct with his critique that if the social is not generated through collective processes it is not more nor less than a private vision of the social. But this represents also an *undersocialised* view of the social entrepreneur and social entrepreneurial processes. Social entrepreneurs must have civic engagement with state, civil society and market in order to formulate and operationalise their social enterprise. The social entrepreneur is not an isolated provider who can stay at 'arm's length' from other stakeholders. This applies to the social domain and even more so to the BoP domain, though there are different factors at play. In the social domain there are many more other actors, organisations and institutions active, and these represent important social and institutional barriers that the social entrepreneur needs to navigate. Sustainable business models at the BoP in many instances require the social entrepreneur to mobilise tangible and intangible assets of poor producers and distributors. Aggregation platforms, strategic coordination in value chains to overcome market and state failure and deep networks to overcome 'last mile' distribution and 'first mile' procurement/bulking challenges are all achieved through collective and joint action of groups of BoP producers/traders, and critically depend on collective learning. Moreover, for capacity building and awareness-raising and for upscaling the social entrepreneur needs to engage and obtain support from NGOs and state actors and agencies. This calls for civic engagement from the social entrepreneur.

Social bricolage is an important phenomenon at the local level where social entrepreneurs face severe resource constraints and have to engage other stakeholders, which would imply deliberative processes in which social ventures will be adjusted for them to become feasible.

Networks play a central role in social entrepreneurial activity. Embedding of such activity in the terms of Granovetter is relevant here. However the role of networks goes beyond generating trust and the role of weak ties. Networks matter in order to reach particular disadvantaged target groups, input suppliers and competitors, and enable two-way or interactive learning about their social needs and how these may be addressed by a social entrepreneurial venture. Knowledge generation, and sharing is a key feature that is distinct from the role of networks for for-profit commercial entrepreneurs who share limited information in the market and purposefully create and maintain information asymmetries for reasons of competitiveness. Furthermore, networks matter to mobilise resources from other stakeholders and play a central role in up-scaling social entrepreneurial initiatives. Last but not least networks, when achieving critical mass, generate new dynamics as they open up opportunities for collective action and advocacy.

To respond to the question formulated at the beginning of this chapter: the social entrepreneur is neither a 'hero' who singlehandedly addresses social or economic needs of underprivileged groups nor a 'villain' who under the cover of a social mission destroys collective or public processes. In both the social and the BoP domain, the social entrepreneur engages other stakeholders and can be successful because (s)he builds bridges between public, private and civil actors and the groups they seek to serve to mobilise resources as well as political and economic support so as to overcome resistance and to create sustainable social enterprises. It is not just the social mission but also this process of civic engagement that is characteristic of the social entrepreneurial process.

Notes

1 The concept of 'Fortune at the bottom of the pyramid' first appeared in a joint article by the late Indian born American management consultant C.K. Prahalad together with S. Hart in the journal *Strategy & Business*. The concept became

well known thanks to Prahalad (2004). Their main contention is that corporations did not focus their business on the bottom 4 billion consumers. Others criticised this bias towards large corporations and claimed that more attention needs to be given to involve micro, small and medium enterprises at the base of the pyramid. This has led to emphasising the 'base of the pyramid' itself. This changed meaning is used here.

2 In their view one can distinguish between 3 lines in the literature: i) those that see social entrepreneurship as not-for-profit initiatives in search for alternative funding; ii) socially responsible business that seeks cross sector partnerships; and iii) social entrepreneurship as a means to alleviate social problems and catalyse social transformation (Mair, Robinson and Hockerts 2006).

References

Alvord, S., Brown, L.B. and Leffs, C.W. (2004) 'Social Entrepreneurship and Societal Transformation: An Exploratory Study', *Journal of Applied Behavioral Science* 40(3): 260–282.

Becchetti, L. and Borzaga, C. (2010) 'Introduction', in Becchetti, L. and Borzaga, C. (eds) *The Economics of Social Responsibility. The World of Social Enterprises*. Milton Park: Routledge, pp. 1–15.

Bieckman, F. (2013) 'Editorial: Enabling Genuine Social Entrepreneurship', *The Broker Online*. Accessed 30 July 2014 <http://www.thebrokeronline.eu/Articles/Editorial-Enabling-genuine-social-entrepreneurship>.

Borzaga, C. and Defourny, J. (eds) (2004) *The Emergence of Social Enterprise*. London: Routledge.

Borzaga, C. and Tortia, E. (2010) 'The Economics of Social Enterprises: an Interpretative Framework', in Becchetti, L. and Borzaga, C. (eds) *The Economics of Social Responsibility. The World of Social Enterprises*. Milton Park: Routledge, pp. 23–39.

Cheriakova, A. (2013) 'The Emerging Social Enterprise. Framing the Concept of Social Entrepreneurship', *The Broker Online*, 28 October. Accessed 30 July 2014 <http://www.thebrokeronline.eu/Articles/The-emerging-social-enterprise>.

Cho, A.H. (2006) 'Politics, Values and Social Entrepreneurship: A Critical Appraisal', in Mair, J., Robinson, J. and Hockerts, K. (eds) *Social Entrepreneurship*. Basingstoke, New York: Palgrave MacMillan, pp. 34–57.

Dacin, T.M., Dacin, P.A. and Tracey, P. (2011) 'Social Entrepreneurship: A Critique and Future Directions', *Organization Science* 22(5): 1203–1213.

Dees, J.G. (1998) 'Enterprising Nonprofits', *Harvard Business Review* (Jan/Feb): 55–68.

Dees, J.G. (2001) '*The Meaning of "Social Entrepreneurship"*' (Original draft: 1998), Durham: Duke University.

Dees, J.G., Anderson, B.B. and Wei-Skillern, J. (2004) 'Scaling Social Impact: Strategies for Spreading Social Innovations', *Stanford Social Innovations Review* 1(4): 24–32.

Dees, J.G., Emerson, J. and Economy, P. (eds) (2002) *Strategic Tools for Social Entrepreneurs: Enhancing the Performance of Your Enterprising Nonprofit*. New York: John Wiley & Sons.

Defourny, J. and Nijssens, M. (2008) 'Social Enterprise in Europe: Recent Trends and Developments', *Social Enterprise Journal* 4(3): 202–228.

Depedri, S. (2010) 'The Competitive Advantage of Social Enterprises', in Becchetti, L. and Borzaga, C. (eds) *The Economics of Social Responsibility. The World of Social Enterprises*. Milton Park: Routledge, pp. 34–55.

Desa, G. and Koch, J.L. (2014) 'Scaling Social Impact: Building Sustainable Social Ventures at the Base of the Pyramid', *Journal of Social Entrepreneurship* 5(2): 146–174.

Di Domenico, M., Haugh, H. and Tracey, P. (2010) 'Social Bricolage: Theorizing Social Value Creation in Social Enterprises', *Entrepreneurship Theory and Practice* 34(4): 681–703.

Driver, M. (2012) 'An Interview with Michael Porter: Social Entrepreneurship and the Transformation of Capitalism', *Academy of Management Learning and Education* 11(3): 421–431.

Edwards, M. (2008) *Just another Emperor? The Myths and Realities of Philanthrocapitalism.* Demos: A Network for Ideas and Action, New York: The Young Foundation.

Elkington, J. and Hartigan, P. (2008) *The Power of Unreasonable People. How Social Entrepreneurs Create Markets that Change the World.* Boston, MA: Harvard Business Press.

Fowler, A.F. (2014) *Innovation in Institutional Collaboration. The Role of Interlocutors.* (ISS working papers. General series, no 584). The Hague: International Institute of Social Studies.

Granados, M.L., Hlupic, V., Coakes, E. and Mohamed, S. (2011) 'Social Enterprise and Social Entrepreneurship Research and Theory: A Bibliometric Analysis from 1991 to 2010', *Social Enterprise Journal* 7(3): 198–218.

Granovetter, M. (1985) 'Economic Action and Social Structure: The Problem of Embeddedness', *American Journal of Sociology* 91(3): 481–510.

Hockerts, K. (2006) 'Entrepreneurial Opportunity in Social Purpose Business Ventures', in Mair, J., Robinson, J. and Hockerts, K. (eds) *Social Entrepreneurship.* Basingstoke, New York: Palgrave/MacMillan.

Hudson, R. (2009) 'Life on the Edge: Navigating the Competitive Tensions between the "Social" and the "Economic" in the Social Economy and in its Relations to the Mainstream', *Journal of Economic Geography* 24: 493–510.

Hulgard, L. (2010) 'Discourses of Social Entrepreneurship. Variations on the Same Theme? Centre for Social Entrepreneurship', Roskilde University: EMES European Research Network. Working Paper 10.

Kieng, S. and Quack, E.J. (2013) 'Balancing Social and Entrepreneurial Values. NGOs Embracing Social Entrepreneurship', *The Broker Online.* Accessed 30 July 2014 <http://thebrokeronline.eu/Articles/Balancing-social-and-entrepreneurial-values>.

Kubansky, M., Cooper, A. and Barbary, V. (2011) *Promise and Progress. Market Based Solutions to Poverty in Africa.* Johannesburg: Monitor Group.

Maas, J. (2013) *Transitions to Social Entrepreneurship. Stimulating Social Entrepreneurial Behaviour in Adverse Environments.* (PhD thesis VU Amsterdam). s'Hertogenbosch: BOXPress.

Mair, J. and Marti, I. (2006) 'Social Entrepreneurship Research: A Source of Explanation, Prediction and Delight', *Journal of World Business* (41): 36–44.

Mair, J. and Noboa, E. (2006) 'Social Entrepreneurship: How Intentions to Create a Social Venture are Formed', in Mair, J., Robinson, J. and Hockerts, K. (eds) *Social Entrepreneurship.* Basingstoke, New York: Palgrave Macmillan, pp. 122–136.

Mair, J., Robinson, J. and Hockerts, K. (2006) 'Introduction', in Mair, J., Robinson, J. and Hockerts, K. (eds) *Social Entrepreneurship.* Basingstoke, NewYork: Palgrave MacMillan, pp. 1–15.

Newth, J. and Woods, C. (2014) 'Resistance to Social Entrepreneurship: How Context Shapes Innovation', *Journal of Social Entrepreneurship* 5(2): 192–213.

108   *A.H.J. (Bert) Helmsing*

Nichols, A. (2011) 'Social Enterprise and Social Entrepreneurship', in Edwards, M. (ed.) *The Oxford Handbook of Civil Society.* Oxford: Oxford University Press, pp. 80–93.

Nyssens, M. (ed.) (2006) *Social Enterprise: At the Crossroads of Markets, Public Policies and Civil Society.* London: Routledge.

Peredo, A.M. and McLean, M. (2006) 'Social Entrepreneurship: A Critical Review of the Concept', *Journal of World Business* 41: 56–61.

Perez de Mendiguren Castresana, J.C. (2013) 'Social Enterprise in the Development Agenda. Opening a New Road Map Or just a New Vehicle to Travel the Same Route?', *Social Enterprise Journal* 9(3): 247–268.

Perrini, F. and Vurro, C. (2006) 'Social Entrepreneurship: Innovation and Social Change Across Theory and Practice', in Mair, J., Robinson, J. and Hockerts, K. (eds) *Social Entrepreneurship.* Basingstoke, New York: Palgrave MacMillan.

Porter, M.E. and Kramer, M.R. (2011) 'Creating Shared Value', *Harvard Business Review* 62 (Jan/Feb): 62–78.

Prahalad, K. (2004) *Fortune at the Bottom of the Pyramid. Eradicating Poverty Through Profits.* Philadelphia: Wharton Business School.

Robinson, J. (2006) 'Navigating Social and Institutional Barriers to Markets: How Social Entrepreneurs Identify and Evaluate Opportunities', in Mair, J., Robinson, J. and Hockerts, K. (eds) *Social Entrepreneurship.* Basingstoke/New York: Palgrave MacMillan, pp. 95–120.

Smith, B.R. and Stevens, C.E. (2010) 'Different Types of Social Entrepreneurship: The Role of Geography and Embeddedness on the Measurement and Scaling of Social Value', *Entrepreneurship & Regional Development* 22(6): 575–598.

Utting, P. (2013) 'Social and Solidarity Economy: A Pathway to Socially Sustainable Development?' UNRISD. Accessed 30 July 2014 <http://www.unrisd.org/unrisd/website/newsview.nsf/%28httpNews%29/AB920B156339500AC1257B5C002C1E96?OpenDocument>.

Zahra, S.A., Gedajlovic, E., Neubaum, D. and Shulman, J.M. (2009) 'A Typology of Social Entrepreneurs: Motives, Search Processes and Ethical Challenges', *Journal of Business Venturing* 24: 519–532.

6 Civic innovation in value chains

Towards workers as agents in non-governmental labour regulation

Karin Astrid Siegmann, Jeroen Merk and Peter Knorringa

Introduction[1]

Neo-liberal governance of production has been accompanied by a rise of insecure work across different regions of the world, across sectors, even in formal establishments. Trade unions, NGOs and other advocates of labour rights, have long criticised these poor labour conditions as a result of a 'race to the bottom' in globalised and more competitive value chains since the 1990s. Transnational corporations (TNCs), in particular, have responded to this critique with the development and implementation of different types of non-governmental labour regulation, often labelled corporate social responsibility (CSR) initiatives, which have gradually involved a wider range of stakeholders (Newitt 2012).

Yet, rampant violations of labour rights in workplaces monitored in the context of CSR initiatives clearly bring to the fore their failure. The collapse of the Rana Plaza building in Dhaka in April 2013, burying more than 1,000 workers in Bangladesh's heavily audited garment industry, became the symbol of the breakdown of trust in conventional CSR (Kumar and Mahoney 2014: 187–188). We consider the lack of workers' active role in the design and implementation of the present generation of CSR initiatives a key reason for their widespread failure to effectively improve labour conditions in value chains. Workers who are covered by non-governmental codes of labour practice are largely seen as passive objects for social auditing. Trade unions and other labour organisations play rather marginal roles in the multi-stakeholder initiatives that set and implement these private codes. In addition, for instance, Barrientos (2008) shows that the most precarious workers rarely benefit from non-governmental labour regulation. Our chapter starts with the assumption that a next generation of non-governmental codes of labour practice can only lead to more decent labour conditions when it puts workers' agency at the centre (Siegmann, Merk and Knorringa 2014).

In recent years, a Polanyian perspective to understand the increase in labour precariousness and to identify pathways to empower workers has experienced a revival. Polanyi (1944) argued that a self-regulating market system could not possibly work in practice (Block 2014: 1450). A market economy involves the commodification of all factors of production, including 'fictitious commodities', such as labour. A fictitious commodity relates to an essential factor of production, which was never meant to be commodified and whose commodification threatens its essential character (Burawoy 2010: 310). Resulting from this, he discerns commodification of labour as both being an integral part of, but simultaneously causing the destruction of market society. This threat to the fabric of society generates 'spontaneous counter-movements to defend society' (Burawoy 2010: 301). Polanyi's lens has been welcomed as offering a 'real utopia' of a labour-led counter-movement against the disembeddedness of labour in the era of neo-liberal globalisation (e.g. Burawoy 2003, 2010; Munck 2004; Silver and Arrighi 2003; Webster, Lambert and Bezuidenhout 2011). Yet, Webster, Lambert and Bezuidenhout (2011: 5) point out that, while Polanyi recognised different responses to labour commodification, he under-theorised how labour-led counter-movements emerge and when and how they manage to protect precarious workers.

Our chapter addresses these questions in the context of non-governmental labour regulation. Drawing on case studies from diverse geographical contexts and economic sectors, we investigate workers' power potentials that helped them to craft innovative arrangements to counter labour precariousness. Moreover, two of us have been involved in campaigns for non-governmental labour regulation as participant observers.[2] With Standing (2011: 10), we understand precarious labour conditions as characterised by a range of work-related insecurities. They include the lack of adequate income-earning opportunities, employment and job insecurity, insufficient protection against accidents and illness at work, the inability to gain skills and use competencies, income as well as representation insecurity, with the latter referring to the lack of a collective voice in the labour market. Moreover, we acknowledge that precariousness goes beyond the workplace: it often emerges in the context of social marginalisation, e.g. on the basis of gender or immigration status, and leads to insecure livelihoods, which further weaken workers' bargaining power (Arnold and Bongiovi 2013: 299–300).

We develop our argument as follows: in the next section, we derive lessons about the power resources that have enabled precarious workers to challenge commodification from a review of earlier studies. The section 'Worker-driven Social Responsibility' presents the persistent and creative struggles and thinking of the Coalition of Immokalee Workers (CIW), a migrant farmworker organisation in Florida, USA in more detail. The CIW has campaigned to raise the incomes and better the working and living conditions of Florida tomato pickers since 1993. Their campaigns have resulted in partnerships with over a dozen multinationals in the food chain that evolved into their Fair Food Program (FFP) in 2010. In the following section, we discuss what can be learned from the FFP about how worker-driven labour regulation emerges. Based on this discussion, in our 'Conclusion', we arrive at an initial sketch of the possible roles of various actors pushing forward a next generation of non-governmental labour regulation in which worker's agency becomes a normal feature of legitimate initiatives and contributes to more decent labour conditions. We believe our discussion of precarious workers' struggles and the innovative arrangements that emerged from them hold broader lessons for civic innovation. We therefore conclude with an outlook for civic innovation research and practice.

Precarious workers' power potentials

Studies that document the failure of non-governmental labour regulation to bring about improvements in precarious workers' working conditions are legion (e.g. Brown 2013; Taylor 2011; Utting 2008). Workers' passive roles as 'human capital' in the production process and as object for monitoring of codes of labour practice have been pointed out repeatedly as reasons for why conventional CSR does not work for workers. In this section, we synthesise findings from earlier studies of three worker-driven forms of non-governmental labour regulation that effectively challenged precariousness. We pay particular attention to the power resources that have enabled precarious workers to counter commodification.

Three cases of worker-driven innovation in value chains

Workers in Honduran factories of the US garment brand Fruit of the Loom (FOTL) reversed a situation of union oppression and poverty wages through a landmark collective bargaining agreement. International collaboration between the Honduran workers' local union affiliated with the union federation *Central General de Trabajadores* (CGT) and activists of the US student organisation United Students against Sweatshops (USAS) catalysed the first collective bargaining agreement in May 2011. The TNC is both the largest private employer in Honduras and one of the biggest producers of US-American collegiate apparel. It committed to honouring workers' organising rights in response to US student protests of the closure of a newly organised plant that led to the termination of several universities' contracts with the brand. As an innovation in globalised production where responsibility for labour standards is often blurred by complex value chains, the local union directly and successfully negotiated with the Kentucky-based brand as their indirect employer (Anner 2013: 29–36; Compa 2013; Kumar and Mahoney 2014: 195–200).

In contrast, the Brazilian rural trade union *Sindicato dos Trabalhadores Rurais* (STR) in the grape cultivating São Francisco valley used the existing voluntary industry standard for global agricultural practices GLOBALGAP to effectively pressurise farmers for better working conditions. Selwyn (2013: 84) describes how, initially, working conditions in the valley's export grape sector were characterised by low and often ad hoc pay, lack of employment security and even the use of child labour. Working on grape farms could be very dangerous, including regular exposure to agricultural chemicals without protective gear. At the heart of STR's strategy of pressuring employers to ameliorate workers' conditions had been the threat, or use of, strike action. In the context of the perishable export product, the deleterious consequences of work stoppage for fruit quality and its sale price make exporters vulnerable. With the increasing relevance of industrial standards such as the GLOBALGAP good agricultural practices as a signalling tool to international fruit buyers, STR has realised since 2004 that they can also use the reference to labour-related stipulations of this code to pressurise farmers. Leading exporters were fearful that new farmers might undermine the GLOBALGAP standards and hence the valley's reputation and therefore appreciated the STR's role as a watchdog. They were therefore ready to make concessions to the union (Selwyn 2011, 2013).

Finally, in the context of severe union repression in Indonesia, the establishment of the Protocol on Freedom of Association (FoA) that was signed by Indonesian trade unions, large Indonesian sportswear manufacturers and major multinational brands in 2011 represents a significant achievement of negotiations led by local unions. It was catalysed by the collaboration among different Indonesian unions who had joined hands with labour solidarity groups in other countries. They had worked together intensively in the context of the international Play Fair campaign that sought to push sportswear and athletic footwear companies, the International Olympics Committee, as well as national governments to take concrete measures to address violations of workers' rights in sportswear supply chains. The Protocol that emerged as a non-governmental guarantee of workers' representation security sets out to regulate the interaction between trade unions and management within sportswear producing workplaces, providing unions with clear guidelines on how to operationalise their activities within the factory premises (Siegmann, Merk and Knorringa 2014).

Precarious workers' power potentials

In the three examples outlined above, precarious workers successfully challenged their marginalisation in globalised production and the associated poor and insecure labour conditions, bringing greater income and representation security. Which sources of power did they tap for their struggles? And which contextual factors facilitated the emergence of worker-driven non-governmental labour regulation – or rendered it more difficult?

Wright's (2000) conceptualisation of workers' power is an important point of reference for both the analyses of the STR's use of the GLOBALGAP to improve labour conditions in Brazilian grape cultivation (Selwyn 2011, 2013) and the emergence of the FoA Protocol in the Indonesian sportswear industry (Siegmann, Merk and Knorringa 2014). In his game-theoretic model of class relations, power is 'the capacity of individuals and organizations to realize class interests' (Wright 2000: 962). He distinguishes two sources of power: 'Associational power' results from the formation of workers' collective organisations, while workers' 'structural power' emanates from their location within the economic system (Wright 2000: 962).

A united agenda strengthened workers' associational power in the examples above. It acted as a lever for better working conditions both in the case of

STR's use of the GLOBALGAP standard and in the case of the negotiations for the Indonesian FoA Protocol. Selwyn (2011: 1312) quotes an STR trade union officer explaining that initial concessions for labour were significant, because the employers' side was not prepared and not united. Siegmann, Merk and Knorringa (2014: 16) highlight the catalytic role of Indonesian trade unions' collaboration in the international 'Play Fair' campaign. It helped to overcome the Indonesian labour movement's internal divisions and to forge a joint agenda vis-à-vis producers and buyers of sportswear.

Associational strength helps to mobilise structural power. For instance, the STR's strengthened membership base since the 1990s has enabled them to credibly threaten to prevent grape exports due to labour rights violations (Selwyn 2013: 85). Specific features of this value chain, such as grapes' precise production calendars due to the fruit's perishability enhanced workers' structural power. This in turn enabled them to threaten with the stoppage of production. Selwyn (2013: 78) concludes that:

> while just-in-time systems of production and delivery are designed by firms to reduce their inventory costs and potentially increase their ability to source 'flexibly' from a large number of suppliers, they simultaneously give workers the ability to disrupt the functioning of supply chains through short bursts of strike action at strategic 'choke points' of the chain.

Selwyn (2011, 2013) and Siegmann, Merk and Knorringa (2014) perceive the collaboration between grape exporters and the rural workers' union STR as well as the FoA Protocol in the Indonesian sportswear industry as instances of what Wright (2000: 958) calls 'positive class compromise'. Such collaboration despite antagonistic interests can arise when workers' organisations are in a position to help capitalists to solve their collective action and coordination problems (Wright 2000: 978). In the case of Brazilian grape cultivation, positive class compromise came about when leading grape exporters realised that striking a compromise with a strong STR would enable them to address threats to their business. They involved some exporters' non-compliance with crucial labour-related quality standards such as the GLOBALGAP, whilst free-riding on the sectors' good reputation with buyers (Selwyn 2013: 1323).

Siegmann, Merk and Knorringa (2014: 19) perceive the FoA Protocol as an example of positive class compromise as its ratification strengthens Indonesian unions, while simultaneously addressing producers and sportswear brands' concerns. For producers, it makes the choking of production through labour struggles less likely: In recent years, despite continued union repression in Indonesia, workers' struggles often escalated before even an attempt at finding a resolution could be mounted (Siegmann, Merk and Knorringa 2014: 13). In addition, signing on to the FoA Protocol protects sportswear brands' reputation as a business community that is 'playing fair' with regards to collective labour rights. Franz (2010: 289) highlights that: 'reputational capital is an important factor for the ability of a company to create and capture value', especially in sectors with a strong consumer orientation. TNCs selling goods and services with a greater visibility to consumers are, therefore, more likely to be concerned about their reputational capital. This in turn augments the related structural power for the workers involved in their production. By revealing labour rights' violations in a brand's supply chain, they are in a position to attack its reputational capital and, hence, sales.

Another chain feature that strengthens workers' structural power is manufacturers' difficulty to relocate and/or limits to brands' option to find alternative suppliers (Brookes 2013: 185). Harvey (2001: 24) labels capital's mobility the 'spatial fix', i.e. 'capitalism's insatiable drive to resolve its inner crisis tendencies by geographical expansion and geographical restructuring'. In Honduras, FOTL's subsidiaries included capital-intensive textile mills, which are less mobile than assembly plants (Kumar and Mahoney 2014: 198). Therefore, a 'spatial fix' of labour struggles was not easily available. It is likely that this increased the brand's willingness to negotiate with the CGT. Since the end of the 1980s, Indonesia is one of only three main producer countries for sportswear, alongside China and Vietnam (Siegmann, Merk and Knorringa 2014: 11). On that basis, Siegmann, Merk and Knorringa (2014: 19) argue that: '[g]iven the structure of the athletic footwear chain, Indonesia is the only producing country where such an effort [to demonstrate commitment to collective labour rights] could credibly be made due to the lack of independence of Chinese and Vietnamese trade unions.'

However, precarious workers' income and labour market insecurity limit their capacity for labour struggles. Individually, they are threatened with the loss of income and their job. Strike funds of precarious workers' organisations that could compensate for these risks are commonly quickly depleted or nonexistent in the first place. This factor is particularly relevant in contexts where unemployment and working poverty are high and state transfers to guarantee income security weak (Brookes 2013: 183).

Transnational coalition partners in consumer regions play a key role to address this vulnerability. Brookes (2013: 192) refers to this resource as 'coalitional power', as the 'capacity of workers to expand the scope of conflict by involving other, nonlabor actors willing and able to influence an employer's behaviour'. They strengthen precarious workers, among others by shifting the pressure from brands' supply to their reputation and, hence, sales. This way, coalitions of workers and organisations representing critical consumers combine workers' structural power to stall production with consumers' economic power to boycott or influence sales otherwise. The presence and lobbying of allies in brands' consumer regions, such as the European Clean Clothes Campaign and Oxfam Australia in the case of the FoA Protocol and the USAS in the case of CGT's lobbying of FOTL, therefore enabled workers' organisations to leverage a less risky and more effective threat to brands' sales for labour rights guarantees. Donaghey et al. (2014: 230) have labelled this a potentially 'symbiotic role that consumers may play in global labor governance'. Connections to international organisations responsible for enforcement of the GLOBALGAP labour-related standards played a similar role in STR's struggles. An STR representative pointed out that they pass on information about labour rights violations to their regional and national trade union organisations, which in turn communicate it to the international organisations that are responsible for enforcing GLOBALGAP. As a consequence: 'the firm risks losing its certification and ability to export' (Selwyn 2011: 1319).

This pincer movement of pressure on production *and* TNCs' sales enabled local workers' organisations to target and directly bargain with distant power-holders in the respective value chain. This, too, is a key commonality of the cases of worker-driven non-governmental labour governance outlined above. Targeting the lead firms of value chains in which precarious workers are employed seems to be crucial to effectively deal with the challenges that complex value chain structures pose to workers' collective strength. The Honduran CGT exercised this in their face-to-face negotiations with FOTL executives in Kentucky, USA. Kumar and Mahoney (2014: 200–201) quote a Honduran trade union representative who speaks favourably of her direct interactions with the FOTL chief executive officer: 'If Rick Medlin says he can go five [Lempiras] higher, he means it, instead of stalling. The top executives honor their word and have the power to make decisions.' It is probably for the same reason that the unions which negotiated the FoA Protocol in Indonesia insisted on the presence of sportswear brands at the negotiating table and that brands, too, would be signatories to the Protocol (conversation with Jeroen Merk, Clean Clothes Campaign, 14 March 2013).

While Wright (2000) refers to workers' tangible power potentials, the examples outlined above also point to the role of knowledge and representation in the emergence of worker-driven non-governmental labour regulation. Such epistemological power entails the production of relevant, credible knowledge about workers' real labour conditions. The STR, for instance, carried out an investigation of working conditions in the São Francisco valley in collaboration with the Ministry of Labour. On its basis, the union formulated a set of demands to employers (Selwyn 2011: 1311). The collaboration with state bodies probably added credibility to STR's claims and demands. In the case of the FOTL agreement, strong health and safety committees were established to support a bottom-up flow of knowledge (Compa 2013). Workers' organisations might have to strike a delicate balance here. Anner (2013: 34) warns that while awareness of poor and precarious labour conditions may be necessary to garner support and negotiate with management, framing of workers as helpless victims is likely to lead to ineffective top-down solutions.

Workers' own awareness about their role in the labour process is key to an alternative, empowering frame. Selwyn (2011: 1315) highlights this as an important factor for STR's success: 'We discovered that the worker needs to know the importance of his role in the work process and the production of the wealth. Just as the employers try to avoid alerting workers how important they are, we try and achieve the opposite.' Quan (2008, in Selwyn (2013: 78)) argues that for workers' strategies to succeed: 'workers need to be educated by trade unions as to their strategic power within the chains'. Anner (2013: 34) observes that the FOTL campaign's positive outcomes resulted in part from an 'empowering frame', which is more likely to involve bottom-up worker organisation.

Contextual factors, some of which have been highlighted above, facilitate the use of workers' power potentials. If the number of relevant chain actors is low and/or the value chain relatively 'short', then worker-driven negotiations for improvement of labour conditions are less complex and, as a result, require fewer resources. This is important as workers' organisations and their allies regularly control fewer resources than capitalists. In CGT's negotiations with FOTL, the fact that the union factories in Honduras were the brand's direct subsidiaries catalysed the negotiations (Kumar and Mahoney 2014: 198). The concentration of sportswear production in Indonesia in compara-tively few, large factories made negotiations around the FoA Protocol easier, too (Siegmann, Merk and Knorringa 2014: 19). Furthermore, the leading role of one of the capitalists – preferably an industry leader – may have a catalytic role to bring powerful multinational enterprises or producers to the negotiating table with workers' organisations. In the negotiations for the FoA Protocol in Indonesia, industry leader Adidas took a prominent role in lobbying for the Protocol among other sportswear brands (Siegmann, Merk and Knorringa 2014: 16). More advanced exporters who controlled the grape exporters' association in the Brazilian São Francisco Valley recognised that the union's power could actually benefit them if channelled in particular ways and, consequently, were prepared to make concessions to the STR (Selwyn 2011: 1324).

In sum, in order to challenge precarious labour conditions in value chains, workers' associational power is key. Yet, it is not sufficient to counter their marginalisation. While strong labour organisations enable precarious workers to threaten with stoppage of production with ripple effects through value chains, their poverty makes them vulnerable to income and employment loss. Support by allies intervening in end consumer markets – the use of coalitional power – can help to overcome this dilemma. The resulting pincer movement of workers' associational and coalitional power, strategically targeting brands' reputation as their Achilles' heel constitutes a key mechanism enabling precarious workers to challenge their commodification.

These dynamics are reflected in the CIW's successful campaign for wage increases protection of labour rights in US agriculture. The model of non-governmental labour regulation that emerged from this campaign has been labelled an instance of 'Worker-driven Social Responsibility' (WSR).

Worker-driven Social Responsibility[3]: the case of the Fair Food Program in US agriculture

Productivity at the expense of farmworkers' precariousness in US agriculture

Productivity in US agriculture has increased so much during the past century that a tripled population can be fed from half the amount of farmed land, while agricultural exports have increased eightfold. This productivity increase has not translated into better working conditions for farmworkers (Loo 2014: 797): As in most countries world-wide, US agriculture is an industry characterised by low wages, high health risks, and poor labour conditions. Reflecting the national situation, in the 'Sunshine State' of Florida, the country's leading producer of fresh tomatoes, farmworkers' average hourly wages of US$ 9.69 in 2013 were less than half the State's average (BLS 2014). The piece rate for a bucket of Florida tomatoes has remained unchanged for the past 30 years (Bowe 2008: 8), implying that they had to pick twice as many tomatoes in 2009 compared to 1980 to make the minimum wage (Gottlieb and Joshi 2010: 130). The seasonality of agricultural employment involves long working hours during planting and harvesting and a high degree of labour market insecurity during other periods, including, for example, when it rains. Average hourly wage figures are therefore likely to significantly underestimate actual incomes. In addition, farmworkers are excluded from the legal entitlement to receive overtime pay (Asbed and Sellers 2013: 41).[4] Work insecurity, too, is enormous with farmworkers being often routinely exposed to hazardous chemicals and performing strenuous labour exposing them to risk of injury, while commonly being excluded from access to health care (Loo 2014: 797). As a result, vulnerable and desperate migrant workers, most of whom originate from Latin American countries are highly concentrated in the sector's workforce. In 2001–2002, 75 per cent of farmworkers originated from Mexico and two per cent from Central American countries (US DoL 2005: ix). The share of farmworkers without legal immigration status has been estimated to be as high as 90 per cent (Gottlieb and Joshi 2010, quoted in Loo 2014: 800).

Legal restrictions for collective protests by US unions more generally (Farhang 2012: 663), farmworkers' exclusion from the right to collective bargaining (Asbed and Sellers 2013: 41) and the high labour turnover in agricultural employment (Gottlieb and Joshi 2010: 129) render protest against farmworkers' precarious labour conditions extremely difficult. These difficulties are further augmented by undocumented migrant workers' lack of legal recognition (Loo 2014: 798). Women workers' wide-spread experience of sexual harassment is another consequence of their social, legal and economic marginalisation (HRW 2012; SPLC 2010: 41–53). It also makes migrant farmworkers vulnerable to situations of forced labour (Loo 2014: 798–799).

The Coalition of Immokalee Workers' Campaign for Fair Food

Loo (2014: 800) argues that the only instances where precarious labour conditions in US agriculture improved were those where workers organised to effectively protest poor treatment or negotiate better conditions. The Coalition of Immokalee Workers (CIW), labelled 'arguably the most significant migrant workers' organization to have been born in the United States since the founding of the National Farm Workers Association [...] in the early 1960s' (Drainville 2008: 358) is an outstanding example thereof. The CIW is an organization of farmworkers in Immokalee, Florida that has campaigned to raise the income and better the living conditions of Florida's tomato pickers since 1993. 'More than 33,000 farmworkers, almost all of them undocumented Latinos, produce Florida's annual crop of 1 billion pounds of fresh-market tomatoes, a crop whose wholesale value exceeds $619 million.' (SPLC 2010: 26). The demand for respect, challenging the stereotype of farmworkers incapable of changing their own destiny, became a key motivation for the CIW to organise from below (Gottlieb and Joshi 2010: 130).

During the first several years of its existence, the CIW organised strikes and work stoppages to pressurise growers to increase piece rates. Despite the resulting greater visibility for Florida's farmworkers, the CIW was unable to significantly raise wages or even force growers to the negotiating table (Asbed and Sellers 2013: 43). In 2001, the organisation changed its strategy and started targeting fast food and supermarket chains as the most powerful actors in the food chain. They realised that: 'If the power to negotiate prices is a function of size, then applying that economic presumption to the supply chain explains the reality of falling farmworker wages' (Asbed and Sellers 2013: 44). They did not stop there, though, and have since tried to leverage volume purchasing power to improve labour conditions on Florida's tomato fields. Their demand for 'fair food', including decent conditions for those labouring in the tomato fields followed the material and discursive successes of the anti-sweatshop and fair trade movements. It led to their boycott of fast food chain Taco Bell in 2001. 'Taco Bell was the first target, not because it was the largest purchaser of tomatoes but because as part of the larger Yum Brands conglomerate, it had considerable influence in the fast food industry' (Gottlieb and Joshi 2010: 131). A subsequent campaign targeted McDonalds from 2005 onwards (Brown and Getz 2008: 1187). Using a range of actions from concerts, cross-country speaking tours to the headquarters of food corporations, a consumer boycott, hunger strikes etc. (Asbed and Sellers 2013: 44; Drainville 2008: 359–362), they demanded improvements in wages and wider working conditions that would be passed down to Immokalee workers through tomato growers. The participation of allies, such as student, environmental, sustainable food and agriculture organisations, community, human and labour rights activists, as well as people of faith from various traditions, who have mobilised with Immokalee farmworkers and share a common vision of fair food has been a major component of CIW's campaign since (Walsh 2012: 198). The relationships that the CIW established with these allies gave a visibility to its work that the precarious social and legal status of its members often did not allow (Gottlieb and Joshi 2010: 129–130).

The Fair Food Program – worker-driven labour regulation

The partnerships with multinationals in the food chain such as Yum Brands, McDonalds, Subway and others that resulted from CIW's persistent and creative campaigns evolved into the Fair Food Programme (FFP) in 2010.

The FFP represents a non-governmental form of labour regulation for the improvement of farmworkers' working and living conditions based on a part-nership among farmworkers, Florida tomato growers, and participating buyers. Initiated and designed by workers, it entails that, via 'evergreen' contractual agreements with the CIW, retail food companies commit to purchase tomatoes only from growers participating in the FFP. The implementation of the FFP is overseen by on-going monitoring of participating farms through the inde-pendent Fair Food Standards Council (FFSC) in which CIW members represent half of the directors (FFSC 2014). By early 2015, 13 major fast food chains and food retailers had joined the FFP, with the two most recent members having voluntarily reached out to the CIW. The programme has received wide-spread praise as the best workplace-monitoring programme in the USA (Greenhouse 2014). It has been awarded a range of prestigious national human rights awards and was invited to present its model in international forums, such as the UN Forum on Business and Human Rights (FFSC 2014: 5; UN 2014).

The FFP covered 90 per cent of Florida's tomato industry in 2011 (CIW 2014) and directly affects the lives and working conditions of over 100,000 workers through wage premia, worker-to-worker education, changes in har-vesting operations and independent audits of growers, among others (FFSC 2014: 13). This partnership is codified in triangular contracts between buyers, growers and harvesters of tomatoes. The CIW has contracts with buyers, and agreements with growers. Based on those, failure to comply with the FFP rules can become one of the reasons for buyers to stop purchasing tomatoes from a grower. The CIW argues that the FFP's reliance on contract law effectively addresses agricultural workers' lack of coverage by existing US labour regulation and the anti-labour bias of both legislation and the judicial system (phone conversation with Hitov, CIW, 9 September 2014).

The pillars of the FFP are a commitment to wage increases in the form of a premium of a 'penny per pound' of harvested tomatoes, compliance with the Fair Food Code of Conduct, the provision of worker-to-worker education sessions, a worker-triggered complaint resolution mechanism, as well as the establishment of health and safety committees on every participating farm. The code covers core labour rights, such as the abolition of forced and child labour as well as discrimination, but also a detailed list of industry-specific 'provisions designed to get at longstanding abuses that only workers could know, the forms of exploitation and humiliation unique to each particular industry that workers have experienced for generations, but no outside "expert" could ever divine' (CIW 2014). Prominent examples include the elimination of the traditional requirement to overfill the picking buckets, a practice that resulted in workers effectively picking one unpaid 32-lb bucket of tomatoes for every ten for which they were paid, or the requirement to provide shade and time clocks in the fields (FFSC 2014: 7).

Its probably most important stipulation is the establishment of the so-called 'penny per pound' premium paid by participating buyers, which ranges from

1.5 to 4 cents per pound, depending on the type of tomato purchased. This Fair Food Program Premium is designed to combat the poverty wages common in tomato harvesting by effectively raising the piece rate per bucket of tomatoes by 60 per cent (SPLC 2010: 27). The CIW therefore describes the 'penny per pound' as the 'reverse princess and the pea principle', referring to the fairy tale in which a princess feels a little pea even under dozens of matrasses: 'change can be felt at the bottom of the food industry with an imperceptible change at the top' (Bell and Fields 2013). Participating buyers remit the premium payments to the participating growers, who subsequently distribute them to workers as a bonus on their pay cheque. The FFSC monitors the supply chain to ensure proper disbursement of the premium.

Sexual harassment is considered among the most severe violations of the code, leading participating buyers to decline to purchase tomatoes from such growers unless any offender is immediately fired. While in 2012 and 2013, three long-time supervisors were terminated for sexual harassment as a result of FFSC investigations, the 2013–2014 season saw the elimination of reported cases of sexual assault at participating farms (FFSC 2014: 14). Overall, participation in the FFP implies that violation of the code leads to the risk of losing revenue for the growers. The CIW perceives this as harnessing the market mechanism to achieve better outcomes for precarious farmworkers (Asbed and Sellers 2013: 44). Regular audits of participating growers are being conducted by FFSC auditors. FFSC reported 7,500 worker interviews over the course of 100 comprehensive audits until 2014 (FFSC 2014: 13).

CIW members themselves are involved in the implementation of the programme through their responsibility for worker-to-worker education sessions. They have reached more than 20,000 workers through training sessions and more than 100,000 through training materials (FFSC 2014: 13). Furthermore, enforcement is ensured through workers' health and safety committees on every farm as well as a worker-triggered complaint resolution mechanism. A toll-free call to a hotline answered by an FFSC investigator leads to investigation, corrective action plans, and, if necessary, suspension of a farm's participating grower status. So far, more than 600 complaints have been recorded and resolved (FFSC 2014: 6–7, 13).

The CIW sees the fact that the FFP puts workers' agency at the centre as the key to its success: 'The Fair Food Program is a workers' rights program that is designed, monitored, and enforced *by the workers whose rights it is intended to protect*' (CIW 2014, italics in original). The CIW label this approach Worker-driven Social Responsibility (WSR) – in contrast to corporate-led CSR approaches to non-governmental labour regulation. In WSR approaches, 'workers are not just at the table, they are at the head of the table' (CIW 2014). Because of the central role of workers 'with a vital and abiding interest in seeing that their rights are effectively monitored and enforced' (CIW 2014), with the FFP, they have constructed an effective system for workers' rights' protection. This is based on the experience that legal change and won lawsuits are not enough to revert farmworkers' indecent labour conditions as these formal changes do not address migrant workers' marginalisation: Lucas Benitez, one of the co-founders of the CIW, argues that, unless workers become aware and campaign themselves: 'who cares what happens to a bunch of *pelagatos* – a bunch of nobodies?' (Bowe 2008: 26).

The CIW continues its Campaign for Fair Food. Current targets include the retailers Publix, Ahold and Kroger, as well as the fast food chain Wendy's. Publix and Kroger – two of the largest retailers in the USA – and Wendy's – the only one out of the top five fast food chains in the USA that has not signed the FFP, yet – supply the CIW's home market. With the Dutch retail giant Ahold, however, for the first them the CIW's campaign targets a company headquartered in a country outside the USA. Jointly, its subsidiaries Giant and Stop & Shop are the fifth largest retailer and the leading online grocer in the USA, contributing more than half to the company's sales and income (Ahold 2015a: 5). While, in contrast to Publix and Wendy's, no on-the-ground campaign has been launched, as yet, since 2010, indecent labour conditions in the Dutch retailer's supply chain have been brought to the table of each Ahold Annual General Meeting (AGM). Until 2014, during each meeting, Ahold raised new arguments in order not to participate. The 2015 AGM was different. Ahold's CEO Dick Boer announced that the company has 'been engaged in very productive conversations with CIW. We intend to continue those discussions in the hope of announcing something positive in the near future' (Ahold 2015b).[5]

Learning from the Fair Food Program about worker-driven innovation

What can we learn from the FFP about how worker-driven labour regulation emerges? More specifically, which strategies are useful and what are possible roles of various actors in and around worker-driven non-governmental labour regulation that effectively protects precarious workers?

The experience of the FFP reaffirms our initial assumption exemplified in other cases, namely, that workers' central role in the design, governance and implementation of, as well as awareness-raising about non-governmental labour regulation is key to its success in protecting precarious workers. The bad news is that this implies that WSR does not offer a blueprint for immediate replication in other locations or along other value chains. Rather, each case of worker-driven innovation that we discuss represents a response to a specific labour process and the particular features of a value chain, including their public and private governance. The good news is, though, that WSR offers important principles that can inspire other forms of worker-driven innovations. If workers are directly involved in their design and implementation, they will be empowered to monitor their own workplaces, end abusive conditions, and will have a voice in discussing how to improve working conditions. This way, for instance, the FFP ended the age-old practice of forced overfilling of harvesting buckets in Florida's tomato harvest (FFSC 2014: 7). In this process, the epistemic violence (Spivak 1988) done to those considered 'nobodies' in globalised supply chains through silencing their voices and demands – a process that translates into material precariousness – is countermanded.

In order to achieve such epistemic and material justice, similar to the other cases of worker-driven innovation, the CIW combines the strength of their own organisation with that of their allies. Coalition partners raise awareness among and mobilise groups of critical consumers. Hence, Florida farm-workers' counter-movement, too, relies on a 'pincer movement' that connects workers' associational with coalitional power targeting buyers in end consumer markets. The coalition partners' pressure on corporations' reputation and sales has a crucial, yet, primarily catalytic role. Brown and Getz (2008: 1192) have called into question the ability of consumers as a collective to make better-informed individual choices as they do not consider the fundamental class-based power imbalances. The FFP, however, addresses this concern by harnessing consumers' economic power to bring capital to the table and, hence, catalyse 'positive class compromise', yet, allies do not negotiate on behalf of Immokalee workers.

In contrast to the other examples of non-governmental labour regulation outlined above, though, the CIW completely shifted the target of their cam-paign to the reputation and, indirectly, sales of multinational brands in the food supply chain. The geographical proximity between the different nodes in the respective value chain may help to explain this difference: in the case of the CIW's Campaign for Fair Food, workers, buyers and consumers are located in the same country. Moral outrage about poverty wages can be mobilised more easily among conscious groups of consumers, such as the CIW allies, if the overall normative (social and legal) framework is shared by workers and consumers. As a result, they are able to use some form of 'symbolic leverage' as 'the ways in which structurally marginal groups of workers invoke notions of collective morality to cultivate a 'positional advantage' over more powerful social actors and institutions' (Chun 2008: 446). The innovative idea of the 'penny per pound' wage premium stipulated in the FFP is an example for how collective morality and narratives can be evoked: the 'reverse princess and the pea principle' embodied in this wage premium suggests that a small change in the consumer price at the top of the food chain has a significant impact at the bottom of the chain. The power of this metaphor is derived from the shared knowledge of this fairy tale in the USA. It suggests that the 'penny per pound' means that a fairy tale can come true, bringing justice for farmworkers. This way, the 'penny per pound' connects to collective narratives with a twist. It implies smallness of action with great impact to those who are the target of the Campaign for Fair Food, namely consumers and branded companies.

Targeting brands as the real power holders in the food chain is a strategy that the CIW shares with other cases of worker-driven innovation. Fair Food Agreements are signed between the CIW and individual participating large retailers and fast food chains rather than with growers as farmworkers' immediate employers. The question is how to scale up these innovations beyond the level of one brand? In the context of US labour legislation biased against workers, in general, and farmworkers, in particular, the CIW does not target the state apparatus for broader coverage of worker-driven innovations. Norm cascading (Sunstein 1997, quoted in Finnemore and Sikkink 1998: 895) is the alternative chosen by the CIW. This process is set in motion through the two-legged strategy of mobilising groups of critical consumers and targeting market leaders in their Campaign for Fair Food. With Taco Bell, the CIW actively targeted a subsidiary of one of the most influential fast food corporations in the USA. Taco Bell later took the lead in bringing on board other companies in the Yum Brands conglomerate to commit to the CIW demands (Gottlieb and Joshi 2010: 131–132). The CIW uses market leaders' participation for wider acceptance of the norms incorporated in its Fair Food Code of Conduct. Vis-à-vis non-participating companies, the coalition argues that they should sign on to the FFP in order not to lag behind their competitors (e.g. CIW 2015a; Lappé 2013; SumOfUs 2013).

The relationship of the FFP and other forms of worker-driven non-governmental labour governance with the state is multi-faceted. On the one hand, the weakness and poor enforcement of public protection of labour rights at the national and international level has led to the emergence of non-governmental forms of labour regulation. In the USA, farmworkers are being excluded from key labour rights, e.g. under the National Labor Relations Act (NLRA). Linder (1987: 1371) points out that the anti-farm labour bias in US labour legislation is rooted in racial discrimination and the fact that it guaranteed good business for white farmers. Interestingly, legal exclusion also proved an advantage to the CIW. According to the NLRA, secondary boycotts are prohibited for unions. A secondary labour action refers to efforts to influence, for instance, a tomato grower by exerting some sort of economic or social pressure against entities dealing with that grower, such as their buyers (Farhang 2012: 664). 'The CIW recognized that since it was not a union, it could undertake a secondary boycott while exploring how to increase the visibility of such a campaign' (Gottlieb and Joshi 2010: 131).

As pointed out above, the CIW consciously does not seek public enforcement of farmworkers' rights through national labour legislation. Unlike most private regulatory initiatives that lack any legal enforceability mechanism the FFP is underpinned by contract law as the CIW's agreements with buyers and agreements with tomato growers could be enforced by private litigation. So far, this mechanism has not yet been used. The CIW considers the threat of consumer action more important for enforcement of the FFP (e-mail communication Asbed, CIW, 17 April 2015). Yet, one can argue that legal norms embodied in contract law are sufficiently internalised in the corporate sector to make them effective in preventing violations of the Fair Food Code of Conduct (e-mail communication Sabonis, NESRI, 27 January 2015). The state has an ambiguous role here: causing the search for alternative forms of labour rights guarantees where it fails to provide sufficient protection against abuse, yet, also offering enforcement tools that strengthen innovative accountability mechanisms. This echoes research that points to potential synergies between state regulation and non-governmental forms of labour regulation (e.g. Amengual 2010; Gereffi and Lee 2014; Locke, Rissing and Pal 2013). Brookes (2013: 188) refers to this 'capacity of workers to influence the behavior of an employer by invoking the formal or informal rules that structure their relationship and interactions' as 'institutional power'.

Conclusion and outlook for civic innovation practice and research

In this chapter, we have defined worker-driven innovation in value chains as institutions contributing to decent work in which workers play a central role in design, governance and implementation. In the context of non-governmental governance of value chains, we consider them counter-movements against workers' structural subordination to a logic of profit maximisation. They are opening horizons that alternatives to this logic are available and inspire social change elsewhere. That way, they represent significant contributions to the 'mosaic of responses' to twenty-first-century neo-liberal capitalism that the notion of civic innovation refers to (Biekart, Harcourt and Knorringa, this volume, pp. 00).

Especially the discussion of the FFP illustrates how precarious workers' counter-movements emerge and lead to worker-driven innovation. The 'pincer' of workers' associational and coalitional power is a particularly relevant tool in the context of farmworkers' income and employment insecurity. While workers' collective voice and agency is the point of departure of worker-driven innovation, other civic actors who share workers' vision of justice along the value chain have a crucial role to play. The resulting 'pincer' has the potential to revert the precariousness that workers experience as a result of marginalisation on the basis of their class and other social identities. Besides, it takes into account the spatial dispersion of production in global value chains that blurs the effectiveness of conventional public accountability mechanisms centring on the direct employment relationship. Workers and their allies target different spaces along value chains in an effort to move those with most power to influence labour conditions, namely branded corporations. Despite the class-based biases and gaps in public enforcement of labour rights that also necessitated, e.g., the CIW's struggles, worker-driven innovation is strengthened by connections to legal enforcement mechanisms. In the case of the FFP, the legal underpinning by contract law supports this innovative model through 'institutional power'.

We believe that more general lessons for civic innovation research and practice can be derived from our analysis. They concern civic actors' sources of power, the scale and normative content of civic innovation as well as the significance of an intersectional approach in civic innovation research and practice, respectively.

We see our conclusions regarding the emergence of precarious workers' counter-movements and worker-driven innovation as specific instances of civic innovation. They show that progressive social change is rooted in and legitimised by marginalised actors' own collective agency, denoted 'associational power' in Wright's (2000) class-focused analysis. Their own organisations are strengthened by allies that provide them with 'coalitional power' (Brookes 2013). Shared, empowering frames play an important role in building such coalitions (Anner 2013; Chun 2008). The 'reverse princess and the pea' narrative that the CIW uses to mobilise support across social identities is an example of such an empowering frame. This parallels insights from social movement theory. For instance, McAdam, McCarthy and Zald (1996: 5) argue that such framing processes are necessary for social mobilisation as 'the impetus to action is as much a cultural construction as it is a function of structural vulnerability.' Mobilising frames form bridges between opportunity structures and burgeoning movements.

We have cautioned that these opportunity structures do not lend themselves for simple replication. Rather, social movements, including those mobilising around precarious work and livelihoods, are shaped by the political constraints and opportunities unique to the national context in which they are embedded (McAdam, McCarthy and Zald 1996: 3). In addition, as we have shown above, the specific labour process and value chain governance may provide civic actors with unique opportunities and, hence, structural power.

This is relevant for the question whether and how civic innovation can be scaled up. Biekart, Harcourt and Knorringa (this volume, pp. 00) point out that bringing innovation to scale may imply the risk of trading coverage with effectiveness. A similar critical question can be raised about worker-driven innovations. Do they offer privileges and protection to a small group of workers only, this way widening the gap between different segments of workers and further marginalising the majority? Wright (2000: 999) anticipates such dualistic tendencies as a result of positive class compromise 'dividing the labour force along the line of privileged access to the guarantee of their labour rights' (Siegmann, Merk and Knorringa 2014: 20). Wright (2000: 999) assumes, however, that such dualistic tendencies can be muted if the norms embodied in worker-driven governance are diffused through the economy. He foresaw a key role for strong trade unions and pro-labour compromises in the political sphere in these processes.

In the globalised context of value chains, we also perceive efforts to bring worker-driven non-governmental labour regulation to scale. For instance, the Indonesian FoA Protocol has become an industry-wide standard on collective labour rights in one of the three main producer countries already. In case of the FFP, too, one can speak of wide-spread adoption of their model already. The programme covered 90 per cent of Florida's tomato industry in 2011 (CIW 2014). At the same time, the CIW is networking with like-minded organisations that emulate and adapt their WSR model 'to fight worker exploitation in settings as diverse as dairy farms in Vermont, tomato fields in Morocco, and apparel sweatshops in Bangladesh' (CIW 2012). The underlying diffusion model is that: 'Justice anywhere is a threat to injustice everywhere' (CIW 2015b). This seems to indicate that rather than adapting values from their initial activism phase (Biekart, Harcourt and Knorringa, this volume, pp. 00), the CIW's struggles make a dent into the norms governing labour in the food chain, not only in the USA. The fact that industry leaders such as Walmart voluntarily reached out to the CIW can be seen as an indication of such a change in benchmark norms or 'tipping point' (Finnemore and Sikkink 1998: 895) in the industry. As predicted by Sunstein (1996: 2033), reputational incentives have played a role in this process. However, the cases discussed above show that such norm diffusion was not a natural process, but rather influenced strategically by coalitions of civic actors.

Our analysis also highlights how civic actors' intersecting identities can be mobilised for civic innovation. Workers' identities are not only confined to their location in a class structure. They have a gender, race, immigration status, too, to name just a few dimensions. These intersecting identities can help to forge coalitions for civic innovation. Brookes (2013: 191–192) highlights that: '[t]o gain leverage in conflicts with employers, workers can draw on these social connections, especially when conflicts concern issues salient to key stakeholders'. This is one of the reasons why the CIW (e.g. in CIW 2014) commonly defines the problem that gives rise to WSR as a violation of *human* rights, rather than of labour rights (conversation Benitez, 15 April 2015).[6] The evocation of human rights offers a broader umbrella, which can subsequently encompass a range of topical campaigns: protest against female farmworkers' sexual harassment in the fields can be organised jointly with women's organisations. Ending the exploitation of migrant workers' lack of citizenship rights, which channels them into '3D' – dirty, dangerous and demeaning – jobs can be demanded together with migrant organisations. Such broader coalitions that start from, but are not confined to class identities, characterise social movement unionism (Walsh 2012: 194). In another lesson drawn from social movement theory, we understand that framing the precariousness of Immokalee workers' work and livelihoods as a violation of human rights helps to 'fashion shared understandings of the world and of themselves that legitimate and motivate collective action' (McAdam, McCarthy and Zald 1996: 6).

It is worthwhile to highlight some of the structural limitations of worker-driven innovations in value chains. A strategy to target key power holders rather than precarious workers' direct employers only works if these companies are identifiable. This will be more difficult, e.g. when multiple suppliers' products are merged into the finished product, as in the case of gold or computer equipment (e-mail communication Hitov, CIW, 24 March 2015). Besides, less visible lead companies will be less concerned about their reputational capital and reach out to workers for 'positive class compromise'. Knorringa (2014) argues that, beyond fulfilling legal norms, the majority of formal firms globally are actually not much concerned about the social legitimacy of their activities. This reduces workers' structural power to impede brands' sales.

Another more fundamental threat to worker-driven innovation may emerge from weakening associational power. Selwyn (2011: 1325) describes this for the context of the São Francisco valley fruit sector. He argues that the compromise might be undermined by

> a rise in apathy among the STR's membership as a consequence of its compromise and thus a decline in the trade union's associational power, or conversely, a successful challenge from within the trade union with its leadership shifting back to more militant strategies, and perhaps the growth of as yet small and non-influential trade unions in the valley.

This vulnerability is rooted in the unequal distribution of resources between precarious workers' associations and coalitions and the companies whom they target. The question is whether innovations such as the FFP challenge this fundamental inequality or preserve it. Brown and Getz (2008: 1184) argue that non-governmental labour regulation has an ambiguous relationship with the neo-liberal dominance of markets. While it resists the consequences of marketisation in terms of poor and insecure labour relations, at the same time it reinscribes neo-liberal thinking by embracing key neo-liberal principles, such as the primacy of the market as a mechanism for addressing social ills, the privatisation of regulatory functions previously reserved for the public sphere, and the assertion of the individual rights and responsibilities of citizen–consumers. One can argue, though, that worker-driven forms of labour regulation, in contrast, reclaim workers' rights from corporate control '[T]hanks to the workers' leading role in designing the program, its structure, function and, most importantly, results, stand in stark contrast to the traditional corporate-led approach to social responsibility' (CIW 2014).

Notes

1 We gratefully acknowledge helpful comments of participants of a seminar of the International Institute of Social Studies (ISS) Civic Innovation Research Initiative (CIRI), of the 2015 International Labour Process Conference's (ILPC's) stream on 'Precarious Work' as well as by Steve Hitov, Coalition of Immokalee Workers (CIW). All remaining errors are solely ours.
2 Jeroen Merk supported the negotiations around the Freedom of Association Protocol in the Indonesian sportswear industry on behalf of the Clean Clothes Campaign. Karin Astrid Siegmann was involved in the Coalition of Immokalee Workers' (CIW) campaign to convince the Dutch retailer Ahold to sign on to their Fair Food Program (FFP).
3 The CIW has a copyright on this term.
4 Historically, US farmworkers have for the most part been left out of labour law legislative battles in the USA for reasons of racial discrimination (Linder 1992). We thank Peter Sabonis, National Economic & Social Rights Initiative, for pointing this out to us.
5 On 29 July 2015 Ahold announced that it will participate in the FFP.
6 Especially the core labour rights featured in the International Labour Organization's (ILO) 1998 Declaration on Fundamental Principles and Rights at Work, namely freedom from discrimination, forced and child labour as well as freedom of association and collective bargaining, have long been understood as 'human rights at the workplace' by the United Nations and ILO (Alston 2004: 492).

References

Alston, P. (2004) '"Core Labour Standards" and the Transformation of the International Labour Rights Regime', *European Journal of International Law* 15(3): 457–521.

Ahold (2015a) 'Responsible Retailing'. Zaandam: Ahold. Available at https://www.ahold.com/#!/Responsible-retailing-5/Responsible-Retailing-Reports/Responsible-Retailing-Report-2014.htm [accessed 27 April 2015].

Ahold (2015b) 'Ahold CEO Dick Boer addresses Annual General Meeting 2015'. Available at https://www.ahold.com/#!/Media/Ahold-CEO-Dick-Boer-addresses-Annual-General-Meeting-2015.htm?year=2015&type=detail [accessed 27 April 2015].

Amengual, M. (2010) 'Complementary Labor Regulation: The Uncoordinated Combination of State and Private Regulators in the Dominican Republic', *World Development* 38(3): 405–414.

Anner, M. (2013) 'Workers' Power in Global Value Chains. Fighting Sweatshop Practices at Russell, Nike and Knights Apparel', in P. Fairbrother, C. Lévesque and M. Hennebert (eds) *Transnational Trade Unionism: New Capabilities and Prospects: Building Union Power*, pp. 23–41. London: Routledge.

Anner, M.S. (2011) *Solidarity Transformed: Labor Responses to Globalization and Crisis in Latin America*. Ithaca, NY: Cornell University Press.

Arnold, D. and J.R. Bongiovi (2013) 'Precarious, Informalizing, and Flexible Work Transforming Concepts and Understandings', *American Behavioral Scientist* 57(3): 289–308.

Asbed, G. and S. Sellers (2013) 'The Fair Food Program: Comprehensive, Verifiable and Sustainable Change for Farmworkers', *University of Pennsylvania Journal of Law & Social Change* 16: 39–48.

Barrientos, S. (2008) 'Contract Labour: The "Achilles Heel" of Corporate Codes in Commercial Value Chains', *Development and Change* 39(6): 977–990.

Bell, B. and T. Fields (2013) 'A Penny a Pound, Plus Power: The Coalition of Immokalee Workers Changes History', *Huffington Post Blog* 15 May 2013. Available at http://www.huffingtonpost.com/beverly-bell/a-penny-a-pound-plus-power_b_3274169.html [accessed 27 April 2015].

Block, F. (2014) 'Polanyian Themes: From Budapest to the Caribbean', *Development and Change* 45(6): 1449–1456.

Bowe, J. (2008) *Nobodies: Modern American Slave Labor and the Dark Side of the New Global Economy*. New York: Random House Trade Paperbacks.

Brookes, M. (2013) 'Varieties of Power in Transnational Labor Alliances: An Analysis of Workers' Structural, Institutional, and Coalitional Power in the Global Economy', *Labor Studies Journal* 38(3): 181–200.

Brown, G. (2013) 'The Record of Failure and Fatal Flaws of CSR Factory Monitoring', *ISHN Journal* (February): 1–6.

Brown, S. and C. Getz (2008) 'Privatizing Farm Worker Justice: Regulating Labor through Voluntary Certification and Labeling', *Geoforum* 39(3): 1184–1196.

Burawoy, M. (2003) 'For a Sociological Marxism: The Complementary Convergence of Antonio Gramsci and Karl Polanyi', *Politics & Society* 31(2): 193–261.

Burawoy, M. (2010) 'From Polanyi to Pollyanna: The False Optimism of Global Labor Studies', *Global Labour Journal* 1(2): 301–313.

BLS (Bureau of Labor Statistics) (2014) 'May 2013 State Occupational Employment and Wage Estimates Florida'. Available at http://www.bls.gov/oes/current/oes_fl.htm [accessed 19 January 2015].

Chun, J.J. (2008) 'The Limits of Labor Exclusion: Redefining the Politics of Split Labor Markets Under Globalization', *Critical Sociology* 34(3): 433–452.

CIW (Coalition of Immokalee Workers) (2012) 'Consciousness + Commitment = Change'. Available at http://ciw-online.org/about/ [accessed 25 March 2015].

CIW (2014) 'Worker-driven Social Responsibility (WSR): A New Idea for a New Century'. Available at http://ciw-online.org/blog/2014/06/wsr/ [accessed 22 January 2015].

CIW (2015a) 'Nashville Fair Food Takes Publix Protests to the Next Level with the "Amazing Race for Farmworker Justice" this Sunday in Middle Tennessee!' Available at http://ciw-online.org/blog/2015/04/nashville-race/ [accessed 27 April 2015].

CIW (2015b) '"Injustice anywhere..." Farmworker Strike in Mexico Underscores Urgent Need for Real Human Rights Protections on Both Sides of the Border...' Available at http://ciw-online.org/blog/2015/04/injustice-anywhere/ [accessed 3 April 2015].

Compa, L. (2013) 'After Bangladesh, Labor Unions Can Save Lives', *The Washington Post*, 26 May 2013. Available at http://www.washingtonpost.com/opinions/after-ba ngladesh-labor-unions-can-save-lives/2013/05/26/77a8809c-c483-11e2-914f-a7aba 60512a7_story.html [accessed 27 April 2015].

Donaghey, J., J. Reinecke, C. Niforou and B. Lawson (2014) 'From Employment Relations to Consumption Relations: Balancing Labor Governance in Global Supply Chains', *Human Resource Management* 53(2): 229–252.

Drainville, A.C. (2008) 'Present in the World Economy: The Coalition of Immokalee Workers (1996–2007)', *Globalizations* 5(3): 357–377.

FFSC (Fair Food Standards Council) (2014) *Fair Food Program 2014 Annual Report*. Sarasota, FL: FFSC.

Farhang, S. (2012) 'Legislative–Executive Conflict and Private Statutory Litigation in the United States: Evidence from Labor, Civil Rights, and Environmental Law', *Law & Social Inquiry* 37(3): 657–685.

Finnemore, M. and K. Sikkink (1998) 'International Norm Dynamics and Political Change', *International Organization* 52(4): 887–917.

Franz, M. (2010) 'The Potential of Collective Power in a Global Production Network: UNICOME and Metro Cash & Carry in India', *Erdkunde* 64(3): 281–290.

Gereffi, G. and J. Lee (2014) 'Economic and Social Upgrading in Global Value Chains and Industrial Clusters: Why Governance Matters', *Journal of Business Ethics*, published online 14 September 2014. Available at http://link.springer.com/article/10. 1007%2Fs10551-014-2373-7#/page-1 [accessed 11 January 2016].

Gottlieb, R. and A. Joshi (2010) *Food Justice*. Cambridge, MT/London: MIT Press.

Greenhouse, S. (2014) 'In Florida Tomato Fields, a Buys Progress', *The New York Times*, 24 April 2014. Available at http://www.nytimes.com/2014/04/25/business/ in-florida-tomato-fields-a-penny-buys-progress.html [accessed 22 August 2014].

Harvey, D. (2001) 'Globalization and the Spatial Fix', *Geographische Revue* 2(3): 23–31.

HRW (Human Rights Watch) (2012) *Cultivating Fear: The Vulnerability of Immigrant Farmworkers in the US to Sexual Violence and Sexual Harassment*. New York: HRW.

Knorringa, P. (2014) 'Private Governance and Social Legitimacy in Production', in A. Payne and N. Phillips (eds) *Handbook of the International Political Economy of Governance*, pp. 361–378. Cheltenham: Edward Elgar Publishing.

Kumar, A. and J. Mahoney (2014) 'Stitching Together: How Workers are Hemming down Transnational Capital in the HyperGlobal Apparel Industry', *WorkingUSA* 17(2): 187–210.

Lappé, A. (2013) 'Human Rights and a Burger Giant'. Available at http://civileats.com/2013/12/10/human-rights-and-a-burger-giant/ [accessed 27 April 2015].

Linder, M. (1987) 'Farm Workers and the Fair Labor Standards Act: Racial Discrimination in the New Deal', *Texas Law Review* 65: 1335–1393.

Linder, M. (1992) *Migrant Workers and Minimum Wages: Regulating the Exploitation of Agricultural Labor in the United States.* Boulder, San Francisco, Oxford: Westview Press.

Locke, R.M., B.A. Rissing and T. Pal (2013) 'Complements Or Substitutes? Private Codes, State Regulation and the Enforcement of Labour Standards in Global Supply Chains', *British Journal of Industrial Relations* 51(3): 519–552.

Loo, C. (2014) 'Towards a More Participative Definition of Food Justice', *Journal of Agricultural and Environmental Ethics* 27: 1–23.

McAdam, D., J.D. McCarthy and M.N. Zald (1996) 'Introduction: Opportunities, Mobilizing Structures, and Framing Processes – Toward a Synthetic, Comparative Perspective on Social Movements', in D. McAdam, J.D. McCarthy and M.N. Zald (eds) *Comparative Perspectives on Social Movements: Political Opportunities, Mobilizing Structures, and Cultural Framings*, pp. 1–20. Cambridge: Cambridge University Press.

Munck, R. (2004) 'Globalization, Labor and the "Polanyi Problem"', *Labor History* 45(3): 251–269.

Newitt, K. (2012) *Private Sector Voluntary Initiatives on Labor Standards*, Background Paper World Development Report. Washington, DC: World Bank.

Polanyi, K. (1944) *The Great Transformation.* Boston: Beacon Press.

Quan, K. (2008) 'Use of Global Value Chains by Labor Organizers', *Competition and Change* 12(1): 89–104.

Selwyn, B. (2011) 'The Political Economy of Class Compromise: Trade Unions, Capital–Labour Relations and Development in North East Brazil', *Antipode* 43(4): 1305–1329.

Selwyn, B. (2013) 'Social Upgrading and Labour in Global Production Networks: A Critique and an Alternative Conception', *Competition & Change* 17(1): 75–90.

Siegmann, K.A., J. Merk and P. Knorringa (2014) 'Voluntary Initiatives in Global Value Chains. Towards Labour-led Social Upgrading?', CIRI Working Paper 3, The Hague: ISS.

Silver, B.J. and G. Arrighi (2003) 'Polanyi's "Double Movement": The Belles Époques of British and US Hegemony Compared', *Politics & Society* 31(2): 325–355.

SPLC (Southern Poverty Law Center) (2010) *Injustice on our Plates. Immigrant Women in the U.S. Food Industry.* Montgomery: SPLC.

Spivak, G.C. (1988) 'Can the Subaltern Speak?', in C. Nelson and L. Grossberg (eds) *Marxism and the Interpretation of Culture*, pp. 271–313. Basingstoke: MacMillan Education.

Standing, G. (2011) *The Precariat: The New Dangerous Class.* London, New York: Bloomsbury Academic.

SumOfUs (2013) 'Wendy's: Support a Fair Deal for Farm Workers'. Available at http://action.sumofus.org/a/ciw-wendys/?sub=taf [accessed 27 April 2015].

Sunstein, C. (1997) *Free Markets and Social Justice.* New York: Oxford University Press.

Sunstein, C.R. (1996) 'On the Expressive Function of Law', *University of Pennsylvania Law Review* 144(5): 2021–2053.

Taylor, M. (2011) 'Race You to the Bottom… and Back Again? The Uneven Development of Labour Codes of Conduct', *New Political Economy* 16(4): 445–462.

UN (United Nations) (2014) *Report of the Working Group on the Issue of Human Rights and Transnational Corporations and Other Business Enterprises. Addendum: Visit to the United States of America.* New York: UN.

US DoL (Department of Labor) (2005) 'Findings from the National Agricultural Workers Survey (NAWS) 2001–2002'. Washington, DC: US DoL. Available at http://www.doleta.gov/agworker/report9/naws_rpt9.pdf [accessed 20 January 2015].

Utting, P. (2008) 'The Struggle for Corporate Accountability', *Development and Change* 39(6): 959–975.

Walsh, J.S. (2012) 'A "New" Social Movement: US Labor and the Trends of Social Movement Unionism', *Sociology Compass* 6(2): 192–204.

Webster, E., R. Lambert and A. Bezuidenhout (2011) *Grounding Globalization: Labour in the Age of Insecurity.* Maiden, Oxford, Victoria: Wiley-Blackwell.

Wright, E.O. (2000) 'Working-Class Power, Capitalist-Class Interests, and Class Compromise', *American Journal of Sociology* 105(4): 957–1002.

7 Civic innovation by family farmers in the face of global value chain inclusion

Between material conditions and imagined futures

Lee Pegler and Wanessa Marques Silva

Introduction/framing the debate

This chapter adds to a growing critical body of evidence that questions whether small-scale producers and communities gain by being inserted in global systems of production (Global Value Chains – GVCs). Despite the argument by some think tanks and international organisations that incorporating and main-streaming of local production and workers into value chains will improve their social conditions, others question the prospect of social upgrading and query its achievement (Barrientos, Gereffi and Rossi 2011; Knorringa and Pegler 2006).[1]

This chapter looks at the impacts of inclusion into GVCs on producer/communities by looking at two Amazonian studies of rural small-scale producer involvement in value chains, one with açaí and the other with palm oil.[2] We ask: What representational dynamics are involved? And as a contribution to this volume on civic innovation, we look at what the experiences of small-scale rural producers bring to our understanding of civic innovation?[3]

In discussing the cases in relation to the social upgrading debate, we look at representational dynamics of civic innovation via three interrelated components. As chains develop and become up-scaled and mainstreamed – 1) Can inclusion of small-scale producers be retained? 2) Can evolving social relations take into account the complex and varied subjectivities/positions in the value chain? And 3) How can we see these social changes as a civic action process?[4] All of these questions need to take into account the context of power and, within this, considerations of agency and representation of the small-scale rural farmers.

One positive, dynamic, civic innovation in the smallholder context is how they push for representation at various levels of the process. Interactions between producers, other private sector actors and government can promote social upgrading or greater levels of security at the work place and these may spill over into the communities in which small-scale farmers take part. Yet involvement in global production chains may also be constraints to social upgrading. Drawing an analogy from the literature relating to small firm economic upgrading in chains (Humphrey and Schmitz 2002[5]), one hypothesis for local level horizontal social upgrading within a vertical chain might be that lasting, inclusive social upgrading depends on: 1) the length and complexity of the chain; 2) the nature of regulation such as the codification of products, in the case of firms, of rights in the case of labour; and 3) the capacity of the 'supply base' – communities/local labour market – to coordinate and control inputs such as labour power and collective action. We reflect on these conditions in our analysis of civic innovation success in Amazonia.

The broader framing of civic innovation and social upgrading which informs this chapter combines vertical (chain) and horizontal (local custom/traditions/values) perspectives. Our specific analysis of representation and social upgrading takes up the concepts of agency/voice and power in the specific rural (livelihoods) context.[6] We analyse the concepts of agency/voice in terms of the 'politics of production' (Burawoy 1985, 2000). In this analysis, outcomes for labour are seen as situational rather than fixed and are determined by a combination of macro level processes (e.g. the state), the interrelations of actors at the meso level and by micro level labour processes (i.e. what tasks people do, what they feel about it, and how they respond at that level).

In looking at the politics of production we argue that labour processes/livelihoods are both objective and subjective but also ambiguous. This is different from earlier versions of labour process theory (Braverman 1974), based more on agent's alientation.[7] We argue that is important to recognise the multiplicity as well as the ambiguity of 'production politics' in people's tasks and in their hopes and desires for secure livelihoods in the future (Gasper 2009, 2010a; Pegler 2011). It is in this dynamic context that we see the potential of civic innovation in production chains in our studies of the Amazon.

The resolution of competing 'logics' – efficiency by chain drivers vs well-being/social improvement for family producers/communities at source – is under pressure as chains evolve. The likelihood of representational security to promote labour gains depends on a delicate balance of thematic foci and local vs broader level structural embedding and legitimation. All of these dynamics we explore in the chapter as we look at the key concepts of social upgrading, agency and power relations and the contrasting and (often) ambiguous representational outcomes for peasant farmers in the Amazon. Our conclusion is that the chances of achieving a durable and inclusionary process of civic innovation, leading to social upgrading, is determined by the spatial intersection, as well as different negotiation capabilities, of the different interests involved in the representational process.

Gains from chain inclusion – social upgrading, agency/voice and power and representation

The literature on global chains has moved from the view that the involvement of firms and communities in global sourcing will necessarily lead to gains in skills, opportunities, material benefits and well-being. Even if firms and communities do integrate and economically upgrade, these can be led to ambiguous social gains, even social downgrading (Barrientos, Gereffi and Rossi 2011). This is especially the case where chain integration promotes a move away from diversified production to greater specialisation and reliance on a limited product and market focus. This is often the case in rural, agricultural and family farming situations.

Income/expected income is only one piece of the social upgrading story (Milberg and Winkler 2010). Others (Barrientos, Gereffi and Rossi 2011) put forward a more variegated classification of social upgrading as measurable and process based rights. Measurable rights improvements are generally more visible and objective – like health and safety standards, for example. Process rights are more intangible and include aspects of work conditions such as participation and representation. They are very hard to measure in effective terms but often determine a person's position and options. Without voice, most other rights and benefits are unachievable. Nevertheless, while this categorisation represents an advance, more is needed to help us understand the civic innovation process. It is important to look at the dynamics of power, subjectivity and normative positioning – occurring within and between families and communities in rurally based production settings.

Selwyn (2013) offers a view of social upgrading that focuses on the role of 'grass roots' representation for the achievement of better working conditions. He argues that meaningful social improvements at the work place are not promoted by firms, governments or international organisations. Beyond a certain point, firms simply choose not to implement social improvements because this would represent an additional cost of production, which could generate losses in competitive advantage. Meaningful social upgrading depends on change in the balance of power between workers and chain drivers. Civic innovation arising from the associational power of workers, in the form of unions (or other collective ways of representation – e.g. farmers associations; cooperatives), can strengthen their bargaining power and enable them to pressure firms towards more decent work conditions. Selwyn (2013) puts 'grass roots' representation at the core of the discussion on how workers and small-scale producers may achieve social upgrading, and in contrast to the ambiguous spaces within the 'politics of production' sees virtually no prospect that the state and other private actors can be significant movers of positive change in labour conditions. This view underlines an important and ongoing debate in respect to participative and representative dynamics. Nevertheless, representation as a way to achieve social improvement requires us to consider more explicitly notions of agency and power relations.

Labour geography literature has contributed to the notion of labour agency, linking work to the study of global value chains. Katz (2004) describes worker's agency as a multi-level conception that includes three main strategies. The first is resilience – small acts that help people to cope with their everyday reality but do not change social relations, e.g. migration (Sportel 2013). The second is reworking – improvement of material well-being, adjusting power relations and the distribution of resources, for example, through the expansion of access to education (Katz 2004). Thirdly there is resistance that challenges historically and geographically oppressive social relations, e.g. the organisation of collective campaigns to improve labour rights (Sportel 2013). These last two strategies of reworking and resistance are acts of civic innovation that may not only lead to decent work conditions through a change in dominant power relations, but also bring about deeper social improvements for entire communities.

Labour geography literature also treats agency as shaped by social (power) relations and subsequent livelihood strategies – which can be both enabling and hindering of people's decision making and agency potential and are embedded in a wider economic and cultural environment. For example, gender based social dynamics can restrict women's agency such as the division of labour within households (Carswell and De Neve 2013). This perspective is grounded in a broader notion like civic innovation that sees worker's agency in both vertical (the governance structures of the chain) and horizontal dimensions – local social relations and livelihood strategies (Coe and Hess 2013; Lund-Thomsen 2013).

Power in these processes can be very explicit, somewhat neutral (as with the 'rules of the game' e.g. for labour relations) or implicit in terms of 'messages'/ ideas which are suggestive as to how people should think, for example the idea of 'voluntarism as the process to achieve corporate social responsibility' (Valentin and Murillo 2009; see also Lukes 1977; Pegler 2011; Huxley 2008; Prince and Dufty 2009). All such forms of power affect peoples' ability to have agency in respect to which tasks they undertake and in their attitudes to the labour process. In this regard, it is important to modify labour process analysis in relation to family farming and by taking a futures/values perspective. Such an approach helps us to probe the nature of social upgrading more deeply from the perspective of these people involved in the process of civic innovation.

The multiple modalities of power relations within GVCs may enable family farmers to coordinate and mobilise ways to pressure for better conditions, but they can also constrain participation, representation and voice. In our case, both studies explore forms of representation, how these civic innovation processes evolved and whether people feel more secure and empowered as a result. At the same time, they define the boundaries within which family farmers have agency to upgrade, on their own terms. The varied nature of agency (i.e. either as a process of change (Giddens 1984) or as a typology of forms – e.g. tacit, accepting, rejecting, quietly modifying (Katz 2004)) requires careful study. Both cases used in this chapter are based on bottom up and power sensitive approaches to the people in the study, and take note of their actual vs desired and imagined futures. After a brief description of the case study contexts, the following subsections compare these labour process and representational dynamics from the perspective of civic innovation and the 'politics of production'.

Amazonian peasants – context, labour processes and representational dynamics

Amazonian peasants – açaí and oil palm cultivation

Açaí is[8] a black berry grown on a variety of palm tree (mainly in the Amazon region, especially in the state of Pará) that has been eaten by locals (*ribeirinhos*) for many centuries. The last decades have seen its rise in popularity as a healthy 'super' berry, in juices or other products, by consumers in broader Brazil and internationally. Most production appears to be based on traditional production techniques, which are very labour intensive. Mainly men and boys are involved in climbing and obtaining bunches of fruit whilst women and girls sometimes add sorting tasks to their traditional household and gardening chores.

The rising breadth and depth of demand of Açaí has raised questions concerning the impact of market demand on the livelihoods of

Amazonian workers, families and communities who cultivate açaí. These questions are set within a context where *ribeirinhos* move quite flexibly between tasks (gardening, fishing, transport, wood culling, retail and services) across quite a wide area. In this context it is also important to note that, while the state sometimes promotes small-scale (açaí) farmers, most of its support has been for large-scale commercial operations and the efficiency of their productive processes such as via land purchase subsidies, technology assistance and codification support (Pegler 2015b). The case study drawn from in this chapter is based on secondary and primary data on a number of small communities and families living to the west of Manaus/Codajás (in the state of Amazonas) and who supply late season, highly demanded product to these centres (Pegler 2015a, 2015b).

Oil palm (*Elaeis Guineensis*), unlike açaí, is not typical of the amazon region. It is a species native to West and Central Africa's rainforests. Due to specificities of its growth, 95 per cent of existing oil palm plantations in the world are located in a latitude range 10° north and south of the Equator line, restricting crops to tropical areas. In Brazil, the state of Pará is the biggest producer, representing 90 per cent of the country's entire production. Brazil is the country with the greatest capacity to produce palm oil in the world (Meijaard and Sheil 2013). However, Brazil's current palm oil production is insufficient to meet the country's internal demand. To overcome this situation the Brazilian government has been strongly investing in the expansion of oil palm plantations through the implementation of various public policies (some favouring small growers, others favouring more large-scale operations).

Most recently, these governmental policies have led to public–private partnerships (PPP) between the government, large companies and family farmers in order to increase income and improve family farmers' well-being and to promote sustainable agricultural practices in the Amazon region. This initiative was based on a pilot project started in 2002 with 150 family farmers from the municipality of Mojú located in the northeast of Pará. In this pilot partner-ship, the government was responsible for providing land and credit for the farmers, the company was responsible for buying production (oil palm seeds/fruit) and assisting with technical support, and the family farmers for culti-vating oil palm. An NGO (Peabiru Institute) entered this process as a social facilitator due to the need of the company to have civic involvement in order to gain certification credentials. The case study drawn on for this chapter is based on primary data collected in three small communities (Arauaí, São Vicente, and Soledade) where most of the family farmers from the pilot project reside (Marques Silva 2014).

What binds these two case studies is that both concern Amazon peasants whose working lives have traditionally combined a mix of products and tasks. Each group is now feeling pressure to specialise in products for (global) value chains. Work and the division of labour bring the family, community and the market very close together, determining local dynamics and power relations. Involvement in the chain will further shift these work processes, both practically and figuratively, complicating how people see their present and future pro-ductive relations.

The families' material conditions, representational situation and future prospects provide points of comparison. Palm oil is a shorter/clearer chain with one buyer, and the company needed civic support to gain quality credentials, creating an environment for civic innovation and social upgrading along with a fairly institutionalised representational process for these communities. In contrast, both market and buyer control is 'at a distance' in the case of açaí. There is no close-by lead firm or actor involved in chain governance. Yet there is a strong 'message' and coalition pushing for value capture, improvements in efficiency, and the codification and formalisation of production. Production relations are inefficient and representation is a long and broadly distributed process with various local and regional points and actors of importance.

It is possible that, under certain conditions, a move to a shorter, clearer chain for açaí could improve representational processes and social upgrading out-comes. Yet, a move to a less complex chain based, for example, on monoculture would remove the issue of labour representation completely as *ribeirinhos* would no longer be involved in production. The a priori view that açaí offers a clearer win-win-win sustainable ecological option for families, consumers and ecology would thus lose force under such a monoculture based scenario.

The following sections discuss further the civic innovation processes and social outcomes for these two case studies.

Amazonian peasants – economic upgrading and human security in labour processes

Açaí,[9] is showing considerable growth in demand, in Brazil and externally. Given this expanding market opportunity both *ribeirinho* suppliers and other actors have attempted to derive greater income and value. In terms of an income based vision of well-being improvement, despite the margins gained by transporters (*atravessadores*), families, especially those most involved in açaí, are making considerable returns from even a basic level of picking and sale. However, there remain questions as to how this has affected choices/options in terms of the division of labour, the degree to which market incentives are influencing behavior and in what this means for *ribeirinhos*' sense of human security, both now and in the future.

For example, in terms of livelihoods and labour processes, there is a mix between market specialisation and livelihood diversification. Income generation and upgrading has led to some modification in the structure of family work and a re-allocation of members amongst tasks such as plant care, climbing, picking, sorting and packing. An additional strategy is often to make (higher value added) açaí juice. Our study shows that there were clear limits to the degree to which labour is reallocated, the use of wage labour and in respect to a strategy based of producing higher 'value added' juice. Some families were well integrated in the açaí market but were not any more oriented more towards 'efficiency' than those less integrated in a market 'logic'.

This mixed result may reflect the newness of the chain and thus an uneven impact of pressures to adopt capitalist production and labour processes and be more fully commodified. It could also illustrate reworking and a certain degree of social or culturally based resilience or resistance to change. In either case, these mixed outcomes for labour processes do seem to underline a degree of uncertainty about markets/livelihoods (this product in particular, and livelihoods in general) and a need for families to find a balance between independence and dependency in evolving market conditions.

On the other hand, a sense of powerlessness and dependency is more clearly pronounced for women family members. For example, to be involved in açaí has required modified task structures, with women becoming involved in sorting, occasional tree climbing and decisions in respect to which children work with açaí (vs traditional tasks) or even with other new tasks – e.g. working the new, now affordable washer. Yet in contrast to other studies (Fraze, Witkoski and Silva 2011) which highlight women's key role in some activities, few indications emerged of how women's roles were recognised in either income or non-income terms. There were some instances of women taking on other forms of work outside the house. However women had a restricted role with respect to this 'new black gold'. Only men close the bags and decide on sale/pass them on whereas, whilst silent, women were regularly observed to take on aggressive stares and posturing at point of sale. Women were, however, more vocal about the destabilising impacts of youth 'vagrancy' on local communities and social relations, especially by youth who were making considerable cash sums from occasional picking and sale to transporters.

Asking about their human security and dependency revealed further important insights (Pegler 2015b). For instance, few beyond the most poor saw açaí as a threat to their traditional ways. It is seen as 'another wave in the rise and fall of the rivers'. This sense of uncertainty was not perceived as a problem per se, people said they would wait and see what it brought for their security of life. Many wanted açaí to be more strongly promoted for them and their community.

From a socio-ecological point of view, their answers to questions were quite disconcerting. In contrast to a view that açaí offers a win-win-win option, those most involved in açaí were not acting with an awareness of ecological impact for the future. Those most involved in açaí were also likely to be engaged in illegal logging. They were positioned somewhere between what has been called 'wise forest managers' and 'chain saw peasants'[10], at least until açaí offers a more secure livelihood than wood sales (Pegler 2015b).

The mixed picture of labour processes, opportunities and human security as a result of inclusion in the açaí chain illustrates various levels of agency and resistance by Amazonians. To some degree there is acceptance and even positive support for what the market is 'proposing'. At the same time, they take a wait and see approach to the future, one that many see in positive terms when considering acai. Yet there are other members of these communities who are not so central. This includes youth who can gain large amounts of cash from casual açaí work but who are often perceived as part of broader social problems. Women are also excluded from the wealth, power and prestige being generated by this 'new superfruit'. The problems of voice for youth and women are more pronounced for this less developed (açaí) region (Amazonas) than in the state of Pará where trade and cooperative processes are more evolved for both açaí and palm oil.[11] The sense of exclusion and lack of opportunities for youth underlines frustration with local development prospects and explains the resultant movement of the young away from such localities.

In contrast, at the beginning of the palm oil partnership, women and men worked together planting and caring for the plantations (Marques Silva 2014). However, as a perennial species oil palm does not require intensive care after the stabilisation of production; after its third year the main task in the field is harvesting, which removes women from plantation work. The acquisition of animals or machineries and the reduction in the workload also spares women from heavy and dangerous work with the oil palm crop. In addition to taking care of household tasks, women cultivate subsistence crops (cassava, rice, maize), look after family businesses (including grocery stores and restaurants) and take on other roles in the community such as civil servants and sellers. Adult male children usually help their parents in oil palm production as well as being involved in other work activities or studying.

Our research found that family farmers experience a substantial increase in their income due to (oil palm) cultivation activity, which led them to contract local workers to help with production. These contract workers were usually paid per day of work or per ton harvested.[12] Whilst this type of work agreement is illegal according to Brazilian legislation, because it does not fully guarantee labour rights to workers, many family farmers used to hire, on average, up to three workers to harvest their production. Since the beginning of 2014 this practice has been eliminated. In order to comply with the Roundtable on

Sustainable Palm Oil Principles and Criteria (RSPO P&C),[13] the firm that participates in the PPP agreement demanded the regularisation of work in the family farmers' plantations using the threat of rescinding the partnership contract if such subcontracting continued.

When the government first proposed the partnership for the cultivation of oil palm, family farmers were afraid to participate. Oil palm plantations were not common amongst family farmers in the region because they did not have the expertise in its cultivation. Notwithstanding, after more than 10 years producing oil palm seeds, the large majority of those interviewed declared that their income and material well-being had improved considerably. Family farmers also pointed to the availability of credit as another one of the main benefits of partnership. Before starting to cultivate oil palm many farmers did not have a bank account or access to credit. This situation changed with the increase in their income and security due to the PPP arrangement. Currently, a local bank offers family farmers credit facilities which enables them to invest in oil palm production (e.g. purchasing tractors or horses) or in other activities (e.g. the cultivation of other crops or the establishment of small business), as well as in the purchase of consumer durables.

The increase in family farmers' income also benefitted their communities. Local businesses were developed (e.g. grocery stores, restaurants and a transportation company were opened) and jobs were created. This new situation arrested the degree of migration from rural to urban areas and brought people back from cities to the villages. Moreover, the creation of the partnership was crucial for the construction of roads and the establishment of power services in the region. A reduction in deforestation was also noted as an important improvement in the region since the establishment of the partnership. Many family farmers used to work with illegal wood exploitation before entering the oil palm project. Additionally, the PPP may have prevented land from being taken over and exploited by big farmers and cattle raisers, which often resulted in environmental degradation and migration to urban areas.

These values, activities and impacts can be seen as positive community spinoffs from social upgrading. They contrast significantly with the example of açaí where youth are moving away, wood exploitation sees little change and where women are quite silent but frustrated. We look below at the nature of civic innovation involved in these representational processes and the balance of power and dependency within the 'politics of production'.

Civic innovation by Amazonian peasants – representational strategies and the politics of production

As suggested earlier, the power context surrounding agency and security in this fledgling açaí value chain situation is more splayed than for the palm oil study area. Distances between homesteads, ports and processing are considerable and the transport process can be complex. Yet formal market structures and rules are rapidly evolving and encroaching on the social relations and activities of these *ribeirinhos* (see Pegler 2015a), as is summarised below.

In 2000 the local centre and hub of açaí in the region (Codajás) became home to a government supported factory and cooperative. Up to 2009 the factory produced blocks of açaí (up to eight tons per day) for various Brazilian and overseas markets but since then has encountered problems due to disputes over quality processes. It built on the reputation of the town as a cultural referent for acai, with an Açaí Festival since 1987, and sought to supply and run the factory via a cooperative of local producers.

Original ideas were that the cooperative would pay average rates (smooth incomes) during the season and deliver benefits to producer members through training, employment opportunities, technical advice and (later) even credit. Yet few of these benefits emerged and any generalised sense of collectivity appears to have evaporated. The majority of local production moves through the town's port but not through the factory. Most factory workers are family of the managers and most suppliers are traders offloading excess capacity, not local producer families.

Despite this, there are various plans (Pegler 2015a) to regain factory certification and reassert Codajás as a dominant centre for açaí value added and trade. This includes tapping into state and federal guaranteed local purchase schemes and technical assistance programmes and sorting out quality, certification and logistics difficulties via links with prominent regional buyers. Various factions and power figures at a local level (also producers) are involved in this process. These factions are also in competition to be the key promoter of a more formalised, codified and efficient model for açaí supply and sale.

The coordination process and key drivers of this process are evolving, yet the message of formalised efficiency is clear. Still, few local producers express any affinity with this process, the cooperative or with key power brokers who sometimes pass by their communities with information on production issues/ government programmes or just for a chat. To be effective other actors must find a way to offer these families a trusted alternative avenue of representational security.

Alternative avenues for voice for the açaí producing families, as opposed to the Codajás cooperative, include the union of rural workers (Sindicato dos Trabalhadores Rurais – STR), a Fish Cooperative, an Association of local Codajás growers and a myriad of local associations. The STR is an established institution, it offers social benefits and has been linked to successful efforts to improve land tenure/reduce land insecurity. Yet distances, resources and their agricultural connection make it difficult for STR to connect to these disparate communities. The local açaí association shares these geographical problems and has even fewer of these benefits.

On the other hand, the fish cooperative represents producers (including açaí producers) of another newly emerging and profitable product – Amazon fish – and has cleverly linked sustainable concerns and income security for local residents via its out of season fish subsidy and technical assistance programmes. Another popular actor, local resident associations, raise and discuss both economic and social issues at regular, albeit male dominated, meetings in the communities.

As suggested earlier, few local producers show faith in or link to the cooperative in Codajás. Some older family members were still connected to the STR and various families divide membership of family members between the STR and fish colony. The sample was also divided (Pegler 2015a) between those with quite an economic and individualised perspective (the most advanced producers), and those with social, sustainability and collective sector development desires of their representatives – most of the middle level producers. Nearly all respondents, on the other hand, appreciated the immediate local focus of the local associations but lamented their lack of influence in respect to state based services such as welfare, education and health.

Representational insecurities (see Pegler 2015b) were registered amidst growing concern that powerful agents and plans are on their way for the formalisation, codification, taxation and control of their newest (market based) value generating product. Representational demands are both horizontal (local) but also vertical (chain based) and this makes the task of any representative agency particularly challenging. Moreover, responses underlined a variety of views within these *ribeirinho* communities. At times they highlight, for example, purely economic vs sector/community concerns, while at others the group was divided between idealism and pragmatism in relation to açaí cultivation vs wood extraction.

The study shows that *ribeirinhos* live a fluid existence. They have flexible tasks and move between the formal and informal sectors. Ironically this may be holding back both the encroachment of sector governance by powerful actors, and also rendering more difficult the task of representative agencies and social sustainability actors to make further inroads into their representation and the further promotion of sustainable futures. The voice and opportunities of youth and women family members appear quite minimal within this new wave of value chains in the Amazon.

In contrast, representation is more institutionalised and representative. Two associations were created to represent the family farmers involved in oil palm cultivation. Each family farmer association, the Association of Arauaí (with 100 members) and the Association of Soledade (with 50 members), has a director elected by the members of the association by simple majority and a board chosen by the director to assist her or him. Only members of the association can apply to be director and the mandate lasts two years. The director and her/his board do not earn a salary or any other formal benefit as a result of their positions. In addition to representing the interests of family farmers, the associations' boards are also responsible for the associations' budgets (Marques Silva 2014).

There is one open meeting with the director/board and family farmers every month in each association, at which representatives of the private company also participate. The government should be present in these meetings as well, but they have not attended any of these since the establishment of the PPP. In meetings, any associate who desires to express an opinion or raise a complaint has the right to do so.[14] However, usually less than half of the association's members attend meetings.

The majority of the interviewees declared that they were satisfied with the work of their respective boards, and that they believe the associations well represent the interests of family farmers (Marques Silva 2014). However, some farmers claimed that the associations' boards could be more efficient and look for better conditions for them. Previous directors of the Association of Arauaí and Soledade stated that the board works to bring benefits to the farmers and their communities. However, they feel that it is sometimes difficult to make improvements because they do not have enough strength to pressure the government or the company. Their bargaining power is weak since they occupy a very vulnerable position within the PPP.

With the absence of the government and having just one buyer (until few years ago the firm with whom they are in partnership was the only company buying oil palm seeds in the region)[15] family farmers have developed a highly dependent relationship with the firm. In addition, their low levels of education, minimal expertise in oil palm cultivation and markets, and (perhaps oddly) their satisfaction with their income, all contribute to this dependency. Family farmers are dependent on the company for the running of their entire production and, consequently, their freedom to make their own decisions is constrained. For instance, it is the enterprise that provides them with fertilisers, pesticides and safety material. The firm buys the chemicals and equipment and resells them to the family farmers, controlling quantities to be used and how they will be managed within the plantation. In this scenario family farmers are not independent producers, they become (effectively) more like employees of the company and their capacity to resist or change this situation (their agency) is hindered by this ambiguous reality.

In this sense, despite having freedom of association, institutionalised representation and (alleged) high levels of satisfaction with their representatives, the accomplishment of better social and work conditions (e.g. safety equipment, better roads, education, healthcare, etc.) by family farmers is limited and depends primarily on the firm's good will. The fact that much of this good will may have been due to the company's need to gain certification adds caution as to the durability of this situation. Further, the way in which the partnership has been configured hinders the degree of agency of family farmers and their capacity to take responsibility for their business. Their inclusion in the palm oil global network has certainly increased income and the livelihood strategies of family farmers, but this status quo is very fragile. It is highly dependent on the company and thus not sustainable.

These family farmers have the potential room for manoeuvre to become more independent. Many of them can count on other livelihood activities or envisage stopping producing the fruit which could put the company in a very sensitive situation with its buyers and consumers. But they are afraid to lose what they have gained; they were very poor and had so little before the PPP. This situation constrains the accomplishment of further and perhaps more varied and fundamental, social and economic benefits.

In contrast to the açaí situation, the palm oil example suggests that having both more local and more institutionalised representation does not necessarily mean that small-scale producers will have voice or will be heard. The way in which these family farmers are inserted both helps and constrains their agency and consequently a fuller attainment of social upgrading. Chain simplicity and proximity may help bring some benefits but do not necessarily help to promote an active, independent and enduring civic innovation process. The balance of power in relations between producers and other chain actors in the 'politics of production' and the degree of clarity of governmental support underwrite the probability and types of social upgrading which can emerge as a result of civic action.

Summary: reflections and implications

Our study illustrates the representational dynamics of civic innovation – how durable, inclusive and respectful of diversity can such engagements in value chains be? The analysis confirms the mosaic of market, subjectivities and actor dynamics inherent in civic innovation. While both cases involve small-scale, rural Amazon producers supplying value chains, it is important to note the chain and context when considering whether civic engagement could improve well-being.

Using the framework of the 'politics of production' helps to see that civic innovation in these contexts can lead to cautiously positive but also ambiguous outcomes for these two groups of family farmers. The mix of personal, collective, local and global values are tainted by uncertainty. The two case studies provide both distinct opportunities and threats to family farmer welfare. Notwithstanding these differences, in both cases it remains uncertain to what extent larger scale commercialised production enables or inhibits family farmer welfare. This was not helped by a state that displayed an ambiguous role via its support for both small-scale and large-scale commercial production.

What is important is whether the representational processes involved in these forms of civic innovation can lead to less dependent relations and support producers' ambitions, for family farmers overall, and in particular for women and youth. The ability to exercise agency remains central. Overall, actors need to find an acceptable balance between local and global sources of influence on their livelihoods. It was here that the closeness of actors within the chain clearly had important, visible and immediate impacts on the potential for representation and expression in the case of palm oil families. It is interesting to note that the palm oil case seems to provide a broader and more optimistic model for participation and voice than the representational situation facing açaí producing families. It is based on a PPP, a state endorsed civil society based model of local cooperative relations and demonstrable gains, in which also women, youth, the environment and local development processes have been helped. All these outcomes contrasted starkly with the case of açaí.

However, despite the looming threat of monoculture plantations for açaí, an ironic (albeit perhaps temporary) outcome for açaí workers is that the 'spaces' for fuller expression and representation may be more open for them due to the distances and present logistical complications of the açaí production chain. Palm oil producing families working in a short, sharp and clearer commercial relationship are dependent on the good will of one company, which allowed their representation in order to illustrate the necessary credentials to receive market certification. Pivot or pressure points are necessary but are quite possibly still temporary and not sufficient guarantees that family farmers will gain voice and representation and thus social benefits from their inclusion in global value chains.

This chapter provides a small step forward in understanding social change and sustainable futures for small-scale producers,[16] bearing in mind that the durability of any social upgrading in the face of market processes is never certain. Chain simplicity/shortness may or may not promote social upgrading and community spinoffs. Codification may also help or hinder social upgrading and representational security. The studies here suggest that social upgrading and representational security depend more on the governance that evolves within the chain and the balance of power embodied in the rules operating in the state and market in relation to worker and producer rights.

What is important for a positive civic innovation outcome – of inclusion and respect of voice/positions (diversity) and their durability – is that all members of supplier families have the independence, space, resources and capabilities to decide, without prejudice, how they engage in markets. It is hard to see, in the types of rural situations reviewed in this chapter, how this can occur without clearer, more unambiguous support for labour and small farmers by state agencies. Processes of civic innovation need to work to ensure that chain inclusion and mainstreaming of small-scale producers are inclusive and promote livelihoods for all the community.

Notes

1 These debates also call into question what we mean by gains (i.e. social upgrading), the materiality of these 'gains' but also their relation to subjective evaluations of one's position and welfare, now and in the future (Gasper 2009, 2010b; Pegler 2011). In a broader and future looking sense, ecological sustainability is just as important as social sustainability/social upgrading and the renewability of the environment places a finite limit (sometimes explicitly, sometimes implicitly) on future exploitation of these resources.

2 One is from Pegler 2015a and Pegler 2015b and the other is from Marques Silva 2014.

3 The evolving civic innovation agenda looks at the prospect of 'responsible" markets; in respect to gendered politics and; in relation to the probability of civic agency between the micro and macro levels.

4 This volume – Introduction, p. 1.

5 This is enhanced if 1) the chain/transactions are simple, 2) the ability to codify product quality/processes is high, and 3) if the capacity of the supply base (firms) is high.
6 I.e. producers = workers; diversified production; various degrees of commodification/ market engagement by activity.
7 E.g. there are multiple points of production (thus possible contestation) for those often carrying out varied, diversified livelihoods.
8 Below is a summary of açaí and its local production process as detailed in Pegler 2015b.
9 See Pegler 2015b, which the following paragraphs summarise/paraphrase, for a detailed discussion of labour processes and human security processes and impacts.
10 First raised as an issue/possible contrast by Nugent 2002 and nuanced/elaborated on in Pegler 2015b.
11 A forthcoming study based on the same methodology but for the region of Curalinho, Marajo (Pará) shows a much higher degree of development and cohesiveness with respect to representative processes and some (but not extensive) differences in women's participation and recognition.
12 One family farmer said he used to pay a worker US$ 8 per day of work and another declared that they paid US$ 22 per ton harvested.
13 In order to maintain the RSPO certification all Agropalma suppliers need to comply with the principals and criteria (P&C) of the certificate, which also includes the family farmers.
14 The meetings normally happen on the first Saturday morning of every month and can last several hours, depending on the numbers of subjects and farmers who want to deliver an opinion.
15 Currently there are other companies operating in the region and also establishing public-private partnerships with smallholder farmers.
16 Civic innovation is understood as inclusionary, accounting for complexity of intersectionalities and these characteristics are durable so that the subjects do not lose their identity when up-scaled (Biekhart, Harcourt and Knorringa – Chapter 1, this volume).

References

Barrientos, S., Gereffi, G. and Rossi, A. (2011) 'Economic and Social Upgrading in Global Production Networks: Developing a Framework for Analysis', *ILO Review*, 150(3–4): 319–340.
Braverman, H. (1974) *Labour and Monopoly Capital*, New York: Monthly Review Press.
Burawoy, M. (1985) *The Politics of Production*, London: Verso.
Burawoy, M. (ed.) (2000) *Global Ethnography – Forces, Connections and Imaginations in a PostModern World*, Berkeley: University of California Press.
Carswell, G. and De Neve, G. (2013) 'Labouring for Global Markets: Conceptualising Labour Agency in Global Production Networks', *Geoforum*, 44(1): 62–70.
Coe, N. and Hess, M. (2013) 'Global Production Networks, Labour and Development', *Geoforum*, 44(1): 4–9.
Fraxe, T.J.P., Witkoski, A.C. and Silva, S.C.P. (2011) 'A Pesca na Amazonia Central – Ecologia, conhecimento traditional e formas de manejo' [Fishing in Central Amazonia: Ecology, traditional knowledge and forms of management], in Fraxe, T.J.P., Pereira, H.S. and Witkoski, A.C. (eds), *Comunidades ribeirinhas amazônicas: modos de vida e uso dos recursos naturais* [Amazonian Ribeirinho communities: modes of life and use of natural resources]. 1st edn. Manaus: EDUA.

Gasper, D. (2009) 'Capitalism and Human Flourishing? The Strange Story of Bias in Activity and the Downgrading of Work', Institute of Social Studies, Working Paper, 469, The Hague.

Gasper, D. (2010) 'Understanding the Diversity of Conceptions of Well-being and Quality of Life', *The Journal of Socio-Economics*, 39: 351–360.

Gasper, D. (2010) 'Climate Change and the Language of Human Security', Institute of Social Studies, Working Paper, 505, The Hague.

Giddens, A. (1984) *The Constitution of Society: Outline of the Theory of Structuration*, Berkeley: University of California Press.

Humphrey, J. and Schmitz, H. (2002) 'How Does Insertion in Global Value Chains Affect Upgrading in Industrial Clusters?' *Regional Studies*, 36(9): 1017–1027.

Huxley, M. (2008) 'Space and Government: Governmentality and Geography', *Geography Compass*, 2(5): 1635–1658.

Katz, C. (2004) *Growing Up Global: Economic Restructuring and Children's Everyday Lives*, Minneapolis: University of Minnesota Press.

Knorringa, P. and Pegler, L. (2006) 'Globalisation, Firm Upgrading and Impacts on Labour', *TESG – Journal of Social Geography* – Special Issue, 97(5): 468–477.

Lukes, S. (1977) *Power – a Radical View*, 3rd edn, London: Macmillan.

Lund-Thomsen, P. (2013) 'Labor Agency in the Football Manufacturing Industries of Sialkot, Paskistan', *Geoforum*, 44(1): 71–81.

Marques Silva, W. (2014) 'What Does Social Upgrading Mean for Small Scale Producers? Family Farmers and Oil Palm Cultivation – A View of Possibilities and Constraints', MA thesis, IOB/University of Antwerp, Belgium.

Meijaard, E. and Sheil, D. (2013) 'Oil-Palm Plantations in the Context of Biodiversity Conservation', in Levin, S.A. (ed.) *Encyclopedia of Biodiversity*, 5(2): 600–612.

Milberg, W. and Winkler, D. (2010) 'Economic and Social Upgrading in Global Production Networks: Problems of Theory and Measurement', *Capturing the Gains*, Working Paper 4.

Nugent, S. (2002) 'Whither O Campesinato? Historical Peasantries of the Brazilian Amazon', *Journal of Peasant Studies*, 29(3–4): 162–189.

Pegler, L. (2011) 'Sustainable Value Chains and Labour – Linking Chain Drivers and "Inner Drivers"', ISS Working Paper, no. 525, Den Haag.

Pegler, L. (2015a) 'Human Security in Evolving Global Value Chains (GVCs): Reconsidering Labour Agency in a Livelihoods' Context', in Newsome, K., Taylor, P., Blair, J. and Rainnie, A. (eds), *Putting Labour in its Place: Labour Process Analysis and Global Value Chains*, London: Palgrave (CPWE – Critical Perspectives on Work and Employment Series), 213–230.

Pegler, L. (2015b) 'Peasant Inclusion in Global Value Chains: Economic Upgrading but Social Downgrading in Labour Processes?' *Journal of Peasant Studies*, November.

Prince, R. and Dufty, R. (2009) 'Assembling the Space Economy: Governmentality and Economic Geography', *Geography Compass*, 3(5): 1744–1756.

Selwyn, B. (2013) 'Social Upgrading and Labour in Global Production Networks: A Critique and an Alternative Conception', *Competition and Change*, 17(1): 75–90.

Sportel, T. (2013) 'Agency within a Socially Regulated Labour Market: A Study of "Unorganized" Agricultural Labour in Kerala', *Geoforum*, 47(2013): 42–52.

Vallentin, S. and Murillo, D. (2009) 'CSR as Governmentality', Copenhagen Business School – Centre for Corporate Responsibiliity, Working Paper, 4/2009.

8 Exploring embodiment and intersectionality in transnational feminist activist research

Wendy Harcourt, Rosalba Icaza and Virginia Vargas

Introduction

This chapter is the outcome of a 'trialogue' across the Atlantic via the Internet on civic innovation. The text is driven by our shared interest in finding possible ways in which our activist-research experiences, marked by troubled but intense dialogue with feminist and non-feminist communities and individuals, could contribute to civic innovation research and praxis. We asked ourselves the question: 'How can the concepts of embodiment, intersectionality, decoloniality and critical interculturality that have been so important to feminist theory and practice inform the concept of civic innovation?' Our conversation reflects on the notion and praxis of embodiment aware of the experiences of the living body (Harcourt 2009) and the importance of intersectionality in feminist analysis (Crenshaw 1989, 2013).[1]

We base our conversation on our own experiences in transnational feminist practice and research. In engaging in this conversation we have co-constructed a critical self-reflection on our own practices as activists-researchers 'doing' civic innovation in Latin America and Europe with a meeting point at the International Institute of Social Studies (ISS). We are consciously drawing attention to our different positionalities as feminists, researchers and gendered beings as we cross diverse knowledge and epistemic boundaries.

The chapter is built up from shared conversations and self-reflections about embodied understanding of intersectional 'identities' in relation to transnational feminist activism. In the chapter we begin with a definition of the main concepts with which we engage – embodiment, intersectionality, decoloniality and critical interculturality. We then share three stories in order to analyse our everyday living and engagement as feminists in different communities, social movements and NGO policy contexts. Each of us describes how our research practices generate ways of understanding embodiment, intersectionality, decoloniality and interculturality. Following the stories we turn to look at how this feminist praxis can contribute to the conceptualization of civic innovation specifically in the university context of the ISS where Rosalba and Wendy currently teach – and where Gina taught in the past. We conclude by reflecting on the importance of research for civic innovation around the issues of embodiment and intersectionality, decoloniality and critical interculturality.

Shaping our common ground

In the process of writing this piece as a critical self-reflection we found ourselves engaged in a particular type of epistemology that required us to identify a common language and agreement about the central concepts to which our different narratives speak. The way we worked together in putting together this chapter was enabled by our meetings in different occasions at the CIRI Forum in 2013, the CIRI 2014 retreat (see the Introduction for more about these two events) as well as private conversations in each other's homes and many email exchanges. In writing the chapter we generated a strong trust in each other's points of view. All three of us were initiators, editors and reviewers. The result is not seamless, but after one person proposed a definition of the key concepts (body politics and embodiment, intersectionality, decoloniality and critical interculturality) we then discussed and redefined them in our face to face and on-line conversations. The end result was that we found common ground from which to co-write the piece and communicate this shared understanding with our readers, while we still thought it important to retain the three stories that we chose as our entry point into the discussions.

Body politics and embodiment

Our understanding of embodiment comes from the rich tradition of feminist theory on the body; international development policy related to bodies and popular writings on the female body as a site of political action. We understand bodies as sites of cultural meaning, social experience and political resistance (Grosz 1994).

Ever since Michel Foucault (1976) explored resistance to systemic power on the body, Western feminist theory has aimed to retell narratives about female embodiment in order to unsettle presumed concepts of biological sex and gender. Judith Butler (1993) has challenged dominant views of embodiment in order to unpack how tradition and modernity are played out on the lived body. Other feminist theorists such as Inderpal Grewal and Cora Kaplan (1994) have contributed to this work challenging the conceptual frameworks that bind male and female embodied experiences in dominant macro frameworks of politics, economics, culture and society. In these feminist writings aspects of female embodiment (such as pregnancy, rape and aging) become privileged sites of significance bearing on how female experience is lived (Shildrick 1997; Young 2005).

Gayatri Chakravorty Spivak (1987, 1999) and Chandra Talpade Mohanty (2003) look at how the experience of female embodiment is informed by sexism, racism, misogyny and heterosexism. Following Spivak and Mohanty feminist writings on body politics in colonialism have explored how bodies, sex and race are intertwined in imperial and colonial medicine and science (Tamale 2011; Wieringa and Sivori 2012). These feminist writings show how the corporeal, fleshly, material existence of bodies is deeply embedded in political relations, from colonialism to population control policies to contemporary biopolitics of migration.

Body politics in the last decades, then, positions the body as site of resistance. Demands for bodily integrity have led to an expansion of rights linking the political dimension of the body with a radical form of democracy (Hartmann 1995; Vargas 2005). Social, cultural and economic institutions and discourses shape and are being shaped by body politics as feminism challenges dominant norms making body politics a key mobilizing force for gender equality, sexuality and human rights.

To include a body politics perspective in the analysis of policy and political economy, means that we consider our bodies as produced and transformed by social relations embedded in the hegemony of colonial hetero-patriarchal capitalism. Hence, our bodies are shaped by exploitative relations and domination as well as by ethnic-racial, sexual and generation discriminations. Our bodies are the primary territory, where mechanisms of domination operate (for example in public health and education or in the biopolitics of security and food). At the same time, it is in our bodies where resistances and rebellions are expressed in the form of ethnic-racial, territorial, gender, transgender, disability movements. In this sense, our bodies are carriers of rights and citizenship (Ávila 2014).

Intersectionality

Our understanding of intersectionality comes from the work of Black feminism and standpoint theoreticians such as Kimberle Crenshaw (1989) and Patricia Hill Collins (2000). Intersectionality emerged as an attempt to challenge the idea of 'woman' as a homogenous category and the experience of oppression for other women when the concept 'white middle class heterosexual women' is taken unquestioningly as the norm.

More specifically, intersectionality as a concept recognizes the inseparability of systems and institutions of oppression such as classism, sexism, racism, homophobia, ageism, ablism and transphobia. It introduces an analysis that is attentive to the complex interactions of these systems of oppression, including their mutual and simultaneous reinforcement, and to their impacts on lives, bodies, sexualities and subjectivities.

As a theory of the social experiences of oppression (McCall 2005), intersectionality analyses the mechanisms and logics that interlock multiple forms of oppression. As such, it should not be confused with an attempt to aggregate abstract identities or social positions that tend to be essentialized or treated as fixed 'in the neoliberal [celebratory] equity/diversity regime' (Bilge 2013: 407). Intersectionality has been used as an analytical device deeply grounded in historical and socio-cultural analysis of incarnated experiences of subjugation in relation to oppressions and power precisely to avoid essential identities or full abstraction of in constant flux identities.[2]

We understand intersectionality not only as a heuristic device or powerful theory of oppression, but as holding 'critical potential for social-justice-oriented change' (Bilge 2013: 405). In this way, intersectionality has allowed us to be politically involved as feminist academics-activists in processes that seek 'generating counter-hegemonic and transformative knowledge production, activism, pedagogy, and non-oppressive coalitions' (Bilge 2013: 405).

Therefore, intersectionality is not only an analytical tool but it is also a political perspective holding epistemic consequences for more complex and democratic understandings. For example, acknowledging the interdependence of oppressions and exclusions allows us to understand in what way they inter-lock to produce structural and political cultural and socio-economic impacts for some but not all people. If we look at where people are placed along the axis where difference and inequality intersect we can see how vulnerability intensifies. In this sense, racism amplifies sexism and affects opportunities (i.e. employment); class exploitation might contribute to reinforce sexism and homophobia; heteronormativity affects lesbian, gays and trans people.

At the same time, in relation to feminisms, an intersectional perspective allows us to understand that women's experiences and histories are multiple and that there is no unique or universal category that expresses what it is to be a woman. This means that it is not possible to analyse discrimination against woman as only linked to gender, or as a product of sexism, racism or class. Instead, what needs to be analysed is the simultaneity of co-existent structures.

Furthermore, the capacity to understand this intersection of exclusions and resistances generates a specific form of knowledge, characterized by a per-spective on the female subject as multiple in her experiences and subjectivities. Women, as subjects of knowledge are embodied and live in material social structures as racialized, sexualized subjects and as such generate situated knowledges (Haraway 2013). Understanding knowledge as situated recognizes that knowledge is not 'pure', 'objective' or 'complete' but partial because it is fed by multiple viewpoints emerging from the many crossing axes of oppression. The partiality of such knowledge, for Amaia Perez Orozco, is 'an epistemic resource that allows us to approach subjects not from our own partiality, but from the acceptance of other forms of understanding the world, social relations, cultures and cosmovisions'. This approach to knowledges makes unavoidable a critical intercultural perspective that overcomes a monoculture of knowledge (Orozco 2014).

Critical interculturality

We use the term critical interculturality as originally developed by Panikkar (2000) and re-worked by Walsh (2012) to refer to dialogues among 'others' which allows us to listen and host differences and radical otherness. The characteristic of this hosting is its capacity to challenge our own presuppositions and assumptions as carriers of partial knowledges. As a practice, critical interculturality has been recently understood as an epistemic and political project that asks about what, why and for what knowledge (Walsh 2012), opening new way of conceiving the building and production of knowledge.

We use critical interculturality in order to retrieve other voices, knowledge and ways of thinking, to appreciate different worldviews that speak of the complexity of reality and the multiple ways of living and being given the complexity of oppressions and privileges that all of us carry. This perspective requires us to recognize the incompleteness of any political proposal that does not dialogue with other forms of life, other ways of building identities and producing knowledge, and asks us to assume an ethical-political commitment with the incorporation of diversity into our ways of living, thinking and coexistence.

From this perspective, critical interculturality has a central role in the democratization of society because it seeks to connect diverse ways of experiencing, thinking and sensing, including those that have been excluded or have been subalternized in modernization processes.

Decoloniality

We engage with the notion of decoloniality as an epistemic and political option to think–act–feel and build relationships and coalitions as feminist academics–activists from the perspective of coloniality. Working from the perspective of coloniality means recognizing those embodied, lived experiences that have been produced in dominant knowledges as absence or as invisible in modern thought, including feminist histories.

Decoloniality is a term coined by the modernity/coloniality/decoloniality group of intellectuals and activists committed to confront and delink from 'the colonial matrix of power' (Mignolo 2011). The colonial matrix of power is understood as the complex interlocking of (read intersectionality of) racism, epistemic eurocentrism, violent and consented westernization of subjectivities and the heterosexual modern/colonial order (Lugones 2010; Mignolo 2007, 2011; Quijano 2000; Walsh 2012).

Therefore, coloniality has been differentiated from colonialism and considered as the dark side of modernity, which implies the domination of others outside the European core as a necessary dimension of modernity. Coloniality is then an epochal condition and an epistemological frame built by capitalism, racism, eurocentrism, westernization and heterosexual order. It is also understood as a logic that justifies oppression, exploitation and violence in the name of salvation, modernity, progress, development and modernization, democracy and freedom.

In its epistemic-knowledge dimension, in the Latin American experience, coloniality expressed since the 'discovery' and subsequent conquest of the Americas in 1492 as the imposition of one valid form of producing knowledge that reclaimed for itself universality.[3] This is the case of positivism and the supposedly objective logic that separates what/whom is being observed (the object) from who observes (the subject).

A decolonial shift in its epistemic dimension would require a reversal of this logic by bringing positionality, hence situated-fleshly-lived knowledges, as a central tenet of critical theorizing, one that is both geographically and body located. From the perspective of decolonial feminism a reinterpretation of capitalism and modernity is undertaken through the historical analysis of the imposition of gender through colonization (Lugones 2010).

Decolonization requires scholars and activists to recover knowledges that have been labelled as folkloric or traditional, acknowledging them as knowledges. For example, Maria Lugones has contributed to the project of decoloniality by showing how the colonial system contains complex interlinkages with race, sex and patriarchy. Maria Lugones' work presents a critical re-consideration of 'gender' as an analytical category that has been widely used and misused in development discourses and interventions in the last three decades allowing for other genealogies to think about women, gender, sexuality and the body that does not belong to the western philosophical tradition. Another example comes from Bolivian feminists who confront state policy with the powerful slogan: there is no decolonization without the elimination of patriarchy (*despatriarcalizacion*).

In the sections that follow, each of us make use of these concepts of embodiment, intersectionality, decoloniality and critical interculturality in order to present our stories of transnational feminist research and praxis and make sense of possible contributions to civic innovation. We do so from different locations and feminist histories, ones that have intertwined in our work together in transnational feminist activism and in our research and teaching at the ISS. We explore our understanding of embodiment and intersectionality as well as the political project of critical interculturality and decoloniality in Latin American contexts but also more experimentally in geographically located European experiences.

Our stories and self-reflections

Virginia (Gina) first reflects on her research and advocacy work in the Latin American feminist 'encounters' (specifically the XIII Latin American and Caribbean (LAC) Feminist Encounter held in November 2014[4]) and the international feminist dialogues of the World Social Forum. She examines how the concepts of embodiment and intersectionality are 'lived' in the discussions and actions that recognize 'difference'.

Rosalba then shares her experiences as a feminist activist researcher politically engaged with indigenous women resistances in Mexico while physically/ professionally based in Europe. She reflects on her research practices as an International Relations scholar and how she has tried to engage with the otherness of the other, radical difference. She reflects on the possibilities of intersectionality and embodied thought to acknowledge different ways of being/knowing/feeling.

Wendy, an Australian living in Europe, ends these stories by reflecting on her experience as a feminist activist researcher in the work of the European Feminist Forum, exploring how intersectionality, embodiment and critical interculturality can be seen to inform feminist practice in the European context.

Gina: learning from (the making of) the Latin American feminist encounters

My contribution elaborates embodiment and intersectionality in transnational feminist research in feminist discourses and practices in Latin America in the twenty-first century in relation to the multiple crises that have impacted social movements (Vargas 2015). From my point of view, these crises have destabilized previous certainties, making visible the new actors, revealing the enormous diversity of races, ethnicities, cultures, sexual options and generational diversity. Leading to new forms of Latin-American feminisms – in the plural. This has been a process of enormous gain but at the same time full of friction, because in their struggle for visibility has become apparent the power relations that the intersectionality of oppression implies.

I explore these 'troubles' from a position of 'situated knowledges', as a feminist activist who theorizes about the politics of feminism. From my position as middle class, urban mestiza, older feminist, I am part of these feminist engagements and at the same time 'other'. The central challenge of civic innovation actions seems to be around the frictions of unequal power relations among women as the intersection of multiple oppressions impacts the lives of some women more than others, and thus feeding hierarchies and power relations.

Latin American feminisms now face the need to create new paradigms rooted in these diverse experiences, perspectives and worldviews, which are yet to enter into feminist analytics. A key lesson has been that the emancipation of women requires confronting not only their subordinate gender status, but also the intersecting systems of oppression based on race, ethnicity, normative heterosexuality, social class, geography, and generation, and the capitalist, colonial and patriarchal systems where these oppressions are generated. These destabilize universal and essentialized visions of women and emancipation.

By recognizing the dissent and the consequent friction it is possible for feminism to break the barriers that exclude black, indigenous, lesbian, transgender, the differently abled, younger and older women. The recognition of the enormous diversity of stories, memories and situated knowledge's speaking from specific realities is of fundamental political importance, because these diversities enrich and create new perspectives of social change.

When intersectionality is acknowledged, it becomes important to make visible those demands or dimensions of reality that have been denied or 'folklorized' by the dominant culture. Such recognition necessarily impacts the knowledge and the way we perceive and construct social movements. Such knowledge is not neutrally located. It is constructed from spaces laden with power relations and exclusions of race, ethnicity, class, age, sex, gender, (dis)ability, and special skills.

In the process of confronting power relations and hegemonic visions within feminisms, new approaches and theories are emerging from the margins. These suggest 'other categories of resistance', other realities, other worldviews, thus subverting and enriching dominant feminist epistemologies. This reflection from the 'borders' emerges in moments of fracture, illuminating the absences in feminist discourse and practice. Thus, it is at the peripheries of power that we learn to live the basis of alternative knowledge systems and counter-hegemonic practices and experiences of life.

To put such different approaches in dialogue with each other is a complex process that expresses the diversity of experiences, cultures and worldviews, and requires an intercultural perspective. As the background document of the XIII Latin American and Caribbean Feminist Encounter held in Lima, Perú (22–25 November 2014[5]) says:

> Critical interculturality allows us to retrieve other voices, knowledge's and ways of thinking, and to appreciate diverse worldviews that speak of the complexity of reality and the multiple ways of living and being a woman. This is not a call to 'celebrate' or 'tolerate' diversity, but a call to recognize the incompleteness of any political proposal that does not incorporate dialogue with diversity, building identities and producing knowledge. This demands that we take on an ethical-political commitment to incorporate diversity in our ways of living, thinking and coming together.
>
> (November 2014)

Within this conceptual and political framework, the primary site of territorial politics is the body. The body is conceptualized as a complex entity, resisted, fought over, and re-appropriated, according to different understandings, experiences and worldviews, while having points of connection that allow the 'translation' of the different approaches. For example, women's autonomy is a point of connection that needs to consider diverse needs, locations, experiences in an intercultural dialogue that contributes to forming a decolonialized body politics.

From this perspective, 'the body as territory' acquires a special meaning as a space of resistance in the Latin American context for the indigenous women's movements in their fight against neo-extractivism and as an expression of a way of life in harmony with the bodies of women and nature. It also incorporates the reconfiguration of the engendered body lived by transvestites and transsexuals, as well as the indigenous and Afro-Latinas. And different understandings of the body are central to the struggle against racism, and in the confrontation against the impact of neoliberal capitalist economy on the bodies of diverse women.

Today, the bodies of women – as carriers of rights – have become a disputed territory. This is what we mean when we say that 'the body is a political category' and that as such it embodies feminist discourses such as the transnational global protest at rape and abductions of girls and women in different locations (Kurian et al. 2015).

Rosalba: struggling for life and the practice of critical interculturality

All over Latin America, indigenous communities are struggling against global capitalist current extractivist focus, as a struggle for life. As I became engaged politically with indigenous women in Mexico, I learnt that their struggle for life is also a collective construction for autonomy from the state and the capitalist market. In concrete terms, this means to establish governing and justice bodies together with learning, healing and productive practices that are parallel to the state and capitalist ones. This autonomy also entails rejecting state-subsidies of any kind, federal and local health/school/security state policies and even state-generated electricity. Moreover, it has involved 20 years of producing and consuming their own food in their own lands.

In this collective construction for autonomy, Oaxaca Zapoteca indigenous women and Zapatista autonomous communities are also transforming those 'traditions' that are specifically violent against women. However, this change is taking place without the intervention of state mechanisms (e.g. political parties, parliamentary quotas) or well-intentioned feminist NGOs interventions, but through the use of their 'traditional ways' (*cambiando la tradicion en la forma tradicional*) i.e. interventions, that change traditions in a traditional way.

A concrete example of a 'tradition' are the communitarian assemblies, which were used in 1993 by Zapatista women to condemn domestic violence, to identify alcohol and drugs consumption as its main cause and in consequence to establish a banning of their consumption in all Zapatista territory. Communitarian assemblies and consultations were also used in 1999 to create the first single mothers, widows and single women weavers cooperative in Teotitlan de Valle, a Zapoteca indigenous community in Oaxaca with various thousands of inhabitants.

For Zapatista women and Zapotec indigenous women, their struggle for life and against global capitalist current extractivism is deeply attached to a defence of their ways of being in the world, or what some called 'traditions' in a colonial relation with 'the modern' ways of being.

So why is it important for feminists doing research on transnational activism to understand indigenous women's struggles for life and autonomous ways of being? Below, I explain how I see this understanding as crucial to feminist coalitions against multiple oppressions.

In recent years, the struggle for life and autonomy through 'traditional' ways by indigenous women that do not call themselves feminist or do not want to be associated with feminism has instigated a deep personal/political/epistemic/ ethical transformation for some feminists in and outside Mesoamerica.

The following testimony, which I heard in January 2008 at CIDECI-UNI-TIERRA Chiapas, from a young Italian feminist who had spent a couple of months as *cooperate* in Zapatista communities, gives an example of the deep transformation to which I refer:

As a feminist, I always questioned immigrant women who arrived preg-
nant in Italy. I always wondered why they wanted to keep their babies.
Pregnancy was simply a burden and abortion was the solution. However,
after being here with the Zapatistas I have learnt to understand the
importance of life for them, and for the first time, also for the immigrant
women that I was 'helping' back home in Italy. I also learnt to understand
my defense for legal abortion in Italy as a recognition of the Italian feminists that were fighting for this right in the streets before me. The right to
abortion is the victory of my grandmother and mother. But most importantly, I have learnt that immigrant and indigenous women defending
their babies is a victory of their grandmothers and mothers too, it is a
defense of their right to be.[6]

From my point of view, this testimony illustrates how 'critical interculturality'
is a practice of dialogue and a learning process of listening. In this listening
there is an attempt to change one's assumptions and presuppositions by
engaging with (not only recognizing or tolerating) the radical difference of
other ways of being (Panikkar 2000). This young Italian feminist spoke of her
life-transforming journey in the process of understanding one of the elements of
Maya cosmology: that every form of human and non-human life is considered
sacred, the river, the mountain, the human and non-human bodies and spirits.
Furthermore, such transformation seemed to entail an understanding of those
who were before us (*ancestras/abuelas/sabedoras*) and are still inhabiting
(*estan siendo*) our common present. In other works, the plurality of times in
the present of resistance became visible for her (Icaza and Vazquez 2013).

Moreover, the testimony seeks to display what critical interculturality as a
practice of listening (or hosting) world-views might mean for the creation of
coalitions across national borders among non-feminist women and feminists
who engage in the defence of life in times of global extractivist capitalism: a
critical reconsideration of social reproduction as part of the struggle for life
and contrary to the capitalist civilization of death.

For some of us, feminists and women rights advocates in/from Latin
America who engage with indigenous womens' struggles for life and autonomy, the act of listening has required dismantling and re-constructing some of
our ontological, epistemic and methodological assumptions and presuppositions
(Gargallo 2014; Icaza 2015; Lugones 2010, 2003; Marcos 2006; Millan 2014).
Some of these shifts we return to below in relation to the ways we think we do
research as feminists and non-feminists on 'civic innovation'.

Wendy: organizing consciousness of otherness in European feminist politics

My contribution reflects on transnational feminist experiences organizing in
Europe in a four year experiment of the European Feminist Forum (EFF) a
loosely organized network of European (East and West) based feminists that
existed from 2004–2008. I analyse the importance of intersectionality and

embodiment in the gender analytics of the EFF as experiment in critical interculturality and decolonialism in Europe.

EFF emerged as a European offshoot of the World Social Forum feminist dialogues which were being held from 2005 (Vargas 2005) and from a dissatisfaction with the mainstream 'NGO-ization' (Alvarez 2009) that dominated European feminist organizations working on 'international' issues in that period – where there was a strong focus on the UN nations and 'solidarity' with women outside of Europe rather than with the various forms of poverty and oppression experienced by women on the social and economic margins of different parts of Europe. The organizations and networks[7] looked at the interlocking issues of racism, sexism, poverty and ageism in Europe. The focus was on migrant women's issues, Roma issues as well as economic justice around trade, youth rights, LGBT issues, body politics and abortion rights. The goal of the Forum was to develop an intercultural space that explored twenty-first-century European feminisms with the impact of the economic and social transitions in 'Europe' on different women as its subject.

The space was mostly virtual which in those days was a much more expensive and complex prospect than in 2015. It aimed to connect diversity of location, race, ethnicity, class as well as gender and sexual identity. The debates held over the four years in different formats and sub groups (using art, dialogue, musical expression) tried to challenge the dominance of the feminisms operating in liberal, white 'professionalized' NGO or policy organizations and to open up the feminist discourse to non-white, non-Western European, non hetero, migrants, young people who were not necessarily wishing to engage in the big economic EURO land project. It also aimed to break down the idea of European feminism in the transnational context as the same as 'gender in development' processes. The EFF searched for a transnational understanding of Europe as connected and engaged with other feminist lives, via resistance to the capitalist project of development. At its core it encouraged discussion among European feminists building from diverse experiences of those who participated. EFF involved over 3,000 women from 20 European countries (within and outside the EU) with around 300 women consistently and actively engaged in the space.

The EFF deliberately aimed to work away from top down organizational principles – working in a horizontal fashion in what Arturo Escobar (2004, 2008) describes as a 'meshwork'. Meshworks bring groups of people together (in cyberspace or in place based events) for the purpose of action and discussion on key issues – there is no membership, the goal is to inform open up possibilities and act politically where people are placed. People do not 'belong' to meshworks, they move in and out of them. Such decentralized flexibility offers possibilities to understand alternative philosophies of life along with the chance to mobilize via self-organizing that enables direct engagement with mainstream politics and economics.

Accordingly there was no attempt to set an agenda or way of working beyond needing to be accountable for funds raised. For three years there was a small secretariat based in IIAV in Amsterdam and a decision making collective made up of the founding European based women's networks.

The Forum was open to all feminists (women, men and transgenders) who self defined as feminist(s) working in Europe. A major innovation, as mentioned above, for that historical period, the Forum was designed to operate in cyberspace. What should be noted is that, perhaps because it was an open space and mostly on the Internet, the majority of participants were young women, from the Central Eastern European (CEE) and (Commonwealth of Independent States) CIS countries.

The three main themes of the Forum were body politics, economy and feminist movement building. The topics selected by the participants for debate during the Forum were diverse: feminist political alternatives; women's physical and sexual integrity, abortion and the politics of ending violence against women; intersectionalities and intergenerational difference; and feminist resource mobilization and building political power.

In terms of decoloniality and intersectional issues, one of the most subscribed topics was migration within Europe and the need to open up European feminism to the experiences of women from the global south in Europe. In terms of body politics, economy and feminist movement building to engage in such intercultural concerns, recognizing diversity at the core of European feminism, displacing white, professional rights for women approaches proved to be a complex and contested issue. Working conditions and integrity issues for Roma women, young queer feminists from CEE and CIS countries, domestic migrant workers and migrant sex workers quickly emerged as central in the discussions. The EFF became, for the short period it survived, a unique space that highlighted the concerns of migrant women who were self-organizing and demanding a variety of rights from the given norms of European feminist mobilizing and movement building.

The dialogues of the EFF revealed how much the cultural, social and economic consequences of migration for women living and working in Europe were not being considered by 'mainstream' feminists in Europe. The dialogue it created brought concerns of women who were on the margins of European feminism to a space where white feminists who were not migrants themselves had to redefine feminist issues within Europe itself. Reflecting on this I asked myself why were these issues and concerns at the margins? What kind of epistemic decisions were made on the basis of which assumptions? Now in conversation with Gina and Rosalba I have become familiar with the decolonial and critical interculturality debates and practices in Latin America and have tried to think further about 'decolonlizing' of European feminism.

This 'decolonizing' of European feminism from within led to many debates and discussion, which led to a shift in the organizing of the Forum EFF secretariat and collective. The original aim of the EFF had been to host a large European 'face to face' Forum, a large international event where these debates could be discussed (something like the Latin American Encuentros (Encounters)). However the complexity and difficulty of the discussions challenged established white professional and liberal feminist behaviour. This meant that instead of a strong authoritative core led by established feminist organizations and groups the Affinity Groups emerged as the main organizing mechanism. The Affinity groups used the possibilities of the early possibilities of that period of Internet to form thematic groups interested in particular issues and activities. The Affinity groups allowed the EFF to cross the power divides among established European women's rights networks and to break down preconceived agendas of old and new Europe (East and West, in and outside the EURO). The self-defined affinity groups were able to work on diverse agendas in Europe as opposed to one imposed from outside (by mainstream feminists working in the EU or the UN or trade unions or other forms of institutions). The EFF experience was an attempt to create spaces where women (and men and transgenders) could feel comfortable to explore differences in identities and histories while at the same time forming connections that could support diverse feminist collective actions.

In conversation with Gina and Rosalba on my experiences in Europe as a feminist activist and now teacher and how I now see the experience of EFF, I would argue that the experiment of the EFF was courageous in acknowledging and working with the tensions in European feminism in order to create new forms of interaction. This particular civic innovation tried to bridge the divisions among European born feminists and migrants, and between Eastern and Western Europe. It tried to create a sense of collective well-being by recognizing that histories, race, ethnicity, as well as gender was part of feminist understanding of oppression and resistance in Europe and transnationally. It recognized that European feminist movements necessarily included migrants and socially excluded women, transgenders, and feminist men and that there were differences between Eastern and Western Europe and within the 27 countries of the EU – making such diversities visible rather than pretending they did not exist, or were not relevant to feminist practice. Key to this process was a search for creative alternatives that built on diverse experiences such as precariousness (of young Romanian and Polish women looking for work in The Netherlands and UK) redefining rights as more than legal rights and movement building as far more fluid than projects (women's equal pay etc., more women CEOs and MPs) that were at the heart of established large liberal and conservative women's organizations. In bringing to the fore such differences, EFF explored power divides within European feminisms. The affinity groups were a conscious attempt to open up to new political spaces where these diverse histories, race, ethnicity and generations could be discussed. EFF saw itself as a mechanism that could encourage connections and dialogue that could, by making differences visible, connect participants in the project beyond their specific geographic, racial, generational, sexual identity and class bound feminist political interests.

As a form of critical intercultural dialogue EFF was an effort 'to build new diverse, open and fluid alliances, which are necessary to understand fully the politics of difference alongside the politics of friendship and the notion of multiple and conflicting identities among inter-movements' (Dutting 2009).

EFF did not solve generational difference, racism and class issues, but it did bring to the fore diverse feminist identities, in terms of ethnicity, class, nationality, age, gender, sexual orientation as part of a new generation of European feminism. Historically it also marked the disillusionment with international politics set by UN agendas that ignored, migration, sexualities, precariousness, feminist art, fundamentalism and intergenerational organizing.

Civic innovation as a mosaic of systems, concepts and practices-experiences

As our narratives indicate, we see civic innovation framed by a mosaic of systems of oppression: patriarchy, capitalism and coloniality, which intersects in different struggles and resistance, creating alternatives or civic innovations. Our narratives illustrate how the civic innovation framework can build on feminist analysis of body politics-embodiment. The concepts set out in the book's introductory chapter such as: 'Activism', 'Intersectionality', 'Knowledge', 'Scale', 'Agency', and 'Establishment' are shaped by civic action in spaces where new forms of social organization show concrete forms of feminist engagement with knowledges and practices from people and communities that have been subalternized by dominant feminist narratives. Such processes challenge power experienced in the bedroom, in the board room, in state institutions, in the academy.

We see civic innovation based on knowledges practices that come out of diverse experiences whether in economically marginal communities, in social movements' struggles or in feminist research and teaching. Through critical intercultural dialogue civic innovation as framework of enquiry focus on alternatives to oppressions can move beyond academic practice that is based on theorizing the 'experience' of marginalized people to be theorized by others.

What we explored in our conversations is how sharing these paradigms and world views is not free of frictions and tensions. The places where we 'talk', feel, want, do, produce wealth, culture and knowledge, are loaded with unequal often invisible power relations. As a result, conflicts can also inform civic innovation on development levels. Nevertheless we think it is important in researching civic innovation to look at the creative frictions between different epistemologies and world views; between different possibilities to access resources, power and recognition. Such frictions and conflicts can be seen as a spur for more inclusive and emancipatory change.

We see civic innovation research as building up from a network of nodes (Panikkar 2000; Escobar 2004). The nodes contribute 'innovative' research practices that have at their core the decolonization of knowledge (including those developed in the university) then we can move to new ways of doing research.

In our conversations we have interrogated from our diverse knowledge and experiences as transnational feminists, how our Western/colonial feminist discourse is built on the modern myth of the individual/individualist being. Such an understanding of what it is to be a modern individual impacts on our notions of 'emancipation', 'justice', 'body', 'gender', 'identity'; determining how, who and what we think about/with and feel. A situated understanding of the privileges-oppressions that inform our subjectivity(ies), requires that civic innovation clearly and systematically demarcates what we are able to think from our different locations. As we are researchers looking at civic innovation in a university, from a position of power and privilege, we need to understand how we can contribute to knowledge in conversations with others outside positions of Western academe and privilege.

To begin with, can we think about multiple bodies and embodiments, going beyond the abstract perfomative body(ies)? Just as we can agree there are some human invariants (Panikkar 2000) of bodily needs (eating, defecation, sex, etc.), then we can also recognize there are multiple and diverse ways of sensing the body, including life and death, spirituality and so on.

One way in which the body is experienced is that of the individual emancipated female being or hegemonic male being in which certain identities are performative. These are not the only experiences of the body. Among diverse indigenous communities in Mesoamerica marked by the coloniality of capitalism-nation-state-Western knowledge and gender (Lugones 2010) the body is a fluid relation (Marcos 2006; Chirix 2010) between male-female and it is permeable by its relations to all that surrounds it: material/immaterial, human/non-human beings, the past, the future (Lugones 2014). This 'other' way of experiencing the body unfolds as a lived relation in practice with others: I am what I do, but also with whom I am doing: feeding, harvesting, nurturing, dancing, thinking, praying, resisting, and so on.

An important implication of this 'other' understanding of the body for civic innovation research is related to the ways in which one thinks what you are doing and with whom. We need be clear in what ways through our teaching and writing are we contributing to specific global struggles for social justice. Through which specific tools and strategies? With whom do we engage and how?

As all three of us have worked in the university environment teaching development studies, we find it crucial to ask whether we can open spaces to learn from the South/colonized experiences? Is it possible to create research-action-learning processes that allow us to put into practice what we are learning from Southern/colonized experiences that we are researching?

For example, in which ways can the emphasis of the Aymara feminist Julieta Paredes (2010) on the myth of the individual being in mainstream feminism contribute to the limits of our teaching-research? From our point of view, the important aspect of Paredes' proposal of 'communitarian feminism' is that she allows us to question whether Western concepts of emancipation and gender justice necessarily need to embrace the individualization of rights.

Another set of questions which interest us in relation to understanding how to do civic innovation research is about the ways Zapotec and Mixtec indigenous communities' understanding of rights are acquired through the fulfilment of duties or cargos and are not seen as inherent in 'human nature'. In what ways does this knowledge contribute to our debates on justice (Maldonado 2002)?

This view of rights was evident in a conversation held by Rosalba in 2014 in Chiapas with a Spanish activist from a cooperative in Valencia where we discussed the challenges of horizontality, autonomy and participatory democratic ways of working within and among cooperatives. This cooperativist stressed that the system of communal duties are a pre-condition for the achievement of rights and was practiced in his and other cooperatives in Spain as one way of countering the power of individualism so entrenched in young neoliberal subjectivities.

One of the questions we were debating is how, by undertaking research on civic innovation in ISS, can we also change our teaching practices in order to explore the limits and tensions of our students as neoliberal subjectivities? Can we create research-action-learning practices that build from Southern/ colonized experiences as in the Valencia cooperatives? We need to take up this crucial/ethical opportunity for civic innovation in the research context.

Similarly, we would like to raise how we can think, research and teach beyond (the coloniality of) gender? Parallel to Julieta Paredes (2010), decolonial feminist Maria Lugones (2003, 2010) proposes to go beyond gender as a universalist and ahistorical category by recognizing its colonial origin as an ordering principle that socializes sexual difference of those considered humans over indigenous people (non-humans/animalized beings). The implication for civic innovation of the critical approach of Lugones is to critically scrutinize the colonial assumptions and pre-suppositions that inform our conceptual mosaic, starting with that of gendered beings. Who was being gendered and when? And who else was being denied a place in the gender system?

We see ISS as an interesting space to engage in civic innovation as a research and teaching practice. Along with the huge diversity of our student body (at least geographically) ISS continues to host many non academics, non Europeans, male, female, transgender, young and old, indigenous, political activists and political refugees who visit as speakers and are recognized as holders of knowledge. In engaging in with embodiment, intersectionality, decoloniality in intercultural dialogues in ISS we see one way to combat the current neoliberalizing of European Universities.

Conclusion

Civic innovation is produced from both marginal and privileged positions. It is therefore important to recognize and even seek to share different paradigms and worldviews. As our stories suggest, when civic innovation is understood as analytical tool, it can benefit from feminist theorizing and critical intercultural debates. When civic innovation is mainly understood as alternatives from people and communities to different and connected forms of oppression, feminist epistemologies and methodologies for collaborative work are able to contribute to framing the debate. And a critical intercultural framework for dialogues as practice of political visibility of those whose knowledge has been subalternized by mainstream knowledges is crucial for critical academic practices.

What we found most interesting in writing up our conversations is how from first being unsure about the usefulness of the term civic innovation, we grew to realise how it resonated with our different experiences. In writing up our conversations we were able to make conceptual connections, as we found ways to bring in our particular interests in embodiment, intersectionality, decoloniality and criticial interculturality. Thinking through civic innovation as a way to make connections, build nodes and engage in other forms of knowledges presents an exciting way to move beyond feminist enclaves. Our common understanding was also something surprising to acknowledge as we were writing from different histories, places and experiences, and even generations (in our 60s, 50s and 40s). The challenge will be to engage more feminists in this conversation around civic innovations from other geographical regions, histories and generations.

Above all, our drive to engage in civic innovation is to undertake research that contributes to social justice. Civic innovation is embedded in the matrix of social relations and shaped by multiple power-oppressions. Using concepts such as embodiment and intersectionality allow us to deepen our understanding of the role of power relations within social, cultural and political relations, in order to challenge multiple oppressions. In writing this chapter we have explored how the concept of civic innovation can help us, as feminist research-activists, to make sense of our practices for change, fully aware of the colonial notions that lurk within our work and even the term civic innovation. We have aimed to make explicit the unravelling of our previous certainties as particular types of feminists, as we recognize the contradictions of our different histories, the diversity of races, ethnicities, cultures, sexual options and generational diversity. We hope that our chapter has illustrated, in its unruly manner of writing, the potential of feminist knowledge and practice for civic innovation. And, in sharing our diverse histories and ideas, our uncertainties and concerns, we hope to have shown how the mosaic of terms that give meaning to civic innovation can inform our understanding of struggles for social justice. We would hope that future research in civic innovation around the issues of embodiment and intersectionality, decoloniality and interculturality can engage many more in these conversations.

Notes

1 Intersectionality looks at how racism (discrimination/hatred/fear of people of colour), sexism (discrimination/hatred/fear on the basis of gender – usually women), homophobia (discrimination/hatred/fear of people who practice homosexuality) transphobia (discrimination/hatred/fear of trans gender people), ableism (discrimination/hatred/fear of people who are differently abled, xenophobia (prejudice against/hatred/fear of foreigners), classism (prejudice against people of other economic classes) are interconnected.
2 See the discussion on the coloniality of gender by Maria Lugones in https://globalstudies.trinity.duke.edu/wp-content/themes/cgsh/materials/WKO/v2d2_Lugones.pdf (Accessed 22 January 2016).

3 Discussions in Europe, Asia and Australia have also taken up these critiques of the violence of modernity and development in currently evolving decolonizing projects. See for example the French feminist Houria Bouteldja's post on the project of decolonial feminism: http://indigenes-republique.fr/feminist-or-not-thinking-about-the-possibility-of-a-decolonial-feminism-with-james-baldwin-and-audre-lorde/ (Accessed 22 January 2016).
4 See the manifesto that was produced for the 13th LAC regional feminist conference: 'For the Emancipation of our Bodies', which articulates the ways in which women's bodies are impacted by the social and political conditions. See XIII Encuentro Feminista de América Latina y el Caribe, in Lima, Peru (22–25 November 2014) http://www.13eflac.org/.
5 For more information about the 13th LAC regional feminist conference (13 Encuentro Feminista de América Latina y el Caribe) in Lima, Perú (22–25 November 2014) visit: http://www.13eflac.org/.
6 CIDECI/UNITIERRA international seminar on anti-systemic movements, 2 January 2008.
7 The networks were: The Polish Federation for Women and Family Planning, Babaylan–Philippine Women's Network in Europe, IFOR's Women Peacemaker's Program (WPP), KARAT Coalition, The Network of East–West Women (NEWW–Polska), the Joint Roma Women's Initiatives (JRWI), Network Women in Development Europe (WIDE).

References

Alvarez, S. (2009) 'Beyond NGO-ization? Reflections from Latin America', *Development* 52(2): 175–184.
Ávila, M.B. (2001) 'Feminismo, ciudadanía e transformação social, [Feminism, citizenship and social transformation]' in *Textos e Imagens do feminismo: mulheres construindo a igualdade* [Feminist texts and images: women building equality], Recife, Brasil: SOS Corpo.
Bilge, S. (2013) 'Intersectionality Undone: Saving Intersectionality from Feminist Intersectionality Studies', *Du Bois Review*, 10: 405–424.
Butler, J. (1993) *Bodies That Matter*, London: Routledge.
Chirix, E. (2010) *Ru rayb'äl ri qach'akul. Los deseos de nuestro cuerpo. Antigua Guatemala* [The desires of our bodies. Ancient Guatemala], Guatemala: Ediciones del Pensativo.
Collins, P.H. (2000) 'Gender, Black Feminism, and Black Political Economy', *Annals of the American Academy of Political and Social Science*, 568: 41–53.
Crenshaw, K. (1989) 'Demarginalizing the Intersection of Race and Sex: A Black Feminist Critique of Antidiscrimination Doctrine, Feminist Theory and Antiracist Politics', *University of Chicago Legal Forum*: 139–167.
Crenshaw, K. (2013) 'Mapping the Margins: Intersectionality, Identity Politics and Violence Against Women of Color', *Stanford Law Review*, 43: 1241–1300.
Dutting, G. (2009) 'Feminists in Europe Responding to the Financial Crisis,' *Development*, 52(2): 338–344.
Escobar, A. (2004) 'Other Worlds are (Already) Possible: Self-organisation, Complexity and Post Capitalist Cultures', in Sen, J., Anand, A., Escobar, A. and Waterman, P. (eds) *World Social Forum: Challenging Empires*, New Delhi: The Viveka Foundation.
Escobar, A. (2008) *Territories of Difference: Place, Movements, Life, Redes*, Durham: Duke University Press.
Foucault, M. (1976) *The History of Sexuality. Volume 1*, Harmondsworth: Penguin.

Gargallo, F. (2014) *Feminismos desde Abya Yala. Ideas y proposiciones de las mujeres de 607 pueblos en nuestra América* [Feminisms from Abya Yala: Ideas and proposals from women of 607 peoples in our America], Mexico: Editorial Corte y Confección, 1st digital edn, January. Online: http://francescagargallo.wordpress.com/ (Accessed 22 January 2016).

Grewal, I. and Kaplan, C. (1994) *Scattered Hegemonies. Postmodernity and Transnational Feminist Practices*, Minneapolis, London: University of Minnesota Press.

Grosz, L. (1994) *Volatile Bodies. Towards Corporeal Feminism*, Bloomington: Indiana University Press.

Haraway, D. (2013) 'Multispecies Cosmopolitics: Staying with the Trouble', Institute for Humanities Research Distinguished Lecture, Institute for Humanities Research, Arizona State University, 22 March.

Harcourt, W. (2009) *Body Politics in Development: Critical Debates in Gender and Development*, London: Zed Books.

Hartmann, E. (1995) *Reproductive Rights and Wrongs: The Global Politics of Population Control*, New York: South End Press.

Icaza, R. (2015) 'Testimony of a Pilgrimage. (Un)learning and Re-learning with the South', in Arashiro, Z. and Barahona, M. (eds) *Women in Academia Crossing North-South Borders: Gender, Race and Displacement*, Lexington: Rowman and Littlefield.

Icaza, R. and Vazquez, R. (2013) 'Social Struggles as Epistemic Struggles', *Development and Change*, 44(3): 683–704.

Kurian, P.A., Munshi, D. and Mundkur, A. (2015) 'The Dialectics of Power and Powerlessness in Transnational Feminist Networks: Online Struggles Around Gender-based Violence', in Baksh, R. and Harcourt, W. (eds), *The OUP Handbook on Transnational Feminist Movements*, Oxford: Oxford University Press.

Orozco, A.P. (2014) *Subversión feminista de la Economía* [Feminist subversion of the economy]. Online: http://www.traficantes.net/sites/default/files/pdfs/map40_subver sion_feminista.pdf (Accessed 22 January 2016).

Lugones, M. (2003). *Pilgrimages/Peregrinajes: Theorizing Coalition against Multiple Oppressions*, Boulder, CO: Rowman and Littlefield.

Lugones, M. (2010) 'Towards a Decolonial Feminism', *Hypathia*, 25(4): 742–759.

Lugones, M. (2014) 'Decolonial Feminism', Middelburg Decolonial Summer School, 25 June. Online: http://decolonialsummerschool.wordpress.com/ (Accessed 22 January 2016).

Maldonado, B. (2002) *Autonomía y comunalidad india. Enfoques y propuestas desde Oaxaca* [Indian autonomy and communality. Approaches and proposals from Oaxaca], Oaxaca: INAH-Oaxaca=/Secretaría de Asuntos Indígenas del gobierno del estado/Coalición de Maestros y Promotores Indígenas de Oaxaca/Centro de Encuentros y Diálogos Interculturales.

Marcos, S. (2006) *Taken from the Lips: Gender and Eros in Mesoamerican Religions*, Leiden: Brill.

McCall, L. (2005) 'The Complexity of Intersectionality', *Journal of Women in Culture and Society*, 30(3): 1771–1800.

Millan, M. (ed.) (2014). *Mas alla del feminismo. Caminos para andar* [Beyond feminism: paths to be walked], Mexico City: Red de feminismos descoloniales.

Mignolo, W. (2011) 'Epistemic Disobedience and the Decolonial Option: A Manifesto', *TRANSMODERNITY: Journal of Peripheral Cultural Production of the Luso-Hispanic World*, 1(2). Online: http://escholarship.org/uc/item/62j3w283 (Accessed 22 January 2016).

Mignolo, W. (2007) 'Delinking', *Cultural Studies*, 21(2–3): 449–514.

Mohanty, C.T. (2003) *Feminism Without Borders. Decolonizing Theory, Practicing Solidarity*, Durham: Duke University Press.

Panikkar, R. (2000) 'Religion, Philosophy and Culture', *Polylog: Forum for Intercultural Philosophy*, 1. Online: http://them.polylog.org/1/fpr-en.htm (Accessed 22 January 2016).

Paredes, J. (2010) 'Spinning Threads from Commutarian Feminism', La Paz, Bolivia: Mujeres creando comunidad.

Quijano, A. (2000) 'Coloniality of Power, Eurocentrism, and Latin America', *International Sociology*, 15(2): 215–232.

Shildrick, M. (1997) *Leakey Bodies and Boundaries. Feminism, Postmodernism and (Bio) Ethics*, London: Routledge.

Spivak, G. (1987) *In Other Worlds: Essays in Cultural Politics*, New York: Methuen.

Spivak, G. (1999) *A Critique of Postcolonial Reason: Toward a History of the Vanishing Present*, Harvard: Harvard University Press.

Tamale, S. (ed.) (2011). *African Sexualities: A Reader*, Oxford: Pambazuka Press.

Vargas, V. (2005) 'Feminisms and the World Social Forum', *Development*, 48(2): 107–110.

Vargas, V. (2015) 'Feminism and Democratic Struggles in Latin America', in Baksh, R. and Harcourt, W. (eds) *Handbook on Transnational Feminist Movements*, Oxford: Oxford University Press, pp. 534–553.

Walsh, C. (2012) '"Other" Knowledges, "Other" Critiques: Reflections on the Politics and Practices of Philosophy and Decoloniality in the "Other" America', *TRANSMODERNITY: Journal of Peripheral Cultural Production of the Luso-Hispanic World*, 1(3). Online: http://escholarship.org/uc/item/6qd721cp (Accessed 22 January 2016).

Wieringa, S. and Sivori, H. (eds) (2012) *The Sexual History of the Global South: Sexual Politics in Africa, Asia and Latin America*, London: Zed Books.

Young, I.M. (2005) *On Female Body Experience: 'Throwing Like a Girl' and Other Essays (Studies in Feminist Philosophy)*, New York, Oxford: Oxford University Press.

9 Towards new perspectives on labour precarity and decent work for sex workers'

Silke Heumann, Karin Astrid Siegmann and Empower Foundation

Introduction

Sex work is often approached as inherently exploitative and conflated with human trafficking (Dworkin 1993; MacKinnon 2005). The moral panic around trafficking is sustained by the convergence of conservative groups with specific groups of feminists, and anti-immigration agendas in the global north. It is fed by a sensationalist media representation with inflated data on 'sex trafficking' and highlighting extreme cases of violence and abuse (Agustín 2007; Bernstein 2010). The conflation of sex work with trafficking has contributed to the increasing predominance of a (neo)abolitionist[1] approach to sex work (Bernstein 2010). This approach situates sex work in the realm of public order, irregular migration and international crime. In other words, it frames it as an issue best dealt with through a criminal law approach centred on border control, persecution of traffickers, and 'saving' women through 'repatriation' and 'rehabilitation' (Bernstein 2010; Crowhurst, Outshoorn and Skilbrei 2012; Doezema 2002; Sullivan 2003). It fails to offer an account of the conditions and mechanisms that contribute to the structural vulnerability of sex workers (Agustín 2007; Bernstein 2010). The highly insecure labour conditions that often characterise sex work are not addressed and frequently aggravated by this approach (Agustín 2007; Bernstein 2010; Empower Foundation 2012a, 2012b; Kempadoo 2005; Peano 2012; Sanders and Hardy 2013).

With so much attention given to precarity and exploitation in the sex industry, it is remarkable that sex work is largely absent from discourses about and interventions for decent work. As a result, the conventional 'tool box' for addressing poor labour conditions is not accessible and applied to those involved in the sex industry. Though many people seem to hold strong views about sex work, there is not enough knowledge about the lived realities of sex work, particularly among political decision makers. Nor is there a concerted effort to ensure the participation of sex workers in the development of decent labour standards.

Our chapter addresses this neglect of sex workers' labour conditions and their structural determinants in international policy debates around decent work. It does so by bringing into dialogue insights from and concerns of gender, sexuality and labour studies, as well as the sex workers rights organisations' knowledge, who have demanded full decriminalisation of sex work as the most effective road from precarious to decent work for sex workers. The chapter is the outcome of collaborative work between two researchers based at the International Institute of Social Studies of Erasmus University Rotterdam (ISS) with the Thai sex workers' organisation Empower Foundation. It has particularly benefitted from their knowledge: Empower Foundation has brought in their previous and ongoing research, the daily challenges they face, and their experience with setting up a work environment that offers a model for good practice in terms of respect for labour rights. In addition, the chapter has benefited from their experience of advocacy and negotiation with a variety of national and international institutions, including the International Labour Organization (ILO).

We argue that recognising sex work as work and acknowledging the diversity of sex workers' experiences opens spaces for policy interventions that effectively contribute to decent labour conditions for those involved in the sex industry as well as to emancipatory movements of sex workers themselves (Bernstein 1999; Doezema 2002, 2005; Kempadoo 2003, 2005; Kempadoo and Ghuma 1999; Truong 2014: 6). Such a labour approach to sex work involves a shift from criminalisation to the effective guarantee of sex workers' labour rights (e.g. Bernstein 1999; Bindman and Doezema 1997; Hardy 2013; Kempadoo 2003, 2005; Shamir 2012). It also means situating sex work within the broader context of neoliberal governance and how it translates into precarious work more generally. By looking at working conditions in the sex industry as a continuum from decent to highly exploitative conditions, including forced labour, we go beyond debates that are caught in a dichotomy of sex work as either choice or coercion, where the discourse of coercion leaves no room for agency and the discourse of choice leaves little room to problematise sex workers' working conditions and experiences of abuse and violence (Doezema 2005).

Specifically, our exploration centres on the debate in the ILO about a Protocol supplementing the ILO Forced Labour Convention, 1930 (No. 29) during the 103rd International Labour Conference (ILC) in June 2014. This debate in the ILO involved controversial discussions of the relationship between sex work and forced labour. On the basis of a discourse analysis of these debates, we try to understand how it came about and what kind of politics prevented the ratification of legal instruments that would acknowledge more explicitly sex work as a form of labour and as a legitimate object of labour protection and regulation. Our analysis of the ILC shows that an opportunity to shift the debate on sex work and its relation to labour exploitation towards an approach based on labour rights and their structural embeddedness was not seized.

Subsequently, we draw on initiatives of sex workers' self-organisation and academic work to outline a labour approach to sex work. We imagine how the Protocol would look if we took sex workers' labour rights seriously. Gasper and Apthorpe (1996: 2) point out that 'discourse analysis can strive for demolition or look for ways forward'. By offering an alternative framing of sex work, based on a patchwork of sex workers' own and academic voices, including our own, we hope to contribute to a way forward – to different practices regarding sex work that are more in line with notions of decent work.

To us, both the topic and methodology of this chapter exemplify how 'civic innovation research' can be put into practice. Our interest in coalitions involving marginalised societal groups, such as sex workers, whose lobbying results in alternative policies and regulation that prioritise human flourishing over narrow definitions of national security and macro-economic development directly addresses civic innovation. Our approach revolves around a dialogue across disciplines and academic boundaries that makes audible voices that are commonly excluded from official discourses. We consider this a fruitful way of doing research that is directly relevant for a more just and inclusive society.

Sex work: definition, decent work deficits and deficits in the Decent Work Agenda

In this chapter, we refer to sex work as the exchange of sexual services for material gain.[2] A range of activities may be covered here, such as direct sexual services, erotic dance, pornography and phone sex (Cohen et al. 2013: 4). Public perceptions of sex work over-emphasise sexual aspects of the work, whereas the working day of a sex worker may include surprisingly little of it. Rather, it can involve a number of other activities, such as singing, dancing, and drinking beer (Empower Foundation 2012b). This further underlines the diversity of experiences and meanings that might be associated to sex work.

With Hardy (2013: 52) we start from the assumption that '[i]t is necessary [...] to recognize prostitution as work, even if that work is deeply exploitative – as many other forms of labour are – in order to create better working conditions and reduce the stigma and violence associated with sexual labour.' Following Bernstein (1999) and others (Agustín 2007; Doezema 2005; Kempadoo 2003; Shamir 2012), we consider that the question whether sex work is exploitative and degrading or a dignified and empowering occupation is not a theoretical, but an empirical one. Answering it requires detailed attention to the context and conditions in which sex work is taking place as well as to the subjective meanings attached to it.

Sex workers' conditions of work range from comparatively secure indoor environments to more precarious non-venue-based, e.g. street-, work. Precarious work refers to a range of work-related insecurities, e.g. related to income, employment access and stability, occupational safety and health as well as representation (Standing 2011: 10). Sex work often offers higher income earning opportunities compared to labour market alternatives (Berg 2014: 694; Gall 2007: 83). However, incomes vary depending on the sub-sector and geographic location of employment. Street workers' earnings are commonly far lower than the incomes that brothel workers, escort service providers or porn actors can generate (Bernstein 1999; Gall 2007). Yet, in Thailand, brothel earnings can be much lower than those of non-venue based sex workers.

Uniformly, however, the restrictive legal environments in which most sex workers operate render their income-earning opportunities insecure (Gall 2007: 79). Risks for sex workers' health and safety are also high. They include, but are not limited to, sexually transmitted infections (STIs) and the risk of violent encounters, but also a significant degree of psychological stress (Alexander 1998; Sanders 2004). As a result of law enforcement, sex workers become more vulnerable to pressure to abandon safer sex practices, thereby further increasing their risk of contracting STIs, including HIV (Alexander 1998: 78; Boynton and Cusick 2006: 191; Goodwin 2012: 21–22). These decent work deficits in the sex industry are aggravated by sex workers' insecure representation. In comparison with other occupations, few organisations exist that represent their concerns and demands. Where they have organised, labour organisations' wide-spread hesitance to recognise sex workers as workers, alongside social stigmatisation and criminalisation, ensures their collective voice in the labour market goes unheard.[3]

Precarious work has been shown to emerge in a context of social marginalisation beyond the workplace (Arnold and Bongiovi 2013). In relation to sex work, for instance, Bernstein's (1999) analysis of sex work in San Francisco shows how young age, whiteness and higher education are associated with sex workers' prospects to achieve decent working conditions. For an improvement of sex workers' working conditions in their diverse work places, the mediating roles of gender, education, migration status, class, etc. need to be taken into account. At the same time, workplaces need to adhere to standards that are safe and fair regardless of differences in these characteristics.

In addition to social marginalisation, neo-liberal governance of the economy has been highlighted to aggravate labour precarity by shifting risks from businesses and governments to workers (e.g. Hewison and Kalleberg 2013: 395–396). These policies that rely on a flexible labour force are seen as the orthodoxy for delivering 'progress' and 'development'. Authors who embed sex work in their structural – economic, political and social – context, have pointed towards the connections between the growth of the sex industry and the impact of global economic restructuring (Bernstein 2007; Cabezas 2004; Kempadoo 1999; Padilla et al. 2007). For example, Bernstein (2007: 185) argues that

> [i]t is precisely these trademark policies of neoliberal globalization which encourage indebted nations to respond to economic crises through the development of local tourist industries [...] and to enhance local cash flow through migrant workers' remittances (including those garnered through sexual labour). As such, policies pertaining to globalization may be far more consequential than either the decriminalization, criminalization, or legalization of prostitution in shaping the size and formal contours of the sex trade.

In addition to these, other economic policies have aggravated labour precarity. For instance, restrictive migration governance has added to the precarity of migrant workers, leaving informal and often illegal work in the sex industry as one of the few viable employment options available to them (e.g. Agustín 2007). Besides, the priority given to (foreign) investment-led growth, associated with unfair land deals, has led to wide-spread proletarisation in rural areas in the global south. The withdrawal of the welfare state in rich economies increases livelihood insecurities (Sanders and Hardy 2014). These and other dynamics push people into jobs that they might not have chosen otherwise, including in the sex industry.

Considering that, in many contexts, sex work is carried out under highly precarious working conditions, surprisingly little attention has been devoted to sex work in international labour-related discourses. While the ILO's Decent Work Agenda considers all forms of work and asserts that all workers have rights to decent labour conditions (ILC 1999: 3),[4] sex work is hardly addressed. Kempadoo and Ghuma (1999: 294–295) already noted the absence of an ILO Convention on sex work in 1999. The then emerging efforts to look at sex work in the context of child labour seemed to suggest a promising move towards regulating sex work within the international labour rights framework (Kempadoo and Ghuma 1999: 294). HIV/AIDS has opened another venue of intervention. One can argue that, implicitly, sex work is being recognised as work in ILO standards such as the ILO Recommendation 200 on HIV and AIDS (ILO 2010; Ouedraogo 2012). Yet, cautious efforts within the ILO to address the precarity of sex work through explicit recognition of the sex industry as an economic sector triggered controversy within conservative and feminist groups: while migrant and sex worker networks hailed the report on 'The Sex Sector: The Economic and Social Bases of Prostitution in Southeast Asia' (Lim 1998) as 'progressive and humane' (Agustín and Weldon 2003: 31), abolitionists perceived it as 'the height of economic opportunism to argue for the recognition of the sex industry based on transforming women's sexual and economic exploitation into legitimate work' (Raymond 2003). The latter outcry in combination with the implicit refusal to see work and employment as related to people's sexuality in labour-related discourses (Cabezas 2004: 1003) might explain the subsequent silence on sex work in the debate about and interventions for decent work.

Analysing discourses on sex work and 'sexual exploitation' during the 103rd ILC

In this context, the predominant international framework to address problems of labour exploitation in the sex industry has become the UN Protocol to Prevent, Suppress and Punish Trafficking in Persons, Especially Women and Children, supplementing the United Nations Convention against Transnational Organized Crime.[5] Conflating sex work with trafficking and slavery has historical roots in the nineteenth-century moral panic around 'white slavery' that emerged out of anxieties related to the migration of European women to the then colonies (Doezema 1999). The negotiations for instruments supplementing the ILO Forced Labour Convention during the 2014 ILC represented an opportunity to move problems of forced labour in the sex industry away from the criminal law approach represented by the UN Anti-Trafficking Protocol and into the realm of labour regulation. It is for this reason that we decided to analyse the debates around instruments to address forced labour that emerged during the 103rd ILC as well as the resulting Forced Labour Protocol.[6]

A key motivation for the debate and subsequent ratification of the Forced Labour Protocol[7] as well as a Recommendation on Supplementary Measures for the Effective Suppression of Forced Labour[8] (ILC 2014b, 2014a) was precisely that trafficking was seen as an important new context for forced labour today. Building on a series of ILC debates (e.g. ILC 2012, 2005) and ILO background research on the scope of forced labour (ILO 2014, 2012; ILC 2005), it was argued that the context of forced labour has changed significantly since the ratification of the Forced Labour Convention in 1930, with the use of forced labour by private individuals and enterprises having become more common than by (colonial) state authorities (ILC 2013: 1). 'Commercial sexual exploitation' was identified as a major share, representing about a quarter of the use of forced labour in the private sector (ILO 2012: 13). Furthermore, a new feature of forced labour was perceived in its embeddedness in the context of international migration, with some 44 per cent of forced labourers having migrated prior to the exploitation of their labour, according to ILO estimates (ILC 2013: 1–2). A new regulatory instrument was therefore deemed to be necessary (ILO 2012, 2013). The conference concluded with the approval of a new Protocol as well as a Recommendation on forced labour (ILC 2014c: 3).

In this chapter, we analyse key documents describing the debates on forced labour surrounding the 103rd ILC, asking how sex work and 'sexual exploitation' are represented. First of all, this concerns the Report of the Committee on Forced Labour (ILC 2014c). It describes the proposed and endorsed changes in the texts of the Protocol as well as the Recommendation that were discussed in 18 sittings of the originally 174 committee members representing governments, workers and employers during the 103rd ILC. In addition, several reports submitted to the conference were reviewed to shed light on how the discourse on the connection between sex work and forced labour changed in the run-up to the ILC. These documents contain background information about the international and legal context of forced labour (ILC 2013), the replies and comments of ILO members on an ILO's questionnaire related to the Protocol and Recommendation to be drafted before the 103rd ILC (ILC 2014d) as well as the resulting text of Protocol and Recommendation proposed in March 2014 (ILC 2014e). Their consideration for our analysis was motivated by the fact that these reports were referred to by the committee during the ILC (ILC 2014c: 2).

In our analysis of the ILC debates, we combine tools from argumentation analysis and elements from Goodwin's (2011) adaptation of Bacchi's (2000) 'What's the Problem Represented to be' (WPR) approach to policy analysis. In line with argumentation analysis, we map the different positions regarding representations of sex work in the debate of the Committee on Forced Labour, their premises, implications and silences. Inspired by WPR, we look at how the different positions relate to different representations of the problem of 'sexual exploitation' and 'labour exploitation', as well as different proposed policy solutions. We trace the assumptions underlying the argumentation, and connect them to broader debates around sex work and forced labour. This way, we identify what is at stake in terms of sex workers' labour rights and the possibility of structurally addressing problems of precarity in the sex industry.

During the ILC meetings, ILO member states are represented by a tripartite delegation consisting of two government delegates, an employer delegate, a worker delegate, and their respective advisers.[9] The Committee on Forced Labour included 28 worker members and several international organisations, governmental and others, as observers. While all delegates have the same rights, only the Committee's Vice-Chairperson for the workers' group spoke on workers' behalf. The Employers' Vice-Chairperson had the same role for the employers' group. Some global union federations, such as the International Domestic Worker Federation (IDWF) were represented. Yet, sex workers' organisations, including the Global Network of Sex Work Projects (NSWP), representing more than 237 sex workers' organisations in over 70 countries across the globe, were not invited.

In the absence of sex workers' own representatives, two important debates took place during the Committee meetings (ILC 2014c) that are relevant to our concern of a more effective approach to addressing precarious work in the sex industry: one was about the status of sex work as work and its relation to labour exploitation. It was addressed in the debate around the meaning of 'sexual exploitation' and its relation to forced labour. The second debate concerned the issue of appropriate prevention and intervention strategies to address forced labour more generally. These discussions will be analysed in the following two sections.

Debating 'sexual exploitation' and its relation to labour exploitation

In the committee discussions, neither 'sexual exploitation' nor labour exploitation were defined explicitly. Nevertheless, both terms were the object of heated debate, in particular, the question of whether or not to mention the term 'sexual exploitation' in the Protocol, and in which relationship to labour exploitation.

Three positions on these questions can be distinguished in the discussions about the Protocol: on the one hand, the Workers' and Employers' group within the ILO regarded 'sexual exploitation' and labour exploitation as distinct from, but *closely related* to each other and both connected to trafficking. Especially the Worker Vice-Chairperson supported this formulation because it mirrors the formulation of the UN Anti-Trafficking Protocol. Both the Workers' and Employers' group therefore strongly supported the draft formulation of the Protocol that emphasises the increasing role of 'trafficking in persons for the purposes of labour or sexual exploitation' for the emergence of forced labour. The emphasis of this debate was on the relation of the Protocol to the Anti-Trafficking Protocol as another international regulatory instrument, rather than on forced labourers' material conditions. This builds on, but goes beyond the observation of the ILO Committee of Experts, a committee whose task it is to examine the government reports submitted to the ILO on ratified conventions, that the notion of labour exploitation in the UN Anti-Trafficking Protocol's definition of trafficking allows for a link to be established between this instrument and the Forced Labour Convention No. 29. In both instruments, exploitation of labour is defined as 'including the threat or use of force or other forms of coercion, abduction, fraud, deception, abuse of power or of a position of vulnerability'. In both cases, hence, labour exploitation is regarded the flipside of a voluntary offer to supply labour (ILC 2013: 12). This position that perceives 'sexual exploitation' and labour exploitation as distinct from, but related to each other does not actually engage with the meaning of the term 'sexual exploitation', however. Instead, it can be seen as a discussion between international regulatory bodies over discursive domains and fields of intervention and specifically as an effort of the ILO actors to claim trafficking as a central concern within the forced labour realm (ILC 2014c: 17–18).

An alternative stance was to see 'sexual exploitation' as a *form* of labour exploitation. This view was most strongly expressed by the Government of Cameroon who saw exploitation in the sex industry as one among many other sectors affected by forced labour. In consequence, she[10] 'stated [her] opposition to singling out sexual exploitation as a form of forced labour, as there were many other forms that would need to be mentioned, including domestic work.' (ILC 2014c: 19). Drawing parallels between labour exploitation in domestic work and 'sexual exploitation' implies that the Government of Cameroon understood the term 'sexual exploitation' as synonymous with labour exploitation in the sex industry.

A third view was that sexual exploitation could *not be considered a labour issue*. This view was connected to a keen interest in situating 'sexual exploitation' outside the realm of labour. It was expressed by the Governments of Sweden, India, Ireland and Spain (ILC 2014c: 19–20). The Government member of India voiced this position most clearly. She 'insisted that reference to labour exploitation was sufficient [in the Protocol's preamble], taking into account the fact that sexual exploitation was not a labour issue but rather a serious offence under criminal law' (ILC 2014c: 18).

The final formulation in the Protocol accommodated the first and the third positions: it refers to the term 'sexual exploitation' in its preamble only, stating that 'trafficking in persons for the purposes of forced or compulsory labour, which may involve sexual exploitation, is the subject of growing international concern' (ILC 2014b: 2). Even the Government of India could join this consensus: 'as reference was made here to sexual exploitation as a consequence of forced labour' (ILC 2014c: 20).

In comparison to the preparatory discussions within the ILO (ILC 2013) and among ILO members (ILC 2014d), it is interesting to note that, during the 2014 ILC, the term 'sexual exploitation' was being used in a rather unspecific manner: in the ILC background document 'Strengthening Action to End Forced Labour' (ILC 2013: 1), forced commercial sexual exploitation is mentioned explicitly as part of forced labour, yet, different from forced labour among 'productive activities'. This probably reflects the lack of international recognition of sex work as an economic activity according to the UN System of National Accounts.[11] In a consolidated response of a number of ILO members to the draft Protocol, they propose to list the sex industry and prostitution among a range of sectors at risk to forced labour (ILC 2014d: 12). Here, in contrast to the lack of explicit recognition of the occupation in UN fora, sex work is treated as one economic activity among others. This contrasts with dominant strands of the discussion during the ILC itself, which separated the broader and vaguer term 'sexual exploitation' from 'labour exploitation'. This framing and the result of the ILC debate about the status of sex work as work and its relation to labour exploitation can be seen as a step back in terms of recognition of sex work as an economic activity that deserves protection through labour legislation.

Debating forced labour and how to tackle it

The second question that informed our analysis was: which measures were debated and finally agreed upon in order to address forced labour? Did they emphasise criminal law or labour rights and regulation? Articles 1 and 2 of the Protocol address measures for the suppression of forced labour. Relevant aspects of the debate around their formulation included the involvement of workers' organisations in policy formulation to combat forced labour, the coverage of the informal economy by the Protocol as well as the use of labour legislation to prevent forced labour.

A red thread running through the discussion of Article 1 was the resistance of the Government member of the United States (US) to the involvement of workers' (and employers') organisations. She opposed a formulation that emphasised the requirement for competent authorities to coordinate with workers and employers' organisations in the development of national policy for the suppression of forced labour, as proposed by the Workers Vice-Chairperson (ILC 2014c: 33–34). Alternatively, she suggested weaker formulations, such as the use of the word 'may' instead of 'shall' or the qualification of coordination 'as appropriate'. She reasoned that: 'there were times when competent authorities had to work alone, without coordinating with the social partners, and this sub-amendment would allow for this' (ILC 2014c: 34). Yet, this stance may also be interpreted in light of the generally union-unfriendly context of US regulation. Besides, and more relevant to sex work, the 2003 US Global AIDS Act, which was only declared unconstitutional in 2013, established that no government funds may be used to promote or advocate the legalisation or practice of prostitution or sex trafficking (Saunders 2004: 184), and forced any organisation receiving funding from the US Agency for

International Development (USAID) to an 'anti-prostitution pledge' (NSWP 2013b). In addition, based on the US Trafficking Victims Protection Act, funding through USAID cannot be provided to '[o]rganizations advocating prostitution as an employment choice or which advocate or support the legalization of prostitution' (Saunders 2004: 186). The final formulation of the Protocol's Article 1, Paragraph 2 reflects the US Government member's proposal:

> Each Member shall develop a national policy and plan of action for the effective and sustained suppression of forced or compulsory labour in consultation with employers' and workers' organizations, which shall involve systematic action by the competent authorities and, *as appropriate*, in coordination with employers' and workers' organizations, as well as with other groups concerned.
>
> (emphasis by the authors)

The Government member of the US was also at the forefront to resist language that explicitly included employers in the informal economy in measures to prevent forced labour. This would have been an important clause in the context of sex workers' labour conditions as the bulk of their employment is informal. The Worker Vice-Chairperson proposed to add a new subparagraph about 'educating and informing employers, including private employers, in order to prevent their becoming involved in forced or compulsory labour practices' (ILC 2014c: 40). This provoked a discussion about whether 'private'/informal employers, as employers hiring domestic workers, should be mentioned explicitly and in which way. The US Government member questioned whether countries should be made responsible for educating 'all' employers as this would represent an obligation difficult to fulfil (ILC 2014c: 41). In the final formulation, the sub-paragraph was included, but in the vaguest form possible. It does not specify the kinds of employers targeted and omits the term 'all'. This discussion and its result are relevant insofar as a very modest proposition, namely to include informal employers in awareness-raising measures on forced labour, evoked strong resistance, especially from the Government members of the US and Canada. As a result, the Protocol does not explicitly mention the coverage of 'all' workers, neither implicitly nor explicitly highlighting the coverage of informal workers, too.

Last but not least, the Protocol's formulation of Article 2 on measures to prevent forced labour situations does not provide solid grounds to strengthen a possible role of labour legislation in addressing existing situations of forced labour, including forced sex work. Firstly, measures based on labour legislation are confined to the prevention of forced labour, rather than including the protection and redress for persons who are in forced labour situations. Secondly, the Protocol's proposed text of Article 2 included 'shall' clauses regarding the broadening of 'the coverage of legislation relevant to forced or compulsory labour, including labour law' (ILC 2014e: 8). The final text, however, toned this down to: 'undertaking efforts to ensure that: (i) the coverage and enforcement of legislation relevant to the prevention of forced or compulsory labour, including labour law *as appropriate*' (emphasis by the authors). This was the outcome of a discussion in which the Workers' Vice-Chairperson proposed to emphasise the enforcement of relevant legislation, while the relevance of labour legislation to the prevention of forced labour was questioned by the Employers' Vice-Chairperson (ILC 2014c: 43). During this debate, the Government member of Belgium, too, emphasised the role of labour legislation to prevent forced labour by arguing that: 'Many situations which amounted to forced labour, such as cases where workers were required to work long hours, were covered by labour law and that needed to be enforced' (ILC 2014c: 43). Again, a formulation proposed by the US Government member bridged these divergent concerns through the insertion of the qualification 'as appropriate'. In the end, this formulation leaves member states room for interpretation. They may consider the 'coverage and enforcement' of labour law as inappropriate for the prevention of forced labour.

Clearly, the resulting Protocol provides few guarantees of forced labourers' labour rights. Even the ILO background document (ILC 2013) and the Protocol draft prepared by the ILO (ILC 2014e) did not consider labour legislation as a way to strengthen people in forced labour, improve their conditions and enable them to exit their situation. Rather, both confine its role to the prevention of forced labour. Therefore, questions raised by the Office in the document providing ILO members' replies and comments on the Protocol's draft (ILC 2014d) also refer to labour law only in the context of prevention.

Despite this restrictive framing, many responses of ILO members did acknowledge the relevance of labour legislation not only to prevent but also to address forced labour situations. Among actors demanding stronger labour rights' guarantees for those in forced labour, the Colombian trade union federation *Confederación General del Trabajo* (CGT) called for explicit inclusion of sex workers in broadened coverage with and strengthening of the application of labour laws (ILC 2014d: 25). Some governments, in contrast, respond to the perceived risk of the possibility that coverage of forced labour with labour legislation effectively normalises it. Germany, for instance, responded to the Office draft that: '[i]f labour laws are applied to cases of forced labour, there is a risk that forced labour will be recognized as normal employment' (ILC 2014d: 23). Such concerns possibly motivated the confinement of a role of labour legislation in the Protocol to the prevention of forced labour.

Yet, the Protocol can be said to emphasise forced labourers' labour rights more in comparison to the mere treatment of forced labour as a criminal offence, as some ILO members proposed. The stipulation that workers' organisations are to be heard for the development of national policy and a plan of action for the suppression of forced or compulsory labour is relevant as it opens a channel for workers' collective voice, including those in forced labour. The prevention of forced labour delineated in Article 2 of the

Protocol shall include efforts to ensure the coverage of all workers and all sectors of the economy with and enforcement of labour law – with the qualification 'as appropriate'. Labour inspection services are to be strengthened, as well.

However, the course of the discussion about the possible inclusion of 'sexual exploitation' in the Protocol's preamble and its results discussed in the previous section suggest that sex workers are unlikely to benefit from this strengthened labour approach to forced labour. Dominant voices in the ILC debate emphasised 'sexual exploitation' as qualitatively different and separate from labour exploitation. Even the Worker Vice-Chairperson recognised that in some – not further specified – circumstances, legislation other than labour law might be necessary as a preventive measure. As a result, sex workers, who are implicitly addressed here, could be excluded from the ambit of labour legislation: ILO members who claimed that 'sexual exploitation' falls under the ambit of criminal law are likely to argue that sex workers should be excluded from the realm of labour legislation.

In principle, the outcome of this new regulation seems similar to the one of the Anti-Trafficking Protocol (Doezema 2002; Sullivan 2003): its ambivalence allows for different interpretations and implementations according to different legal frameworks regulating sex work in different countries. In countries where sex work is legal, the new legal instruments, which also cover improvements in labour conditions, can be tools to address indecent working conditions of sex workers. In other contexts, where buying and provision of sex work is criminalised, they do not apply.

This way, the Protocol fails to address the exclusion of sex workers from a decent work agenda – whether they are in forced labour situations or otherwise. Instead of setting (new) international labour standards that countries should comply with, it accommodates the different national legal frameworks. This is made explicit in the Protocol's Article 6, which states that '[t]he measures taken to apply the provisions of this Protocol and of the Convention shall be determined by national laws or regulations'. Hence, it even applies when those frameworks – often based on the use of criminal law – play a crucial role in perpetuating sex workers' precarious working and living conditions.

In addition, while some official statements imply an occasional acknowledgement of a spectrum of forced labour situations (e.g. ILC 2005: 8), by and large, ILO labour standards, research and policy debates see forced labour, including 'trafficking for sexual exploitation' as an exceptional situation, in which entry into the labour relation is assumed to be involuntary, and exit envisioned as the only goal (Lerche 2011: 10; Shamir 2012). This framework, narrowly focused on 'saving' the victims and punishing perpetrators, does not address the legal environment and wider social and economic structures that allow bad working conditions to go unchecked. As a result – whether voluntary or forced – the labour conditions remain exploitative.

From a criminal law to a labour approach to sex work

A criminal law approach to forced labour treats forced labour as an 'exception' and a discrete category, clearly distinguishable from the voluntary provision of labour. It is seen as belonging to the realm of crime, criminal law and criminal organisation, rather than the realm of labour. Its focus is on targeting and punishing migration networks and employers of forced labour. Victims are to be 'saved' through exit from exploitative conditions, and given eventual compensation and 'repatriation', often regardless of the wish of the victim (Skilbrei and Tveit 2011).

This individualistic, victim-centered approach is very problematic. Research has shown that it is not only ineffective, but also harmful for those that it intends to protect, namely the very persons who are subjected to conditions of forced labour (Agustín 2007; Baye and Heumann 2014; Bernstein 2010; Crowhurst 2012; Empower Foundation 2012a, 2012b; Peano 2012).

In particular, a criminal law approach to forced labour has been regularly applied in the context of anti-trafficking measures. The 'trafficking' discourse is used as a pretext to crack down on the sex industry and tighten border controls. It bypasses the problem of why people migrate, and that returning to their countries brings them back to where they were when they decided to migrate, namely to a situation without prospects of a decent livelihood. Furthermore, it ignores the extent to which restrictive migration governance increases people's dependency on migration brokers. Such restrictive governance reduces people's bargaining power and leaves them unable to denounce situations of abuse, because they risk deportation. Finally, the notion of 'victim' is based on an assumed (and necessary) absence of agency (Agustín 2007; Doezema 2002). These binary notions of agency and victimisation are problematic because they leave little room for capturing the much more complex actual situations of forced labour. For instance, temporary bonded labour may be the result of loans that enabled people to travel (Peano 2013). A criminal law approach leaves victims in a very ambivalent and vulnerable social and legal position that some people have called the 'victim/criminal paradigm': if they cannot prove they are victims, then by default they are active participants in illegal, criminal networks and/or illegal migrants. As such, they are subjected to abuse, involuntary detention and deportation (Crowhurst 2012; Crowhurst, Outshoorn and Skilbrei 2012; Peano 2012; Testaí 2013). The focus on extreme cases makes it difficult for victims to prove their case. In addition, prioritising the persecution of international smuggling networks has translated in practice into making support for the victim conditional to their role in denouncing and actually capturing the brokers, exposing the victim (and their families back home) to reprisals of these groups. The sole focus on individual exit rather than transforming precarious working and living conditions, means that nothing changes on a structural level: punishing migration brokers also does nothing to change exploitative labour market conditions or to achieve citizenship for undocumented migrants.

Rather than improving exploitative labour conditions, the criminal law approach has been shown to aggravate conditions. Take, for example, Thailand's sex workers' precarious labour conditions: due to the criminalisation of sex work and restrictive immigration regimes in Thailand, access to remunerative employment is difficult in the first place (Empower Foundation 2012a: 4–5). In addition, the risk of raids as part of anti-trafficking measures means that sex workers easily lose their job and livelihoods. This way, trafficking laws have been used to control voluntary sex work in Thailand (Goodwin 2012: 24). Empower Foundation (2012a: 58) has found that in anti-trafficking raids and rescue operations undertaken in Thailand, for every person that is identified as victim of trafficking, eight non-trafficked migrant sex workers are arrested, detained and deported.

Detention results in income insecurity, in addition to representing a major human rights abuse. Empower Foundation (2012a: xiii–xvi) describes how migrant sex workers in Thailand have been detained as witnesses for periods up to a year as part of anti-trafficking measures. During those periods, neither witnesses nor victims of trafficking have access to compensation for lost earnings. Besides endangering sex workers and their families' livelihoods, anti-trafficking measures have undermined programmes to improve sex workers' health (Goodwin 2012: 24–25).

Rather than separating 'sexual exploitation' from 'labour exploitation' and applying a binary definition of exploitation, when a selected set of exceptional conditions is met, our perspective on sex work starts from the assumption that labour exploitation is a continuum (Lerche 2011; AP Forced Labor Net 2014: 6–7). It affects sex workers as well as workers in other industries (AP Forced Labor Net 2014: 6–7).

Equally important is that a labour approach to sex work acknowledges that sex work is work, and that there must be respect for sex workers' knowledge and demands. The recognition of sex work as work is the first principle of the three core values of the sex workers' global network NSWP (2013a), which underlines that sex workers are entitled to labour rights. The guarantee of labour rights, rather than criminalisation, plays a key role in the prevention of forced sex work and the protection of those in forced sex work (e.g. Bindman and Doezema 1997; Hardy 2013; Kempadoo 2005; Shamir 2012).

Respecting sex workers' knowledge and demands implies that sex workers and their representatives have to be involved in policy debates at the national and international level. Fundamental, 'enabling' rights that need to be guaranteed effectively are freedom of association and the right to collective bargaining. This, too, represents one of the core values of the NSWP (2013a). The empowerment of workers – in the sex industry and elsewhere – through collective representation and guarantee of labour rights is crucial to preventing and putting an end to exploitative working conditions. Given that sex workers tend to be excluded from policy arenas, respect for these two basic principles will lead to re-definitions of how (in)decent working conditions in the sex industry are understood.

A labour approach to sex work also considers and addresses the structural, globalised determinants of labour precarity in the sex industry through neo-liberal economic policy and restrictive immigration governance (e.g. Jordan 2012: 9–12).

In the following section, we build on this understanding to reflect on the possibilities of approaching labour precarity in the sex industry in a more effective way.

Imagining a different discourse: the discursive and material consequences of recognising sex work as work

If the principles of the labour approach outlined above had been taken up by ILC participants, what shape could the debate in the Committee on Forced Labour have taken? And: what could have been the result?

In this section, we imagine that 'another 103rd ILC debate is possible' during which sex workers themselves raise their voices. The alternative – hypothetical – discussion outlined in this section aims to open new discursive spaces to address the material insecurities confronted by sex workers. Similar to the actual ILC debate, our imagined alternative would also be composed of a tripartite delegation of government delegates, an employer delegate, a worker delegate, and their respective advisors. However, while sex workers' national and global representatives were excluded from the actual ILC debate, now these organisations, such as NSWP and Empower Foundation, would be included as members of the ILO workers' delegations or as their advisors. Observing international non-governmental organisations, such as the Association for Women's Rights in Development (AWID) and Amnesty International (2015c), which have supported sex workers' demands for recognition and decriminalisa-tion, would speak out, too. The positions taken by the actors in this hypothetical debate reflect existing statements of sex workers' organisations and their allies whose spirit (and, often, wording) we have tried to preserve. With this hypothetical, more inclusive debate, we intend to demonstrate that the involvement of marginalised societal groups, such as sex workers themselves is likely to shift discourses towards alternative policies and regulation that prioritise human flourishing over narrow definitions of national security and macro-economic development.

We imagine the global sex workers' representative would be able to point out that freedom from slavery-like practices such as forced or bonded labour and servitude should be considered as a basic human right for people employed in the sex industry as much as for everyone else (NSWP 2013a: 8). S/he[12] would not consider the notion of 'sexual exploitation' helpful in the debate about effective measures to prevent forced labour and protect those in forced labour situations – sex workers or others: 'Framing sex work as violence or as inherently exploitative renders sex workers' realities invisible by not recognising sex work as work' (NSWP 2013a: 8). The global sex workers representative would therefore demand the omission of the term 'sexual exploitation' from the Protocol's preamble due to this misleading use of the term. Instead, s/he would demand that: '[T]hese abuses should be addressed through a labour and industrial relations framework that includes access to justice for all sex workers' (NSWP 2013a: 9).

A representative of Empower Foundation would add that the use of the term 'sexual exploitation' in a labour context, in practice, deprives sex workers from effective access to justice on the basis of labour rights:

> If we are exploited sexually as women we would want to use criminal sexual assault and similar laws to seek justice. Prevention of sexual exploitation is the mainstream prevention of sexual violence by men. If we are exploited in our work we want to use criminal forced labour laws or other labour laws to get justice as workers. Prevention of exploitation of our labour is the mainstream prevention of labour exploitation. When we feel exploited or forced to work we don't use language like 'sexually exploited' we use work terms 'forced to work' 'ripped off' or 'cheated at work'.

She would point out that sex workers working in diverse parts of the industry and in different regions of Thailand have consistently identified labour conditions that they associate with the exploitative extreme of a decent work continuum. Such exploitative conditions include, for instance, daily quotas related to the number of customers and/or alcohol consumption; advances on the salary with more than 20 per cent interest; as well as a split of their salary with more than half going to the employer (Empower Foundation forthcoming)[13]. According to the representative of the Empower Foundation, singling out sex work as 'sexual exploitation' in the Protocol is motivated by an obsession with sex as extra-ordinary. Such treatment diverts attention from a recognition of sex workers' rights:

> when people discuss human trafficking into the Entertainment Industry they call it 'sex trafficking' and the word 'human' disappears. They don't use similar terms like sewing trafficking or fishing trafficking. The focus isn't on our human rights after all, but rather the problem seems to be that we are having sex.
>
> (Empower Foundation 2012a: 21)

We go on to imagine the global sex workers' representative would pick up the demand to treat sex work as any other work vulnerable to exploitation. Along the lines of the consolidated position of workers' organisations expressed in the comments on the Protocol's draft (ILC 2014d: 12), s/he would argue that: 'Sex work has always been a part of the informal economy!' (D'Adamo 2015: 9). Similar to other largely informal occupations providing intimate labour, work involving physical or emotional closeness such as domestic work, sex work has been excluded from basic labour standards, putting sex workers at risk of becoming victims of forced labour. They should therefore be mentioned explicitly in the Protocol's preamble – alongside other vulnerable sectors and groups of workers. Her/his view would be seconded by the representative of Amnesty International. She would argue that, over and above the lack of labour rights guarantees for sex workers, evidence and the real-life experience of sex workers themselves show that criminalisation makes them less safe.

> We therefore advocate for the decriminalization of all aspects of consensual adult sex. We believe that decriminalization would help tackle forced labour. When sex work is decriminalized, sex workers are better able to work together and demand their rights, leading to better working conditions and standards and greater oversight of commercial sex and potential forced labour within it. When they are not threatened with criminalization, sex workers are also able to collaborate with law enforcement to identify traffickers and victims of trafficking.
>
> (Amnesty International 2015a, 2015b)

Regarding effective prevention of forced labour situations and protection of those in such situations, we picture the international sex workers' representative arguing in favour of a central role of workers in related measures:

> In efforts to prevent and protect workers at risk to or in forced labour situations, their own position needs to be strengthened. Sex workers should therefore be invited and meaningfully consulted to ensure that their expert opinions are included when sex workers' lives and work are discussed by government and other bodies.
>
> (NSWP 2013a: 3)

This is in line with a consolidated position taken by workers' organisations in the preparation of the Protocol's text (ILC 2014d: 22–23), which, however, was ignored during the actual debate. This stance is being seconded by the Association for Women's Rights in Development (AWID) which participates in our imagined Committee deliberations as an observer. Their representative would state that:

> We also believe that it is vital to recognize the human rights of sex workers and stand in solidarity with them in their struggles and organizing processes. AWID considers sex workers as key actors in the effort to eliminate all forms of violence against women, including trafficking and sexual exploitation.
>
> (AWID 2015: 4)

In the discussion around measures to prevent situations of forced labour, the representative of Empower Foundation reiterates the need to entitle sex workers to labour rights in order to reduce their vulnerability to exploitation rather than policing them and that way heightening their precarity. Her imagined position draws on the more general point made by the Government member of Belgium in the actual ILC debate that labour law needed to be enforced to address forced labour (ILC 2014c: 43). She would also agree with the demand that figured in the actual ILC debate that labour inspection had to be strengthened to prevent forced labour (ILC 2014c: 45). This, they would argue, should be applicable to all workers, and include informal and sex workers. Empower also suggests that sex workers' organisations be supported to play a pivotal role in designing labour inspection appropriate for the sex industry that are not camouflage for raids.

But more would be demanded as delegates recognise that economic and migration governance have a crucial role in mediating the precarious labour conditions that sex workers encounter. Representatives of Empower would point out, for instance, how despite the need that many countries have for migrant workers, there is a lack of government assisted migration or employment recruitment agencies, a void that is then filled by informal employment systems, i.e. brokers. In consequence, 'migrants must take a chance as to whether the broker they are dealing with is fair or exploitative. This will influence not just the migrant's travel costs and safety, but also to a large extent the working conditions at the end of their journey' (Empower Foundation 2012a: 4–5). The international sex workers' representative would agree with the Empower Foundation's position and add that, in order to address root causes of forced labour, all workers, including sex workers, should be provided with: 'safe, legal, and equal channels to migrate and obtain work visas for sex work or other work' (NSWP 2013a: 22).

Our imagined, alternative ILC debate could shift the consensus about how to address sex work in debates on forced labour from criminalisation to recognition and greater empowerment for sex workers. It would be in line with the ILO's implicit recognition of sex workers as workers, in research (e.g. Lim 1998) or in labour standards (e.g. ILO 2010). We imagine a resulting seventh preambular paragraph on trafficking in persons as part of a changing context of forced labour that does not single out the unclear element of 'sexual exploitation'. Instead, as proposed by several countries in response to the first draft of the Protocol (ILC 2014d: 12), the imagined Protocol's preamble would recall that certain groups of workers have a higher risk of becoming victims of forced labour, and would list those working in the sex industry along with other groups with heightened vulnerability in this regard. Furthermore, in line with our proposed labour approach to sex work and with the demands of several actors contributing to the ILC debate on forced labour, the envisaged Protocol would be more specific in Article 2 regarding how to address the root causes and factors that heighten the risks of forced or compulsory labour. For instance, as proposed by the US-American union federation AFL-CIO (ILC 2014d: 20), safe migration processes and supply-chain monitoring can contribute to less exploitative labour conditions.

Such an alternative debate would help to create a discursive space that makes visible, includes and strengthens sex workers' collective agency for improvement of the conditions of their work and livelihood.

Conclusion

In this chapter, we build on research that shows that the dominant criminal law approach to sex work and forced labour silences sex workers' legitimate demands to implement policies that really end exploitative labour conditions in the sex industry. We propose that to effectively address labour precarity in the sex industry, an approach is required that acknowledges sex work as work and looks at labour exploitation as a continuum. We argue that this helps to strengthen sex workers' agency to improve their working conditions. We imagine how such an alternative approach that enables the effective representation of sex workers' demands would have shifted the course and outcomes of the 2014 ILC debate on forced labour. The acknowledgement of sex work as work and sex workers as entitled to empowerment and protection through labour rights' guarantees is necessary, yet, not sufficient. Sex workers' precarious labour conditions need to be understood in the context of a global (neoliberal) political economy that marginalises the majority of workers world-wide. Only then would action to empower them economically and socially succeed.

Our approach attempts to address rifts and holes in the landscape of discourses on sex work. We argue that a labour approach to sex work can help bridge the divide in feminist discourses. While in this polarised debate, sex workers' free choice or the coercion they experience, respectively, are highlighted to justify diametrically opposed policy stances regarding sex work, we argue that the concern for sex workers' precarious labour conditions that form the normative benchmark of a labour approach to sex work is a shared motivation of antagonistic feminist discourses.

The silences surrounding sex work in labour studies and advocacy for decent work, despite the fact that it represents a large occupational group characterised by a high degree of decent work deficits, can be seen as an expression of the implicit refusal to analyse work and employment in relation to people's sexuality. Our chapter addresses this neglect of sex workers' working conditions. It is innovative in making explicit the relevance and analytical value of conceptualisations of precarious work for sex work. This involves embedding a labour approach to sex work in a critique of neo-liberal capitalism, in line with Bernstein (2007: 185–6) who maintains that 'feminists and other social commentators who are concerned about the existence and augmentation of contemporary sex markets would be wise to identify the fight against corporate globalization (in both its transnational and local guises) as pivotal to their interests'.

Last, but certainly not least, we have aimed to make sex workers' own (diverse) voices more audible in research, arguing with Gall (2007: 76) that it is of critical importance for sex workers' interest representation that they, supported by allies, develop the discourse themselves. The choir of their voices in our imagined, alternative ILC debate offers an impression of how policy discourses that are likely to shape material conditions could change when the people concerned get a chance to voice their demands and present their ideas for greater social justice.

Notes

1 According to (neo)abolitionist feminists, sex work is inherently exploitative. It is seen as an act of violence against women (MacKinnon 2005).
2 In the following, we refer to 'sex work/er' as a broader and less stigmatising term (Berg 2014: 693) compared to 'prostitution/prostitute'.
3 See Gall (2007) and Hardy (2010) for exceptions.
4 According to the ILO, decent work 'involves opportunities for work that is productive and delivers a fair income, security in the workplace and social protection for families, better prospects for personal development and social integration, freedom for people to express their concerns, organize and participate in the decisions that affect their lives and equality of opportunity and treatment for all women and men' (ILO 2015).
5 In the following, we refer to this as the 'UN Anti-Trafficking Protocol'.
6 We focus on the analysis of the Forced Labour Protocol as the legally binding instrument.
7 Referred to as 'Protocol' in the following.
8 Referred to as 'Recommendation' in the following.
9 The ILO constitution allows for a maximum of two advisors for each item on the agenda of the ILC (ILO 1974).
10 The use of personal pronouns in the analysis of the Committee on Forced Labour follows ILC (2014c).
11 One can argue, however, that code 9609 'Other personal service activities n.e.c.' of the UN International Standard Industrial Classification of All Economic Activities, Rev.4 captures most of the activities covered by our definition of sex work either explicitly or implicitly (UNSTATS 2008).
12 We use the term 's/he' as personal pronoun for the international sex workers' representative in order to reflect the diversity of sex workers, including women, men and transgendered persons.
13 Empower has been working on describing sex work according to the real experiences of sex workers aligned with ILO and other definitions of labour practices. They began in 2013 with workshops in six provinces in Thailand. To date 220 sex workers have joined the project to create a continuum that describes sex work in Thailand starting with Decent Work across the spectrum to situations that would fit with the UN Protocol definition of trafficking. The work was partially funded by the international women's fund Mama Cash, but currently has no specific funding and is undertaken within their core work. The data presented here is part of that research.

References

Agustín, Laura María (2007) *Sex at the Margins: Migration, Labour Markets and the Rescue Industry.* London and New York: Zed Books.
Agustín, Laura María and Jo Weldon (2003) 'The Sex Sector: A Victory for Diversity', *Global Reproductive Rights Newsletter* 66/67(2/3): 31–34. Amsterdam: Women's Global Network for Reproductive Rights.
Alexander, Priscilla (1998) 'Sex Work and Health: A Question of Safety in the Workplace', *Journal of the American Medical Women's Association* 53(2): 77–82.
Amnesty International (2015a) 'Q&A: Policy to Protect the Human Rights of Sex Workers'. Available at: https://www.amnesty.org/en/qa-policy-to-protect-the-human-rights-of-sex-workers/ [accessed 3 September 2015].
Amnesty International (2015b) 'Sex Workers' Rights are Human Rights'. Available at: https://www.amnesty.org/en/latest/news/2015/08/sex-workers-rights-are-human-rights/ [accessed 3 September 2015].

Amnesty International (2015c) 'Decision on State Obligations to Respect, Protect and Fulfil the Human Rights of Sex Workers'. Available at: https://www.amnesty.org/p olicy-on-state-obligations-to-respect-protect-and-fulfil-the-human-right s-of-sex-workers/ [accessed 25 January 2015].

Arnold, Dennis and Joseph R. Bongiovi (2013) 'Precarious, Informalizing, and Flexible Work Transforming Concepts and Understandings', *American Behavioral Scientist* 57(3): 289–308.

Asia Pacific Forced Labour Network (AP Forced Labor Net) (2014) 'Online Discussion Report: What is Forced Labour, Human Trafficking and Slavery? Do Definitions Matter, and Why?' Marja Paavilainen (moderator) and Na Eun Mun (facilitator). ILO Regional Office for Asia and the Pacific. 22 April–2 May 2014.

Association for Women's Rights in Development (AWID) (2015) *Sex Workers Transforming Economic Power to Advance Women's Rights and Justice. Post 2012 AWID International Forum Innovation Seed Grants.* Toronto: AWID.

Bacchi, Carol (2000) 'Policy as Discourse: What does it Mean? Where does it Get Us?', *Discourse* 21(1): 45–57.

Baye, Eneze and Silke Heumann (2014) 'Migration, Sex Work and Exploitative Labor Conditions: Experiences of Nigerian Women in the Sex Industry in Turin, Italy, and Counter-Trafficking Measures', *Gender, Technology and Development* 18(1) 77–105.

Berg, Heather (2014) 'Working for Love, Loving for Work: Discourses of Labor in Feminist Sex-Work Activism', *Feminist Studies* 40(3): 693–721.

Bernstein, Elisabeth (1999) 'What's Wrong with Prostitution? What's Right with Sex Work? Comparing Markets in Female Sexual Labor', *Hasting Women's Law Journal* 10: 91–117.

Bernstein, Elisabeth (2007) *Temporarily Yours. Intimacy, Authenticity, and the Commerce of Sex.* Chicago and London: The University of Chicago Press.

Bernstein, Elisabeth (2010) 'Militarized Humanitarianism Meets Carceral Feminism: The Politics of Sex, Rights, and Freedom in Contemporary Antitrafficking Campaigns', *Signs* 36(1): 45–71.

Bindman, Jo and Jo Doezema (1997) *Redefining Prostitution as Sex Work on the International Agenda.* Vancouver: Commercial Sex Information Service.

Boynton, Petra and Linda Cusick (2006) 'Sex Workers to Pay the Price', *British Medical Journal* (Clinical research edn) 332: 190–191.

Cabezas, Amalia L. (2004) 'Between Love and Money: Sex, Tourism, and Citizenship in Cuba and the Dominican Republic', *Signs: Journal of Women in Culture and Society* 29(4): 987–1015.

Cohen, Rachel Lara, Kate Hardy, Teela Sanders, Carol Wolkowitz (2013) 'Introduction: The Body/Sex/Work Nexus', in Carol Wolkowitz, Rachel Lara Cohen, Teela Sanders and Kate Hardy (eds) (2013) *Sex/Body/Work: Intimate, Sexualized and Embodied Labour.* Basingstoke: Palgrave.

Crowhurst, Isabel (2012) 'Caught in the Victim/Criminal Paradigm: Female Migrant Prostitution in Contemporary Italy', *Modern Italy* 17(4): 493–506.

Crowhurst, Isabel, Joyce Outshoorn and May-Len Skilbrei (2012) 'Introduction: Prostitution Policies in Europe', *Sexuality Research and Social Policy* 9(3): 187–191.

D'Adamo, Kate (2015) 'Beyond Sex Work as Work', *Research for Sex Work* 14, September, pp. 9–10. Available at: http://www.nswp.org/sites/nswp.org/files/R4SW%202015_ issue 14_PDFV.pdf [accessed 25 January 2016].

Doezema, Jo (1999) 'Loose Women or Lost Women? The Re-Emergence of the Myth of White Slavery in Contemporary Discourses of Trafficking in Women', *Gender Issues* 18(1): 23–50.

Doezema, Jo (2002) 'Who Gets to Choose? Coercion, Consent, and the UN Trafficking Protocol', *Gender and Development* 10(1): 20–27.

Doezema, Jo (2005) 'Now You See Her, Now You Don't: Sex Workers at the UN Trafficking Protocol Negotiation', *Social & Legal Studies* 14(1): 61–89.

Dworkin, Andrea (1993) 'Prostitution and Male Supremacy', Speech at a symposium entitled 'Prostitution: From Academia to Activism', sponsored by the Michigan Journal of Gender and Law at the University of Michigan Law School, 31 October 1992.

Empower Foundation (2012a) *Hit and Run: Sex Worker's Research on Anti Trafficking in Thailand*. Nonthaburi: Empower Foundation, Thailand.

Empower Foundation (2012b) *The Prevention and Suppression of Human Trafficking Act 2008: Impact on Sex Workers. A Report by Empower Foundation*, Bangkok Art and Cultural Centre, 21 February 2012. Available at: http://www.empowerfounda tion.org/sexy_en.php?id=5 [accessed 3 September 2015].

Empower Foundation (forthcoming) *Empower Community Research 'Decent Sex Work in Thailand'* (working title). Nonthaburi: Empower Foundation, Thailand.

Gall, Gregor (2007) 'Sex Worker Unionisation: An Exploratory Study of Emerging Collective Organisation', *Industrial Relations Journal* 38(1): 70–88.

Gasper, Des and Raymond Apthorpe (1996) 'Introduction: Analysis and Policy Discourse', in Raymond Apthorpe and Des Gasper (eds) *Arguing Development Policy: Frames and Discourses*, pp. 1–15. London: Frank Cass.

Goodwin, John (2012) *Sex Work and the Law in Asia and the Pacific. Laws, HIV and Human Rights in the Context of Sex Work*. Bangkok: United Nations Development Programme.

Goodwin, Susan (2011) 'Analysing Policy as Discourse: Methodological Advances in Policy Analysis'. In L. Markauskaite, P. Freebody and J. Irwin (eds), *Methodological Choice and Design: Scholarship, Policy and Practice in Social and Educational Research*, pp. 167–180. Sydney: Springer.

Hardy, Kate (2010) 'Incorporating Sex Workers into the Argentine Labor Movement', *International Labor and Working-Class History* 77(01): 89–108.

Hardy, Kate (2013) 'Equal to Any Other, but Not the Same as Any Other: The Politics of Sexual Labour, the Body and Intercorporeality', in Carol Wolkowitz, Rachel Lara Cohen, Teela Sanders and Kate Hardy (eds), *Sex/Body/Work: Intimate, Sexualized and Embodied Labour*. Basingstoke: Palgrave.

International Labour Conference (ILC) (1999) *Decent Work. Report of the Director General to the International Labour Conference's 87th Session*. Geneva: ILC.

ILC (2005) *A Global Alliance Against Forced Labour. Report of the Director-General. Global Report under the Follow-up to the ILO Declaration on Fundamental Principles and Rights at Work*. Geneva: ILO.

ILC (2012) *Recurrent Discussion under the ILO Declaration on Social Justice for a Fair Globalization and the Follow-up to the ILO Declaration on Fundamental Principles and Rights at Work. Report of the Committee for the Recurrent Discussion on the Strategic Objective of Fundamental Principles and Rights at Work*. Geneva: ILO.

ILC (2013) *Report IV(1). Strengthening Action to End Forced Labour*. Geneva: ILO.

ILC (2014a) *Text of the Recommendation on Supplementary Measures for the Effective Suppression of Forced Labour*. Geneva: ILO.

ILC (2014b) *Protocol to the Forced Labour Convention, 1930, Adopted by the Conference at its 103rd Session, Geneva, 11 June 2014*. Geneva: ILO.

ILC (2014c) *Fourth Item on the Agenda: Supplementing the Forced Labour Convention, 1930 (No. 29), to Address Implementation Gaps to Advance Prevention, Protection and Compensation Measures, to Effectively Achieve the Elimination of Forced Labour. Report of the Committee on Forced Labour*. Geneva: ILO.

ILC (2014d) *Report IV (2A). Strengthening Action to End Forced Labour*. Geneva: ILO.

ILC (2014e) *Report IV (2B). Strengthening Action to End Forced Labour*. Geneva: ILO.

International Labour Organization (ILO) (1974) *ILO Constitution*. Geneva: ILO. Available at: http://www.ilo.org/dyn/normlex/en/f?p=1000:62:0::NO:62:P62_LIST_ENTRIE_ID:2453907:NO [accessed 10 July 2015].

ILO (2010) 'HIV and AIDS Recommendation, 2010 (No. 200)'. Geneva: ILO.

ILO (2012) *ILO Global Estimate of Forced Labour: Results and Methodology*. Geneva: ILO.

ILO (2014) *Profits and Poverty: The Economics of Forced Labour*. Geneva: ILO.

ILO (2015) *Decent Work*. Geneva: ILO. Available at: http://www.ilo.org/global/topics/decent-work/lang–en/index.htm [accessed 25 August 2015].

Jordan, Ann (2012) 'Slavery, Forced Labour, Debt Bondage and Human Trafficking: From Conceptual Confusion to Targeted Solutions', American University Center for Human Rights & Humanitarian Law Issue Paper, No. 2. Washington, DC: Center for Human Rights & Humanitarian Law.

Kempadoo, Kamala (2003) 'Globalizing Sex Workers Rights', *Canadian Woman Studies* 22(3, 4): 143–150.

Kempadoo, Kamala (2005) 'Introduction: From Moral Panic to Global Justice: Changing Perspectives on Trafficking', in Kamala Kempadoo et al. (eds) *Trafficking and Prostitution Reconsidered: New Perspectives on Migration, Sex Work and Human Rights*. Boulder/London: Paradigm.

Kempadoo, Kamala and Ranya Ghuma (1999) 'For the Children: Trends in International Policies and Laws in Sex Tourism', in Kamala Kempadoo (ed.) *Sun, Sex, and Gold: Tourism and Sex Work in the Caribbean*, pp. 291–308. Lanham: Rowman & Littlefield Publishers.

Lerche, Jens (2011) 'The Unfree Labour Category and Unfree Labour Estimates: A Continuum within Low-End Labour Relations', *Manchester Papers in Political Economy*, No. 10. Manchester: University of Manchester.

Lim, Lin Lean (1998) *The Sex Sector: The Economic and Social Bases of Prostitution in Southeast Asia*. Geneva: International Labour Organization.

MacKinnon, Catharine A. (2005) 'Pornography as Trafficking', *Michigan Journal of International Law* 16: 993–1012.

Global Network of Sex Work Projects (NSWP) (2013a) 'Consent Statement on Sex Work, Human Rights, and the Law'. Edinburgh: NSWP.

Global Network of Sex Work Projects (NSWP) (2013b) 'Update on USAID v AOSI Case on Anti-Prostitution Pledge'. Edinburgh: NSWP. Available at: http://www.nswp.org/resource/nswp-update-usaid-v-aosi-case-anti-prostitution-pledge [accessed 10 July 2015].

Hewison, Kevin and Arne Kalleberg (2013) 'Precarious Work and Flexibilization in South and Southeast Asia', *American Behavioral Scientist* 57(4): 395–402.

Ouedraogo, A. (2012) 'A Labour Rights Approach to HIV and Sex Work', Presentation during 19th International AIDS Conference, Washington DC, 22–27 July 2012, 'Turning the Tide Together'.

Padilla, Mark B., Jennifer S. Hirsch, Miguel Munoz-Laboy, Robert Sember and Richard G. Parker (eds) (2007) *Love and Globalization: Transformations of Intimacy in the Contemporary World*. Nashville: Vanderbilt University Press.

Peano, Irene (2012) 'Excesses and Double Standards: Migrant Prostitutes, Sovereignty and Exceptions in Contemporary Italy', *Modern Italy* 17(4): 419–432.

Peano, Irene (2013) 'Bondage and Help: Genealogies and Hopes in Trafficking from Nigeria to Italy', in Joel Quirk and Darshan Wigneswaran (eds) *Slavery, Migration and Contemporary Bondage in Africa*. Trenton, NJ: Africa World Press. Available at: http://www.academia.edu/4498855/Bondage_and_help_Genealogies_and_hopes_in_trafficking_from_Nigeria_to_Italy# [accessed 3 September 2015].

Raymond, Janice G. (2003) 'Legitimating Prostitution as Sex Work: UN International Labour Organization Calls for Recognition of the Sex Industry', Sisyphe.org, 1 October 2003. Available at: http://sisyphe.org/spip.php?article689 [accessed 3 September 2015].

Sanders, Teela (2004) 'A Continuum of Risk? The Management of Health, Physical and Emotional Risks by Female Sex Workers', *Sociology of Health & Illness* 26(5): 557–574.

Sanders, Teela and Kate Hardy (2013) 'Sex Work: The Ultimate Precarious Labour?', *Criminal Justice Matters* 93(1): 16–17.

Sanders, Teela and Kate Hardy (2014) *Flexible Workers: Labour, Regulation and the Political Economy of the Stripping Industry*. Abingdon and New York: Routledge.

Saunders, Penelope (2004) 'Prohibiting Sex Work Projects, Restricting Women's Rights: The International Impact of the 2003 US Global AIDS Act', *Health and Human Rights* 7(2): 179–192.

Shamir, Hila (2012) 'A Labor Paradigm for Human Trafficking', *UCLA Law Review* 60: 76–136.

Skilbrei, May-Len and Marianne Tveit (2011) 'Mission Impossible? Voluntarily and Dignified Repatriation of Victims of Trafficking to Nigeria', in Thanh-Dam Truong and Des Gasper (eds), *Transnational Migration and Human Security*, pp. 135–146. Heidelberg: Springer Publications.

Standing, Guy (2011) *The Precariat: The New Dangerous Class*. London, New York: Bloomsbury Academic.

Sullivan, Barbara (2003) 'Trafficking in Women', *International Feminist Journal of Politics* 5(1): 67–91.

Testaí, Patrizia (2013) 'Victim Protection Policy in a Local Context: A Case Study', in Mary Burke (ed.) *Human Trafficking: Interdisciplinary Perspectives*, pp. 3–23. Abingdon and New York: Routledge.

Truong, Thanh-Dam (2014) 'Human Trafficking, Globalization, and Transnational Feminist Responses', ISS Working Paper Series No. 579. The Hague: ISS.

UNSTATS (United Nations Statistics Division) (2008) 'Detailed Structure and Explanatory Notes ISIC Rev.4 code 9609'. Available at http://unstats.un.org/unsd/cr/registry/regcs.asp?Cl=27&Lg=1&Co=9609 [accessed 30 July 2015].

10 Resistance and hope

Youth responses to the economic crisis in Southern Europe

Paulina (Sat) Trejo-Mendez, Paula Sánchez de la Blanca, Laura Santamaría Buitrago, Emma Claire Sardoni, Guilia Simula with Wendy Harcourt

Introduction and framing of the chapter[1]

This chapter looks at civic innovation in youth responses to the current economic crisis in Southern Europe. The chapter is an intergenerational dialogue held over several months about the experience of youth and the economic crisis in Rome, Italy, Madrid and Malaga, Spain. It sets out to question dominant negative narratives about the current economic crisis by looking at resistance and hope. These two main concepts reveal the strong and passionate way young people perceive their futures in terms of resistance as an act and practice that challenges and creates new possibilities outside the mainstream narrative and equally strongly as a sense of hope expressed as positive emotions about the possibilities of a future that they will live and determine.

As activist scholars we have put together the chapter via a series of discussions among ourselves as young people aged from 16–30 in dialogue with Wendy Harcourt one of the editors of the book. All of us have lived or undertaken research in Spain and Italy. Paulina Trejo-Mendez from Mexico, did research in Madrid, Spain for her MA at the International Institute of Social Studies (ISS) at Erasmus University and is now doing her PhD at ISS; Paula Sánchez de la Blanca, from Spain is doing her MA at ISS in The Netherlands, Laura Santamaría Buitrago, from Colombia did research in Malaga, Spain for her MA at ISS, and is currently working in peace building projects with young men and women in Bogotá and other regions of Colombia; Emma Claire Sardoni, from Italy is studying at the Tasso Classical High School, Rome and undertook research in Rome, Italy, and Giulia Simula, from Italy is doing her MA at ISS; Wendy Harcourt, from Australia with Italian citizenship lives and undertakes research in Italy and teaches at ISS.

We have experimented in writing the chapter as a series of conversations about theory, experience of resistance and possibilities of hope told in the interviews and conversations. We have drawn from our own experiences shared with other young activists in dialogue with different theories about social movements, embodied research and youth studies. We contribute to research on civic innovation by reflecting on our individual and collective experiences of change, looking at how youth are navigating changing social relations in Rome, Italy and Madrid and Malaga in Spain. Methodologically we position the researcher as part of the experience, challenging the binary division between the researcher and the researched. Our epistemological position also aims to break down the division between academic knowledge and activist knowledge. In doing so, we aim to explore new (embodied) ways of doing research that look at generational positionalities, privileges and epistemologies.

Our theoretical grounding comes from some of the social movement literature and the ongoing debates around youth responses to the crisis by Jenny Pearce (2013) and the work of Ana Dinerstein (2014) in her discussions of the organizing of hope in Latin America. This literature points to how and why young people see the potential for civic innovation in a time of crisis.

Our study looks at the impact of the economic crisis on progressive students and youth living in Madrid, Malaga and Rome from the perspective of youth's own experiences rather than expert opinions on youth. In focusing on youth's own experiences and opinions we are taking up Arturo Escobar's proposal of 'political ontology' (Escobar 2015) as a way to question dominant hegemonic narratives. This means that contrary to traditional understandings of ontology that emphasise a notion of a unified, abstract, individual universal complete self, we are interested in the politics of being or becoming or 'knowing by doing', investigating the power-laden processes through which life is experienced and lived. We see the struggles of becoming actively engaged as civic beings as based in everyday resistances arising from everyday experiences of oppression.

The civic innovation we are interested in exploring in this chapter is the active engagement in social change processes by young people in response to the economic crisis as they are living it, in the period from 2012–2014, in Madrid, Malaga and Rome. In these three cities there are specific histories and traditions of social resistance, but we do not to seek to chronicle those traditions as such, only when they touch on the perception of the youth in the study. In this way we focus on the doing and being of youth in their own understanding of politics in this period of time. These responses by youth we understand as civic innovation not because there is something new in youth and student movement resistances and struggles, as such, but rather there is something innovative in this specific historical moment. In other words, we look at how youth resistance is creating innovative ways to challenge the contemporary dominant order of things and in this way are creating alternatives to current dominant economic practices. We see our interest in youth critical attitude to the status quo as relevant for critical thinking and practices of social resistance.

In looking at these particular civic innovations by youth in Madrid, Malaga and Rome, we see ourselves as building knowledge that supports youth as part of social and economic transformation processes. We see the study as counter to the crisis narratives that depict youth as marginal and victims of economic crisis. By exploring how youth are engaged in creative responses to crisis, we focus on the sense of hope and possibility that we see as necessary to generate alternative discourses. These responses include, among other initiatives, locating traditional ways of living and working alongside oppressive practices. We analyse how youth position themselves as political beings and how youth have brought social relations and traditionally non-political categories to the centre of their struggles.

We are also experimenting in our way of writing by acknowledging the emotions felt during these struggles. We see emotions as not something to ignore, but rather to help us to understand the different ways the economic crisis is experienced. We argue that an analysis of the economy cannot be separated from our felt emotions and bodily sensations. There is fear generated by crisis narratives, the struggle by youth is in this sense to remain hopeful and to forge new ideas of how to live through crisis and precarity and how to change consciously the way we relate to each other, society and nature. There is a struggle to rethink the economy beyond material lack and loss, in order to go beyond the narrative crisis, and to think about what is possible. In this aim to rethink the economy, we have also been in conversations with theorists who are looking critically at dominant economic theory. In particular we have been inspired by the conversations of J.K. Gibson Graham that look at non-market transactions, or non-waged labour as legitimate economic processes. We have welcomed their approach to dismantle 'capitalocentrism' of economic discourse and to value economically diverse activities as something that can complement rather than be totally contained within capitalism (Gibson-Graham 2008: 37). In our research we have pushed this analysis further by considering how rethinking the economy impacts on the bodies of the young, and how such bodies become the locus of resistance and struggle, moving from just the 'individual' subject to becoming 'collective subjects' through mutual support. As we go on to elaborate below, the youth in coming together forge webs of support, which results in the construction and strengthening of a collective body, proposing a new alternative against the solitude and individualism characterizing capitalism and states of crisis. In considering the different experiences of students and youth in Italy and Spain we found the conceptual analysis of Gibson-Graham moving beyond 'capitalocentricism' useful. They invite us to question capitalism understood by macro theory and policy as the ominprescent narrative: bounded, hierarchically ordered, driven by the growth imperative (Gibson-Graham 1996, 2006). The hegemony of dominant capitalist narratives makes the very idea of a noncapitalist economy difficult to imagine. Our chapter instead looks at daily non capitalist economic practices as part of innovative forms of anticapitalist politics and economic imaginaries (Osterweil 2005).

We are also responding to questions raised by writers such as Nancy Fraser who asked: 'Why is there no European-wide movement against austerity?' And, why has the current economic crisis failed to 'produce a clear counter hegemony to capitalism and marketization with a coalescence around alternatives' (Fraser 2013: 127)? We would answer Fraser by saying that this study of youth in southern Europe illustrates how youth networks are working to form alternatives in ways that differ from older more traditional struggles of class and capital. We see youth as part of a contemporary form of protest today that is resisting inequalities and responding to global consumer capitalism in ways that go beyond the old class/capital battles. In negotiating current relations and futures youth are dealing with issues like generation, gender, sexuality, race/ethnicity, care and environment. We explore how these concerns lead to more messy and heterogeneous modes of organizing, chronologies and agendas. The new forms of relations particularly linked to non-hierarchical ways of organizing are not entirely new, but can co-exist with previous experiences of collective leadership (e.g. long-term *autonomistas* (autonomy) and anarchist traditions in Spain).

Our chapter's focus on the narratives of youth reshapes our understanding of generational difference in political, economic and social relations. We see this historical moment of economic crisis in Southern Europe as opening up questions about economic innovation and social change. By bringing together the interpretations and narratives as told by youth themselves we aim to displace the gloomy unemployment statistics and economic forecasts and instead present the crisis as forging possibilities for a change of the current social, economic and political order (Lantier 2013). As the Spanish based movement 'Youth without Future' state, they came together first in order to make their plight visible as youth 'without a home, without a job' but also as people 'without fear' for the future. High school students in Rome occupied their school for ten days to demand changes in the education reforms from a 'centre left' government, protesting in joyful marches in their thousands when politicians and their teachers were grimly just accepting the cuts to education facilities and bowing to the demands of austerity. University students together with young social entrepreneurs hold classes in the alternative university in Rome (in the disused central city abattoirs) and travel from town to town in order to hold public teach-ins on alternative money systems. And in Malaga, as described below, the collective 'Zambra Malaga' tries to find new ways of living life by privileging collectivity in economic dynamics and through communitarian ways of living. These young people, tired of the effects of the crisis over their lives, are trying to live the world they are envisioning by placing care and collectivity at the centre of their struggle.

The chapter is told via several voices: some collective, some individual as indicated in the text. This introduction and the following section set out our collective understanding of the dominant crisis narratives on youth and the economic crisis. Sat and Paula then look at the experiences of youth in Madrid followed by Laura on Malaga. This is then followed by Emma Claire reflecting on high school students' experience in Rome, and Giulia more generally on Italy. Wendy, reflecting on those experiences and her own intergenerational engagement, then discusses shifting economic imaginaries. We conclude by collectively analysing civic innovation in the search for a politics of place and youth within it.

Generations in times of crisis

As stated above, in our exploration of youth we are also interested in the concept of generation. Edmunds and Turner (2002) define an age group as a generation when the historical context in which they exist has shaped a shared cultural identity. The concept 'generation as actuality' applies when there is a strong connection forged between those who feel they belong to a generation. Edmunds and Turner mention the impact/role in social change of a generation can only be clear with time. Not all age cohorts become generations (Roberts 2011). The youth collective activities now emerging in southern Europe are building a collective awareness marked by precariousness, vulnerability and struggles. They are engaging in collective activities to find alternatives in ways that would not have been imaginable before the crisis. Similarly, the students in Rome see themselves as a generation that needs to act even as they face uncertain futures. What will define them and whether they become a generation or not, remains to be seen. The University students in their discussions are preparing themselves to make new economic communities in the face of uncertain jobs, but also shifts in the climate and concerns around loss in agricultural production.

How are we defining youth from this generational perspective? Is the age of youth now an expanding category with the delayed incorporation of this generation into a 'stable' job market? Are extended education careers and precariousness prolonging the 'youth life stage'? (Roberts 2011). In the conversations with young people in Spain in their twenties and early thirties, and among the same age group in Italy, they define youth not only in terms of age but also in relation to the conditions in which they are forced to live – precariousness, instability and insecurity. They are constantly wondering if they can afford to pay rent, if they will keep temporary contracts or work with no contracts at all (Trejo Mendez 2014). They are, as in the discussion in Italy, aware that precarity or 'austercide' (the violence caused by austerity measures) is impacting not only them but also older generations. The prosperity that their parents, the generation of late 'baby-boomers', is visibly declining with a shrinking welfare system and failing labour market. There is a noted tension among generations, with younger people seeing their parents as the beneficiaries of the post-war social democracies that have led to neoliberal politics that they, the younger people, are now suffering (Roberts 2011: 483). A generational divide is emerging as the crisis bites and the apparent prosperity is evaporating along with questioning the idea of economic progress linked to dominant practices of the capitalist system. In this essay we use the category of generation in our research as we collectively speak from our ages and experiences, trying to transcend the rigid division between generations and to construct collective knowledge from our generational positionalities.

Challenging the dominant crisis narratives

With few jobs, homes and little hope of 'retirement' and pensions, youth are becoming stereotyped in European media and the broader public imagination as the 'lost generation'. According to the European Commission (2013) 7.5 million young Europeans are neither studying nor employed or in training (NEETS). According to the statistics of the European Commission more than one in five young people cannot find a job in southern Europe. In Spain one in two young people are unemployed (European Commission 2013) with the official registered unemployment level at 53%. Media reports speak of 'ballooning youth unemployment rates' and the Generation E (Expat, Erasmus, Exilium, Exodus, Escape, Easyjet) (Ottaviani 2014). In 2012, approximately 55% of the population of 25 years and younger couldn't get a job and nearly 30% of them had been looking for a job for more than two years (Mateos and Penades 2013); 54% of the people age 18 to 34 were living with their parents (López Biasco in Taibo 2013: 156).

The November 2014 figures from ISTAT, the National Statistical Institute of Italy, record a national youth (15–24) unemployment rate of 43.9%[2] with even once wealthy central Italian towns such as Viterbo experiencing 49% youth unemployment. South of Rome in the 'mezzogiorno' the figures are 60.9% for young people – in some place close to 90% for young women.

Reading these statistics, youth are well aware that they cannot expect to enjoy the prosperity or stability of their parents as the resources for not only the working class but also the middle class of the future are shrinking. In the face of such dire predictions, youth are considering how to live beyond such negative classifications of their lives and their future. The everyday experience of the crisis has brought with it the search for alternatives to dominant economic and social structures. Youth in resistance are building different relations to politics, capitalism and the state. In Spain, for instance, there are increasing numbers of autonomous mobilisations: In 2012 the number of protest marches reached 42,000: approximately 60 a day, six times more than the previous decade (Observatorio Metropolitano 2011). Throughout these experiences youth is turning the dominant narratives upside down, as we explore in the following stories below.

Madrid: youth without a future (Paulina (Sat) Trejo Mendez)

Sat began her connections with Youth Without a Future (YWF) during a trip to Madrid in Summer 2013 and has since been engaging with, observing and interviewing youth activists in Spain, The Netherlands and Germany. In Madrid, she spoke with youth in their twenties and thirties who were involved in protesting and different alternative community initiatives. People in YWF are mostly students, some are unemployed, and some with precarious jobs. In the interviews they shared that they cannot plan their life in the way their parents did and that many of the problems they face today and in relation to their future need to be dealt with differently. They spoke of the need for solutions that go beyond meeting their momentary needs and inherited expectations. They challenged the old imaginaries of what a 'successful life' looks like. Some spoke of the dominant economic system as clouding other ways of existing and portraying alternatives as undesirable, or simply not possible.

YWF denounced the precarious working conditions, inaccessible housing, temporary contracts, and disguised exploitation presented as 'non-paid internship opportunities'. The resilience strategies of young people use virtual as well as traditional protest (marches and occupations) in their refusal to accept the image of unemployed youth existing hopelessly on the margins. Their actions aim to show a broader public how young people are resisting the dominant homogenizing discourse that flattens their realities.

Youth are responding in many ways as they build new types of relations to others – to their neighbours, parents, the economy, the state, the school. In March 2013 YWF launched the campaign: 'We are not leaving they are kicking us out' connecting youth leaving Spain looking for opportunities elsewhere. They developed an interactive map where they asked young people to write themselves into the map, with stories about their experience – the statement is that precariousness and nomadic lives are now the way of life for young people (Trejo Mendez 2013: 16). The action illustrated how many Spanish youth were leaving their homes in the search for decent living conditions and jobs but also how they were looking to form new relations, make new communities and use virtual means to protest and be visible. Through this virtual network they organised protests in over 30 countries. This initiative underlined that these young people refused to be read or defined merely through sterile statistics that cannot capture their lived realities. In Berlin, Spanish youth who are looking for employment opportunities have formed 15MGAS (Grupo de Acción Syndical – Syndical Action Group). With the slogan 'in exile and exploited? Defend yourself!' they form a platform for Spanish youth who travel to Germany providing information in 'a precarious office' (Doncel 2014).[3]

There is a sense of hope in these shifting relations and building alternatives alongside and outside the system that is failing to provide jobs, education, housing and well-being. The focus is on creating the reality they want today – not waiting for tomorrow either for utopia or for further economic and political failure. In the Madrid neighbourhood assemblies are formed all over the city. Initiatives by people from 15M, neighbours and activists provide food for people who cannot afford it through self-managed food banks and popular free meals in the squares (Trejo Mendez 2013: 21).

YWF also joined with other resistance movements in neighbourhoods, bringing together young with old illustrating new relations among generations, a radical move given the stereotype of young people as disconnected consumers, ignoring other relations (especially the old) as they connect to abstract consumer 'things'. *Yayoflautas* is an example of a group formed by the older generation (mostly retired, often grandparents) that is actively involved in demonstrations – *flautas* – against injustice and in solidarity with other movements such as youth with similar aims (Yayoflautas Madrid 2014). With slogans such as 'Unjust laws are not to be followed', the 'Asamblea de vivienda centro' or community of neighbours in Madrid and nearby Toledo have organised 'to take that which is ours' (Lavapies 2014). They have taken over buildings to provide housing to families who are in need giving shelter to 30 young, families, single mothers and single youth facing precarious conditions (Lavapies 2014).

The vibrancy of these civic innovations can be illustrated by the activities held from 17–18 May 2014 when 50 collectives, groups and assemblies gathered at Campo de Cebada, the self-managed, autonomous space of the barrio 'La Latina' in Madrid, in order to celebrate the anniversary of 15M; with workshops and cultural activities they are building existing alternatives 'to the dominant regime' (15M 2014). Campo de Cebada is an example where neighbours, families and young people create together alternative economies: community gardens, open workshops, classes, free art and cultural activities, cooperatives, exchanging school textbooks, popular food banks, organizing politically (Trejo Mendez 2013). These are all examples of civic innovation as youth are finding themselves in solidarity, resistance and hope in relation with others and to one and other (Autoconsulta.org 2014).

In Campo de Cebada a popular university was set up in the summer of 2013 for people of all ages. Everyone was free to join the courses meeting in the space that had held a now demolished public sports centre. People contributed to the university not only in intellectual discussion – for example the wooden movable benches were made by the wood collective and the edible garden is tended by the people of the barrio (Trejo Mendez 2013: 43). These are all examples of new forms of relations to people, the community and environment, as youth create a learning community space in the Campo de Cebada.

The politics of place: 15M as a bonding experience (Paula Sanchez de la Blanca)

Paula shares her direct engagement with 15M as a youth activist in Spain and as a student in The Netherlands.

Youth struggles may not be anything new. Yet it is difficult not to recognise that there is something new about the way Spanish youth faces the idea of 'youth without future'. On 15 May 2011, under the call for *Real Democracy Now!* (*Democracia Real Ya!*) a demonstration took place in Madrid. It soon quickly evolved into the occupation of the city's central square (Plaza del sol) by many hundreds of *indignados* – indignant, outraged people – who ate, slept, and lived on the square for the following weeks. They turned the square into their collective living- and bedroom for several weeks. Anyone walking in the city centre could join the camping or just breathe some of the excitement and hope emerging on Plaza del Sol, where the metro signs were refashioned to state its new name: Plaza de la Solución (solution square).[4]

The occupying of public squares spread across Spain from the capital to other cities (see below about the experience in Malaga for example), and lasted several weeks before the city governments decided to put an end to them. Nonetheless, 'The 15M' is still very much alive through the many local city assemblies which have continued to convene regularly up to the present day (Rivas and Gámez 2013). The 15M also lives on in other movements and initiatives that started up from the occupation of the squares and assembly decision-making.

Many of the Indignados were young people who identified with 'Youth without future'. The 15M experiences meant the opening up of new 'places' for youth struggles; places from which we could re-imagine what we wanted our futures to be like. The 15M was also about claiming a new way to be a political subject. As Eklundh (2014) argues, the Indignados cannot easily fit into Habermas's notions of *deliberative democracy*. According to Eklundh, Habermas's deliberative democracy has as its starting point a notion of rational communication, where consensus is the absence of dissensus. This implies a violent exclusion of *noise*, as different from *voice* (Rancière in Eklundh 2014). In many senses, Habermas could not explain – and was 'violently excluding' non-deliberative based concepts and practices such as the Indignados' refusal to succumb to the idea of representation or rationalised organisation.

Moreover, the Indignados reframed what 'speaking' means. During mobilisations we use a repertoire of protest methods that appeal to emotions such as the name or the use of noise/silence. We express an explicitly strong detachment both from government's policies and its forms. The crisis situation and material discontent melted together with a deeper questioning of democracy and legitimacy (Juventud sin Futuro 2013).

By challenging the current idea of what and where politics is, the Indignados are bringing in disagreement over what a political subject is, and they question what counts as a political statement. It is in this instance, where we think that they do not make sense, or that their claims are unintelligible, unattainable or simply wrong, that politics is being reintroduced (Eklundh 2014: 232–233).

This 'collectively taking back politics' was not a clear and unified process. Quite to the contrary, 15M assemblies faced regular debates. In the context of emerging new political parties there are dilemmas that continue to require an answer: Is horizontal democracy possible? How can we deal with exclusion? How can we generate social change using political parties? How can we assure that a political party meets our demands?

Such a new way of being a political subject also implies moving beyond the traditional nation-state set-up, in that we simultaneously contest local, national and European policies, neoliberal capitalism, growth-led development, etc. We do not even need to be inside Spain. In fact, many of us were engaged from abroad as part of an increasing youth community in exile, studying or working in other countries.

In these exiled communities, moreover, engagement seemed to grow rather than diminish. Personally, when I arrived in 2012 in Strasbourg for an exchange programme I immediately searched and joined the 15M groups there. Later, I found myself speaking in a labour union seminar to a local collective in Strasbourg about the 15M experience and the current activism of the Spanish Platform for the Mortgage Victims (*La Plataforma de los Afectados por la Hipoteca*).

Back in a still pulsating Madrid, the link between the global and the local was becoming increasingly clear to me. The experience of having collectively occupied the capital's main square for several weeks left us with a taste for reclaiming more of our public spaces. Indeed, YWF was busy reclaiming the whole city. Under the slogan 'Madrid is not a city for young people' (*'Madrid no es ciudad para jovenes'* referring to the film *No Country for Old Men*), the YWF collective held a campaign to support young people's needs and proposals for Madrid.[5]

Taking back the local also meant 'taking back the economy' (Gibson-Graham, Cameron and Healey 2014). Alternative local economic practices (bartering, time banks, local exchange trade systems, etc.) were spreading across urban and rural Spain, as we discuss further below.[6]

Through all of these initiatives, youth in Spain defy the image of *'ninis'* (*'ni estudia ni trabaja'*: neither studying nor working). We oppose the image of youth travelling abroad just for fun, as idle adventurers. Neither do our protests fit easily in a naïve repetition of 1968 as elder generations would label us. This refusal of easy labelling, however, does not mean a rejection of intergenerational solidarities. In fact, there has been a deep involvement of elderly people in the 15M movements, many of whom were also involved in the resistance movements during Franco's dictatorship.

Zambra Malaga: embodied resistance from collectivity (Laura Santamaría Buitrago)

Laura explores how one of the movements that strengthened its action during the Spanish 15M occupations and mobilisations was feminism. A renewed strand of the movement, committed to resist the effects of the crisis on women's lives, focused on the search for alternative economies and exploring new body politics. Several groups were born from the discussions and manifestations in the plazas, and continued their work in their cities, in alliance with other groups at a national level.

One such collective is Zambra Malaga, an autonomous activist group that works in the city of Malaga, Spain. During 2014 Laura Santamaria Buitrago undertook research in Malaga sharing daily experiences, and maintaining conversations and travelling with the young people of the collective. She shares her activist research experiences here.

Zambra Malaga aims to resist the effects of the crisis over their lives and to act in solidarity with people living in marginal neighbourhoods in which the collective works. They search for alternatives to the capitalist/hetero-patriarchal crisis by opening spaces for debate and direct action. The collective

202 Trejo-Mendez et al.

came together when they met as part of the 15M in the 'Plaza de la Constitución' in Malaga, where 15M activists stayed during the '*acampadas*' (camping). It is not an exclusive radical feminist group, as young men and women belong to it, however feminist ideas broadly guide their action and agenda.

Zambra is 'an example of new grassroots young resistance, framed in *other* ways to struggle against capitalism and hetero-patriarchy' (Santamaría Buitrago 2014: 1). The focus of their activities was to bring new forms of political issues to the centre of their struggles and resistance. Zambra activists use the category of care as the thread through their political action: first from re-thinking the economy by valuing the importance of care within it and by engaging in collective care networks as a lifestyle that they see as re-positioning the bodies of the young in personal and collective levels.

Examples of this focus on care can be illustrated in Akelarre Zambrero a feminist project by Zambra, which aims to deconstruct the patriarchal system from corporality by creating supportive spaces. What is innovative about this project is that it aims to change both private and public ways of caring both through activism that struggles for change in the public sphere and by valuing care as core to the ways of behaving in the collective. They are looking at 'other ways' to be in the world.

Zambra searches for new ways of valuing collectivity: 'while the individual subject is being reconfigured, the collective one is being constructed and enforced, strengthening the union between participants and consolidating the politicization of everyday individual and collective lives' (Santamaria Buitrago 2014: 42).

Zambra validates life as communitarian by defining care in particular practices. Caring and supporting each other is seen as counter-systemic and is about hopeful possibilities to tackle crisis. Thus, care is understood both economically but also as a form of resistance in the everyday. For Zambra, dismantling capitalism/hetero-patriarchy requires a gradual process in all social arenas. It is the embodied experience of care that gives its legitimation as the main path for social reconstruction of life. Care, a non-political category, then is located at the centre of the Zambra's political struggle (Santamaría Buitrago 2014: 23).

As Escobar and Harcourt state, 'bodies are imbricated with the expressions of life in collectivity' (Harcourt and Escobar 2005: 17). Therefore, the deconstruction of stereotypes and oppressions should rise from the same bodies. In the Zambra initiative of Akelarre, the young people from Zambra – both men and women – place their embodied relations at the core of their place-based struggle, so that their bodies become the locus of resistance. In this exercise, the individual body is re-defined in alliance with the bodies of others through reciprocal care and support. Thus, care transforms the collective way of being and creates networked spaces where care is given and allowed to be received.

Activists mention how these dynamics have resulted in losing the fear to claim for their rights in an extremely repressive political scenario. Being-in-common with others has entailed a possibility to resist the crisis, diminishing its effect over their lives, showing that other ways of living are possible and giving them a renewed sense of hope. These young activists try to live in their present the life they envision for the future; therefore resistance becomes a process and not just an ultimate goal.

The possibility of a different world where the young are no longer the ones suffering the effects of the crisis, for Zambra comes from deconstructing oppressions and creating forms of connectivity with others. Working collectively is a way out of the solitude that characterises capitalism. In other words, this is a political engagement parting from subjective transformations framed in the prevalence of being-in-common with others (Gibson-Graham 2006). Every-day practices and its dynamics gain importance over static political agendas, establishing a new political commitment. Networked care is exercised in a conscious manner and becomes a determined concept of resistance, which emerges from horizontal support and the possibility it opens for the young and their futures.

Youth occupation in Rome high schools (Emma Claire Sardoni)

This search for new forms of collectivity and engagement among youth is also evident in the resistance movements in Italy. Youth public protests at precarious futures, including occupation of schools and marches on the streets, are regular events in Rome. Planned and spontaneous demonstrations happen all over the city. For example, in October 2014 young people occupied the ancient his-torical monument area of Porta Pia in Rome outside government buildings, stopping people to talk to them and consider together what economic crisis means for young people who face precariousness in a situation where ISTAT (2014) reports that 80% of young people under 30 live at home. This is just one of many examples of shifting relations in place-based locations.

When speaking to young people in protest, it is evident they are looking for positive forms of cultural identity and politics. They are searching for a col-lective voice and identity. This search is driven by anger and a strong distrust of the national politics and their future in the national and global economy. Young people, along with migrants are employed in the shadow economy, without a contract or access to rights. Particularly in sectors dominated by tourism, with its seasonal or casual work in restaurants, hotels and wine bars, many work in the black economy (with no security and no records of their employment). The shift in attitudes and expectations is evident in the lack of engagement of young people in traditional struggles for labour rights and social protection. Many youth imagine that eventually they will need to move to Germany, England and The Netherlands where they see their chances of jobs as being higher. As described by Giulia Simula below, young people are questioning their understanding of national identity. They are not sure what to expect of the state, or what the state can offer them. Their reflections suggest that in this search, taking them to different locations, it is a generation that expects to be on the move.

Emma Claire Sardoni, a high school student, interviewed students at one of the large inner city high schools in Rome, whose ages range from 14–18 years and who define themselves as politically active. The interviews were held during the occupation of their school in December 2014 held as a protest against the newly elected Prime Minister Renzi's education and employment reforms. The occupation lasted ten days, one day short of its programmed 'itinerary', which aimed to raise awareness among all the students of political issues in Italy. The occupation had been timed to end a day before a very big demonstration held on the 12 December 2014 in Rome but the school authorities evicted the students from the school a day early.

The interviews show how young people engage politically. Their points of view illustrate how youth are emerging as political beings with a mix of uncertainty and a strong willingness to engage. The discussion focused on whether they identified themselves as did the popular media as a 'lost generation', how they saw the older generation, and what they think the State will provide for them in terms of education and work, as well as their individual identity and place in Italy's future in relation to other European countries. They also commented on their engagement in the demonstrations and school occupation, including the images of resistance and hope that were being captured in the photos circulating both in the press and social media.

There are varied opinions of the students about whether or not they are part of a 'lost generation'; they engaged in the question, reflecting on the difference between their own and their parent's expectations. Maciej spoke about himself as 'an in-between' generation, living through a cycle of crisis. Tigre (Alessandro) considers that he and other students are in part a 'lost generation' from a work perspective, differently than his parents' generation. Benjamin doesn't see himself as part of a lost generation, but he feels his generation is left alone. Many older people, he feels, fail to understand the difficulties faced by young people. Marco also does not see himself as part of a lost generation, though the future is very uncertain. Carlo comments: 'We may be a lost generation but there's too much negativity coming from the older generation'. Similarly, Gaia states that her generation is often underestimated. 'It's not a lost generation for now. Together we're managing to succeed against all odds.' Carla also does not see herself as part of a lost generation, rather, it is what all people feel: 'my parents always tell me how also their parents used to have discussions regarding their future and how they used to wonder "where will we go" and "what will happen to our generation?" Time goes by and every generation has its own characteristics.' Margherita states that while some of her generation are disinterested and poorly informed, she sees room for hope in change and growth, if more young people were to engage. She sees indifference being a major issue – making it easier for those in power to claim consensus.

Given that the interviews were held during the protest, it was not surprising that they had strong opinions about the need for protest in order to make their views heard. Though they were not always sure of the effectiveness, they felt they had to engage. Carlo argues that protest is key. He sees marches and demonstrations as important to make noise and show young peoples' dissent in front of the government, regardless of whether the system likes it or not. Tigre sees his future as fighting against the state. He stated that 'every form of protest is important (whether the government listens or not)'. For him, not to protest would be tantamount to giving up. Marco also felt that demonstrations are important as 'polite words are not always heard and more aggressive behaviour can be necessary'. Margherita and Benjamin agree that protest is the way to change things and, additionally for Margherita, protest is an important political tool for citizens:

> Each and every one of us has to be free to share their ideas and their dissent. Protests are accessible to all citizens that have something to say, and they are an instrument that unifies ideas and voices, making all of us part of something bigger than ourselves.

Maciej, in contrast, looks to democracy and voting as ultimately the most effective way to protest, as he does not find demonstrations useful in really challenging government power.

There are varying views on the role of the Italian state among the students. Maciej stated that the Italian state only gives the illusion of freedom, and even after many years of struggle it is the state (those in power) that determines the parameters within which people can choose. Paradoxically, he felt, the current precarious conditions of the Italian education system are producing a resistance that is allowing a more radical future class to emerge. Carlo adds that he sees absolutely no guarantee given by the state for young peoples' rights to employment, particularly if the new Renzi (education) reforms pass (which they did in 2015).

In response to the question about how they saw their own future in Italy or not, several, such as Maciej, are planning to leave to look for work. Carlo states that if things keep going the way they have, Italy will continue to lag behind the other countries and he will probably move from Italy to look for work. Tigre agrees that Italy like Greece and Spain are the most hit by the economic crisis and he cannot foresee any radical change on the horizon and can imagine he might move. Margherita, on the other hand, recognises Italy is in decline but she does not want to see her future outside of Italy even if there seem to be more fertile possibilities outside Italy. Gaia thinks the government is making promises that they won't be able to fulfil and that there is a very doubtful future for young people if they continue to be fooled. She is concerned that the crisis will never end and Italy will become completely subdued by stronger countries. She hopes, this will not happen as she does not wish to move out of Italy because problems have to be dealt with and it will all become impossible if all of the younger generation leaves and abandons Italy. In contrast to the others, Marco is not planning to leave Italy to study as he states there are good faculties and he is confident of finding a job.

These interviews show how the experience of precariousness leads to a process of radicalisation in how youth think about their possible futures. They are forced to move from thinking just about themselves and their future to consider something larger as they engage in bigger economic, social and political questions and the need to innovate beyond their parents' generation. Their immediate engagement and shaping of politics in their daily life express an innovative vision of social change and also political ways of living as well as economic alternatives. The changing expectations of precarious youth (of both genders and working and middle class) determine how they think about their future in very different ways from their parents and, as a consequence, how they act. What is evident in the marches and occupation is that the students are enjoying building their own sense of self that refutes directly the power of the state. They are building a sense of collectivity as they organise, with a sense of being part of history that they are making for themselves. The unruliness of street demonstrations happened alongside care and concern for each other as a generation building community spirit. Their political expression is in the spontaneous marches and meetings that are not determined by any party politics or dogma. Their enjoyment and connection together as a generation taking their future into their hands, forming a sense of collectivity as Generation E (in a very different way than is meant by their critics), can be seen in the hundreds of Facebook photos posted by participants in the demonstrations.[7]

Countering mainstream narratives and shifting places of struggle among Italian youth (Giulia Simula)

As discussed by the Roman high school students, the dominant narratives around the crisis and austerity measures in Italy have depicted young people as 'the precarious generation'. Giulia explores how two narratives illustrate this well. In October 2012, the Minister of Labour and Social Policies Elsa Fornero,[8] called young people 'choosey'. The Minister argued that young people should be more active, that they should not stay home waiting for the perfect opportunity but should rather take job opportunities as they come along without being picky (Corriere della Sera 2012). In the same year the Minister of Internal Affairs Cancellieri labelled young people '*mammoni*' (dependent on their mothers) implying that they do not want to leave their home and that they are not flexible enough to move in order to find a job.

These two storylines, which were given considerable media attention, mirror the dominant narrative that depicts young people as lacking the will and capacity to react, and who are only able to complain rather than take action. These views are disconnected from the realities on the ground. Many young people around the country are far from waiting for the opportunities to materialise; they are not waiting for the state or their families to provide a job for them.

As Emma Claire describes the situation in high schools in Rome, many more high schools and universities around Italy have been the sites of struggle between 2009 and 2014, the time of the study, with thousands of marches in the street or occupation of school and university buildings. The 'Rete della Conoscenza' (the knowledge network) is an important example of students' organisation that connects university students from around Italy who reject the dominant narratives about young people as 'lost' and fight against the privatisation of schools. They define themselves in defiant terms: 'We are a new social subject, not a class or a generation, but a set of identities, a complex subject with strong connotations of neither class nor generation.' They go on to state: 'For the state bureaucracy we are citizens-users of the education service; for private corporatism we are consumers-customers of the product "knowledge". For our part, we claim the leading role in the production of knowledge and know-how in our society'.[9]

The occupations and marches of schools as described above link students from the *rete della conoscenza* as they continue to protest against the Jobs Act proposed by the prime minister Renzi and against the education reforms '*la buona scuola*' (the good school) referred to by Carlo above, that aim to institutionalise a corporate mentality into schools through continuing waves of privatisation of services. Italy has also witnessed the rise of *centri sociali* (social centres) as spaces in which to create subaltern knowledge, to make politics through art and music, and to organise and unite. In all of these actions, forging new relations among students and different generations, there is a strong mobility with connections back and forth among regions in Italy and abroad.

Another common narrative that youth challenge is that young people who leave the country (and there is a huge migration of youth leaving Italy in search of jobs in other parts of Europe) are giving up on the struggle against injustices. Yet this story also proves to be incomplete. Some young people leave with the idea of enriching their experiences and coming back home to create alternatives.

I am one of the many young Italians who go abroad and decide to stay there and continue their struggle from abroad in solidarity with people back home. All these lived struggles are the examples of young people who decide not to accept the single narrative imposed on them and who decide to still believe in an alternative future that they aim to create. I have been living abroad for six years and everywhere I go I join the local groups' struggles against austerity measures, against the neoliberal dictates and try to join local initiatives that aim at creating alternatives and challenging the current system. I believe this is a strong sign of the changing role of the 'modern state' and the borders that it represents.

Part of the way young people struggle is by uniting regardless of where they are; and by doing so they strengthen community values rather than market, individualistic values. Therefore young Italians struggle for real democracy and real alternatives not necessarily relating towards a specific state but rather they recognise the international dimension of the current crisis and act accordingly.

Shifting economic imaginaries (Wendy Harcourt)

In the above narratives by youth in Spain and Italy we see that the media hype and policy rhetoric of a lost generation is countered in the actions and responses of the students. They are not seeing the crisis as a glitch moment where young women and men are temporarily worse off, looking to the state and business to provide projects to reinstate them in the labour market. They are responding to what they see as a deeper systemic crisis, and their actions are part of a possible historical transition of global neoliberal capitalism as it is lived out in Southern Europe. They do not see the crisis as something insurmountable and paralytic; rather it is forcing creative and innovative possibilities for change.

Wendy explores how young people expose systemic contradictions and the failures by the state and dominant economies that, at the same time, contain within them the hopes for social change. They challenge political and economic prescriptive givens contributing to a search for new ways of living and new economic imaginaries (see Gibson-Graham 2007).

The 'Rethinking Economics' student movement is spreading around Europe. I have been working with a community based group in Punti Di Vista, a community based organisation in Bolsena, Italy, two hours north of Rome, that has organised and participated in several meetings of university students and young Italian entrepreneurs in 2013 and 2014. These public workshops, teach-ins and summer schools have perceived the economics crisis as forcing a rethinking of economics along with questions about environment, gender relations, rural and urban living, the practice of permaculture.

Another example of young people shifting economic imaginaries is Carlo Mancosu from Sardinia who went to study in Leeds and came back to Sardinia to create an alternative currency. He found the inspiration while studying in Leeds and was motivated to return hoping to create the Sardex. Sardex allows small businesses to have credit (by lending to each other) without having to pay an interest. Small firms are now able to make investments that they could not have afforded otherwise. Mancosu explains how Sardex emerges from a different idea of money and society: 'from the moment that I take from a community – as is the case in Sardex – I am in debt towards that community; when I settle that debt with the community, I have given what I have received.' In this way, '[Sardex] is money that serves an end', rather than being an end in itself. This is just one example of many alternative economy initiatives, including time banks, etc. These initiatives incentivise other types of exchange and other values and expose the failures of the current dominant economic narratives.

Such discussions and activities by young students and youth in Italy resonate with other activities throughout Southern Europe as they take back the economy (Gibson-Graham 2014). Alternative local economic practices (bartering, time banks, local exchange trade systems, etc.) are spreading across urban and rural Spain.[10] In her research about the local community currency (*Puma*) in Sevilla, Medina concludes that the currency was a way of micro-political resistance beyond the crisis context: 'Puma LETS was more than simply a temporary patch on the hardships of recession; Puma LETS promoters envisaged community currency as an emancipatory micro-political tool of resistance to reinvent their economic practices in more autonomous, humane and ecological ways' (Medina Prado 2014: 54).

In Campo de Cebada, Madrid (see above) Sat Trejo Mendez shares that the discussions in the summer public university looked at new alternative economic models that are emerging from economic crisis (Trejo Mendez 2013: 46). Debates around alternative economies, communities and societies are led by Galvez Manoz a professor of economic history from Seville who gives seminars on alternative economics – both to her students at the Pablo De Olavide University and to students of community universities in the piazzas in her town – and the need for alternative economic models to overcome what she called 'austercide' (killed by the austerity measures).

In Malaga, Zambra proposes the *Renta Basica de las Iguales* initiative (Basic Income of the Equals) as an alternative economic model looking to give value to a 'dignified life' over the market value. Each person has the right to receive periodically a determined amount of money to fulfil his or her needs independently of his or her ethnicity, gender, age or existing income. This functions as a way to validate care work and gives the possibility to decide between having a job or not, opening the possibility to choose whether or not to enter into the market. The term *las iguales* refers to a communal fund which is built up in order to fulfil collective needs (sanitation, infrastructure, housing, etc.) as defined by the communities. At the beginning 80% goes to every individual and 20% to the fund, but this percentage will gradually increase. The rationale behind it is that a dignified life must be ensured in a communitarian way, a proposal that is an alternative to capitalism and the individual subject (Santamaría Buitrago, 2014).

New values extend from alternative monies to youth actions of solidarity and support. For example, a youth collective in Crete produces organic olive oil, part of the money is used to support political prisoners in Greece. This olive oil can be bought at Café Cralle in Berlin, a space for Queer politics, cultural and social activities. Popular kitchen evenings in Amsterdam in places like Kraakschool Antartica or Joe's garage are where many young people gather to share food that would be thrown away otherwise. These are the same spaces used to organise and fundraise for youth political prisoners such as those facing trial linked to La Ciutadella protest in Barcelona (Joe's Garage 2014). Zambra Malaga occupied a bank office in Palma-Palmilla, the most excluded neighbourhood in the city, and adapted it as a communitarian dining room where nowadays more than 100 impoverished people eat daily. It is supplied by a communitarian garden maintained by the same occupants of the neighbourhood (Santamaría Buitrago 2014).

Young unemployed people are at the heart of many of these initiatives. While these collective projects are not necessarily recognised as prosperous entrepreneurial endeavours, they are effectively contesting the labels that are imposed on unemployed youth.

The search for a politics of place and youth within it

In looking at these examples in different places in Italy, Spain and Europe, it is possible to point to new forms of localised economic politics where different community economies are connecting to create an ethical and political rather than structural conception of economic dynamics. In this imaginary, the economy is seen as a diversified social space. At the centre of these forms of economies are new economic subjects and ethical practices of self-cultivation. Place can be conceptualised as a site of becoming and the ground where global economic politics in local practices negotiate power. In this way, place-based globalism can be seen as an alternative logic of politics and economics, one that invests not in what is to be replaced, but in what is to become. These youth based activities and alternative ways of being show the specificity of economic identities and capacities rather than seeing them as just nodes in a global capitalist system (Gibson-Graham 2008: 39). In this economic imaginary, local economic transformation is about ways of cultivating economic subjects with different desires and capacities and greater openness to change and uncertainty. Place becomes the site and possibility of becoming, the opening for politics:

> In the place-based imaginary, every place is to some extent 'outside' the various spaces of control; places change imitatively, partially, multi-directionally, sequentially, and space is transformed via changes in place ... Place-based globalism recognizes that there is a continual struggle to transform subjects and places and conditions of life under circumstances of difficulty and uncertainty.
>
> (Gibson-Graham 2008: 34)

Activists adapt themselves to the particular dynamics of their places. Thus, they become changeable, heterogeneous and open. The participants of Zambra Malaga, for instance, affirm their rejection to be enfranchised in particular ideologies or strands of a movement; they move along with the urgent and specific needs of their territory in a particular moment and depending on the social and political scenario. They are eclectic and fragmented, which is very typical of contemporary place-based struggles (Santamaría Buitrago 2014).

The young Italian entrepreneurs referred to above are engaged in rethinking economics, are experimenting in new projects – from permaculture to solar powered housing to ecological wine production. They show the potential for new imaginaries, combining economies, politics, concern with environment and community, and as a counter to the global big chain stores and businesses.

Conclusion

Innovative modes of activism require innovative ways of doing research and pose questions about the positionality of the researcher (Harding 2005). We see ourselves as tackling hegemonies and proposing alternative ways of being and doing in our own way of doing research. By listening to stories and visions of the future, while constantly examining our own assumptions as youth engaging and working in civic innovation, the traditional division between research and the other is blurred. Writing about these civic innovations is part of the project to create other knowledges. We have aimed to move beyond capitalocentricism in research that reflects on civic innovation in relation to how young people are living and becoming part of social change. In undertaking this research we are also engaged in this search for community, new values, alternative economies and forms of politics that reflect how young people are living and working in response to the crisis.

We see youth not as lost but rather as building forms of civic innovation; searching for alternative forms of economics, revaluing care, creating places for discussion, and creating new forms of relations. Youth are searching for change, not as part of political parties or organised NGOs or even social movements but rather in their own ways of living precarity and loss and uncertainty. In this we see youth as going beyond dominant hegemonic ideologies of economics, politics and society and challenging even the idea of what is southern Europe – and what type of futures youth are creating now.

The value of writing this chapter as an intergenerational dialogue is to show the intertwining of diverse experiences and modes of resistance across southern Europe. The dialogue reveals crosscutting concerns, and points to similar ways in which youth are re-thinking themselves, their present and future. By writing this chapter we are constructing a web of knowledge about resistance, as well as opening the hopeful possibility for links between these different collectivities and people. This is not merely a picture about the youth in southern Europe and their striving for alternatives. It is also a challenge to the neoliberal academic assumptions about who is supposed to create knowledge and how it is supposed to be created. And it is, most importantly, an expression of our wish to interconnect and co-produce knowledge about our experiences in a pluriversal dialogue about the need for both resistance and hope.

Notes

1 Thank you to Rosalba Icaza, Roy Huijsmans, Jacqueline Gaybor Tobar and Kees Biekart for comments on earlier versions of this chapter.
2 See http://www.istat.it/en/files/2015/01/201411_PressRelease.pdf?title=Employment +and+unemployment+(monthly)+-+7+Jan+2015+-+Full+text.pdf (accessed 22 January 2016)
3 Youth across Europe have also protested against austerity measures. 'We don't owe, we don't pay', (*vuestra deuda no la pagamos*), 'International solidarity against Capitalist Europe' (*solidarité internationale contre l'Europe du capital*) were some of the rallying cries in blockupy Frankfurt where thousands of people of all ages from Spain, Greece, Italy, Netherlands, Germany and other parts of Europe came together to block the central European bank in Madrid in 2013 (Trejo Mendez 2013).
4 See http://madrid.tomalaplaza.nethttp://madrid.tomalaplaza.nethttp://madrid.toma laplaza.net (accessed 2 October 2015).
5 See YWF Website of Madrid: 'No es ciudad para jóvenes' [No city for young people], http://www.noesciudadparajovenes.com/ and http://www.noesciudadpara jovenes.com (accessed 2 October 2015).
6 See the Map of alternative economic initiatives: http://mapa.vivirsinempleo. org/map/ (accessed 2 October, 2015).

7 For reasons of privacy we cannot reproduce the photos of the students but see examples on student organisation websites such as http://www.retedellaconoscenza. it (accessed 6 October 2015).
8 The Minister was part of the Monti administration, the non-elected 'technical government' which was chosen to implement austerity measures.
9 See http://www.retedellaconoscenza.it (accessed 6 October 2015).
10 See the Map of alternative economic initiatives http://mapa.vivirsinempleo.org/map/ (2 October 2015).

References

Autoconsulta.org (2014) 'Transformations, projections, alternatives and convergences 15M'. Accessed May 2014 <http://autoconsulta.org/mutaciones.phphttp://auto consulta.org/mutaciones.php>.

Corriere della Sera (2012) 'Fornero ai giovani: «Sul lavoro non dovete essere schizzi-nosi». E si scatena la polemica' [Fornero to youth: 'In the workforce you can't be so fussy'. And the controversy is set loose], 22 October 2012. Accessed 6 October 2015 <http://www.corriere.it/economia/12_ottobre_22/fornero-scende-in-piazza-se-m i-invitano_b156df5c-1c3e-11e2-b6da-b1ba2a76be41.shtml>.

DinersteinA. (2014) *The Politics of Autonomy in Latin America: The Art of Organising Hope.* London: Palgrave Macmillan.

Doncel, L. 2014 'Trabajadores Espanioles en Alemania se organizan contra las injus-ticias laborales' [Spanish migrant workers in Germany organize against labour injustices], *El Pais.* Accessed 29 June 2014 <http://sociedad.elpais.com/sociedad/ 2014/06/29/actualidad/1404060780_813802.html>.

Eklundh, E. (2014) 'Who is speaking? The Indignados as political subjects', *Global Discourse* 4(2–3): 223–235.

Edmunds, J. and B.S. Turner (2002) *Generations, Culture and Society: June Edmunds and Bryan S. Turner.* Buckingham: Open University Press.

Escobar, A. (2015) 'Degrowth, postdevelopment, and transitions: a preliminary con-versation', *Sustainable Science* 10: 451–462.

European Commission (2013) 'EU measures to tackle youth unemployment'. Accessed May 2014 <http://www.eesc.europa.eu/resources/docs/youth_unemployment_leaflet_ en.pdfhttp://www.eesc.europa.eu/resources/docs/youth_unemployment_leaflet_en. pdf>.

Fraser, N. (2013) 'A triple movement? Parsing the politics of crisis after Polanyi', *New Left Review* 81, May–June.

Gibson-Graham, J.K. (1996) *The End of Capitalism (As We Knew It): A Feminist Critique of Political Economy*, Oxford: Blackwell Publishers.

Gibson-Graham, J.K. (2006) *A Postcapitalist Politics*, Minneapolis: University of Minnesota Press.

Gibson-Graham, J.K. (2007) 'Economic imaginaries', Web edition. Accessed May 2014 <http://www.communityeconomies.org/site/assets/media/KatherineGibson/Veni ce-gibson-graham.pdf>.

Gibson-Graham, J.K. (2008) 'Place-based globalism: a new imaginary of revolution', *Rethinking Marxism* 20(4).

Gibson-Graham, J.K., J. Cameron and S. Healey (2014) *Take Back the Economy: An Ethical Guide for Transforming our Communities.* Minneapolis: University of Minnesota Press.

Harcourt, W. and A. Escobar (2005) *Women and the Politics of Place*. Bloomingdale, CT: Kumarian Press.

Harding, S. (2005) 'Rethinking standpoint epistemology: What is "strong objectivity"?' in A.E. Cudd and R.O. Anderson (eds) *Feminist Theory. A Philosophical Anthology*, pp. 218–236, Oxford: Blackwell Publishing.

ISTAT (2014) 'Nel 2013 persi 478mila posti lavoro. Disoccupazione al 12,9%, record dal 1977' [In 2013 478,000 jobs were lost. Unemployment is at a record 12.9%], *Il Fatto Quotidiano*, Web edition. Accessed May 2014 <http://www.ilfattoquotidiano. it/2014/02/28/istat-nel-2013-persi-478mila-posti-di-lavoro-tasso-disoccupazione-giova ni-al-424/897056>.

Joe's Garage (2014) 'Info-night and benefit: Surround the Parliament, Barcelona'. Accessed May 2014 <http://www.joesgarage.nl/>.

Juventud sin Futuro (2013) 'We do not go away even if they try to push us out'. Accessed May 2014 <http://www.nonosvamosnosechan.net/http://www.nonosvam osnosechan.net/>.

Lantier, A. (2013) 'Europe's economic crisis: unemployment hits record highs in Spain, France'. Accessed May 2014 <https://www.wsws.org/en/articles/2013/04/26/euro-a 26.html>.

Lavapies (2014) 'La Asamblea de Vivienda Centro recupera un tercer bloque dentro de la campaña estatal de Obra Social de la PAH' [The Central Assembly reclaims a third block within the national Social Work campaign of the PAH]. Accessed May 2014 <http://lavapies.tomalosbarrios.net/2014/05/12/la-asamblea-de-vivienda-centro-recup era-un-tercer-bloque-dentro-de-la-campana-estatal-de-obra-social-de-la-pah/>.

Mateos, A. and Penades, A. 2013. 'España: crisis y recortes' [Spain: crisis and cut-offs], *Revista Ciencia Política* 33(1): 161–183.

Medina Prado, Cristina (2014) 'Our money: Our place. Exploring Puma LETS as a micro-political tool in the context of economic crisis'. Master Thesis of Governance, Policy and Political Economy (GPPE). Accessed May 2014 <http://hdl.handle.net/ 2105/17402>.

ObservatorioMetropolitanode Madrid (2011) 'Crisis and revolution in Europe: People of Europe, Rise Up!' Madrid: Traficantes de Sueños.

Osterweil, M. (2005) 'Place-based globalism: theorizing the global justice movement', *Development* 48(1): 23–28.

Ottaviani, J. (2014) 'Crowdsourcing youth migration from southern Europe to the UK', *The Guardian* Data blog, first published Thursday 2 October 2014. Accessed 22 January 2016 <http://www.theguardian.com/news/datablog/2014/oct/02/crowd sourcing-youth-migration-from-southern-europe-to-the-uk>.

Pearce, J. (2013) 'Power and the twenty-first century activist: from the neighbourhood to the square', *Development and Change Forum* 44(3): 639–663.

Rivas, A. and Gámez, M. (2013) 'Feminismos 2.0 y 15-M: cuestionando los cambios en la esfera pública' [Feminisms 2.0 and 15-M: Questioning changes in the public sphere], in R. Zallo and A. Casero (eds), *Comunicación y regeneración democrática: Castellón, ULEPICC-Universitat Jaume I de Castellon. Actas del IV Congreso Ule- picc España Comunicación y regeneración democrática* [Communication and Democratic Regeneration: Report of the IV Congress Ulepicc Spain[, pp. 345–357. Universitat Jaume I de Castellón.

Roberts, K. (2011) 'The end of the long baby-boomer generation', *Journal of Youth Studies*, 27 February 2012 web edition. Accessed May 2014 <http://dx.doi.org/10. 1080/13676261.2012.663900>.

Santamaría Buitrago, L. (2014) 'Together somewhere, anywhere alone: Zambra Malaga, care as an embodied feminist resistance'. *Social Justice Perspectives (SJP)*. Accessed May 2014 <http://hdl.handle.net/2105/17423>.

Taibo, C. (2013) 'The Spanish Indignados: A movement with two souls', *European Urban and Regional Studies* 20(1): 155–158.

Trejo Mendez, P. (2013) '"Juventud Sin Futuro": Subjective experiences of Spanish youth. Resistance and organization in the context of economic crisis', ISS Working Paper Series 581: 1–53.

15M (2014) 'Jornadas abiertas 15M' [15M open days]. Accessed May 2014 <https://www.facebook.com/events/703124593064258/https://www.facebook.com/events/703124593064258/>.

Yayoflautas Madrid (2014) 'Quienes somos?' [Who are we?] La web de l@s yay@-flautas de Madrid. Accessed 1 August 2014 <http://yayoflautasmadrid.org/?page_id=2http://yayoflautasmadrid.org/?page_id=2>.

11 Civic activism and social accountability

A quantitative approach

Anderson Macedo de Jesus and Irene van Staveren

Introduction: why a quantitative approach

Does civic activism contribute to the social accountability of governments? If so, how? And how is civic activism measured? And can we measure social accountability in a meaningful way?

These are typical questions that cannot be answered at the individual country level. If we agree that, in country X, governments do a bad job in providing the population with access to good quality health care services, how can we improve this? If it is a fragile state, with an armed conflict, or recovering from a natural disaster, or a deeply corrupt state, it is likely that these are the factors standing in the way of adequate service delivery. If country Y is among the poorest ten counties in the world, it is very likely that it is a lack of financial resources – income and public expenditures on health – which constrains the delivery of adequate health care services to all people, urban and rural, rich, middle class and poor. But if country Z is not a low-income country and not a fragile state, and we nevertheless agree that its health care services are underperforming, can we expect that civic activism will contribute to better service delivery? Of course, we can follow a country like Z over time to see if civic activism generates the social transformation pushing for more social accountability of the government of country Z. But if health care services improve over time in this country, how do we know this is not because of economic growth? Or because a new government spends more money on health care? How do we know whether civic activism really plays a role that makes a difference? Moreover, how do we measure whether health care services improve – do we measure the number of hospital beds available, or the number of doctors per one thousand inhabitants? Can we be sure that it is not a more intensive use of health care services by the middle class rather than wider access for the poor? Is there a more accessible service in cities than in rural areas?

There are many questions. And they cannot be answered with a case study at the country level because there are so many factors at play and we cannot compare country Z with other countries that have a different level of GDP, lower or higher health expenditures, and better or worse health care services, or more or less social exclusion. So, whatever we find for country Z cannot be generalized because all the variation of all relevant variables is limited to 1. With a one-country study we have only one level of GDP per capita, only one level of health care spending, only one level of government effectiveness, and only one level of health care services. In other words, the sample size is one – and this does not allow us to analyse how different levels of the relevant variables just mentioned influence better health care service delivery.

The advantage of using a cross-country quantitative approach is that the analysis can make use of a large sample size, even including all developing countries (as long as the data allow, of course). The variation thus created in the sample allows us to find statistical relationships between variables. These relationships may be positive or negative, large or small, and statistically significant rather than occurring by chance (the standard probability used for a true relationship is 95%, with 90% as the lower alternative and 99% as the higher alternative).

What is more difficult to assess with a quantitative study is the direction of causality. But this is an important question. If we assume that civic activism improves health care services, we should be able to eliminate the possibility that better health care services create more civic activism (through shifting people's priorities from their family's health to social issues), or that better health care services generate higher incomes (through healthier workers). Can quantitative studies do this? Well, let us first see if qualitative studies can eliminate reverse causality. Would an in-depth case study of civic activism and health care services in country Z be able to uncover a one-directional relationship from civic activism to health care? There is no guarantee that better health services contribute to more civic activism, perhaps in an indirect way, by shifting people's priorities. A quantitative study suffers from a similar weakness when it comes to eliminating the possibility of reverse causality.

However, there are econometric techniques available that at least help to check for the reverse causality; first, a time-consistency test of changes in the dependent variable and changes in the explanatory variable. If, as we assume, the explanatory variable causes the dependent variable, increases in the explanatory variable should precede increases in the dependent variable over time; just like the application of fertilizer precedes the growth of plants in time. The econometric test for this is the Granger-causality test. This simply compares the data over time of two sets of variables to see if changes in the one variable (increases or decreases) precede changes in the other (increases or decreases) variable. In a regression analysis, the idea behind this test can also be integrated by using time-lags in explanatory variables. So that variable X_{t-1} is used as the explanatory variable in a regression with Y_t as dependent variable. For example, t is the year 2010 and t-1 is the year 1999. Or you may want to use t-5 for a five-year time-lag, so that the X variable used is for the year 2005, whereas the Y variable used is for the year 2010. If then X has a statistically significant and sizeable relationship to Y we may well assume that X is a causal factor of Y rather than the other way around.

However, this test can only be applied for time-series data, and not for cross-section data, which uses data from countries at only one point in time. A second test can be applied for panel data. This is a dataset for which there is data available for more than one year per country. It has the following structure: country X year 1; country X year 2; country Y year 1; country Y year 2; etc. The dataset that we will introduce in this chapter has five data points per country, so, year 1 until 5. With such a panel of data we can 'switch off' the variation within countries over time in the analysis and only use the variation between countries. In this way, we are able to disregard that country X undergoes significant changes over time, such as a military coup or a drought or a change of government. So that at least such changes cannot cause any changes in the explanatory variables. So, such kind of reversal causation is 'switched off'. A third econometric test for reversed causality is the most advanced and requires data for an additional variable, often a historical variable that logically cannot be influenced by the dependent variable. This is called an instrumental variable (often referred to as IV). For example, if the dependent variable is better maternal health care services, and we want to be sure that this does not have any causal influence on civic activism, we need an instrumental variable, which substitutes for civic activism but cannot logically be influenced by better maternal health care. Perhaps a law allowing or prohibiting civic activism would be a suggestion for such an instrumental variable. Because it is not likely that an improvement of maternal health care will cause a law change on demonstrations.

Finally, our question as stated in the first sentence, whether civic activism can help governments' social accountability, can only be addressed meaningfully when we also take other factors into account that are likely to improve social accountability. In econometrics we call these control variables. Because we need to control for their influence. If civic activism has a sizeable, positive and statistically significant relationship with maternal health care, and we have tested for reverse causality, can we be sure that all the improvement in maternal health care is indeed caused by civic activism? Here we see the difference between what is called a bi-variate regression analysis and a multi-variate regression analysis. The first analyses the relationship between only two variables: a dependent variable and an explanatory variable (also called independent variable). The problem with this is that it does not control for other factors that may also have an influence on the dependent variable. Multi-variate regression analysis includes control variables. The results will show the effects of each variable on the dependent variable. Hence, we can compare the influence of each variable. It allows us to see which variable has the biggest influence (size effect), and whether all variables are statistically significant or not, or only some. For example, with high economic growth and some civic activism, maternal mortality rates may go down. But the effect of civic activism may be very small compared to the effect of higher incomes. Or the effect of civic activism may seem big but it is not statistically significant, at least not at the 95% level of probability. So, multi-variate regressions allow us to estimate the influence of each individual variable, to compare their relative influence, and to add up all effects to find the total effect.

However, quantitative analysis has its own weaknesses. These vary from problems of measurement at the cross-country level and data limitations, to the fact that causality can never be established with full certainty. Moreover, not everything that matters can be measured. So, quantitative analysis and qualitative analysis are generally complementary. We argue in this chapter that this is also the case for research on civic activism and social accountability.

In this study, we present and critically discuss the why and how of quantitative analysis of the relationship between civic activism and social accountability. An important variable that we include is press freedom, because it provides the necessary information that both parliamentarians and civil society need in order to be able to demand social accountability from the government. Hence, the section below discusses the literature on these three variables: social accountability, civic activism, and press freedom.

Quantitative literature on social accountability, civic activism and press freedom

We will first review the quantitative literature about the relationships between social accountability, civic activism, and press freedom. This will provide an overview of what we know and what we do not know yet from a macro-level perspective. It gives insights into relevant variables and relationships and gaps and disagreements in the current empirical debate.

Social accountability

Government accountability has a social dimension, concerned with adequate service delivery, and a political dimension, concerned with democracy. Social accountability is concerned with the extent to which governments deliver what people demand (and pay for with their taxes), in particular universal public goods such as health care and education. We use the definition of service-delivery focused government accountability in line with Khemani (2005: 186), who gives three criteria. A public agency is accountable for service delivery if it (1) assumes and is assigned responsibility, (2) has some minimum resources and capacity, and (3) undertakes appropriate actions towards service delivery, given resource and capacity constraints. For this understanding of social accountability, Shah (2008) has argued that citizen-centric governance is the most effective approach to enforce service delivery. Both definitions are reflected in a recent study by the Institute of Development Studies (IDS), in which citizens' engagement is regarded crucial for governments to enable people to realize their right and gain access to resources (IDS 2006).

Social accountability may also have a more transformational purpose, in the sense of empowerment. But we focus on the actual delivery of what governments are obliged to their populations: service delivery, and hence, the development dimensions of social accountability (Gaventa and McGee 2013).

This social accountability model for service delivery implies, according to Shah, responsiveness, fairness, responsibility, and judicial accountability. This would result, among others, in public services consistent with citizen preferences, improvements in economic and social outcomes and quality of life, improvements in quantity, quality and access of public services, including for the poor, minorities and disadvantaged groups, and better and cheaper services.

A literature review by IDS on accountability and service delivery makes a distinction between social and political accountability. It recognizes that social accountability of government is through 'a continuous relationship of citizen's demands through street protests and mobilizations, public naming and shaming, signing of petitions, etc.' (Mejia Acosta 2010: 13) Social accountability is particularly focused on service delivery, according to IDS:

> The core feature of social accountability mechanisms is to exert direct political influence on government officials to extract increased – and effective – government action in the short run. Through social accountability mechanisms, citizens have organized to demand service provision from government officials in charge of specific sectors (health, water, sanitation), sometimes even bypassing some elected bodies (national legislatures, city councils).
>
> (Mejia Acosta 2010: 13)

The IDS desk review of sixteen case studies is qualitative but interestingly, it uses rather similar criteria for social accountability as quantitative analyses:

- demand for social accountability (production and use of independent media)
- responsiveness in service delivery (social expenditures)
- standards for service delivery (health and educational outcomes)
- enforceability (rule of law, government effectiveness)

On the basis of the qualitative desk review, the IDS report suggests 'a positive association between effective accountability and the adequate provision of government service' (IDS 2006: 28). However, the report admits that it cannot say anything about size effects and causality. Here is where quantitative analysis can come in to provide complementary insights.

Qualitative studies on social accountability and civil society emphasize the role of interlocution, and the process through which civic activism leads to states becoming more effective in delivering to their populations (Tembo 2013). But such a process is difficult to measure. This study will measure social accountability through one of the four measures identified by IDS for quantitative studies: standard for service delivery.

Civic activism

Civic activism is concerned with civic voice, with the monitoring and agenda setting roles of civil society vis-à-vis government. These roles of civil society have been referred to by Glasius (2010) as a mix of social capital, citizens active in public affairs, non-violent action, fostering public debate and counter hegemony. Fowler and Biekart (2008) therefore refer to these roles as the dynamic and agency dimensions of civil society, labelled as civic-driven change. Civic-driven change is in their view a combination of three dimensions: civic agency, collective action, and empowerment. This change, or at least this demand for change, by civil society, is the complement of the representative democratic checks and balances of governments.

The empirical literature is rather silent on the effectiveness of civic activism in holding governments accountable. An empirical study by Williamson (2009) has assessed the relative effectiveness of the informal institutions of civil society (pro-social norms, trust, cooperation, demonstration, etc.) vis-à-vis the formal institutions of the state, such as the rule of law. She finds that 'countries that have stronger informal institutions, regardless of the strength of formal institutions, achieve higher levels of economic development than those countries with lower informal institutional scores' (Williamson 2009: 377). A recent United Nations Development Programme (UNDP) report on inequality notes about the role of civil society that 'coordinated mobilization is indispensable for people who wish to pursue a common interest and (...) claim specific policies' (UNDP 2013: 263).

A recent overview study of social capital carried out for the Organisation for Economic Co-operation and Development (OECD) distinguishes four channels through which civic activism impacts upon well-being: through (1) fostering trust and cooperative norms, (2) improving the performance of formal institutions, (3) having a direct impact on individual well-being, and (4) building networks and civic skills (Scrivens and Smith 2013). Of these four, channels two and three are the two which are most likely to represent social accountability. In other words, these two channels are most likely to contribute to adequate service delivery by governments.

A recent study with International Institute of Social Studies (ISS) data on civic activism found that an increase in civic activism of 10% is associated with a statistically significant 4% poverty reduction (van Staveren and Webbink 2012). The strong and statistically significant association of civic activism with poverty reduction indicates that the activities of civil society have an important effect on development outcomes and may therefore also stimulate social accountability.

Civic activism, social accountability and independent media

Empirical research on press freedom has demonstrated the importance of the free press for government accountability. In particular, studies by Pippa Norris (2006) have shown the importance of this production dimension of independent media. In her 2006 study, Norris distinguished between three roles of the media: watch-dog, civic forum, and agenda-setter. Interestingly, these roles are very similar to the roles recognized in the literature on civil society, as the key roles that civic activism plays in holding governments accountable. This suggests that civic activism and press freedom are complementary, and mutually related: they feed into each other. The results of the empirical analysis in Norris (2006) show that press freedom is positively associated with greater political stability, rule of law, government efficiency in the policy process, regulatory quality, and low corruption. However, the study did not analyse the impact of press freedom on service delivery. Moreover, the regressions were only cross-country (hence, for a single year), without time-lags, and do not use controls for formal institutions and social expenditures. This leads to over-estimation of effects. For example, when the level of GDP per capita is ignored, regression results tend to over-estimate the effect of the explanatory variable, as if economic development does not matter. But we know from the literature that GDP does matter: more highly developed countries tend to have more press freedom. So, part of the effect measured by Norris may well be due to economic development rather than to press freedom alone.

Tran et al. (2011) found a positive association between press freedom and human development. The sample size, however, is small, with only 65 countries in a hierarchical regression analysis. Interestingly, they found endogeneity effects: press freedom seems to both influence human development and is in turn influenced by human development.

Becker and Vlad (2011) summarize the empirical literature in a detailed overview of the effects of independent media on development. They conclude that press freedom correlates negatively with corruption and positively with various development outcomes.

Studies on independent media recognize that press freedom is not in itself a sufficient indicator of information use. For example, Price (2011a: 12) states that 'even a media system that is diverse and pluralistic may not achieve the goals of "voice"'. Price also recognizes that none of the three available measures of independent media addresses 'voice'. They measure the *production* of information, not how civil society *makes use* of it. And as Norris has made clear, one of the three roles of independent media is the creation of a civic forum – this is precisely the space that civil society is likely to fill.

The literature review points out that both press freedom and civic activism support government accountability. But there are clearly only very few wide-ranging quantitative studies available, and none of them includes both press freedom and civic activism. Hence, an adequate analysis of the role of civic activism in government accountability needs to fill the gaps in the literature in the following ways:

- include all relevant variables and make an informed choice about particular measures

- identify specific service delivery variables, as the standards of social accountability
- include all developing countries and preferably over a medium or long period of time.

A framework for quantitative analysis

Drawing on the causal chain approach to social accountability by Anuradha Joshi (2014), we simplify the model of mutual influences between the three variables in that model of information, citizen action, and state response. We measure these three variables as:

- press freedom
- civic activism
- service delivery

Whereas the causal chain approach assumes causal relations between these three in two directions, we focus on the causal relationships from information (press freedom) to state response (service delivery) and from citizen action (civic activism) to state response (service delivery), whereas our model allows for mutual influences between press freedom and civic activism as well.

Variables and measurement

This section identifies the relevant variables to measure government accountability, civic activism, the intermediate variable of independent media, as well as control variables. Next to this, it will explain the existing measures and discuss their strengths and weaknesses.

Social accountability

The government social accountability data are the outcome measures of public service delivery. They measure the extent to which people's well-being has improved. We have selected two areas of wellbeing: health and education, with four variables in each area. The health outcome variables that we use are: infant mortality, under five mortality, immunization DPT (Diphtheria, Tetanus, Pertussi) and immunization measles. The data are all from the World Development Indicators by the World Bank.

Infant mortality rate (IMR) is measured as deaths of children under one year per 1,000 live births. Under five mortality (U5MR) is similarly measured as deaths of children under five years per 1,000 live births. The two immunization rates (ID and IM) are percentages of children between 12 and 23 months old.

Civic activism

ISS has a unique database, Indices of Social Development.[1] The ISD database is explained in a recent article by Foa et al. (2013). The database contains six indices, including one on the use that civic actors make of the media: Civic Activism Index (CA). This measures citizen's use of the media (listening to radio and television news, reading newspapers and using internet to learn about political developments) and support for and participation in civic activities such as in demonstrations and petitions, as well as the strength of civil society (based on Civicus ratings).[2] The ISD measure of the strength of civic activism uses 33 indicators on the extent of engagement in civic activities such as signing petitions or joining peaceful demonstrations, studies of the organization and effectiveness of civil society, access to sources of media information, levels of civic awareness and information on political matters and concerns, and the extent to which civil society organizations are connected to broader, international networks of civic activity.

We could also use the variable Voice and Accountability Index (VA) of the Worldwide Governance Indicators by the World Bank, although it is not a very suitable variable for the research question at hand, because it includes press freedom and it focuses on political accountability. And it is constructed on the basis of expert opinions only: it lacks objective measures and attitudinal measures of the population. Voice and Accountability (VA) 'captures perceptions of the extent to which a country's citizens are able to participate in selecting their government as well as freedom of expression, freedom of association, and a free media.'[3]

Independent media

Empirical research into independent media uses either the Press Freedom Index put together by Freedom House, or the Press Freedom Index developed by journalists themselves through Reporters without Borders. A more recent index is the Media Sustainability Index by IREX. The IREX started in 2000 covering only European countries. It extended its measurement to the Middle East and North Africa in 2005 and to Africa in 2007, and covers 80 countries today; although not Asia and Latin America. The Media Sustainability Index measures, like the two press freedom indices, media independence. But it covers it slightly more broadly.[4] It includes an indicator on whether the public media reflect the views across the political spectrum, are nonpartisan, and serve the public interest; there is also an indicator on whether a broad spectrum of social interests are reflected and represented in the media, including minority-language information sources. But the large majority of indicators overlap with or are identical to those in the two press freedom indices. And none of the three independent media indicators includes investigative journalism or other indicators of the depth of independent media.

Two studies that have compared the two press freedom indices of Freedom House and Reporters without Borders contradict each other in their findings about their similarity. They both compared the indices indirectly, by comparing their explanatory power in regression analyses with democracy and related variables. Norris (2006) concludes that they work out quite similarly in econometric analyses, whereas Tran et al. (2011) find the results in regression analyses to be very different. A recent and more thorough and direct analysis of the two measures of press freedom confirms Norris: the two measures are found to be quite similar, over time and even across differences in country choices. Using correlation coefficients on each of the indicators making up each press freedom index, Becker and Vlad (2011: 38) conclude that: 'The Freedom House measure and the Reporters without Borders measure are highly correlated. At present there is little to distinguish them.' The average correlation (measured as r) between the two for the period 2002–2008 is 0.83. Hence, 70 per cent (measured as r^2) of the variation in the one can be explained by the other. This is, statistically seen, quite high. Hence, it does not matter really which of the two press freedom measures is used in a quantitative study. We opt for the Freedom House variable because it is available for more countries. The Press Freedom Index (PF) developed by Freedom House measures media independence of print, broadcast, and internet media. It consists of 109 indicators in three areas[5]: legal environment (laws, regulations, guarantees, and independence of the judiciary bodies), political environment (political control such as censorship, news diversity, intimidation and violence against journalists), and economic environment (transparency and concentration of ownership of media sources, selective withholding of advertising or subsidies, and bribery).

It is important to note that The Press Freedom Index is measured negatively. PF of 0 means full press freedom and 1 means no press freedom at all. All other variables are measured positively. So, for example, a Civic Activism score of 0 means no civic activism and 1 a very high level of civic activism.

Control variables

Control variables are expected, on the basis of the literature, to also have an influence on the service delivery outcome variables of health and education. The most important one is the level of economic development of a country, measured as GDP per capita (GDP). The richer a country, the more likely it is that the government will have the capacity for adequate service delivery. GDP per capita is measured in dollars, and varies from a few hundred per year in the poorest countries to several thousand dollars per year in middle income countries. In line with econometric practice, the income data must be normalized by taking the logarithm: lnGDP pc.

The higher the share of government expenditures on health care or education, the more resources available for social service delivery. We therefore use the share of GDP spent by government on health care and on education (percentages). Together, we sometimes refer to these variables as the social expenditure variables. The data for Expenditures on Health (EXPH) are provided by World Bank's World Development Indicators.[6]

With an adequate rule of law in place, a country is more likely to be able to deliver services effectively. Rule of Law 'captures perceptions of the extent to which agents have confidence in and abide by the rules of society, in particular the quality of contract enforcement, property rights, the police, and the courts, as well as the likelihood of crime and violence'[7]. It is a comprehensive index of formal institutions representing the effectiveness of government to protect citizen's rights. The Rule of Law index (RL) is part of the Worldwide Governance Indicators of the World Bank. Rule of Law (RL) is measured in rank percentiles between 0 and 1, with 1 the highest level of rule of law.

Table 11.1 provides an overview of all the relevant variables, their measurement, and their sources, categorized over three variable categories: dependent variable, explanatory variable, and control variable.

Table 11.1 Variables

Type	Category	Name	Definition	Source
social accountability	dependent variable	IMR	number of deaths per 1,000 live born	World Development Indicators
	dependent variable	U5MR	number of deaths per 1,000 live born	World Development Indicators
	dependent variable	ID	percentage immunized of 12–23 years old DPT	World Development Indicators
	dependent variable	IM	percentage immunized of 12–23 years old measles	World Development Indicators
civic use of media	explanatory variable	CA	index of civic activism as rank 0–100	Indices of Social Development
	explanatory variable	VA	index of voice and accountability as rank 0–100	Worldwide Governance Indicators
production of media	explanatory variable	PF	index of press freedom as rank 1–0	Freedom House
level of development	control variable	GDP	logarithm of GDP per capita	World Development Indicators
social spending	control variable	EXPH	percentage health expenditures of GDP	World Development Indicators
governance	control variable	RL	index of rule of law as rank 0–100	Worldwide Governance Indicators

Insights from quantitative analysis

Bi-variate regression analysis

Before going into the multivariate regression analysis, let us start with the more intuitive statistical relationships with the help of scatterplots. The four diagrams below show the statistical relationship between two variables in Table 11.1 plus the regression line of best fit.

The first two scatter plots show on the vertical axis the two explanatory variables: press freedom (PF) in the first diagram and civic activism (CA) in the second diagram. The horizontal axes show two dependent variables, both social accountability variables: primary school completion rate (PCR) and under-5 mortality rate (U5MR). Hence, the two diagrams give a rough indication of how the explanatory variables are related to the dependent variables. Both show a negative relationship, and more or less the same size (the regression line has the same slope). Remember that PF is measured negatively: 0 means full press freedom and 0 means absence of press freedom. Hence, the first diagram indicates that the more press freedom, the higher primary completion rate. In other words, the more independent the media, the lower the school drop out. But does this mean that we can attribute higher completion rates to press freedom?

The second diagram (Fig. 11.1b) indicates that the more civic activism, the lower child mortality. This seems a desirable result of an active civil society –

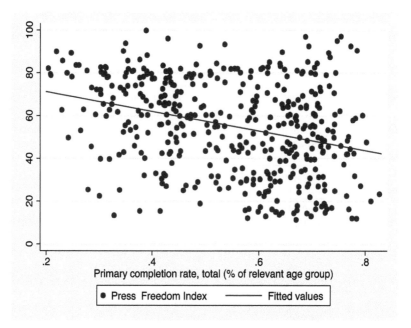

Figure 11.1a–d   Scatter plots between relevant variables

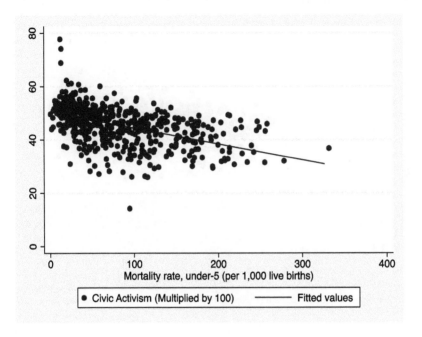

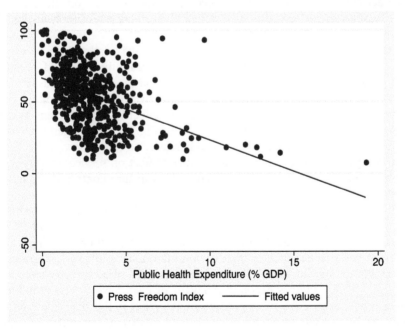

Figure 11.1a–d Continued

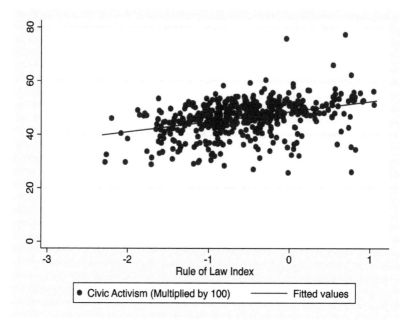

Figure 11.1a–d Scatter plots between relevant variables (Continued)

civic activism seems to be able to force governments to deliver more effective child health care services. But are lower child mortality rates simply attributable to an active civil society?

The third and fourth diagrams point out that the relationships of the first two scatter plots are not so straightforward. Diagram three (Fig. 11.1c) shows that press freedom is also positively related (mind the negative measurement!) to health expenditures. Perhaps the positive effect of press freedom on the reduction in child mortality is not a direct effect at all, but runs through higher health care budgets. Diagram four (Fig. 11.1d) suggests a similar indirect effect. Civic activism is positively related to rule of law in this scatter plot. So, perhaps civic activism has no direct effect on service delivery at all, but only on a more effective rule of law, which in turn contributes to a more effective service delivery.

Bi-variate correlations are a very crude method to measure statistical relationships. Because they do not control for the influence of other variables, which may be equally important or even more influential. That is why we need to do multi-variate regression analysis. This allows for estimating the simultaneous influence of all relevant factors. Which factors are most relevant? Which factors become irrelevant or even have a reverse influence when other factors are taken into account? What is the size of the effects? And what is their probability of being estimated correctly (statistical significance)?

Multi-variate regression analysis

A multi-variate regression analysis starts with a model. This shows the expected relationships between the various categories of variables. Figure 11.2 shows the model that we introduced at the end of the literature review.

The multi-variate regression analysis consists of four estimations, for each health care service delivery variable one. And each estimation includes five independent variables: two explanatory (press freedom and civic activism) and three control variables (GDP, public expenditures on health, Rule of Law). The results are given in the following terms:

a   size of the parameter, indicating how big the influence is of each individual independent variable on the dependent variable
b   sign of the parameter, indicating whether the effect is positive or negative
c   statistical significance of the parameter, indicating the probability that the parameter estimated is the true value (generally 99%, 95%, or 90%)
d   strength of the model, expressed as R square, with values above 30% generally considered to be strong.

The results allow a comparison between parameters, because the regression analysis returns parameter values for each variable. We will interpret here the results for a model estimation, based on our panel regression analysis (with fixed effects for countries) as carried out in the underlying quantitative study (Macedo de Jesus and van Staveren 2014a and 2014b). The sample included five years of data (1990, 1995, 2000, 2005, and 2010) and all developing countries (except those with missing data for certain variables, which makes the sample size per estimated equation vary between 168 and 457 country-year cases). We also run the same regressions with time-lags for the independent variables, to test for time-consistency of the estimations. This is, next to the fixed-effects estimations, another test for causality: if the values of the independent variables of five years back still have substantive parameter sizes and are statistically significant, it is more likely that the regression results show the expected direction of causality.

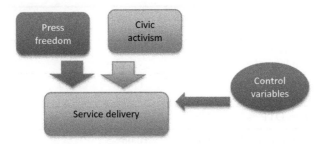

Figure 11.2 Model with service delivery determinants

Table 11.2 shows a summary of the results for the case that the value of an independent variable increases. What happens when there is 10% more civic activism? The table shows that in that case there are 8.9 fewer children dying under the age of one year old on average for developing countries, and even 17.1 fewer children dying under the age of five years. Also, the immunization rates go up: 6% for DTP and 4% for measles. But, the table shows that money has a bigger effect; 1% more economic growth has a ten times bigger effect on under-5 mortality, for example. And 10% more health expenditures by the government reduces child mortality more than twice as much as compared to 10% more civic activism ... But Rule of Law is less effective than any of the other variables. The signs of the parameters are positive for civic activism on all explanatory variables. Also, statistical significance is strong for civic activism for all four health outcome variables. But not for press freedom – that is why press freedom does not appear in the table.

The results imply that:

1   Civic activism has a positive influence on social accountability in the area of health outcomes.
2   Press freedom does not have a statistically significant effect.
3   Money has stronger effects on health outcomes, both income and public expenditures of health.

Weaknesses

Finally, we would like to draw attention to the weaknesses of our analysis. First, the service delivery variables, as outcome variables, not only refer to government efforts but also include efforts of the private sector and communities to deliver better health outcomes. Second, for various variables, there is missing data for individual country-year combinations. We have been able to address this partially by using data for the years close to the selected years. This is justifiable, because also the CA index is constructed with data for the two years below and above the selected year. For example, where data was

Table 11.2 Results

Model	10% more CA	1% more GDP	10% more RL	10% more EXPH
(1) Infant mortality (number of children)	−8.9	−12.3	−1.5	−20.3
(2) Under-5 mortality (number of children)	−17.1	−17.1	−3.0	−40.1
(3) Immunization DTP %	+0.06	+0.07		+0.13
(4) Immunization Measles %	+0.04	+0.08		

missing for a variable for 2005, but available for one of the years 2003, 3004, 2006, or 2007, we included the observations for the closest available year of these four alternative years for the 2005 data. Third, although we did causality checks, the results can never provide 100 per cent reliability of the direction of causality. But, compared to the empirical literature discussed above, our estimations address the endogeneity issue more extensively, in three complementary ways. We did this through a Granger-causality test for the independent media variables, we used a fixed effects estimation, and we did a robustness check with time-lagged variables for independent media.

Conclusions

A comprehensive quantitative analysis of the role of civil society can provide complementary insights to qualitative analyses. In particular, a quantitative analysis results in size effects of each variable (How big is the effect?), probabilities (How likely is the effect to occur?), signs (Is the effect positive or negative?), and allows for comparing the effects of all the variables (Which one is bigger or most likely to occur?). The overall conclusion from our analysis is that a quantitative analysis of the role of civil society in development is possible and meaningful, but not entirely on its own. Its results are most meaningful in combination with qualitative analysis, either through the use of primary data analysis, or through a thorough literature review of a variety of qualitative research method results.

Notes

1 www.IndSocDev.org
2 http://www.indsocdev.org/civic-activism.html
3 http://info.worldbank.org/governance/wgi/pdf/va.pdf
4 http://www.irex.org/resource/media-sustainability-index-msi-methodology
5 http://www.freedomhouse.org/report/freedom-press-2012/methodology#. U4MMHy80zeY
6 http://data.worldbank.org/data-catalog/world-development-indicators
7 http://info.worldbank.org/governance/wgi/index.aspx#home

References

Becker, Lee and Tuder, Vlad (2011) 'The Conceptualization and Operationalization of Country-level Measures of Media Freedom', in Monroe Price, Susan Abbott and Libby Morgan (eds) *Measures of Press Freedom and Media Contributions to Development – Evaluating the Evaluators*, pp. 23–43. New York: Peter Lang.

Foa, Roberto with Ellen Webbink, Arjan de Haan and Roberto Foa, 'The Last Mile in Analyzing Wellbeing and Poverty: Indices of Social Development', *Forum for Social Economics*, 43 (1) 2014, pp. 8–26.

Fowler, Alan and Kees Biekart (2008) 'Civic Driven Change: A Narrative to Bring Politics back into Civil Society Discourse', Working Paper no. 529. The Hague: Institute of Social Studies.

Gaventa, John and Rosemary McGee (2013) 'The Impact of Transparency and Accountability Initiatives', *Development Policy Review* 31(S1): S3–S28.

Glasius, M. (2010) 'Dissecting Global Civil Society: Values, Actors, Organizational Forms', Working Paper no. 14. The Hague: Hivos.

IDS (2006) 'Making Accountability Count', IDS Policy Briefing issue 33, November.

Joshi, Anuradha (2014) 'Reading the Local Context: a Causal Chain Approach to Social Accountability', *IDS Bulletin* 45(5).

Khemani, Stuti (2005) 'Local Government Accountability for Health Service Delivery in Nigeria', *Journal of African Economies* 15(2): 285–312.

Macedo de Jesus, Anderson and Irene van Staveren (2014a) *Production and Use of Independent Media: Road to Government Accountability?* The Hague: Institute of Social Studies.

Macedo de Jesus, Anderson and Irene van Staveren (2014b) 'Production and Use of Independent Media: Road to Government Accountability?' Working Paper 2014-1. Indices of Social Development. The Hague: Institute of Social Studies. Online: http://www.indsocdev.org/resources/Working_Paper_2014-1_Production_and_Use_of_Independent_Media.pdf (accessed January 2016).

Mejia Acosta, Andres (2010) *Democratic Accountability and Service Delivery – a Desk Review*. Brighton: Institute of Development Studies (IDS).

Price, Monroe, (2011) 'Press Freedom Measures: An Introduction', in Monroe Price, Susan Abbott and Libby Morgan (eds) *Measures of Press Freedom and Media Contributions to Development – Evaluating the Evaluators*, pp. 1–19. New York: Peter Lang.

Norris, Pippa (2006) 'The Role of the Free Press in Promoting Democratization, Good Governance and Human Development'. Paper for UNESCO Meeting on World Press Freedom Day. Colombo, 1–2 May.

Scrivens, Katherine and Conal Smith (2013) 'Four Interpretations of Social Capital: An Agenda for Measurement', OECD Statistics Working Papers 2013/06. Paris: OECD.

Shah, Anwar (2008) 'Demanding to be Served: Holding Governments to Account for Improved Access', Policy Research Working Paper 4643. Washington DC: The World Bank.

Tembo, Fletcher (2013) *Rethinking Social Accountability in Africa: Lessons from the Mwananchi Programme*. London: ODI.

Tran, Hai, Reaz Mahmood, Yong Du and Andrei Khrapavitski (2011) 'Linking Measures of Global Press Freedom to Development and Culture: Implications from a Comparative Analysis', *International Journal of Communication* 5: 170–191.

UNDP (2013) *Humanity Divided: Confronting Inequality in Developing Countries*. New York: United Nations Development Programme.

Van Staveren, Irene and Ellen Webbink (2012) 'Civil Society, Aid and Development: A Cross-Country Analysis', IOB Study, Ministry of Foreign Affairs of the Netherlands, The Hague, June.

Williamson, Claudia (2009) 'Informal Institutions Rule: Institutional Arrangements and Economic Performance', *Public Choice* 139(3): 371–387.

12 Minding the gap between activism and academia – or bridging it?

Reflections on how to do civic innovation research

Kees Biekart and Karin Astrid Siegmann

Introduction[1]

KARIN: I think my entry into academia was somehow motivated by the question: How to change the world by doing research?

KEES: Hmm, I have never thought about it this way. I always looked at it differently: How can I make use of the academic world to promote social transformation?

In the Civic Innovation Research Initiative (CIRI) we aim to contribute to 'liberating knowledge', that is, knowledge that embodies progressive social change. This may refer to research undertaken 'with' rather than 'about' groups that struggle for recognition, equality and empowerment. It may also relate to knowledge generated by activists in an academic setting, produced according to academic standards, but applied within processes of transformative social change. As two people interested and involved in exploring new research methodologies, but also keen to link activist and academic work, we are asking ourselves: 'Is there a specific way of doing civic innovation research?' 'Doing civic innovation research' for us has two dimensions. On the one hand, it refers to features of research that investigate processes of progressive change. On the other hand, it denotes research that embodies, i.e. promotes, is part of, and leads to progressive change or civic innovation. In this chapter, we focus on this second dimension.

Efforts to make knowledge generation more relevant to progressive change are not new in social science research. For instance, key tenets of Participatory Action Research include to *'improv[e] social practice by changing it* and learning from the consequences of change' (McTaggart 1989, italics in original; see also Fals-Borda 2006). Flyvbjerg (2001) envisages an alternative social science dedicated to enhancing socially relevant forms of knowledge. His book has triggered research into ways to address and act upon social problems in a particular context (Flyvbjerg, Landman and Schram 2012: 1). Feminist theories of knowledge provide us with another important source of inspiration. They have pointed out that values and partiality are part and parcel of all knowledge generation (e.g. Haraway 1988; Longino 2004), that departing from the perspectives of the marginalised helps to move towards greater social justice (e.g. Harding 1992) and that knowledge needs to be expressed in accessible terms to be useful for change (e.g. Patai 1988).

Yet, these perspectives do not represent the mainstream in the social sciences – and conventional research approaches may even form an obstacle to progressive social change. In the next part of this chapter ('Business as usual' in research – and where has it brought us'), we therefore sketch problematic features of 'Business as usual' in social science research that we hope to address with an alternative. We discuss criteria for knowledge production and aspects of such an alternative approach in 'Doing research for progressive change – whose knowledges, which approaches?'. It would be naïve, however, to ignore that there are many challenges to such a different way of doing research. This is why, in '(En)countering dilemmas in doing civic innovation research', we engage with the questions: Which dilemmas do we encounter in doing civic innovation research? And: How can they be addressed? We conclude with ideas about pathways for civic innovation researchers: in our view, descending from the academic ivory tower, respecting and deploying multiple knowledges for civic innovation, approaching them through participation, patient dialogue and experimentation are key features of knowledge that embodies progressive social change.

We developed our ideas about how to do civic innovation research by having a live dialogue. This was partly because we found that an interactive conversation would better fit an engagement with civic innovation, but also because we wanted to experiment and have fun. In our first exploratory conversation, we soon agreed to bring along our drawing gear, as well as pictures and videos of our work to visualise our ideas. The series of creative encounters that followed allowed us to get to know each other and our ideas better – and to further develop them jointly. We had six drawing and brainstorming sessions between May and August 2014. Each session was recorded and transcribed. Colleagues also contributed to these dialogues, especially during a CIRI retreat in August 2014. The ideas emerging during these dialogues constitute the basis of this chapter.

'Business as usual' in research – and where has it brought us

In 'business as usual' in social science research, the objectives of academics and activists are commonly not aligned. Both groups seem to move on different 'tracks'.

KEES: You say: "Business as usual" in doing social science research may form an obstacle to progressive social change.' I probably agree. But why is that?
KARIN: When I studied economics I often heard: 'Here at the university, we are doing science. Application of this knowledge is someone else's responsibility.' As a result, people are made to believe that these are two different and separate logics and spheres. Why can't you generate knowledge *and* use it for change? Academics have moved into an ivory tower and

have developed a language that ordinary people do not understand. How can you contribute to change that way?

Part of the problematic 'business as usual' is how knowledge is defined: as separate from values, requiring distance of the researcher from what s/he is trying to understand. This position is inspired by positivist criteria for knowledge generation. Here, values or personal interest are assumed to interfere with the generation of a valid account of social realities (Sayer 2000: 58). Positivists therefore distinguish the justification of research – which can be motivated by values – from the investigation itself, which should be value-neutral. For many scholars, this legitimates a retreat in the 'ivory tower', a distancing from individuals, groups, and institutions, which also produce and use knowledge for change, yet, in non-academic settings, as well as a non-engagement with the realities of power relationships.

The separation of academia from the rest of society has been associated with increasing disciplinary specialisation within the academic field. In the twenty-first century, this specialisation has been augmented by the rising commoditisation of knowledge. In this context, time has become money for scholars whose 'business' is – time-consuming – reflection. Academic institutions are increasingly branding and marketing themselves to attract students and funding. For academic researchers, this translates into pressure to 'produce outputs' that support their institutions' 'competitiveness'. Academic publications are therefore prioritised over more accessible and possibly more influential forms of communication.

At the same time, powerful actors – from government, via corporations to international organisations – often exert significant influence about which questions are being asked in research and which ones are silenced, as well as which frameworks are considered legitimate to inform policies and interventions. This commonly happens through the provision of research funding and conditions attached to grants. Its restricting effects on research contrast with the idea of 'better' knowledge emerging from open rational deliberations. Rather, it is the result of the power to '[keep] issues and actors from getting to the table in the first place' (Gaventa and Cornwall 2001: 71). Such influence is unlikely to promote knowledge generation that challenges the status quo and embodies change.

KARIN: Together with a colleague at the research institute in Pakistan, where I worked for several years, I did research on human dimensions of water management in Pakistan. This became a background paper for the World Bank's national water strategy.[2] Yet, because the World Bank saw water management largely as a technical problem rather than as issue of inequitable access, our recommendations hardly figured in their final water strategy.[3]

The separation of the 'tracks' of academia and activism as well as the greater influence of powerful rather than marginalised actors in shaping research questions are two important obstacles for civic innovation research.

Jointly, they lead to a hierarchical relationship between academics and activists, which forms a third, separate hurdle.

KEES: For me, another central problem is that people who are in an activist setting are often being 'strangled' by academic researchers. A lot of mainstream research is taking away – 'extracting' – knowledge, without bringing in new knowledge or really contributing anything to change processes.

KARIN: That's also what I experienced while working in Pakistan. A lot of research on the country was generated by foreign academics in collaboration with Pakistani researchers and activists. It was being published in international journals, earning the authors academic brownie points. But these journals often cannot be accessed from Pakistan: non-governmental organisations, but even universities are too resource-strapped to pay for their expensive subscriptions ...

In most academic settings in the global North, researchers are evaluated on the basis of the quantity of their publications in leading academic journals. These journals are often not accessible to activists or even to scholars in the global South: their subscriptions are expensive and controlled by the big academic publishing companies, which block open access to academic publications. This also leads to a form of 'knowledge extraction' that Sousa Santos (2014: 42) has called 'cognitive injustice'. While – lower paid – sub-contracted research partners in the global South are crucial to conduct research, the results of their work are not formally accessible to themselves. And if the publications are available to a wider readership, for example via 'open access' web pages, they are often written in a language that is not easily accessible to actors who may take new ideas forward. Hence, conventional academic outputs seldom inform progressive social change in the interests of giving language to and empowering marginalised people.

The process described above is also triggered by the increased pressure to specialise within one particular academic discipline. Due to competition for funding, this tendency of mono-disciplinarity has led in many fields to a hyper-specialisation of academics and greater specialist technical language. Even if it is asserted that researchers work together in multi-disciplinary teams, this often implies in practice that a mono-disciplinary division of labour is even reinforced (Max-Neef 2005). In the next section, we explore how interdisciplinary and transdisciplinary approaches are dealing with this, alongside other features of alternative forms of knowledge production.

Doing research for progressive change – whose knowledges, which approaches?

What can characterise an alternative to this – admittedly simplified – conventional way of doing social science research? An alternative that has more potential to promote civic innovation?

KARIN: In our conversations, you have often asked: Is there anything like a methodology for doing civic innovation research? That implies that there is something clearly different, doesn't it?

KEES: You know what I think? There is a civic innovation approach, which takes different existing sources of inspiration into consideration and is conscious of it. Whether it really brings something new: I don't know. But I don't find that particularly interesting either. If it brings fun, if it brings inspiration, if it brings empowerment – then I want to use and further develop it in my research!

In this section, we argue that civic innovation researchers descend from the academic ivory tower, respect and deploy diverse forms of knowledge and express this in research approaches that transcend disciplinary boundaries and in which academics work alongside marginalised people, based on participation and dialogue.

Descending from the academic ivory tower

In order to do research differently, the first question to ask is whether we can understand ourselves as different from the isolated scholar in an ivory tower?

KEES: I had just started to study political science at the University of Amsterdam. Studying there initially was great and exciting, but I soon found the urban squatters' movement politically much more interesting than the lectures at the political science department. So I felt I was in between two tracks: the squatters' movement and academia, and that it was impossible to combine the two. This also had to do with an anti-intellectual bias in this movement. Later, after dropping out of the movement, travelling abroad and writing a book, the desire to reflect on what we had been doing in terms of social transformation in previous years became stronger. Back in the library and taking time to read and reflect, I realised that action and reflection were actually not disconnected at all, but closely related.

KARIN: This reminds me of ideas that I encountered while doing research in Niger for my MA thesis. The development organisation that I worked with was inspired by Freire's 'Pedagogy of the oppressed'. It emphasises that the three critical steps for change are observation, reflection and action. Hence, my colleagues in Agadez saw reflection as part of transformation.

When we discussed this during a CIRI retreat, our colleagues Loes Keysers and Wendy Harcourt emphasised that there is no need to force the apparently separate 'tracks' of academic and activist logics together. They are embodied in us anyway, as people who generate knowledge and try to deploy it for progressive social change:

LOES: There is the assumption that we are the academics or activists, and there is 'the other' we research on. Yet, in my life I have done a lot of research on my own movement, the sexual and reproductive health movement. Many of the reflections, engagements, the crying, and the coming out, and all the contradictions, were ploughed back into the movement. As a committed activist researcher, I felt that this really was my contribution.

WENDY: This means that we can look at ourselves as embodied activist researchers. The activist researcher: I feel that is me. I always felt I was border crossing all the time between academe and movements, and also within movements, I was border crossing a lot, too. So, border crossing for me is the metaphor that I find useful. And the embodied experience in all of this: commitment to certain values, emotions, etc.

Feminists have long pleaded for knowledge production to be grounded in people's lived lives (e.g. Harding 1991). Among others, such embodiment implies that knowledge generation is always interwoven with values (Longino 2004). Feminist philosophers of science have argued that this acknowledgement should motivate researchers to commit themselves and their work to values promoting human flourishing (Intemann 2010: 781).

Deploying multiple knowledges for civic innovation

Feminist perspectives on knowledge production also emphasise the idea of research as a collective endeavour, where people who look at the world from different perspectives based on their history and situatedness can complement and validate each other's insights (Intemann 2010; Jackson 2006). Similar arguments have been used to motivate the use of mixed methods approaches: besides the combination of qualitative and quantitative techniques leading to stronger and more holistic understandings, Dzurec and Abraham (1993: 76–77) emphasise that mixing methods can support the 'pursuit of innovation' in knowledge creation. This implies work that goes beyond mono- and multi-disciplinarity. Such transdisciplinary approaches are therefore keen to look outside established disciplines as well as outside academia, and to work towards a common set of questions, frameworks, and values. These questions might not be commonly asked or even actively disliked in wider academia. We have tried to implement this approach in the present book. Here, knowledge production is seen as a more holistic and integrative process in which non-academics can be as much 'experts' as the academic researcher (Max-Neef 2005). This is in line with Sousa Santos (2014: 42) who argues for a new epistemology, 'which contrary to hegemonic epistemologies in the West, does not grant a priori supremacy to scientific knowledge (heavily produced in the North). It must allow for a more just relationship among different kinds of knowledge'.

Such deployment of multiple knowledges for civic innovation takes sides with marginalised groups and their movements, generating knowledge 'with' rather than 'about' them (Fals-Borda 2006; Harding 1992; Simmons 2012). The recognition that different types of knowledge exist and matter results in modesty regarding our ability to know: clearly, it is not the 'academic experts' who know best.

KARIN: In our study of undocumented people's access to healthcare in Dutch cities, colleagues and I trained undocumented women and men to become researchers themselves. They conducted the interviews, have been involved in their analysis and in writing a policy brief. The approach is inspired by a Participatory Ethnographic Evaluation and Research methodology.[4] But it goes beyond it: the 'researched' become researchers through all stages of the process.

JENNY: Our idea of non-extractive and interactive research last year led into the new 'community university' in Bradford with community researchers and with various kinds of activists and levels of activism. They never would use that word 'activist', but still they were making change. For example around community gardens, which is one of the most important ways in which people were seeing they can make change. So through the actual doing it I have learned most about what are the challenges we face. I do not want to diminish the value of good academic knowledge, yet, I do not privilege it either. It is the encounter with experiential knowledge and 'other knowledges' that is enriching.

Approaching civic innovation research through participation and dialogue

What are the methodological implications of such an epistemology of modesty and plurality?

First and foremost, the acknowledgement that multiple knowledges need to be mobilised for civic innovation has to be translated into an involvement of all co-researchers in choices about relevant topics and adequate ways to generate, analyse and disseminate knowledge (Sinha and Back 2014: 478). For civic innovation researchers, this may involve giving up privileges.

KEES: For me, it is important to work in a participatory manner in which ideas are generated collectively, and are benefiting the political action of social movements. In my view, such Participatory Action Research, in which you make yourself inferior as an academic, step back, and certainly step out of your ivory tower is one methodology for social change. And for you?

KARIN: I agree. But, apart from academics, there are powerful groups within social movements, whose voices are more prominent, whose knowledge gets more recognition. Spivak (1988) raised the question whether the marginalised can actually be heard as they do not speak the language of power. The challenge is how to enable them to participate in knowledge production. But maybe it is not that difficult at all and we simply have to unlearn some privileges. This reminds me of the shareholder meeting of the Dutch multinational Ahold that I attended last year on behalf of the Coalition of Immokalee Workers (CIW), a farmworker organisation in Florida. Lucas Benitez, a farmworker from Mexico and co-founder of the CIW demanded living wages in Florida's tomato fields. Peter Sabonis, a human rights lawyer supporting the CIW was given the microphone first, although Lucas had stood up earlier. But we had discussed earlier that we wanted Lucas to speak first in case we'd be interrupted by the chairman of the meeting. Peter got the microphone first, though, and I think that this was on the basis of racist prejudice ... He, a white gentleman, appeared neater to the meeting's Dutch audience than a Latino who probably comes with an inconvenient story. But Peter said: 'I'd would like this gentleman to speak first'. And that was accepted.

Besides unlearning privilege in order to make space for marginalised voices, careful listening is necessary for participatory research. This enables dialogue between different people and groups committed to progressive change. Sinha and Back (2014: 482) also argue that fostering sociable dialogues in research – besides being more respectful towards research participants – also supports an orientation towards collective analysis of social problems and community action. During the conversations informing our contribution to this book, we realised that creating open listening time – the resource that is economised so much in conventional academic knowledge production – is crucial for such sociable dialogue.

KEES: This process also requires patience, time. Reminds me of our visit to the '*Universidad de la Tierra*', the University of the Earth, in the autonomous indigenous region in Chiapas (Mexico). We came with a group of people participating in a knowledge exchange between activists and academics on the practice of civil society building in Central America.[5] The people we met there were also both researchers and activists. We first thought: 'They are talking endlessly.' But it was a very special encounter. They first asked us to tell them something about ourselves, and what our questions were. Then they withdrew and consulted amongst each other, returning after two hours. Then they answered all our questions in detail during four hours! They called it a dialogue. At that time, I thought of dialogue in a completely different manner, but we accepted their approach: it was their way to pursue a dialogue. The time was simply subordinate to the quality and depth of the exchange.

In order to enable truly participatory generation of knowledge, civic innovation researchers also have to step out of their comfort zone. A research orientation towards problem-solving and contributing to alternatives involves forward-looking research. Social sciences have long tried to understand how processes of political and economic domination inhibit people's flourishing, assuming that their explanation would give clues about how to end or revert them. However, in an open world in which actors and their relations change, such structural identity between explanation and prediction that Hempel and Oppenheim (1948) posited is unlikely to hold. Critical realists emphasise that we live in an open world in which actors and their relations constantly change. Therefore, it is unlikely that explaining, for example, experiences of poverty and social marginalisation is sufficient to understand how to *combat* poverty and marginalisation. For research to embody progressive change, therefore, focusing on how alternatives have come about is necessary alongside the analysis of marginalising dynamics. Case studies that contextualise local effects and responses to processes of structural change are therefore an important approach to civic innovation research (Ackroyd 2009).

Stepping out of our comfort zone also affects the toolbox of methods we apply.

KEES: For that, taking the risk to experiment is important, as many traditional academic methods basically undermine our creativity. At the CIRI Forum last year, we therefore experimented with an open microphone, an approach coming from activist circles. I saw it for the first time in the early 1980s when I was part of the Amsterdam urban squatters' movement. We made a tour through Germany and Switzerland, and ended up in the Autonomous Youth Centre in the Red Factory in Zürich. There, we witnessed how 800 young activists discussed their strategy towards the government via just one open microphone. The only rule was that the person using the mike had the right to speak, and the others would have to shut up and wait for their turn to speak. I had never seen this before. There was no chair, it was self-facilitating. It was amazing! If you don't have a leader and you share this sort of responsibility then this gives enormous power to your movement. Hence, doing things experimentally has a goal. It's not just trying something new.

Communicating research powerfully

Openness for experiment is important for communicating civic innovation research, too. Commonly, researchers are trained to write academic publications in an academic language targeted at an academic audience. Does this form of communicating knowledge catalyse progressive social change? Civic innovation research has to be communicated to wider audiences of potential change makers if it wishes to produce liberating knowledge. A crucial step in the production of knowledge that has the potential to embody progressive change is the possibility to discuss and assess its adequacy for that change with a wider range of actors. But that implies a descent from the ivory tower, leaving behind the comfortable furniture of an academic, or even more specialised disciplinary jargon.

KARIN: You mentioned that the 'right' way of communicating knowledge also relates to power. What did you mean?

KEES: What I found a very moving example is what happened when, in June 2014, I participated in the conference of the European Association of Development Research and Training Institutes, together with other CIRI colleagues. We had agreed that, actually, we wanted to do our civic innovation-related panel without powerpoint presentations. The only type of slides that you were allowed to bring were photographs. Mary Rutenge, a CIRI PhD student, brought pictures for her presentation on gold mining multinationals and communities in Tanzania. She presented an amazingly strong story about the local resistance against the mining companies because she talked to her pictures, which became vivid! People sat with open ears and eyes to listen because it was such a powerful story. And why was that? Because she also broke with a traditional academic way of communicating which did not suit her anyway. For her, this was a moment of discovery: You can communicate your research differently, and through that you can be understood much better, you can have more impact. For me, that is an example of how experiments can be empowering. Visuals, the presentation only had visuals – that was it! If you use visuals, then you can also address people who are not very much talented with words, but who are talented in being triggered by symbols and colours.

IRENE: We are still stuck in the stereotypes of outputs … In academia, we spend months and years publishing academic articles and books. But in our activist personae we do it without asking any money and pay with own time, teaching courses, or writing pamphlets. Perhaps it is also our responsibility to use channels in between; some are writing blogs. I use Twitter, though I could do that a lot more.

As in Mary's case, who felt more comfortable with her photographs guiding her through the narrative of her research results than a wordy presentation, the greater flexibility in the choice of 'language' we use in itself might actually be a liberation for many of us. Visualisation, for instance, can help to trigger conversations, which overcome language ambiguities, as well as rational and linear arguments. For the training and practice of civic innovation researchers, this implies that serious engagement with and proficiency in plural forms of communication with a range of target groups is required. Drawings, as well as video and theatre can be equally important and powerful media to generate stories and knowledge 'from below' as text. Training and practice in communication via print, electronic and social media is crucial for civic innovation researchers apart from the standard courses in academic writing. A wider range of communication tools available means that we can broaden the circle of people we communicate with, to include those who can relate to an image of resistance against mining rather than to a theory of social movements.

Embracing a story-telling, narrative approach, rather than appeals to logic and statistical significance alone, as a valid and important way of communicating knowledge that embodies civic innovation is another lesson to be learned from Mary's experience. Often, it is not the deductive logic of an argument, but the ambiguity of a narrative that initiates reflection (Polletta et al. 2011: 122). Narration more powerfully reminds us of the partiality of the story-teller – her/his specific angle, her/his commitments. This is something that teaches modesty to civic innovation researchers and highlights the need to position ourselves more explicitly (Polletta et al. 2011: 113).

(En)countering dilemmas in doing civic innovation research

Of course, there are risks and dilemmas in any research that seriously engages with the epistemological and methodological principles outlined above. In this section, we flag key challenges for doing civic innovation research and discuss ways of dealing with them. They involve tensions that civic innovation researchers may experience within their home institutions. Power relations and hierarchies between and within academic and activist fields may complicate our commitment to participatory research. Finally, what some may consider constructive critical reflection on efforts to promote progressive change, might be seen as detrimental to these efforts by others.

As researchers keen to embody progressive social change in our work, we ourselves might feel comfortable with the descent from the ivory tower – but will our employers and funders? Our colleagues addressed this question towards the end of the CIRI retreat when we were discussing a large paper collage of our dialogue outside on the beautiful moors.

ALAN: If you try to bridge academic and activist worlds, then part of the challenge is to accept, within either one of the tracks that you try to hold together, that you are marginalised in both! You are not a good enough academic, because you are not 'pure' enough and you are not good enough as a practitioner because you are not offering up enough. So, one chooses to be willingly on the periphery of two tracks, but we do realise the costs ...

KEES: That was also our experience when we did Participatory Action Research with the Dutch development organisation Hivos in Central America, together with three different social movements. We had this ambiguous feeling: this is ambitious, but certainly not easy. We actually did what we wanted to do: working in a genuinely participatory manner with the movements in the driver's seat and local academics in a supportive role. In fact, we only facilitated the process rather than imposing it as Northern researchers. Neither did we publish anything, as the movements published the findings themselves. But then, afterwards Hivos asked us: 'Why did you not do "normal research", which would have generated articles from you as senior researchers in highly ranked academic journals?' Initially we did not understand this comment, but later we realised that Hivos did not have any prior experience with participatory research.

So it was rather disappointing they did not value this, also since we had made great efforts to step back as academics to create conditions for movement-led participatory research. Even some of our ISS colleagues suggested we had wasted our time by not producing any academic output from this project ourselves.

WENDY: The real key word is 'we', the group and how we can work together? The tension here is that of a group working in an academic environment. This is generally not accepted. We are trying to break with that dynamic, consciously and with courage. Particularly for younger researchers, those who have not climbed particularly high on their career ladder ... We have to recognise that as it is a sacrifice, as it is much easier for an academic to sit there individually and to do your own thing.

PETER: I think that the dilemma is simultaneously the solution: embarking on civic innovation research as a collective adventure will improve the quality of your work. That way, you can contribute to change – and convince funders and publishers!

This conversation touches upon the discussion on societal relevance – so-called 'valorisation' – of research. In recent years it has become more accepted – and it is even stimulated by funders of research – to make sure that research becomes valuable for and relevant to society. The problematic point here is

Figure 12.1 Researchers discussing how to do civic innovation research at CIRI retreat, Hilversum, The Netherlands, August 2014
Source: Kees Biekart

that this valorisation commonly takes place in hindsight, rather than during or even prior to research activities. This way, relevant questions and research approaches are being defined without the participation of those to whom new knowledge matters most. In civic innovation research, in contrast, we take a more direct route to social relevance, aiming for effective participation at all stages of knowledge generation. From this perspective, it is so obvious that research has to be relevant to change agents in society, and we therefore often do not emphasise this clearly enough.

The commitment to participatory research as an expression of respect for a plurality of knowledges is beautiful in theory. In practice it is problematic. The views of different actors often do not complement each other to one coherent whole, but are contradictory and contest each other's basis to know. The inextricable connection between knowledge and values implies that each potential participant in our dialogue on civic innovation brings her/his own interests to the deliberative table. How to decide whose agenda is most in line with the value of progressive social change? And: Who may rightfully claim the authority to take this decision? One feminist solution to these dilemmas, namely to ground claims in the perspectives of the marginalised (Harding 1992; Mohanty 2003) has been problematised from the perspective of intersectionality (Crenshaw 1991). The self-reflexive acknowledgement of one's own responsibility for the specific types of knowledge one produces as well as the effort to see things from a range of other perspectives may offer ways out (Anderson 2011). Ignoring these questions, however, may lead to a misrepresentation of the perspectives of the marginalised.

Our colleague Silke pointed to this risk when we discussed our experience with participatory research:

SILKE: The Participatory Action Research on the histories of social movements in Central America taught us important lessons. Movements are heterogeneous, there are internal power hierarchies. Therefore, the question who was assigned to write the history of a movement matters: *Which* history and *whose* history is being written? Our contacts within social movements are probably part of the more powerful players within movements – they are the ones with transnational linkages. What does that mean for participatory research? Through our decision of who participates and who doesn't, we run the risk of reinforcing existing power relations, of legitimising the elite's perspective of the movement.

Silke's statement exemplifies what is referred to in this book's introduction, namely that, amongst activists and social movements, 'internal power relationships often are obscured in order to prioritise "larger" social goals' (Biekart, Harcourt and Knorringa, this volume: p. 9). How to deal with that in the process of knowledge generation? This can be a real dilemma: by choosing to work with a particular movement in participatory research, does one also have to respect the autonomy of the movement up to the point of accepting that critical internal voices are being silenced?

In civic innovation research it is common that one is operating in conflictual settings, so being aware of potential power battles is very important. More importantly, '[r]esearch is as much a process of power as any other sphere of life' (Clegg and Pitsis 2012: 67). Therefore, knowledge production that is not sensitive to – internal or external – power relations runs the risk of undermining change processes or strengthening hierarchies. A 'power check' is therefore recommended when engaging with change agents in order to prevent conflicts between researchers and activists. Simmons (2012: 254) suggests that: '[w]e must resist the temptation where we believe that we have included all voices – we must continuously deconstruct how we continue to privilege or stage certain voices'.

KEES: In our PAR study in Central America, we had this strong idea from the beginning that, in the first place, the outcome of this research would have to be useful to the movements themselves. In the case of Costa Rica it was basically drawing lessons from a campaign against the Free Trade Agreement, looking backward based on empirical data. In Guatemala, the discussion was more forward-looking, which is generally creating more interest of organisations to participate in the discussion. But it also can generate more conflict since you are dealing with ongoing and real existing power struggles. Movements prefer to look ahead (rather than back, which is common in academic research) but they do not like conflict at all, so this is tricky for researchers.

KARIN: This reminds me of a discussion I had with Silke, about her research on social movements in Central America. She felt it was a dilemma to talk about the frictions within the women's movement. On the one hand she wanted to talk about exclusions and power dynamics within the movement. They were hampering the very goals of the movement. On the other hand, she was worried about alienating the movement's leadership as well as of how this information might be used – or rather misused – by their adversaries. But this is not about a neat distinction between activists and academics. As academics we are often activists, too, with loyalties to the aims of movements. It is probably movement leaders who don't want to show divisions, but those who are silenced who have an interest in voicing them. Likewise some academics – like us – will want to explore the contradictions. Others choose to overshadow them and keep a neat public image.

These dilemmas about power, empowerment, and legitimacy are not always easy to resolve. In our discussions we basically identified four ways to deal with this. The first was to be modest about our role and potential as activist researchers. We have to develop and maintain a sense of responsibility about our potential disruptive and steering role in initiating and managing research activities. A second and related condition is to maintain a self-reflective attitude at all times, even if this sounds obvious. It implies that we cannot always put our own research objectives at the centre and that we often have to give in for the interest of the final outcome. A third, and related, point is to make sure we have really prepared ourselves well about the ins and outs of a movement, about the frictions and factions and internal power relations, so that we can take the various voices into account. And the fourth possible perspective to keep in mind is to make sure our research primarily serves the objective of social transformation rather than academic careers or individual hobbies or priorities. This last element is not all easy to comply with: we only know what research outcome looks like after several years. So how to judge this? It is essential to reflect about this jointly and repeatedly.

KARIN: During the Ahold shareholder meeting, I actually had the impression that the things I engage with academically contributed to a better strategy, better arguments in our efforts to lobby the company for better working conditions in their supply chain.
KEES: Yes, apparently you *can* change the world through research. Or contribute to change. That's in fact what you say. You still state it cautiously: 'I had the impression that …' But what is the basis for that impression? And: Who determines that you are effective? Or that you have an impact?
KARIN: See, I have no idea what our efforts at the shareholder meeting have meant for a movement by Ahold towards the CIW. Here, I don't talk about what is going to happen regarding poverty wages or living wages in tomato fields in Florida. What I can assess, somehow, is that particular situation at the shareholder meeting. We had expected that we wouldn't be given space for our demands. We tried to address this strategically, through the division of roles among Lucas, Peter and me, through our distribution across the conference hall, through translation. And that was successful. But how does it fit into the whole campaign? We had a discussion about how to identify instances of civic innovation during a CIRI workshop. We realised that it all depends on what you look at, in terms of the spatial and temporal boundaries of the change you are interested in promoting.

Patchy pathways for civic innovation research

BERT: In these conversations about doing civic innovation research, there is an enormous amount of questioning of what we as academics commonly do. My question is: To what extent can we actually deliver on all the criteria we have developed about how we want to do civic innovation research? And: Can we communicate that in a way that others are able to understand? And can they and we do something with it? I have learned a lot, but I am terribly worried whether we are able to deal with all the questions we raised. Our levels of ambition are enormous.

Descending from the academic ivory tower, respecting and deploying multiple knowledges for civic innovation, approaching them through participation, patient dialogue and experimentation: indeed, this is an ambitious roadmap for the civic innovation researcher. Ambition has to be accompanied with modesty: about what we can know, about the change we can embody in the knowledge we generate, share, and deploy. The pathways for civic innovation researchers are patchy, yet, leading to a thrilling, promising journey.

This journey of doing civic innovation research may sometimes resemble a labyrinth: Can we really use social transformation as a *benchmark* for our research approaches, while simultaneously hoping to *find out* about what this progressive social change entails through co-production of knowledge? There is no easy way out of this labyrinth. Yet, only if you dare to enter in the first place, can you learn how to travel within it. Time spent on dialogue is necessary to explore, understand and negotiate what represents 'civic innovation' from a range of different positionalities. This addresses the question raised by Biekart, Harcourt and Knorringa (this volume: p. 9): 'Who determines which means and ends of activisms are justified and would contribute to the common good (and who decides what is "the" common good)?'.

The role of power in doing civic innovation research is multifaceted. A commitment to 'horizontal sharing of knowledge where all expertise and knowledges are valued and understood as coming from a particular positionality' (Biekart, Harcourt and Knorringa, this volume: p. 17) has to be accompanied with an acute awareness that relations between different knowers are rarely horizontal, but rather shaped by intersecting hierarchies of gender, age, education, race – to name a few. This sensitivity needs to be employed to challenge these very hierarchies and marginalising processes, rather than to corroborate them in research. The knowledge so generated has the potential to contribute to epistemic and material justices, to empowerment.

Such knowledge that embodies progressive social change is produced not by abstract thought, but by people who have bodily experience in different spatial and social spheres. We can produce (academic and other) knowledge *and* use it to change the world – including ourselves. We integrate these experiences, rather than them splitting our personalities into a researcher and an activist self. From this epistemological point of departure, we can travel a journey towards co-generation of knowledge that is informed by visions of a society that enables human flourishing and engages in constant, self-critical reflection about whether the ways we think and act are true to these visions.

At a structural level, our efforts to do research differently, to embody progressive social change, have to address the neo-liberal context in which academic knowledge production is embedded. With Jessop (2007) we aim to re-embed knowledge in society, i.e. make it a public good again, with public benefit.

The most important contribution from a civic innovation perspective is probably to be critical of the processes and actors we study, and to maintain a self-reflective attitude. Learning is essential and that means constant reflection on your process of knowledge production. To stick with the metaphor of the journey: it is no option to stand still, even not whilst reflecting, as permanent movement is required on the bumpy road leading away from the ivory tower and towards knowledge that embodies progressive change ...

Notes

1 We gratefully acknowledge helpful comments by John Cameron on this chapter.
2 See Siegmann and Shehzad (2006).
3 See Briscoe et al. (2006).
4 See Guemar and Hintjens (2013).
5 See Biekart and Icaza (2011).

References

Ackroyd, S. (2009) 'Research Designs for Realist Research', in D.A. Buchanan and A. Bryman (eds) *Handbook of Organizational Research Methods*, pp. 533–548. London: Sage.
Anderson, E. (2011) 'Feminist Epistemology and Philosophy of Science', in E.N. Zalta (ed.) *The Stanford Encyclopedia of Philosophy* (Fall 2012 Edition). Available at http://plato.stanford.edu/archives/fall2012/entries/feminism-epistemology/ [accessed 8 July 2015].
Biekart, K. and Icaza, R. (2011) 'Knowledge Dialogues with Central American Social Movements', Hivos–ISS Working Paper. The Hague: ISS.
Briscoe, J., U. Qamar, M. Contijoch, P. Amir and D. Blackmore (2006) *Pakistan's Water Economy: Running Dry*. Karachi: Oxford University Press.
Clegg, S.R. and T.S. Pitsis (2012) 'Pronesis, Projects and Power Research', in B. Flyvbjerg, T. Landman and S. Schram (eds), *Real Social Science: Applied Phronesis*, pp. 66–91. Cambridge: Cambridge University Press.
Crenshaw, K. (1991) 'Mapping the Margins: Intersectionality, Identity Politics, and Violence Against Women of Color', *Stanford Law Review* 43(6): 1241–1299.
Dzurec, L.C. and I.L. Abraham (1993) 'The Nature of Inquiry: Linking Quantitative and Qualitative Research', *Advances in Nursing Science* 16(1): 73–79.
Fals-Borda, O. (2006) 'Participatory (Action) Research in Social Theory: Origins and Challenges', in P. Reason and H. Bradbury (eds) *Handbook of Action Research*, pp. 27–37. London: Sage.
Flyvbjerg, B. (2001) *Making Social Science Matter: Why Social Inquiry Fails and How it Can Succeed Again*. Cambridge: Cambridge University Press.
Flyvbjerg, B., T. Landman and S. Schram (2012) *Real Social Science: Applied Phronesis*. Cambridge: Cambridge University Press.
Gaventa, J. and A. Cornwall (2001) 'Power and Knowledge', in P. Reason and H. Bradbury (eds) *Handbook of Action Research. Participative Inquiry and Practice*, pp. 70–80. London: Sage.
Guemar, L.N. and H. Hintjens (2013) 'Is the Peer Ethnographic Approach a Suitable Method for Researching Lives of Undocumented Migrants?', *Tijdschrift over Cultuur & Criminaliteit* 2013(3)1: 69–81.
Haraway, D. (1988) 'Situated Knowledges: The Science Question in Feminism and the Privilege of Partial Perspective', *Feminist Studies* 14(3): 575–599.
Harding, S. (1992) 'Subjectivity, Experience and Knowledge: An Epistemology from/for Rainbow Coalition Politics', *Development and Change* 23(3): 175–193.

Harding, S. (1991) 'What Is Feminist Epistemology?', in S. Harding *Whose Science? Whose Knowledge? Thinking from Women's Lives*, pp. 105–137. Buckingham: Open University Press.

Hempel, C.G. and P. Oppenheim (1948) 'Studies in the Logic of Explanation', *Philosophy of Science* 15(2): 135–175.

Intemann, K. (2010) '25 Years of Feminist Empiricism and Standpoint Theory: Where are we Now?', *Hypatia* 25(4): 778–796.

Jackson, C. (2006) 'Feminism Spoken here: Epistemologies for Interdisciplinary Development Research', *Development and Change* 37(3): 525–547.

Jessop, B. (2007) 'Knowledge as a Fictitious Commodity: Insights and Limits of a Polanyian Analysis', in A. Buğra and K. Ağartan (eds) *Reading Karl Polanyi for the 21st Century. Market Economy as a Political Project*, pp. 115–134. Basingstoke: Palgrave.

Longino, H.E. (2004) 'How Values can be Good for Science', in P. Machamer and G. Wolters (eds) *Science, Values, and Objectivity*, pp. 127–142. Pittsburgh: University of Pittsburgh Press.

Max-Neef, M. (2005) 'Foundations of Transdisciplinarity', *Ecological Economics* 53 (1): 5–16.

McTaggart, R. (1989) '16 Tenets of Participatory Action Research (PAR)'. http://www. caledonia.org.uk/par.htm [accessed 24 August 2014].

Mohanty, C.T. (2003) '"Under Western Eyes" Revisited: Feminist Solidarity through Anticapitalist Struggles', *Signs* 28(2): 499–535.

Patai, D. (1988) 'Who's Calling Whom "Subaltern"?' *Women and Language* 11(2) (Winter): 23–26.

Polletta, F., P. Ching, B. Chen, B.G. Gardner and A. Motes (2011) 'The Sociology of Storytelling', *Annual Review Sociology* 37: 109–130.

Sayer, A. (2000) *Realism and Social Science*. London: Sage.

Siegmann, K.A. and S. Shehzad (2006) 'Pakistan's Water Challenges: A Human Development Perspective', SDPI Working Paper, No. 105, Islamabad: SDPI.

Simmons, W.P. (2012) 'Making the Teaching of Social Justice Matter', in B. Flyvbjerg, T. Landman and S. Schram, *Real Social Science: Applied Phronesis*, pp. 246–263. Cambridge: Cambridge University Press.

Sinha, S. and L. Back (2014) 'Making Methods Sociable: Dialogue, Ethics and Authorship in Qualitative Research', *Qualitative Research* 14(4): 473–487.

Sousa Santos, B. de (2014) *Epistemologies of the South: Justice against Epistemicide*. Boulder and London: Paradigm Publishers.

Spivak, G.C. (1988) 'Can the Subaltern Speak?', in C. Nelson and L. Grossberg (eds), *Marxism and the Interpretation of Culture*, pp. 271–313. Basingstoke: MacMillan Education.

13 Conclusion

Moving agendas forward

Wendy Harcourt, Kees Biekart and Peter Knorringa

Introduction

Woven throughout the book's descriptions and analysis of different examples of social transformation, change actors and innovative methodologies is an evolving conceptual discussion of civic innovation. In this conclusion we continue the discussion first raised in the introductory chapter's 'mosaic' as we define more clearly the conceptual interests of civic innovation as an area of research. In what follows we pull out from each of the chapters how key concepts help us to define what civic innovation is in practice. As the book chapters indicate with the myriad of interests and concerns, we look at civic innovation wherever it occurs – whether in the streets, in market negotiations, intergovernmental conferences, NGO planning or in on-line forums. We explore in these places how civic innovation is creating space for exchange and dialogue. What is striking throughout the book is the effort to engage with, but also move beyond, the norms and known categories of the well-worn narratives of labour, institutions, movements, NGOs, class, gender, race and generation.

Our understanding of civic innovation recognises that these categories can be restrictive given how power and knowledge are played out in horizontal as well as vertical interactions. For example, in most of the chapters there is a strong reluctance to adopt the crisis narratives of there is a 'them' oppressing 'us'. Even while acknowledging there is oppression, silencing and worse, the underlying tenor is to build on relations, on what can be done, with feelings of hope in order to move towards positive visions for change where peoples' agency is the driver. The chapters work not in abstractions but look at specificities and actions in localities and then see how they interconnect with the big picture narrative. In this way civic innovation is analysed from the ground as working through a mesh of connections in place linked to global arenas via fluid and loose networks.

In our concluding chapter we present some of the highlights of the chapters looking at what we have identified as conceptual innovations around thematic concerns that form the foundations of civic innovation research reflecting the focus of different sets of chapters loosely looking at 'markets' 'politics' and 'gender, sexuality and youth'. These were the categories from which we began our research, though as we explain, in the writing of the book those initial divisions among the research group have become much more closely interwoven, which is an important part of the conceptual innovations we present here. We follow this summary of the 'highlights' of each chapter with our editorial reflections on the process and methodology of doing civic innovation research, which we have found to be a very important part of the civic innovation initiative and the making of this book. Finally, we set out some of the next steps that we envisage taking as we move forward in this new research field on civic innovation.

Conceptual innovations: some highlights

The big picture of 'innovation'

Our research has been undertaken during a particular historical moment as discussions whirl around the post 2015 development agenda and the uncertainty of big picture narratives. The search for 'what is to be done' in response to perceived crises of security, climate, finance, labour and the geopolitical divides of 'North' and 'South', means that we have taken a politically sensitised lens to our research of grounded and local initiatives of civic innovation. While the European Horizon 2020 agenda and the Sustainable Development Goals (SDGs) also focus on similar concerns through labels such as social innovation and the search for inclusive societies, we position civic innovation as a complementary approach with a more explicit focus on power differentials. Such an explicit power focus and a recognition of difference and diversity allows us to explore more deeply where and when and what type of grass roots initiatives are able to contribute to more empowered and dignified lives for marginalised groups of people in various societies. Unqualified positive outcomes of such struggles are hard to proclaim, but a more nuanced and careful empirical analysis – like in many of the book's chapters – shows that steps towards progressive social transformation are being made in very different arenas. In our emerging civic innovation approach we explore the fine line in between a utopian and a cynical view on societal change. We look at transformational change and the contribution to that change by more marginalised and exploited people, whether due to age, class, gender or geographic location.

Our research on civic innovation aims to make visible what remains hidden in the mainstream development agendas, complementing other development research agendas dealing with the 'big narrative' picture such as that of the Institute of Development Studies (IDS), Sussex University, pathways to sustainability approach[1] which looks at 'engaged excellence for global development', emphasising global as well as local ideals and bringing in their research and capacity building agenda on equality and sustainability and security.

Civic innovation as set out in the book, brings to the fore critical development thinking that questions dominant negative narratives about the current economic crisis by looking at both resistance and hope. Specifically, two chapters (Trejo-Mendez, Sánchez de la Blanca, Santamaría Buitrago, Sardoni, Simula and Harcourt, Ch. 10; and Harcourt Icaza and Vargas, Ch. 8) take up Arturo Escobar's proposal of 'political ontology' (Escobar 2015) as a way to question dominant hegemonic narratives. As explained in Chapter 10 by Trejo-Mendez, Sánchez de la Blanca, Santamaría Buitrago, Sardoni, Simula with Harcourt, this means research on civic innovation is the politics of being or becoming or 'knowing by doing'. Civic innovation research investigates the power-laden processes through which life is experienced and lived as people are becoming actively engaged in everyday resistances. In understanding the everyday quality of these resistances civic innovation analyses political actions and economic activities as closely linked to our emotions and bodily sensations. Civic innovation aims to move beyond the fear of the big narratives of crisis and to remain hopeful by rethinking the economy and to think about what is possible – from youth led collective kitchens to social entrepreneurs doing responsible business.

At the interface of capitalism – markets and civic innovation

Markets and market thinking are often equated in progressive development discourse with all the evils of a neoliberal capitalist hegemony. Our approach shows how civic innovations do occur even in market settings. The chapters that conceptualise the process of civic innovation and the role of social entrepreneurs in markets (Gómez and Ritchie, Ch. 2, and Helmsing, Ch. 5), as well as the thoughtful empirical chapters in which actors operate squarely in a market setting (Siegmann, Merk and Knorringa, Ch. 6; Pegler and Marques Silva, Ch. 7; Macedo de Jesus and van Staveren, Ch. 11) all conclude that qualified opportunities for civic innovations do exist. Actors need to go against the tide, possible gains usually remain fragile and many obstacles and complications confront those engaged in trying to push for progressive social transformations. Nevertheless, we do see a multitude of 'seeds for change', also in market settings. A few such seeds may well enable committed groups to more durably strengthen their relative bargaining positions in markets, especially when they align with like-minded actors at other points in the respective value chain or market. Notwithstanding macro level processes of concentration of power and resources, we also recognise and attach significance to a mosaic of counter movements at micro and meso levels of analysis. Moreover, we are committed to do research together with people who are in the forefront of these struggles, in order to also try to systematise and spread lessons to be learned from various civic innovations, which we hope and expect will contribute to their strength and resilience.

Gómez and Ritchie (Ch. 2) conceptualise the institutional foundations of civic innovation, using institutional economics' theory to embed civic innovation in a theory of institutional change. This posits civic innovation as a politically motivated and endogenously driven collective action process that can successfully challenge and change institutions whose societal outcomes have become unacceptable. Using the elegant stylised simplicity of economic theorisation they show how civic innovation offers a potential way out of otherwise stagnant and oppressive institutional structures. Therefore, Gómez and Ritchie provide an important conceptual foundation for the following chapters that combine specific empirical observations with more applied conceptualisations. The chapter also focuses on the important role of change agents in organising resistance to oppressive institutions and in constructing and consolidating new institutions that offer more potential for progressive transformations.

Helmsing (Ch. 5) focuses on how the social entrepreneurship literature operationalises the social in social entrepreneurship. Building on the ideas from Fowler (Ch. 3) on interlocutors, social entrepreneurs can be seen as hybrid actors who apply their entrepreneurial drive and skills to achieve social goals. Much of the social entrepreneurship literature tends to focus on the heroism of the individual entrepreneur, in line with the mainstream for-profit entrepreneurship literature. Going beyond this approach, Helmsing explores also more critical strands of literature that analyse when social entrepreneurs are more likely to contribute to progressive social transformation. This more critical literature for example posits that the self-defined social goals of 'can do' well-intentioned social entrepreneurs may displace or contradict more locally rooted collective processes of identifying social needs. However, in this conceptual chapter Helmsing convincingly argues that social entrepreneurs' success at least partly depends precisely on the extent to which they actively engage in interacting with other change agents at the local level. Moreover, they may define their social mission in interaction with poorer and more excluded groups, but there are also many 'off the shelf' social missions – like access to potable water – that do not require much deliberation as a goal in itself, while it remains crucial to embed the processes and actors through which such a mission is operationalised.

A major conceptual finding by Helmsing is that some level of civic engagement, networking and embeddedness – as opposed to acting as a 'lone ranger' – is a key feature of success for social entrepreneurs in international development. Given the achievement-oriented behaviour of entrepreneurs, this is a major incentive for social entrepreneurs to invest in such engagements. Therefore, social entrepreneurs who generate innovative ways to address unmet social needs are rather likely to also support or co-create broader processes of localised social transformation.

Siegmann, Merk and Knorringa (Ch. 6) investigate the civic innovation potential of non-governmental labour regulation in value chains, using illustrative findings from the Fair Food programme. They move beyond the disillusionment with private codes of conduct and related attempts at leaving businesses to self-regulate labour conditions in (global) value chains. They begin from the observation that a next generation of non-governmental regulation can only become meaningful when workers themselves occupy a central position in the formulation and implementation of standards. However, workers' agency at the bottom-end of the value chain will in isolation not suffice to achieve significant improvements in bargaining power that may enable broader social transformation processes. The main argument is that chances to achieve more effective and more durable 'decent work' outcomes increase when local collective action among workers can be complemented by social activists' campaigns at other points in the value chain. Such coalitions between directly affected actors like workers and activists who share their struggle for justice can at least partially overcome the geographical, class and cultural gaps along these (often global) value chains. Moreover, it enables such coalitions to concentrate and pinpoint their bargaining power where they have a better chance to 'punch above their weight', through directly targeting consumer facing A brand companies like McDonalds, Walmart or Nike. Therefore, the authors argue that strong localised collective agency is a necessary but not sufficient condition to generate genuine countervailing power in such value chains. Coalitions with civic activists focusing on other actors in the value chains are a strategic asset to enable more durable processes of social transformation.

Pegler and Marques Silva (Ch. 7) present two contrasting case studies from the Amazon in order to illustrate how value chain structures matter for opportunities to create the enabling conditions for social transformation. The case studies bring to life the diversified livelihood struggles by Amazonian rural small-scale producer households, as rather scattered and marginalised participants in various value chains. They compare opportunities for effective agency and representation of communities involved in the palm oil and acai value chains. Next to a number of similarities, like weaker bargaining positions of women and youth in these communities as compared to men, the main empirical contribution of the chapter lies in exploring the differentiated possible gains from value chain inclusion in palm oil versus acai. In palm oil the small-scale producers tend to depend on one main buyer with a strong local presence. This main buyer offers somewhat better economic returns in the short run, while local power differences can be expected to block any attempts at collective action among small-scale producers. Palm oil as an income generating activity requires households to at least partially specialise in this product. In contrast, the acai value chain is characterised by much more loose relationships with less embedded buyers and does not require much specialised effort by households, enabling them to remain flexible and diversified as befitting their overall income generating logic. While economic benefits are relatively less, these types of value chain relationships may offer the rather remote possibility for more effective collective action among small-scale producers. These differences are remarkable and provide more nuance to an often more generic literature that dismisses any option for effective collective action among the most marginalised participants in such value chains. The more nuanced question then becomes how one might assess the 'trade-off' between a little bit more attractive economic gains in the shorter run versus a possible but far from certain longer term perspective on perhaps being able to create a little bit more room to manoeuvre for developing countervailing power in the value chain. With a link to Siegmann, Merk and Knorringa we could argue that this second option might become more attractive when local collective action initiatives are able to construct alliances with civic activists at other levels of the acai value chain. Given that acai is a key input for some of the major global beverage companies, this might offer opportunities for more durable social transformations.

Macedo and van Staveren (Ch. 11) use a quantitative approach to examine whether civic activism contributes to the social accountability of governments. It provides two key contributions to this volume. First, the findings themselves show the complementary value of using a quantitative approach in trying to identify and analyse the constituting elements of civic innovation. The chapter shows in some detail and in a non-technical manner, how with the use of the Indices for Social Development data base one can operationalise such a research question. The chapter explains why it chooses specific sets of variables to test its main hypotheses, and concludes that civic activism does have a positive influence on social accountability in the area of service delivery on health. However, more unexpectedly perhaps, more press freedom does not have a statistically significant positive relationship with more social accountability of governments. Such a provocative finding from a cross-country and longitudinal multi-variate regression analysis should at least make all researchers – whether using more quantitative or more qualitative methods – think hard about often assumed causal relationships that might sometimes be stimulated by wishful thinking and about the reliability of data. This leads to the second and per-haps most important contribution of this chapter. It provides a very clear and useful non-technical introduction to the complementary value of quantitative analysis in trying to understand causal relationships in civic innovation research. The regressions provide insightful results that provide food-for-thought for more qualitatively oriented researchers. The authors conclude that quantitative analysis is a useful complementary approach that can reveal broad patterns in causal relationships between key civic innovation variables over time and across countries.

Politics, power and civic agency

From a perspective of 'politics', the exploration of civic innovation was ela-borated in three chapters: the ones on interlocutors (Fowler, Ch. 3), the chapter on consultants as change agents (Bergh and Biekart, Ch. 4) and the chapter on civic innovation research methodology and knowledge generation (Biekart and Siegmann, Ch. 12). These chapters analyse the power base of change actors in society, irrespective of the sector they operated in. These actors were generally understood in a broad sense, also including Latour's 'actants' who have their power base in information technology. Another common element in these analyses is that labels are given to these intermediary actors for the function they perform: this can be 'interlocution' (for the interlocutors), it can be a role as auditing (of development actors), or rather allying with their agendas for social transformation (auditors or allies).

In the chapter by Biekart and Siegmann, Ch. 12 the role of border crossing between academia and activism is highlighted, a space in which we as embodied activist researchers are operating. The chapter reports on a dialogue between two scholars, using a diversity of narrative techniques they also use in their methodology courses at the International Institute of Social Studies (ISS). They explain why they are often uncomfortable in academic settings, thereby exploring new avenues, concepts and techniques to counter this discomfort. The chapter elaborates on the key role of producing and bringing together multiple knowledges, especially by applying a transdisciplinary approach. That is, looking beyond the various disciplines and using mixed research methods in order to pursue adequate innovation in knowledge generation. Inspired by Sousa Santos (2014) the authors label this an 'epistemology of modesty and plurality', which requires quite a lot of commitment from activist researchers: responsibility, self-reflection, as well as a commitment to social transformation (as a leading principle overriding the priority of advancing individual academic careers). Many of the ideas discussed in the chapter were generated in one of the final sessions of the Civic Innovation Research Initiative (CIRI) retreat, and therefore also reflect the collective advances we have made in our methodological thinking on civic innovation research.

The chapter on development consultants as change agents (Bergh and Biekart, Ch. 4) analyses similar roles, but also emphasises that consultants tend to have different roles at the same time. They can be working within the establishment within a rather mainstream framework when opportunities arise that change the game. There is a tendency to try to keep a distance from the holders of power including those who work for Aidland (Mosse 2011) institutions who hire the consultant. The result is that those involved have to learn to orientate themselves in the process of doing the job, rather than a practice where those entering Aidland are taught what to do. Obviously, such a learning orientation requires creativity and constant innovation, for which there is often no time or resources available. So the concept of autonomy, in this case versus the directives of Aidland, is an important one generated in this chapter. Consultants are constantly moving positions between the constraints of a particular frame of reference generating dependency and disempowerment and the option to work with local networks to overcome the limitations of Aidland and actually managing to generate alternative perspectives.

This element of autonomy and space for manoeuvering is further elaborated in Fowler's chapter on interlocutors as key actors in civic innovation processes. Fowler's central point is that 'while an individual entrepreneur, activist or civic innovator may have a winning socio-economic idea to "change the world", or a meaningful part of it, she or he alone will not bring about significant societal effects; the building and expanding of relationships will be critical' (Ch. 3, p. 42). The networked relationships are managed by intermediary actors called interlocutors. Interlocution is a civic innovation process in itself as it requires dealing with power imbalances trying to prevent any game-changing at all. The concept has its origins in research on social accountability, but Fowler shows how it has a wider applicability which is relevant for civic innovation. Interlocution sometimes also implies strengthening existing power balances, for example via processes of invitation or instigation that seek to retain the status quo, and therefore interlocution cannot be seen as synonymous with civic innovation. The chapter identifies a range of key interlocutor attributes as part of multi-stakeholder initiatives such as leadership quality or the capacity to properly analyse and frame the bigger picture. This is illustrated with seven examples of cases of interlocution, underlining the diversity of interlocution processes. Fowler clearly explains the difference between 'social innovation', also labelled 'solutionism', and 'civic innovation' in which there is an explicit focus on citizen-driven politics in action.

The three chapters emphasise the need to be aware of unpredictable changes in power balances, and to make use of opportunities to trigger game changes. The actors generating this game change – the civic innovators – can have many different appearances, but key attributes seem to be: quality of leadership, integrity as a trust builder, autonomous position towards other actors, ability to connect different levels, ability to speak with several tongues, what Fowler calls being a 'polyglot', and the capacity of maintaining a self-reflective attitude.

Dialogues on sexuality, feminist epistemology, youth and civic innovation

The chapters by Trejo-Mendez, Sánchez de la Blanca, Santamaría Buitrago, Sardoni, Simula with Harcourt (Ch. 10), Harcourt, Icaza and Vargas (Ch. 8) and Heumann, Siegmann and Empower Foundation (Ch. 9) look at how the economy impacts on bodies and how as a result (youth, feminist advocates and sex workers) become the locus of resistance and struggle. The three chapters illustrate how feminist epistemologies have contributed to understandings of resistance and transformation, and offer possibilities for feminist theory to be a strong component of civic innovation as it marks out a new field of research. The chapters are feminist epistemological explorations of transformative processes, using an intersectional lens to look at issues of embodiment, sexuality and decoloniality. The conceptual discussion provides inter-generational, multilayered dialogues on key dilemmas (and divides) of the 'body politic' of hegemonic discourses and practices of development. The engagement with marginal experience narratives of youth, sex workers and movement organisers are offered as ways to unsettle normative ideologies of gender and sexuality. The originality also lies in the structure of each chapter where the differences, complexities and potential solidarities among scholar-activists engaged in the debates are made evident.

Each of the chapters challenges the literature around 'gender and development', women and youth engagement in civil society organising, and concepts of class, state and markets. The chapters listen to and bring in the voices of the actors themselves – feminist organisers, sex work advocates and youth in resistance. In addition, by positioning themselves as part of the practices of civic innovation, the authors push beyond dualities of 'us and them' in their engagement with the fight against capitalism. They reveal how to engage in modes of resistance including listening to the possibilities of imaginaries of feminists, youth and sex workers for different kinds of futures. In all three chapters there is a strong sense of living in a particular moment. On the one hand there are huge challenges and deep inequalities to recognise, resist and overcome, but on the other hand there are potential spaces opening up for change – with the technologies, knowledge and connection that are shifting old norms and hierarchies. All three chapters show the importance of organising in ways that recognise how embodied lives enter into public discourse. They do so by looking not only at economic and social relations but also at how relations are determined by cultural, sexual and racial difference. The chapters are positioned not only with reference to academic debate but also with the voices of the actors in the interviews, direct contributions of the youth, feminist and sex worker organisers as co-authors. In addition, there is a strong self-reflective writing including creative imagining of alternative outcomes in order to guide ways forward for change.

Harcourt, Icaza and Vargas (Ch. 8) introduce some key concepts to the meaning of civic innovation: intersectionality, sexuality, difference, generation, relationality, embodiment, intercultural dialogue, and decoloniality. The authors explain how body politics is created in the interconnection of racism, sexism, homophobia, transphobia, and xenophobia in transnational feminist analysis and practice in Latin America and Europe in their explanation of intersectionality. Building from the authors' experiences as feminist activists, the trialogue examines different events and encounters in order to illustrate how lived intersectional difference is important to an analysis of civic innovation. Embodied understandings of the feminist practice is crucial not only in understanding the divisive effects (and emotions) of racism/xenophobia/transphobia in social movements but also in unpacking how deeply these different (often ignored) lived experiences of the body inform relations in neoliberal capitalist economies.

The chapter also points to 'critical interculturality', or the practice of dialogue and learning processes of listening, as important for civic innovation that tries to change deeply held prejudices and painful forms of oppression such as those experienced by indigenous women, transpersons or Roma women. Civic innovation is required not only when engaging in such dialogues across cultures but also in doing research on civic innovation. The underlying critique of the chapter is how important it is to explore embodied and intersectional difference in civic innovation processes. The effort to open up diverse, open and fluid alliances, working with the politics of difference alongside the politics of friendship can create conflicting identities and fractions within movements. The examples given in the chapter illustrate how civic innovation can be a transformative process as it creates space for feminists of different ethnicity, class, nationality, age, gender, sexual orientation, to work together across border and boundaries. The final conceptual tool, decoloniality, explores how to move beyond an epistemological framework of Eurocentric capitalism, and to unmake that specific historical racist, sexist and heteronormative order that undergirds many developmental studies and policies.

Heumann, Siegmann and Empower Foundation (Ch. 9) also address the issues of heteronormativity and sexuality by looking at civic innovation in efforts to change the working conditions for sex workers. The chapter looks in depth at the difficulty of ensuring the participation of sex workers in the development of decent labour standards. The chapter is an example of inter-cultural dialogue between ISS researchers and the Thai sex workers' organisation Empower Foundation, which maps out sex workers' embodied knowledge and lived realities in the policy arena of the International Labour Organiza-tion (ILO). The chapter illustrates how civic innovation happens through dialogue where grounded academic research can make audible the voices of the sex workers, which are commonly excluded from official discourses. The chapter contributes important empirical and analytical insights to civic inno-vation on the concepts of gender, sexuality and labour through both a reading of policy processes at the ILO, and by listening and engaging with the sex workers' knowledge.

Key to the chapter is the concept of agency for the sex workers, which the authors argue is necessary if sex work is to be seen as work rather than exploitation and oppression in ways that understand labour exploitation as a continuum. In this chapter, the authors show how sex workers' precarious labour conditions need to be understood in the context of a global neoliberal political economy that marginalises many workers world-wide. The chapter pioneers with doing civic innovation research through an active exercise in imaginary futures. The authors rewrite the actual ILO decisions to demonstrate how an imaginary decent work policy could take into account sex workers' demands as agents and workers as part of their hopeful vision for a more equal, inclusive and just future.

Trejo-Mendez, Sánchez de la Blanca, Santamaría Buitrago, Sardoni, Simula with Harcourt (Ch. 10) pioneer a civic innovation method of research in a multi author intergenerational dialogue that looks at civic innovation in youth responses to the current economic crisis in Southern Europe by looking at how young people perceive their futures with both resistance and hope. The chapter challenges the binary division between academia and activisms, youth and adults, women and men, and how to undertake an embodied approach to research. The chapter counters the popular narrative that youth living in Spain and Italy are marginal actors and victims of economic crisis. Instead, it gives multiple examples of how youth locate themselves as political beings and in so doing challenge the concept of precarity as a way of life. The dialogue reveals crosscutting concerns, and points to similar ways in which youth are re-thinking themselves, their present and future. Instead of seeing youth as lost, the chapter proposes that youth are building forms of civic innovation;

searching for alternative forms of economics, revaluing care, creating places for discussion, and creating new forms of relations. They are bringing about change not as part of political parties or organised NGOs or even social movements but rather in their own ways of living precarity and loss and uncertainty. The chapter is an example of how civic innovation can be found in many small experiments in ways of living with a sense of hope for the future despite their economic uncertainty. As the chapter concludes:

> By writing this chapter we are constructing a web of knowledge about resistance, as well as opening the hopeful possibility for links between these different collectivities and people. This is not merely a picture about the youth in southern Europe and their striving for alternatives … it is most importantly, an expression of our wish to interconnect and co-produce knowledge about our experiences in a pluriversal dialogue about the need for both resistance and hope.
>
> (p. 211)

Reflections on doing civic innovation research

The process of making this book on civic innovation has been an organic one, following our different research interests as we shaped the collective research agenda with an openness to new methodologies as well as new cross disciplinary combinations. As a new research group we wanted to analyse how the idea of civic innovation related to our existing research practice. Our curiosity about 'what is civic innovation?', and in particular 'how can a civic innovation approach enrich our research focus', was the starting point for our exploration, each from our own disciplines and our own analytical frameworks. However, as we started to put together the book, in many cases we encouraged each other to co-author chapters across the different conceptual strands. In the process of writing together we had to discuss our different and often opposing views on how economic, political and social transformation are perceived, how they are studied, and what are the important features. As part of the collective exploration we held a Forum and a Retreat, as described in the Introduction, as well as numerous bilateral, trilateral or more meetings. All this generated a diverse and inspiring research process leading to the 11 chapters that we summarise here in the conclusion.

Central in this exercise was creating and trying out new methodologies of research and collaboration. From the very first research meeting we were self-critical about mainstream academic culture based on hierarchy, gender bias or indifference, Northern bias, mono-disciplinarity that can make mainstream academia a fearful and uninspiring place to work in. We agreed to find alternative ways of doing research, meeting in non-hierarchal settings, discussing creative ways of working out our ideas mindful and respectful of all our different conceptual 'baggage', gathering data in ways that included the personal and embodied awareness of what doing research is about. All of these

262 *Wendy Harcourt, Kees Biekart and Peter Knorringa*

processes were essential for providing a space for the exploration of civic innovation as an idea and as a practice. The International CIRI Forum on civic innovation in October 2013 was a key moment to bring together our various research agendas and networks, but also to facilitate cross-border debates. The central conviction was: if we want to pursue an agenda of civic innovation we have to find new ways of exchanging ideas and discuss our differences. Overall, this volume illustrates that we did find new, innovative ways to do research, and the authors are excited about the new ways of working we have experienced and learned together.

All good research requires critical self-reflection in order to continue to engage in open rather than closed questions. In the process of writing the book there were uncomfortable moments where the frictions pointed to unresolved concerns, contradictions as we tried to pull together different histories of engagement in various research approaches, methodologies and experiences. Learning from each other was exciting as well as challenging. We were confronted with different academic terms and concepts and moved out of our comfort zone in terms of experiments in how to break down the barriers to learning about each other's approaches.

There are several moments when we came together in the making of the book, and those created both new ways forward, but also some awkwardness. For example, for some, doing drawings in order to explore and share ideas with each other was familiar and easy. For others it was a new and embarrassing experience. In sharing data some were comfortable with tables and graphs and technical economic terms, whereas others did not have the economic literacy to follow the argument and felt ignorant and not a little suspicious. And again, speaking about the body and gender were central to some peoples' research, while for others it seemed marginal and nothing to do with what they were exploring. When pushed, many terms required explanation. Even the term politics was scrutinised. Some saw politics as resistance and revolution, while others defined the market as a political process determined by particular institutions. We all understood age, gender and the country and personal context to inform our interest in civic innovation, but we could not always speak about how it did as clearly as we would have liked. In short, we found ourselves having to consider creating a new vocabulary to handle the new assemblage of different concepts, material and emotional experiences, histories and contexts.

What we have learnt is that it is a slow and difficult process to bring together activist researchers from different disciplines – particularly for younger people who may not be in a position to engage in a new, yet to be tested, framework. ISS PhD researchers participated in our heated discussions, but we also recognise their reluctance to leave the safe boundaries of their own research project. The question remains as to how we could have encouraged them more to join the project as, in the end, only two of them co-authored a chapter along with some past MA students. We learnt to acknowledge that the current politics of mainstream universities makes collaborative research on the boundaries of academic disciplines something of a risk. Nevertheless, we feel that civic innovation can enrich different disciplines and contribute to other fields of interest, forming as we see it, a mosaic of engagement that we are calling civic innovation. We think civic innovation can help shift narrow disciplinary boundaries, which we see as important if research is to be relevant to the rapidly shifting concerns of today's world.

We are convinced that inter- and trans-disciplinary collaboration is not something you can learn, but simply is a thing one has to do (and sometimes suffer from) in terms of peer recognition. We also learned that our disciplines are not that far apart and that many overlaps exist even though we read other books and favour different authors. We managed to ask each other difficult questions, and sometimes we were even able to answer these. We also learned that civic innovation is an intriguing umbrella, since we can explain its meaning differently, but always in a positive sense. It leads to something new, something that triggers curiosity, something that has to do with the kind of thing people do to realise change in their community and/or society. What we have achieved is to generate even more curiosity about a field of study that seems to generate hope and expectation for social transformation. We want to continue developing a new vocabulary to characterise this and a different set of explanations to understand it.

Probably one of the main achievements is that we have not ended up disliking the concept of civic innovation, but actually became inspired by its potential. As Khalid Nadvi suggested at the CIRI Forum in 2013: we are on a promising track to develop a new narrative, even though we do not know yet where it will lead us. We are also surprised we managed to inspire each other across disciplines, gender divides, and safe paradigms. Here lies the potential for an innovation of our way of working together, doing research and linking it with our daily realities, at home as well as in distant locations about which we theorise and publish, including the fuzzy field of 'development studies'.

Next steps: exploring a new research field

After helping to open up connections among the different strands of thinking on civic innovation, what is the next set of challenges? We are interested in how to use a civic innovation lens to research that is working on ways to understand social transformation. In the book we have presented civic innovation as a useful tool that can be applied in different circumstances. We do not see it as restricted to the particular context, policy or funding frameworks that the different chapters outline. We have the aspiration to build a research network that combines researchers, practitioners and activists building on the broader tradition of ISS that has a strong history of societally relevant research activity as well as working with partner research institutions, movements and organisations. Our interest is in how to expand the network, concerns and issues as we link our research to ongoing discussions on social transformation in academic, policy and movement circles.

The challenge of our book also is to communicate to our academic colleagues what we mean by civic innovation and why we believe it is a valuable framework that needs to be explored further. And even more important, that it is a field that requires critical feedback in order to grow further. How can we implement more coherent forms of civic innovation research? We feel it would be important to look closer at the various aspects of civic innovation we identified in the book: the thrust of the process, the nature of the actors, the tensions in and between the various sectors, the methodological dilemmas, the deeply felt urge to do social sciences differently; more oriented towards society, more self-reflective and not taking academe too seriously, and more linked to a practical and political perspective of social transformation.

The production of this book and our discussions have made possible new research projects and our ideas on civic innovation are now more clear than when we started, even though many new questions have arisen. The central element remains to better understand complex processes of societal transformation from the angle of civic innovation. We are interested to examine how citizens, as well as their multiple organisations and institutions, are creatively responding to the shifting dynamics of life they encounter. This can be individually as well as collectively, this can be from a perspective of producers and consumers, public servants and voters, as well as class-based, gendered and generationally. Civic innovation is after all not about simply exploring change dynamics in civil society, or in markets. It has a profound cross-cutting feature, exploring links amongst and between sectors, leading to hybrid organisations pursuing agendas for societal change.

One of the ideas for a possible civic innovation focus is to look more closely at nowadays middle-income countries that some have called 'emerging economies' (Birdsall 2015). Apart from the better known examples of countries like China, India, Brazil, and South Africa, there are also a dozen other countries in the Global South with quickly growing economies and growing middle classes. What these countries have in common is a 'layer' of society that has moved out of economic poverty – the 'new' middle classes – as a result of sustained rates of economic growth, often also at least partly at the expense of other more marginalised groups in society who continue to be exploited. Notwithstanding these new inequalities, over the next three decades these countries will have produced a proportionally large and globally significant group of people who will identify as middle class.

In terms of our civic innovation agenda, the political effects of these increasing numbers of middle classes are the source of recent academic debate (Wiemann 2015; Knorringa and Guarin 2015; Fowler and Biekart 2013). What is interesting for civic innovation research is how the middle classes are becoming a pivotal political force in many emerging societies, sometimes as positive protagonists for inclusive change and sometimes as negative protagonists by advocating against changes that threaten their newly acquired privileges.

This opens up a new agenda for civic innovation research, which explores how these protagonisms are organised and institutionalised. It allows us to look more closely at the aspirations, visions, and values of the middle classes as expressed, for example in the new and often hybrid organisations such as social business, philanthropic foundations, and social laboratories. It also allows us to explore new types of demands – LGBT rights, youth rights, environmental protection, healthy foods, etc. A few decades back we would probably point at a wide variety of NGOs asserting this type of middle-class protagonism. But this modality is altering drastically due to a dual restructuring of aid-providing welfare states and foreign aid funding. In addition, there is a more conservative approach typical of the middle classes, which is trying to protect its hard won, often still precarious, privileges and achievements (Biekart 2015). For example migrants, particular ethnic groups, or political opponents can be stigmatised as being a 'threat' to those who perceive themselves as the holders of middle-class interests. These frictions are central to tensions generated within and by middle-class growth, and they merit further examination in a civic innovation research agenda.

Even though the authors of the book have not yet formulated a new collective research agenda,[2] what we do agree on is the methodology and the objectives. One of the key words articulated in a recent brainstorm on new research plans was 'dialogue', illustrating that we think differently and are interested to understand the other. Another typical key word was 'empowerment', emphasising the centrality of power in our research, but also expressing the aspiration that our research output will be empowering. The core of the CIRI approach continues to be a combination of interdisciplinarity – accepting that we come from different epistemological backgrounds; and transdisciplinarity – realising that academia and practice are intimately linked. Exploring new avenues for linking our research to change processes as well as to actors for change remains a major challenge (Latour 2005). We plan to be creative and inventive, though innovation is not a goal in itself. We see it as a way to bridge our heterogeneous research interests and agendas. In this way, we look not for one single civic innovation research agenda, but for an eclectic mix of methods and approaches, working together on the basis of a collective curiosity and engagement.

Note

1 For more on the STEPS approach see http://www.ids.ac.uk/project/social-technolo gical-and-environmental-pathways-to-sustainability-steps-centre.
2 As we go to press we have organised a series of discussions on civic innovation at ISS from January – June 2016 and we will be hosting panels on civic innovation at the Development Studies Association in Oxford, September 2016.

References

Biekart, K. 2015, 'The Choice of the New Latin American Middle Classes: Sharing or Self-caring', *European Journal of Development Research*, 27(2): 238–245.
Birdsall, N. 2015, 'Does the Rise of the Middle Class Lock in Good Government in the Developing World?' *European Journal of Development Research*, 27(2): 217–229.

Escobar, A. 2015, 'Degrowth, Postdevelopment, and Transitions: A Preliminary Conversation', *Sustainable Science*, 10: 451–462.

Fowler, A. and Biekart, K., 2013, 'Relocating Civil Society in a Politics of Civic Driven Change', *Development Policy Review*, 31(4): 463–483.

Knorringa, P. and Guarin, A. 2015, 'Inequality, Sustainability and Middle Classes in a Polycentric World', *European Journal of Development Research*, 27(2): 202–204.

Latour, B. 2005, *Reassembling the Social: An Introduction to Actor Network Theory*, Oxford: Oxford University Press.

Mosse, D. (ed.) 2011, *Adventures in Aidland: The Anthropology of Professionals in International Development*, New York, Oxford: Berghahn Books.

Sousa Santos, B. de 2014, *Epistemologies of the South: Justice against Epistemicide*, Boulder and London: Paradigm Publishers.

Wiemann, J. 2015, 'Sharing Global Responsibility: The Role of the Middle Classes on the Way to a Just and Sustainable Global Economy', *European Journal of Development Research*, 27(2): 195–201.

Index

Locators in *italics* refer to figures and tables.

15M (action group) 198–201
24/7 citizens 5, 20–1, 25, 33–4

abortion 157
abuse, gender based violence 2, 9–12, 16
academia, civic innovation: 'business as usual' research 234–6; dilemmas in 243–7; disciplinary position 4, 238, 262–5; relationship to activism 233–4, 247–9, 257; research for progressive change 236–43
açaí farming case study 132, 136–9, 141, 145, 255
acceptable solutions (agency) 31
accountability: *see* political accountability; social accountability
action-information loop 25–31, *26, 30*, 36
activism 9; development consultants 77; feminism 148, 202–3; global scale 6, 10, 11, 16; institutional change 32, 35, 37; labour rights 116–21, 125–6, 255; social accountability 220, *226–8*, 228, *229*, 230; social entrepreneurship 93, 95; youth 192–5, 197–206, 210–11; *see also* academia, relationship to activism; protests
activist researchers 153–4, 238, 246–7, 257, 262–3
actor-network theory 42, 68
advocacy movements 89, 102
affiliation, social entrepreneurship 101
Affinity Groups 160
affordability, social entrepreneurship 98
Africa: behaviours 24; interlocutors 48–9; media 223

age groups 196
AGEing 43, 61, 70–1
agency 5, 9, 256–8; family farmers 133–5, 140–4; forced labour 180; and institutions 25–36; labour rights 124–7; sex work 180, 185, 186, 260; social entrepreneurship 90, 94–5; *see also* change agency
agenda-setters 221
agriculture: *see* farmworkers; tomato industry
Ahold 121, 247
aid effectiveness 74; *see also* development consultants
Aidland 67–8, 70–1, 72–3, 82–3, 257
Aidlish 72–3, 75
AIDS 171, 172, 176–7
Akelarre Zambrero 202
allies (development consultants) 70–1, 76–83
Alvord, S. 99, 100
Amazonian peasants 133, 136–44, 255
ambition, civic innovation 247–8
Amnesty International 184
Anderson, B. B. 100–1
Angola 76–7, 81–2
anti-political agenda 74–6
Anti-Trafficking Protocol 174–5, 179
Aoki, Masahiro 21, 26–7, 31
Apthorpe, R. 67, 79, 169–70
Arauaí, Association of 142–3
argumentation analysis 173–4
Association for Women's Rights in Development (AWID): interlocutors 53–6, *54*; sex work 184
Association of Arauaí 142–3
Association of Soledade 142–3

associational power 112–13, 116, 122, 124, 125, 126–7
auditors (development consultants) 69, 70, 79, 82
austercide 196, 209
austerity 194–5
authority, interlocutors 44, 45
AWID: *see* Association for Women's Rights in Development

backbone organisations 57
Bangladesh, Rana Plaza building collapse 109
Base of the Pyramid (social entrepreneurship): emerging economies 90; scale 101; and social domain 87, 88, 95, 97–100; welfare 104–5
Beckert, Jenss 30, 33
behaviours: and institutions 23–31, 33; interlocutors 46
beliefs *24*, 24–5
Benitez, Lucas 121
Bergh, Sylvia 67
Biekart, K. 67, 220
bifurcation 47
bisexual rights 151, 158, 265
bi-variate regression analysis 226–8, *226–8*
Black feminism 150
blended value creation 99
body, the 4, 258–9; Civic Innovation Research Initiative 6; feminism 149–50, 155–6, 162; Tahrir Square, Egypt 10, 11–12; youth 194, 202; *see also* embodiment
BoP: *see* Base of the Pyramid
boundary spanners 49
Bourdieu, Pierre 23
boycotting 118
brainstorming sessions, Civic Innovation Research Initiative 6–7, 234
Brazil: development consultants 81–2; family farmers 136–7, 139–44
breadth scaling 101
bricolage 29, 99
brokerage 68
brothels 170–1
Brousseau, E. 31, 36
Brown, L. B. 99, 100
'business as usual' research 234–6
Butler, Judith 11, 149

CA (Civic Activism Index) 223, 230–1
Cameroon, sex work 175

Campo de Cebada 199
capitalism 253–6; Civic Innovation Research Initiative 8; labour rights 114; narratives 3–4, 17; Occupy movement 60; social entrepreneurship 89–90; youth perspectives 194–5, 196, 203, 208–9, 210
capitalocentricism 194, 211
careers, development consultants 71–5
Caribbean: *see* Latin America and Caribbean
causality: agency 25–6; social accountability 216–17, 222, 229, 230, 231
CDC (civic driven change) perspective 47
Central America: civil society 240; Fair Trade movement 13; farmworkers 117; Participatory Action Research 243, 245, 246
Central Eastern European (CEE) 159
certification: ethical labels 13, 59; family farmers 141, 145; *see also* Fair Trade movement
CGT (*Confederación General del Trabajo*) 178
'chain saw peasants' 139
change agency 5; development consultants 80–1, 82, 83; Fair Trade movement 12; institutions 25–36, 254; social entrepreneurship 91, 99; *see also* development consultants; interlocutors; social change
chemicals, farming 143
Chiapas (Mexico) 47, 163, 240
China 114
Cho, A. H. 93–5, 103, 104
CIRI: *see* Civic Innovation Research Initiative
civic action 7
civic activism: *see* activism
Civic Activism Index 223, 230–1
civic agency: *see* agency
civic driven change (CDC) perspective 47
civic forums 221
Civic Innovation Research Initiative (CIRI) 3–9; academia 233, 237, 241, 243–4, *244*, 261–3; feminism 149; methodologies 17; social entrepreneurship 88; terminology 5, 6–7, 262
Civic Innovation Research Initiative Forum 5–9, 149, 241, 261–2, 263
Civic Innovation Research Initiative Retreat 149, 234, 243–5, *244*, 257, 261

civic-driven change (CDC) 5, 8, 68, 70, 220
civil society: Civic Innovation Research Initiative 8; social accountability 220; social entrepreneurship 88–9, 91, 94; *see also* public-private partnerships
CIW (Coalition of Immokalee Workers) 110, 117–21, 122–3, 125–6, 240, 247
class relations: power 112–13, 122, 125; youth 197
climate change 59–60
Coalition of Immokalee Workers (CIW) 110, 117–21, 122–3, 125–6, 240, 247
coalitional power 114, 122, 124, 125
Codajás cooperative 141, 142
cognitive injustice 236
collaboration: academia 261, 262–3; interlocutors 43, 48–50
Collaborative Intermediary Organisation 46
collective agency: institutions 21, 28–31, 34–6, 37; interlocutors 51; knowledge 238; labour rights 112–15, 124–6, 255–6; sex work 185; social entrepreneurship 90, 100; youth 194, 200, 202, 206
collective morality 122
colonialism: decoloniality 152–3, 159, 163; feminism 150, 156, 162–3
commodification: development expertise 71; knowledge 235; labour rights 110
common good 9, 248
Commonwealth of Independent States (CIS) 159
communications: academia 241–3, 264; interlocutors 45–6
communications technology: interlocutors 42, 46; political parties 60–1; Tahrir Square, Egypt 10, 12
communitarian feminism 162
communitarianism 202, 209
community responsibility system 24
community university 239
competitive advantages: social entrepreneurship 90; social upgrading 134
complex chains of causality 25
concordance, institutions 31
Confederación General del Trabajo (CGT) 178
conflict management 44, 46
consequence function 26–7
consultancies 50, 69
consultants: *see* development consultants

consumers: Base of the Pyramid 97–100; Fair Trade movement 1–2, 12–14, 17, *54*, 58–9; labour rights 118, 122
contract law 123–4, 139–40
control variables, quantitative studies 217, 224–5, *225*, *229*, 230
cooperatives 163
co-partnership 17
corporate social responsibility (CSR): Foundation Strategy Group 56; labour rights 109, 111; social entrepreneurship 89; *see also* Worker-driven Social Responsibility
counter-movements, labour rights 110, 122, 124–5
creating shared value (CSV) 56–7
creative frictions 6, 161
criminal law, sex industry 168, 169, 173, 175–8, 183–4
crisis narratives 3–7, 193–4, 197, 251, 253
critical interculturality 151–2, 155, 156–7, 259–60
critical mass 100
cross-section data 216, 217
CSR: *see* corporate social responsibility
CSV (creating shared value) 56–7
culture: consultancy 73; good personhood 23–4; institutions 23–5, 29; solidarity 2
currency alternatives 208
cyber protest 10–11

Dacin, P. A. 92–3
Dacin, T. M. 92–3
databases, social accountability 222–3, 224–5
Day of Global Occupation 14, 15
Decent Work Agenda 170–2, 255, 260
decision-makers, interlocutors 48–9
decision-making, horizontal 15
decoloniality 152–3, 159, 163
Dees, J. G. 91, 93, 100–1
deforestation 140
deliberative democracy 200
delimited selection 29
demi-regularities 28
democracy 199–200, 205
democratic participation 47
demonstration effect 13
demonstrations: *see* activism; protests
Department for International Development (DFID) 69, 73
dependency syndrome 89
dependent variables, quantitative studies 216–17, *225*

depoliticisation 74–6
depth scaling 101
Desa, G. 98, 101, 103
despair 4
development: academia 263; crisis
  narratives 3–7; innovation concept
  252; measuring 74–5, 78–9; press
  freedom 221
development consultants 67–8, 82–3,
  257; case studies 76–82; categories
  68–71; constraints on 71–5;
  interlocutors 70–1
DFID (Department for International
  Development) 69, 73
Di Domenico, M. 99–100
dialogue, academia 240, 248, 259, 265
digital natives 16
Dinerstein, Ana 193
disciplinary position, civic innovation 4,
  238, 262–5
disciplinary specialisation, academia
  235, 236
discrimination: intersectionality 150–1;
  see also LGBT rights; women's rights
disempowerment effects 89
dissemination, social
  entrepreneurship 101
distributed authority 45
distribution costs 98, 105
diversity: and institutions 27;
  interculturality 155; and interlocutors
  46, 48, 49
division of labour: civic innovation 236;
  family farmers 137–8; gender 135
domestic violence 156
Douglas, M. 24
drawings, use in research 242, 262
drinking water 94
durability, institutions 31
dynamic institutions 25
dysfunctionality 4, 41, 57

ecological impacts, farming 136–7, 139
econometric techniques 216–17, 224
economic crises: crisis narratives 3–7,
  193–4, 197, 251, 253; youth 192–6,
  260–1; *see also* Occupy movement
economics: growth 215–16, 224–5;
  interlocutors 49; Occupy movement 2;
  social entrepreneurship 96–7; youth
  perspectives 194–5, 196, 203, 208–9, 210
education system, Italy 205
Egypt *see* Tahir Square
email communication 12

embeddedness, social entrepreneurship
  102–3, 105
embodiment: academia 233, 234, 237–8,
  248–9, 257, 260, 261; activist
  researchers 238; civic innovation 1–3,
  8, 8, 9, 16–17; decoloniality 152–3;
  feminism 10, 148–51, 153–5, 157–8,
  161–2, 164, 259; interlocutors 42, 47;
  Tahrir Square, Egypt 11; youth 192–3,
  201–3; *see also* the body
emerging economies 90, 264–5
EMES (European Research Network on
  Social Enterprises) 91, 103
emotions 194; *see also* despair; hope
employment, youth prospects 195, 196,
  197, 209; *see also* labour rights
Empower Foundation 169, 181, 182, 183,
  184–5, 260
empowerment 4, 59; academia 265;
  development consultants 72; labour
  rights 109–10, 121, 125; protests 2
endogeneity 221, 231
endogenous institutional change 21,
  31–6, 37
entrepreneurship, institutional 34–6, 45;
  see also social entrepreneurship
environmental impacts, farming 136–7, 139
environmentalism 42
epistemology 149, 238, 257
equilibria: and institutions 27, 31;
  interlocutors 41
erasing knowledges 42, 47–8, 60
Escobar, Arturo 158, 193, 202, 253
establishment 9, 12–13, 17
ethical labels 13, 59; *see also* Fair Trade
  movement
ethnicity: *see* race
ethnography 239
Eurocentricism 152, 260
European Association of Development
  Research and Training Institutes 242
European Clean Clothes Campaign 114
European Feminist Forum (EFF) 154,
  157–61
European Horizon 2020 agenda 252
European Research Network on Social
  Enterprises (EMES) 91, 103
evaluation of development 74–5, 78–9
evolution (institutional change) 25, *26*,
  28–31, *30*
exogenous institutional change 32, 37
Expenditures on Health (EXPH) 224–5
expertise, development consultants 67,
  71–3

explanatory variables, quantitative studies 216–17, 221, *225*, 230
exploitation: *see* labour exploitation; sexual exploitation
extractivism 156

factors of production 109–10
Fair Food Program 110, 116–23
Fair Food Standards Council 119–20
Fair Trade movement 1–2, 12–14, 17, *54*, 58–9
familiarity, rules 28–9
family farmers 132–3, 144–5; Amazonian peasants 136–44, 255; chain inclusion 133–5
farmworkers: academia 240; Fair Food Program 110, 116–21; precarious workers 111–15
fast food corporations 118, 121, 122–3
Fechter, A. M. 68, 71–2
feminism 163–4, 258–60; the body 149–50, 258; case studies 153–61; and civic innovation 161–3; critical interculturality 151–2; decoloniality 152–3; intersectional embodiment 2, 148–51; knowledges 238; Occupy movement 15; solidarity 11, 12; subjectivities 6; youth 201–3; *see also* women's rights
Feminist Encounter, Latin American and Caribbean 153, 154–6
fertilisers 143
FFSC (Fair Food Standards Council) 119–20
15M (action group) 198–201
financial crises: *see* economic crises
financial sector, Occupy movement 2
financialisation, social entrepreneurship 89–90
financing: academic institutions 235; and interlocutors 46; Occupy movement 60; social entrepreneurship 88–9, 99–100, 101
fish cooperatives 141–2
Five Star Movement, Italy 61
flexibility, production 113, 142
Florida, tomato industry 117–21, 122–3, 125, 240
FoA (Protocol on Freedom of Association) 112, 115
forced labour 173–9, 184–5
Forced Labour Convention (ILO) 169, 172–6, 182–5
Forced Labour Protocol 173–9

forest managers 139
FOTL (Fruit of the Loom) 111, 114–16
Foucault, Michel 33, 149
Foundation Strategy Group (FSG) *54*, 56–7
Fowler, A. 5, 43, 70–1, 81, 220
Fraser, Nancy 194–5
free press 220–2, 223–4, *226–7*, *229*, 230, 256
Free Trade Agreement 246
Freedom House 223–4
freedom of association 143
frictions, civic innovation 1, 4; Civic Innovation Research Initiative 5–6; creative frictions 6, 161; interlocutors 41; Occupy movement 2; power 246, 247
Fruit of the Loom (FOTL) 111, 114–16
funding: *see* financing
fundis, Fair Trade 13

game changing: case studies 53, 56–7, 58, 60; Civic Innovation Research Initiative 7, 7; development consultants 71; interlocutors 45, 46–7, 50, 52, *54–5*, 61–2; *see also* 'rules of the game'
gate keepers 48–9
gay rights 151, 158, 265
GBV (gender based violence) 2, 9–12, 16
GDP (gross domestic product) 215–16, 224–5, 229, 230
gender 4; and colonialism 153, 162–3; Fair Trade movement 13, 59; family farmers 138; and interlocutors 46; intersectional embodiment perspective 2, 16; *see also* feminism; women's rights
gender based violence (GBV) 2, 9–12, 16
general interest goods 90, 103
generalization, institutions 36
generation as actuality 196
generational relations 195, 196, 204, 211
geography, spatial fix 114
Gibson-Graham, J.K. 194
global activism 6, 10, 11, 16
Global Network of Sex Work Projects (NSWP) 174, 177, 181, 182–3
global North, academia 236
Global Partnership for Oceans 50
global South: academia 236, 264–5; feminism 159; sex work 172
Global Value Chains 132, 133–5, 145
global warming 59–60

GLOBALGAP 111–15
globalisation: family farmers 132; labour rights 109, 125; sex work 171, 186; social entrepreneurship 89
globalism, place based 210
good personhood 23–4
governance: family farmers 136–7, 142–3; labour rights 114–15; *see also* social accountability
Granger-causality test 216–17
Granovetter, Mark 27, 35, 97, 105
grape sector 111–15
grassroots agency 42
grassroots representation 134, 202
Greif, A. 24, 26–7, 28–9, 31, 32
gross domestic product (GDP) 215–16, 224–5, 229, 230
growth, economic 215–16, 224–5
GVCs (Global Value Chains) 132, 133–5, 145

Habermas, J. 200
habits (behaviours) 23, *24*, 25, 28–9
habitus 23
Harcourt, W. 192, 202
Harvey, D. 114
Haugh, H. 99–100
health and safety 119, 120, 171
health care: academia 239; press freedom *227*; social accountability 215–16, 222
heroic individuals 92, 104
heteronormativity 6, 151, 260
hierarchies: institutions 27–8, 37; knowledge 248
Hindman, H. 68, 71–2
HIV/AIDS 171, 172, 176–7
Hivos 243–4
Hockerts, K. 91, 95–6, 100
Hodgson, Geoffrey 21, 22, 25, 29
Hollingsworth 31
home ownership 197, 203
Honduran factories, USA 111, 114–16
hope: civic innovation 4, 251, 253; youth 192, 193, 198, 202–3, 204, 261
horizontal interactions: civic innovation 17, 248, 251; institutions 28, 37; meshworks 158; Occupy movement 15, 17; power 9, 10, 135, 251; representation 142; social upgrading 133
hosting, interlocution 58, 62
human capital 111
human development 221; *see also* development

human rights: Fair Food Program 119; family farmers 134; human trafficking 181; labour rights 126
human trafficking 168, 172–3, 174–5, 177, 180–1, 183
hybridity, social enterprises 90, 100, 103, 264–5
hypermobility 75

identities: feminism 161, 162; generations 196; labour rights 126; youth 203
IDS (Institute of Development Studies) 218–19
IDWF (International Domestic Worker Federation) 174
Immokalee, Florida 117–19
implication, interlocutors 45
IMR (infant mortality rate) 222
inclinations (behaviours) 28–9
income: *see* salaries
independent media 220–2, 223–4, *226–7*, *229*, 230, 256
India: sex work 175; underclass 49
Indices of Social Development 222–3, 256
indigenous communities: feminism 156–7; women's rights 162–3
Indignados 14, 60, 199–200
individual roles: development consultants 68; feminism 161–3; interlocutors 42, 48, 51, *55*, 257; social entrepreneurship 87–8, 92, 97, 100, 104, 105, 254; youth 194, 202; *see also* interlocutors
Indonesia 112, 113
industry facilitators 42
inequality 4, 259; emerging economies 264; intergenerational 196; labour rights 127; social accountability 220
infant mortality rate (IMR) 222
informal economy 176, 177, 183
information-action loop 25–8, *26*, 29–31, *30*
infrastructure, farming 140
innovation concept 5, 252–3
INPSSE (Intercontinental Network for the Promotion of Social Solidarity Economy) 58
instincts (behaviours) 23
Institute of Development Studies (IDS) 218–19, 252
institution-action loop 25–31, *26*, *30*, 36
institutional disequilibrium 32
institutional entrepreneurs 34–6, 45
institutional flexibility 36
institutional organisation theory 33

Institutional Political Economy 33–4
institutional power 124
institutionalization: behaviours 31; Fair
 Trade movement 12–13, 17; Occupy
 movement 16
institutions 8, 9, 20–5, 36–7, 253–4;
 academia 235, 243; development
 consultants 75, 83, 257;
 endogenous institutional change 31–6;
 interlocutors 44–5; Occupy movement
 14; social accountability 220; social
 entrepreneurship 96–7; theory of
 institutional change 25–31, 254
instrumental variables, quantitative
 studies 217
intentionality, actions 33
intercessional role, interlocutors 48–9
Intercontinental Network for the
 Promotion of Social Solidarity
 Economy (INPSSE) 58
interculturality 151–2, 155, 156–7, 160–1,
 163, 259–60
interdependence: 24/7 citizen 25;
 interlocutors 50; intersectionality 151;
 rules 28
inter-disciplinary approaches 4, 238,
 262–3, 265
interests, institutional change 33
interface approach 68
intergenerational experiences 195, 196,
 204, 211
interlocution 48–51, 257, 258
interlocutors *8*, 9, 41–3, 61–2, 256–8;
 Association for Women's Rights in
 Development 53–6, *54*; development
 consultants 70–1; Edward Snowden
 55, 61; Fair Trade 12, *54*, 58–9;
 Foundation Strategy Group *54*, 56–7;
 Koch Foundation *54*, 59–60; multi-
 stakeholder role 41, 43–6; objectives
 46–8; Occupy movement *55*, 60–1;
 systematic understanding 51–2, *53*;
 United Nations Research Institute for
 Social Development *55*, 57–8; *see also*
 change agency
International Domestic Worker
 Federation (IDWF) 174
International Institute of Social Studies
 (ISS) 5, 67, 148, 153, 163, 220
International Labour Organization
 (ILO): Decent Work Agenda 170–9;
 sex work 169, 182–5, 186, 260
internet political parties 60–1
internships 198

intersectionality 1–3, 9, 16, 259;
 academia 245; case studies 153–61;
 Civic Innovation Research Initiative 6;
 feminism 148–51, 157–61, 164; social
 entrepreneurship 90
Islamism 11
ISS (International Institute of Social
 Studies) 5, 67, 148, 153, 163, 220
Italy 193, 194, 195, 196, 203–6
ivory tower (academia) 234–5,
 237–8, 239

job prospects, youth 195, 196, 197, 209;
 see also labour rights
Jobs Act (Italy) 207
Joshi, Anuradha 222
justice: cognitive injustice 236;
 indigenous communities 162–3;
 intersectionality 151, 164; labour
 rights 125–6; sex work 183
just-in-time production 113

Kingston, C. 26–7, 28, 31, 32
Knorringa, P. 113, 114, 126
knowledge 9, 251; academia 233–6,
 238–9, 245–6, 248; Civic
 Innovation Research Initiative 7;
 decoloniality 152–3; development
 consultants 72; erasing knowledges
 42, 47–8; feminism 151–2, 154–6,
 161, 164, 238; institutional change
 32; interlocutors 42, 45–6;
 intersectionality 151–2; social
 entrepreneurship 96–7, 105; of
 social norms 23; youth 207
Koch, J. L. 98, 101, 103
Koch Foundation *54*, 59–60

labour conditions: *see* working conditions
labour exploitation 174–6, 180–1, 185,
 198, 260
labour rights: Amazonian peasants
 136–44; Fair Food Program 116–24;
 family farmers 132–5, 144–5;
 precarious workers 111–16; regulation
 109–11, 124–7, 254–5; sex work
 168–70, 183
labour-led counter-movement 110
language: academia 241–3; interlocutors
 45–6; Occupy movement 60; and
 participation 239–40
las Iguales initiative 209
Latin America and Caribbean:
 colonialism 152–3; feminism 154–6

Latour, B. 42, 256
law: *see* criminal law, sex industry; legislation/ policies
layers, institutions 27–8, 37
leadership 43–4, 57
learning: and institutions 27, 30; reflexive learning 17
Leffs, C. W. 99, 100
legislation/ policies: family farmers 136–7; labour 109–11, 123–7, 254–5; policy analysis 173–4; sex work 171–2, 173–8
legitimacy, academia 246–7
Legro, J. 31
LGBT rights 151, 158, 265
life experiences: development consultants 70; social entrepreneurship 96, 100
livelihood strategies 135, 138
local scale: development consultants 67; Fair Trade movement 13, 14; family farmers 132, 144; intersectional embodiment perspective 2; politics of place 209–10
locations, social entrepreneurship 101
logical positivism 4, 43
long haul view 45, 80
'lost generation' 197, 204, 207–8, 211
Lugones, Maria 153, 163

Maas, J. 100
Madrid, Spain 193, 197–201
mainstreaming 8; Fair Trade movement 12–13, 17, 59; family farmers 132; feminism 158, 159
Mair, J. 91
'Making Things Better' 5
Malaga, Spain 193, 195, 201–3, 209
marginalisation: and participation 239–40, 245; precarious workers 110, 116, 124–5; sex workers 171
market failures 94, 98
markets: civic innovation 5–7, 8, 253–6; family farmers 138; social entrepreneurship 89–90, 96, 102
maternalism 11
Maya culture 157
MDGs (Millennium Development Goals) 3, 67
measuring development 74–5, 78–9
media: free press 220–2, 223–4, *226–7, 229*, 230, 256; sex work 168; youth 207–8
Media Sustainability Index 223
mediating actors 68; *see also* interlocutors

men: the body 10, 11; Fair Trade movement 13; family farmers 136, 138; *see also* gender
mercenaries (development consultants) 69; *see also* auditors
Merk, J. 113, 114
meshworks 53, 158
'messy' world 16, 18
methodologies, civic innovation 16–17, 237, 241, 261–2
Mexico: Chiapas 47, 163, 240; feminism 153, 156–7
micro-macro scale 6; *see also* scale
middle classes 264–5
middle-income countries 264–5
migrants: feminism 157, 159; precarious workers 117; sex work 171–2, 185; youth 203, 207
Millennium Development Goals (MDGs) 3, 67
minimum wage 117
mission drift 89
missionaries (development consultants) 69–70; *see also* allies
mobility, development consultants 75
Mobilization for Social Justice 42
modernity 47, 73, 149, 152–3
modesty, academia 239, 243, 248, 257
Mohanty, Chandra Talpade 149–50
Monitor Group 98
monocultures 136–7, 145
morality: development consultants 69–70; Fair Trade movement 59; good personhood 23–4; sex work 168
mosaic concept 8–9, 17–18, 251, 253, 263; *see also* tessera
Mosse, D. 67, 72–3
movementalists 59
movements: *see* social movements
multi-disciplinary approaches 4, 238, 262–3
multi-stakeholder initiatives (MSIs) 49–50
multi-stakeholder partnerships (MSPs) 49–50
multi-stakeholder processes: interlocutors 41, 43–6, 51; labour rights 109; Sustainable Development Goals 62
multi-variate regression 217–18, 228–31

narratives: academia 242–3, 257; the body 149; civic innovation 252; of crisis 3–7, 193–4, 197, 251, 253; feminism 161, 164; youth 193–4, 195–6, 206–7
National Committee for Responsive Philanthropy 59

National Farm Workers Association 117–18
national identity 203
National Labor Relations Act (NLRA) 123
national security 61
NEETS (neither studying nor employed or in training (NEETS) 197
negotiation capabilities 133
neo-extractivism 155
neoliberalism 3
neo-Marxism 24
nested rules, institutions 27–8
Network of Sex Work Projects (NSWP) 174
networks: institutions 27, 30–1, 32–3, 35, 37; interlocutors 257–8; meshworks 53, 158; social entrepreneurship 93–4, 97, 99, 100, 105, 254
neutrality, interlocutors 45, 70–1
New York, Zucotti Park 14–15; *see also* Occupy movement
NGOs: development consultants 69–70, 77, 78; erasing knowledges 47–8; family farmers 137; feminism 158; institutional change 35–6; labour rights 109–10, 116–21, 123; sex work 182; social entrepreneurship 88–9; women's rights 53–6
Nichols, A. 87–8
NLRA (National Labor Relations Act) 123
nodes, research 161
non-governmental organisations: *see* NGOs
non-profit entities: Foundation Strategy Group 56–7; interlocutors 50; social entrepreneurship 88–9, 91
Norm Cycle Models 58
norms, social 21–5; *see also* values
Norris, Pippa 220–1, 224
North, Douglass 22, 25
Northern-based consultants 76–82
not-for profit: *see* non-profit entities
novelty driven change 30, 32, 37
NSWP (Global Network of Sex Work Projects) 174, 177, 181, 182–3

Oaxaca Zapoteca 156
objectivity 6
occupation: Madrid 199–200; Rome 203–6
occupational health and safety 119, 120, 171

Occupy movement 1, 2–3; interlocutors 55, 60–1; temporality 14–16
Occupy Patriarchy 15
OECD (Organisation for Economic Co-operation and Development) 220
oil palm case study 132, 136–7, 139–40, 143–5, 255
Old Institutionalism 21
open microphone approach 241
oppression 9–10, 150–1, 161, 251, 254, 259
optimisation, economics 30
optimism: *see* hope
Organisation for Economic Co-operation and Development (OECD) 220
Orozco, Amaia Perez 151
Ostrom, Elinor 22, 27–8, 51
otherness 157–8
Oxfam Australia 114

Pakistan 235, 236
palm oil farming case study 132, 136–7, 139–40, 143–5, 255
Panikkar, R. 151–2
Paredes, Julieta 162, 163
participation: academia 233, 239–40, 243–6; political accountability 223
Participatory Action Research 233, 239–40, 243–5
Participatory Ethnographic Evaluation and Research 239
patriarchal capitalism 8, 17
patriarchy: activism 202; decoloniality 153; Tahrir Square, Egypt 11
PEA (Political Economy Analysis) 73–4
Pearce, Jenny 193
'penny per pound', Fair Food Program 119–20, 122
pensions, generational differences 197
people trafficking 168, 172–3, 174–5, 177, 180–1, 183
performative identities 162
Perrini, F. 88, 100
personal privacy 61
pesticides 143
phase shifts 47, 126
philanthro-capitalists 92, 96
philanthropy: Foundation Strategy Group 56–7; Koch Foundation 59–60; social entrepreneurship 89, 96
photographs, use in research 242
'pincer movement', worker power 115, 116, 122, 124

The Pirates, Germany 61
place: politics of 199–201, 209–10; spatial fix 114
Play Fair campaign 112, 113
Plaza del Sol, Madrid 199–200
plurality, academia 239, 245, 257
Polanyi, Karl 109–10
policies: *see* legislation/ policies
policy analysis 173–4
political accountability 219, 223
political economy: the body 6, 150; Institutional Political Economy 33–4; interlocutors 46, 59; sex work 186, 260; social entrepreneurship 92
Political Economy Analysis (PEA) 73–4
political ontology 193, 253
political parties, on internet 60–1
political universalism 60
politics 2, 256–8; interlocutors 48–9; meaning of 262; of place 199–201, 209–10; of production 133, 134, 135, 140–4; youth 204
polycentric governance 45
polyglots 46, 57, 60, 258
positionality 17, 153, 210–11, 248
positive class compromise 113, 122, 126
post-modernism 24
potable water 94
potentially codifiable rules 22–3
poverty: and activism 220, 241; development consultants 69, 70; precarious workers 111, 114, 116, 120, 122, 247; social entrepreneurship 89, 92, 95
power 9, 251, 252, 256–8; and academia 239–40, 242–3, 246, 247; colonialism 152; and communication 239–40, 242–3; family farmers 133–5, 140–4; feminism 161; institutional change 29, 33–6; interlocutors 42–3, 45, 52, 62, 256, 258; intersectionality 154–5; labour rights 110, 111–16, 122, 123–5, 126–7; social entrepreneurship 92, 102; youth 193, 210
power checks, academia 246
PPP: *see* public-private partnerships
precarious workers: sex work 168, 170–2, 182, 186; value chains 110, 111–16, 126; youth 196, 198, 206
pregnancy 157
presence, interlocutors 45
press freedom 220–2, 223–4, *226–7, 229,* 230, 256
primary school completion rate *226*
privatisation 87, 104

privileges, academia 239–40
process rights, family farmers 134
production: empowerment 59; factors of 109–10; family farmers 133, 134, 135; labour rights 109–10, 113–15; politics of 133, 134, 135, 140–4; value chains 116–21; *see also* Fair Trade movement
professionalisation, development expertise 71
professionals: *see* development consultants
profit, social entrepreneurship 91
profit maximisation 124
progressive change: *see* social change
prostitution 170, 176–7
Protestant Ethic (Weber) 24
protests: Occupy movement 2; youth 195, 198–200, 204–5; *see also* activism
Protocol on Freedom of Association (FoA) 112, 115, 125
public sector 95; *see also* state
public squares 2, 16, 199–200; *see also* Tahrir Square, Egypt
publications, academia 236, 241–4
public-private partnerships (PPP): family farmers 136–7, 140, 143–5; interlocutors 49, 50
'pull' products 98
Puma LETS 208
'push' products 98
puzzles concept 8

qualitative analysis 218, 231
quantitative studies: measuring accountability 222–6; quantitative analysis 226–31, 256; quantitative literature 218–22; social accountability 215–18

race: feminism 150, 158, 159–60; privileges 240
race to the bottom, labour rights 109
radical imagination 47
radicalisation, youth 206
radio technology 42
Rana Plaza building collapse, Dhaka 109
rational choice 34
rational learning 30
Raynaud, E. 31, 36
realism 241
realos, Fair Trade 13
reconstitutive upward causation 29
reflexive action 29–30
reflexive learning 17

regression analyses 217–18, 224
regulation of labour 109–11, 123–7, 254–5
regulations: *see* legislation/ policies
religious belief 24
Renta Basica de las Iguales initiative 209
Renzi, Matteo (Prime Minister of Italy) 204, 205, 207
Reporters without Borders 223–4
representation, family farmers 132–7, 140–4, 145
reputational capital 113–14, 126
research 3; and activism 233–4, 247–9; 'business as usual' 234–6; dilemmas 243–7; feminism 161–2; for progressive change 236–43; reflections on civic innovation 261–5; *see also* academia, civic innovation; Civic Innovation Research Initiative
Research Institute for Social Development 55, 57–8
resilience 134
resistance: the body 149–50, 151, 155, 258–9; feminism 153, 158, 160; labour rights 135, 138, 139, 177; youth 192, 193, 198–9, 201–3, 205, 261
resources, social entrepreneurship 99–100, 101; *see also* financing
'Rethinking Economics' movement 208
retirement, generational differences 197
reworking, labour 134–5
ribeirinho communities 136, 137–8, 141, 142
rights: *see* human rights; labour rights; women's rights
rights movements 4
Ritchie, H. A. 28, 34, 36
RL (Rule of Law index) 225
Robin Hood taxes 16
Robinson, J. 91, 96–7
Rome, Italy 193, 195, 196, 203–6
Roundtable on Sustainable Palm Oil Principles and Criteria 139–40
RSPO (Sustainable Palm Oil Principles and Criteria) 139–40
Rule of Law index (RL) 225, 228, *228*
'rules of the game': 24/7 citizen 20–1; development consultants 81; institutions 22–31, *24*, 36–7; interlocutors 46–7; power 33–6
Rutenge, Mary 242

safety, occupational 119, 120, 171
salaries: development consultants 71–2; family farmers 134, 138, 139–40;

farmworkers 117, 118, 119–20, 122; sex workers 170–1
Sardex 208
scale *8*, 9; Fair Trade movement 12–14; family farmers 132; global activism 6, 10, 11, 16; interlocutors 42, 44–5; labour rights 125; social entrepreneurship 100–3; *see also* globalisation; local scale
Scaling up Nutrition (SUN) Initiative 44
scatter plots 226, *226–8*
schools 206–7
SDGs (Sustainable Development Goals) 3, 62, 252
secularism 11
security: family farmers 138–9, 142; national 61
self-enforcement, behaviours 26, 31
self-evaluations, measuring development 78
self-governed communes 24
self-help 75, 95–6, 102, 103
self-interest: development consultants 69–70; institutions 27, 36
self-reflection: academia 246–7, 248–9, 262; feminism 148, 149, 153–61; interlocutors 258
Selwyn, B. 111–13, 115, 126–7, 134
servant leadership 43–4
service delivery, social accountability 215–16, 218–19, 221–2, 224–5, 228–30, *229*
sex work 168–70, 186, 259–60; Decent Work Agenda 170–2; forced labour 173–9; labour approach 180–5; sexual exploitation 172–6
sexism: gender based violence 10–11; intersectionality 150, 151, 158
sexual exploitation 172–6, 179, 180–1, 182–4, 260
sexual harassment 117, 120, 126
sexual terrorism 11
sexuality 4, 259, 260
sexually transmitted infections (STIs) 171
SGACA (Strategic Governance and Corruption Analysis) 74
Shah, Anwar 218–19
shock events, development 79
Shutt, Cathy 72
Siegmann, K.A. 113, 114
Sillitoe, P. 72
simplicity, institutions 31
Sindicato dos Trabalhadores Rurais (STR) 111–15, 127, 141–2
skilful actors 30, 34–5

slavery 32, 172–3
Slum Dwellers International 42
small-scale farmers: *see* family farmers
Smith, B. R. 102–3
Snowden, Edward *55*, 61
social accountability 43, 51, 215–18;
    interlocutors 258; measurement 222–6;
    quantitative analysis 226–31, 256;
    quantitative literature 218–22
social activism: *see* activism
social bricolage 99, 105
social bricoleurs 102–3
social capital: activism 220;
    interlocutors 44
social change 4–5, 17–18; academia
    233–4, 236–43, 245, 247; development
    consultants 69, 76–82; family farmers
    132–3; institutions 20, 36; vs 'business
    as usual' 234–6; *see also*
    transformation
social constructionists 102–3
social domain: institutions 90; social
    entrepreneurship 88–9, 95–7, 104–5;
    welfare 104–5
social downgrading 134
social engineers 102–3
social entrepreneurship 87–90, 103–5,
    253, 254; defining 91–5; processes of
    95–103
social franchises 101
social innovation (solutionism) 5, 51–2,
    56, 258
social justice: indigenous communities
    162–3; intersectionality 151, 164
social marginalisation: *see* marginalisation
social media: gender based violence 11;
    global activism 6; Occupy movement
    15; Occupy Patriarchy 15; Tahrir
    Square, Egypt 11–12; youth 206
social movement action 7
social movements: academia 239–40,
    243–4, 245–6; empowerment 125;
    social entrepreneurship 93, 102;
    Tahrir Square, Egypt 11–12; youth
    193, 208
social norms 21–5; *see also* 'rules of the
    game'; values
social relationships 96–7
social science: intersectional embodiment
    perspective 16; and progressive change
    233–4, 240–1
social sector: *see* social domain
social solidarity economy (SSE) 58
social structures, institutions 22–5

social upgrading 132–5, 145
socially acceptable actions 20–1, 22–3
societal relevance, research 244–5
Soledade, Association of 142–3
solidarity: development consultants 77;
    Fair Trade movement 58–9; feminism
    158, 201–3; and local cultures 2;
    Tahrir Square, Egypt 9–12; youth 199,
    201–3, 209
solutionism 5, 51–2, 56, 258
Sousa Santos, B. 236, 238, 257
southern Europe: case studies 197–209;
    politics of place 209–10; youth 192–6,
    210–11
Southern-based consultants 81–2
sovereignty, interlocutors 46
spaces, interlocutors 42–3, 48–9
Spain 193, 194, 195, 197–203, 209
spatial fix 114
spatial intersection 133
specialisation, academia 235, 236
Spinning the Green Web 42
Spivak, Gayatri Chakravorty 149–50
squatters' movement 237
SSE (social solidarity economy) 58
Standing, G. 110
state: Civic Innovation Research
    Initiative 8; labour rights 123–4; social
    entrepreneurship 88, 94–5, 104
statistics: *see* quantitative studies
Stevens, C. E. 102–3
Stirrat, R. L. 69–70, 73, 78–9
stories: *see* narratives
STR (*Sindicato dos Trabalhadores
    Rurais*) 111–15, 127, 141–2
strategic agency 33
Strategic Governance and Corruption
    Analysis 74
street workers, sex work 170–1
strikes 118
structural power 112, 113–14
structuration 41
structures, institutions 22–5
students 195, 196, 206–7
subjectivities 6, 162
sustainability 252; family farmers
    136–7, 139, 141–2; institutions 36;
    interlocutors 49–50; social
    entrepreneurship 104–5
Sustainable Development Goals (SDGs)
    3, 62, 252
sweatshops 111
Swedberg, Richard 27, 35
symbolism, Occupy movement 60

system analysis 44–5, 47
systematisation 51–2, *53*
systems of rules 22

Taco Bell 118, 121
Tahrir Square, Egypt 1, 2, 9–12, 16; and social media 12
taxation, social entrepreneurship 90
technocracy 67, 71–3
technology: *see* communications technology
temporal processes, interlocutors 45, 48–9
Terms of Reference (ToR), development consultants 69, 73, 76, 78
tessera 21, 27, 37; *see also* mosaic concept
textiles industry 111–15
Thailand, sex work 170–1, 181, 183, 260
time-bound presence 45
timely transformation (TT) 47
time-series data 216–17
tipping points 47, 126
tomato industry 117–21, 122–3, 125, 240
ToR (Terms of Reference), development consultants 69, 73, 76, 78
Tracey, P. 92–3, 99–100
trade unions: family farmers 141; labour rights 109, 111–13, 114–15, 125; sex work 178
tradition, and feminism 156–7
trafficking, people 168, 172–3, 174–5, 177, 180–1, 183
Tran, Hai 221, 224
trans-disciplinary approaches 238, 263, 265
transformation 251, 252, 264; academia 237; feminism 156–7; labour rights 255; measuring development 74–5; narratives 3–4; social accountability 218–19; social entrepreneurship 99, 100–1, 102, 104, 254; *see also* social change
translation, development consultants 67
transnational corporations (TNCs) 109, 113–15
transnationalism 42, 56
transsexuals 151, 155, 158, 265
transvestites 155
trust: development consultants 72; interlocutors 44
TT (timely transformation) 47
24/7 citizens 5, 20–1, 25, 33–4

U5MR (under five mortality) 222, *227*
uncertainty: family farmers 138–9, 144; and institutions 30

uncivil actions 41, 87
under five mortality (U5MR) 222, *227*
underclass, India 49
undersocialised view, social entrepreneurship 104
unemployment, youth 195, 196, 197, 209
United Nations Research Institute for Social Development 55, 57–8
United States: Fair Food Program 116–23; sex work 176–8; tomato industry 117–21, 122–3, 125, 240
United Students against Sweatshops (USAS) 111, 114–15
universalism 60
Universidad de la Tierra 240
universities 195, 196, 199, 206–7
University of the Earth 240
unpaid work 198; *see also* voluntary participation
UNRISD 55, 57–8
upscaling: *see* scale
urban squatters' movement 237
USAS (United Students against Sweatshops) 111

VA (Voice and Accountability Index) 223
valorisation, research 244–5
value chains: Fair Food Program 110, 116–21; Fair Trade movement 58; family farmers 132–3; labour rights 109–11, 124–7, 255–6; precarious workers 110, 111–16; worker-driven innovation 121–4
values 9; 24/7 citizen 20–1; development consultants 69–70; institutional change 32–3; interlocutors 45; rules 22–5, *24*; social entrepreneurship 89, 92, 95–6, 99–100; social norms 21–5
Veblen, T. 23, 25
vertical interactions: civic innovation 251; institutions 28, 37; power 9, 135; representation 142; social upgrading 133
victimisation 180
Vietnam 114
violence, gender based 2, 9–12, 16
viral campaigns 16
visualisation, use in research 242
voice: academia 246, 247; development consultants 74, 81, 83; family farmers 133–5, 141, 145; and institutional change 35; interlocutors 46; labour rights 110, 121–2, 124; resistance 258–9; social accountability 220, 221

Voice and Accountability Index (VA) 223
volatility, markets 98
voluntary codes of practice 109
voluntary participation: development consultants 80; interlocutors 43–4; social entrepreneurship 89
voluntary work 198
Vurro, C. 88, 100

wages: *see* salaries
Walmart 126
Walsh, Catherine 6, 151–2
Washington consensus 56
watch-dogs 221
water, drinking 94
water management, Pakistan 235
'we are the 99%' slogan 15, 60
Weber, Max 22, 24
Wei-Skillern, J. 100–1
welfare: social accountability 215–16; social entrepreneurship 88, 104; youth perspectives 196–7
West Africa, interlocutors 49
What's the Problem Represented to be (WPR) approach 173–4
whistle-blowers 61
'wise forest managers' 139
women's rights: the body 155–6; development consultants 81; family farmers 138; indigenous communities 162–3; intersectional embodiment perspective 2; labour rights 117, 120, 126; Tahrir Square, Egypt 2, 10; *see*

also Association for Women's Rights in Development
Worker-driven Social Responsibility (WSR) 116, 120–1, 126
working conditions: farmworkers 117; sex work 168, 169–70, 186
World Bank: and academia 235; depoliticisation 75; development consultants 73
World Shift 52
World Social Forum 158
World Summit on Sustainable Development 49
WPR (What's the Problem Represented to be) 173–4
Wright, E. O. 112–13, 115, 125
WSR (Worker-driven Social Responsibility) 116, 120–1, 126

Yayoflautas 198–9
youth 260–1; case studies 192–3, 197–209; crisis narratives 197; family farmers 138; generations 196; politics of place 199–201, 209–10; southern Europe 192–6, 210–11
'Youth without Future' movement 195, 197–201

Zahra, S. A. 102
Zambra Malaga 195, 201–3, 209, 210
Zapatistas 47, 156–7
Zimbabwe 82
Zucotti Park, New York 14–15

For Product Safety Concerns and Information please contact our EU
representative GPSR@taylorandfrancis.com
Taylor & Francis Verlag GmbH, Kaufingerstraße 24, 80331 München, Germany

www.ingramcontent.com/pod-product-compliance
Ingram Content Group UK Ltd.
Pitfield, Milton Keynes, MK11 3LW, UK
UKHW021012180425
457613UK00020B/906